Deploying Microsoft Exchange Server 5

Rand Morimoto, MCSE

Osborne **McGraw-Hill**

Berkeley New York St. Louis San Francisco
Auckland Bogotá Hamburg London Madrid
Mexico City Milan Montreal New Delhi Panama City
Paris São Paulo Singapore Sydney
Tokyo Toronto

Osborne **McGraw-Hill**
2600 Tenth Street
Berkeley, California 94710
U.S.A.

For information on translations or book distributors outside the U.S.A., or to arrange bulk purchase discounts for sales promotions, premiums, or fundraisers, please contact Osborne/**McGraw-Hill** at the above address.

Deploying Microsoft Exchange Server 5

1234567890 DOC 9987

ISBN 0-07-882314-5

Publisher
Brandon A. Nordin

Editor in Chief
Scott Rogers

Acquisitions Editor
Wendy Rinaldi

Project Editor
Mark Karmendy

Editorial Assistant
Ann Sellers

Technical Editor
Chris Amaris

Copy Editor
Michelle Khazai

Proofreader
Stefany Otis

Indexer
Rebecca Plunkett

Computer Designer
Roberta Steele

Illustrator
Lance Ravella

I dedicate this book to my parents and to my wife. To my parents, Edward and Victoria Morimoto, for teaching me that hard work and perseverance is the key for me to attain my goals. To my wife, Kim Morimoto, for providing me with the encouragement and support as I wrote day and night, seven days a week, to complete this book and meet a very aggressive timeline.

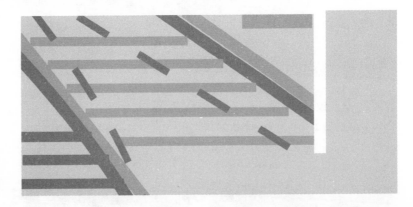

Contents at a Glance

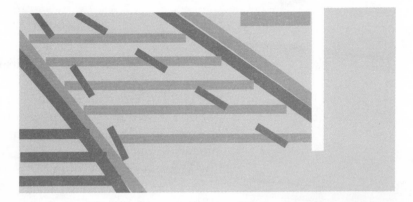

Contents

PART III

Administering, Optimizing, Tuning, and Managing a Microsoft Exchange Environment

PART IV

Advanced Business Uses for Exchange

PART V
Appendixes

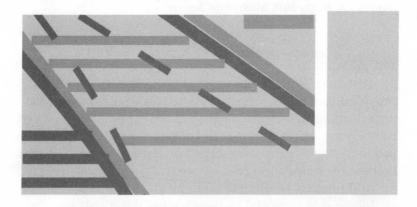

Acknowledgments

There have been a number of people who have been instrumental in helping to get this book to print. From Scott Rogers, editor-in-chief, who gave me the opportunity to have this book published by Osborne/McGraw-Hill. To Wendy Rinaldi, my acquisitions editor, who has given me guidance and support from chapter to chapter to turn a vision into reality. To my project editor, Mark Karmendy, and his team of editors, Michelle Khazai and Cynthia Douglas, who helped to turn my technical thoughts and ideas into readable sentences and paragraphs. To Chris Amaris, my technical editor, who read through every piece of the book to make sure everything was technically correct. To production director, Marcela Hancik, and her team, who set the pages beautifully. And last, to Anne Ellingsen, Polly Fusco, and Ann Sellers who have helped to market and promote the book so that you, the reader, would be made aware of this project and hopefully the valuable content it has to offer.

I would also like to acknowledge the effort and support I have received from Microsoft Corporation, including the Microsoft Exchange development team, Microsoft Consulting Services, and the Microsoft Northern California district. With their assistance and support, they have provided my company and me with the technical resources to gain the expertise in the Exchange product long before the product was publicly available. They have also provided us with the opportunity to work with some of the largest organizations in the country to gain the experience in designing, planning, prototyping, implementing, and supporting the Microsoft Exchange Server product—experience necessary to produce the knowledgebase that has become the foundation of this book.

And finally, I would like to thank all of the senior consultants and project engineers at Inacom Oakland, as well as the clients we serve who create and implement the business processes and technical solutions in order to utilize the capabilities of the Microsoft Exchange Server product. There have been thousands of hours already spent in working with previous Exchange solutions, summarized in this book, that will hopefully translate into making your experience with Exchange one that leverages the lessons learned from many before you.

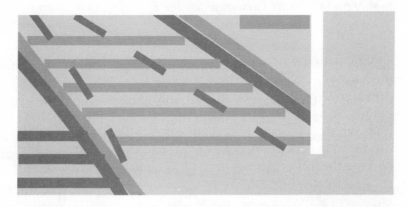

Introduction

In the twenty years that I have been in the computer industry, I have seen companies and products come and go. There have also been a number of monumental events in these twenty years that have had drastic effects on the way we utilize information technology. One of the earlier events was the invention of the IBM Personal Computer in the early 80s. For the first time, a computer was designed for businesses and made affordable to the general public, and as a consequence, the way we viewed computer technology was changed forever.

When I was given the opportunity to view the plans for the Microsoft Exchange product many years ago, I knew I was looking at a technology that was, again, going to have significant impact on the way we were going to do business. As my company, Inacom Oakland, started to work with major corporations with the design, prototyping, and testing of the Exchange Server product in its early beta releases, my belief was confirmed in how Microsoft Exchange Server was going to change the way we were going to be able to do business in the future. Microsoft Exchange was not just another "me too" product that was going to be here today, and quickly replaced by something new and better tomorrow. The Exchange Server product fundamentally changes the way we think about workgroups, about communications, and about business processes.

What I set out to accomplish in this book was not to rewrite an installation guide or general product information manual, but rather to take a couple years of practical experience with the Exchange product and highlight what other organizations around the world are doing to leverage the capabilities of Microsoft Exchange to improve the way they do business. Like with any product, there are a number of "gotchas" in the planning, implementation, or support of the product that you usually don't realize until you make the mistake of heading down the wrong path, and then need to find ways to work around the problem. By taking the experience of hundreds of previous installations of the Exchange Server product, it is the hope that the information in this book will help to prevent you from making the same mistakes, and to guide you through the planning and implementation of a highly functional communications infrastructure that the Microsoft Exchange Server product provides.

How this Book Is Structured

A Microsoft Exchange Server implementation logically breaks into four separate segments that make up the four parts of this book, and you'll find a supportive fifth section as well.

Part I provides a background to what Microsoft Exchange is, what the standard features and functions of the product are, and how the product works. If you have heard about Microsoft Exchange or want to know more about the core features that make up this communication infrastructure environment, this first part provides that background information.

Part II focuses on the planning, installation, and migration to a Microsoft Exchange environment with an emphasis on the designing and planning portion of the installation or migration. Far too often have we seen organizations start from an idea and jump straight into prototyping or testing an installation without giving much thought to what the final solution would entail. Every successful installation or migration that we have participated in had a majority of the time spent in detailing every component of the technology solution, so that when the project was completed, it met the original goals and expectations of the organization. Part II highlights the key success factors in preparing a successful installation.

Once an organization has installed Microsoft Exchange, the need to tune, optimize, and manage the installation is crucial in making the system run more efficiently and effectively. In Part III of this book, we took the approach of making the Exchange environment more efficient by supporting more users and groupware functionality, rather than by adding faster processing speeds and more servers which would only mask the inefficiencies of a poorly-tuned system. Maintaining the Exchange environment is critical in getting the most out of the product's capabilities.

And where most books stop once the software has been installed and tuned, we have elected to add Part IV that details third-party add-ins to Microsoft Exchange, as well as business solutions that help to leverage the true capabilities of the Exchange product. For some organizations, the add-ins to Exchange, like enterprise faxing, document management, or remote communications, may be the core reason for the organization's implementation of Microsoft Exchange. Other organizations may not realize the potential of the Exchange product and are under-utilizing the capabilities of the technology. Part IV covers business solutions for the Exchange Server product that highlight how Microsoft Exchange can fundamentally change the way we view information and improve the way we communicate.

Finally, Part V contains a number of appendixes for your reference: a glossary of terms used throughout the book, a list of new components found in Exchange v5.0, some hints concerning the upgrade from Exchange v4.0 to v5.0, a list of considerations when dealing with Microsoft Exchange on an international level, and a list of some third-party applications and where you can find them.

There is a lot covered in this book; however, the Microsoft Exchange product is a very robust communication environment. It is our hope that you will be able to use the information in this book to get the most out of the product as you plan, design, migrate to, deploy, maintain, and support a Microsoft Exchange environment

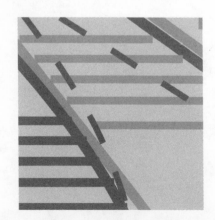

PART ONE

Overview of the Microsoft Exchange Environment

CHAPTER 1

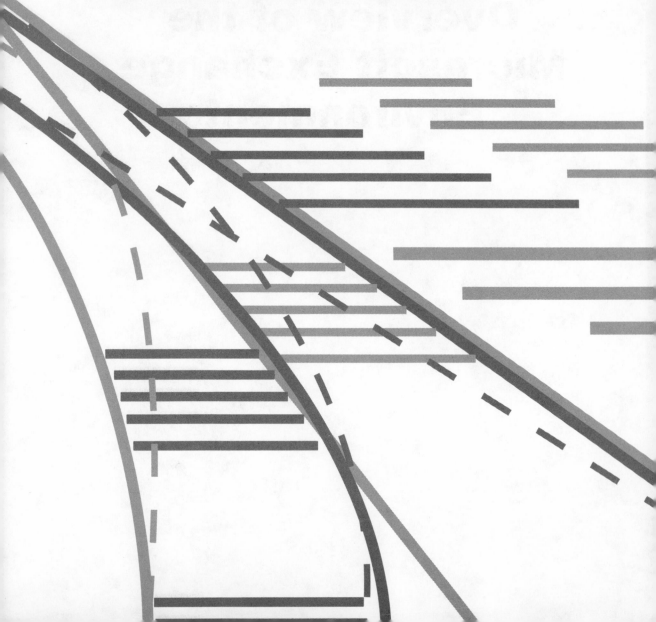

Introduction to Microsoft Exchange and Groupware

Microsoft Exchange is the latest entry in the evolution of local area network (LAN)-based electronic messaging systems. Although electronic mail (e-mail) has been available for a few decades on mainframe and mini-computer-based systems, it wasn't until the emergence of the local area network in the mid-to-late 1980s that personal computer-based electronic messaging systems became available. In just the past decade, millions of personal computers have been sold and subsequently connected by local area networks or to the Internet. It is this ability to interconnect computer systems that has enabled and expanded the functionality and accessibility of personal computer-based electronic messaging.

Connectivity to a LAN or to the Internet has created the infrastructure for a workgroup or a company-wide messaging system. The flexibility of a graphical user interface (like Microsoft Windows, the Macintosh OS, OS/2, and X-Windows) has enabled the proliferation of sophisticated features and functions in the evolution of e-mail systems. In addition to electronic mail, a new class of applications called *groupware* have arrived which contain enhanced capabilities, such as group and resource scheduling, forms and intranet information management.

Microsoft Exchange is one of the five components of the Microsoft BackOffice product family, shown in Figure 1-1. Microsoft BackOffice includes the SQL Server Client/Server database system, the Internet Information Server Internet Web server, the SNA Server for LAN-to-mainframe connectivity application, the System Manager Server network management software, and the Microsoft Exchange electronic messaging and groupware environment.

What is Microsoft Exchange?

While Microsoft Exchange Server is one component of the Microsoft BackOffice product family, the Exchange Server product itself includes three major applications. They include Microsoft Exchange client, Microsoft Scheduler, and Microsoft Electronic Forms Designer.

Electronic Mail

Electronic mail (e-mail) has become the communications backbone of many companies and is quickly replacing voicemail and facsimile copies as the preferred means of relaying messages and information. The popularity of e-mail stems from the user's ability to document communications in a format that can be cut and pasted into a database or personal information

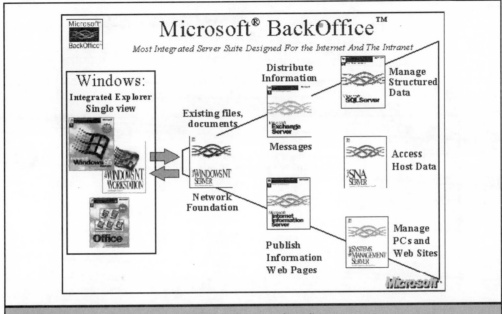

Figure 1-1.   *The Microsoft BackOffice product line*

management software package, and to attach documents and other files to the e-mail message. E-mail software also allows users to expedite their communications with almost immediate transport.

Best known for its capabilities as a robust e-mail system, Microsoft Exchange is the direct beneficiary of Microsoft's seven-plus years of experience with their highly successful Microsoft Mail messaging program. The core function of an e-mail system is its ability to reliably send and receive electronic messages. Microsoft Mail has provided this basic level of reliable electronic messaging for years, and Microsoft has enjoyed the benefit of having the largest installation base of all personal computer/LAN-based e-mail systems. Figure 1-2 shows what a message looks like when it is created and ready to be sent.

Scheduling

Personal and group appointment scheduling was the next progression in the evolution of electronic messaging and group communications. By notifying other group members of their availability, groups of users can plan and

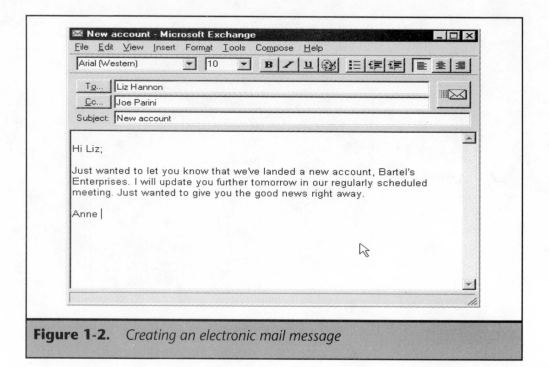

Figure 1-2. *Creating an electronic mail message*

schedule meetings or times when they can communicate non-electronically. Microsoft Exchange's built-in calendar function, as shown in Figure 1-3, can be used to schedule individual or group appointments or to allocate resources (such as conference rooms, shared laptop computers, or company vehicles).

Users of the Microsoft Exchange Scheduler software can view their appointments on a daily, weekly, or monthly basis.

Forms

As electronic messaging within a workgroup evolves, users in an organization find ways to create standardized methods to exchange thoughts or ideas. Companies have used e-mail as a means for employees to submit purchase order or helpdesk support requests and ask for office supplies. The problem with a freeform e-mail process is that pertinent information does not necessarily end up getting sent with the message. An employee may forget to note the quantity of the items they are requesting, or possibly a ship-to address. The electronic forms in Microsoft Exchange (similar to a form depicted in Figure 1-4) enable users to create forms with questions and fill-in

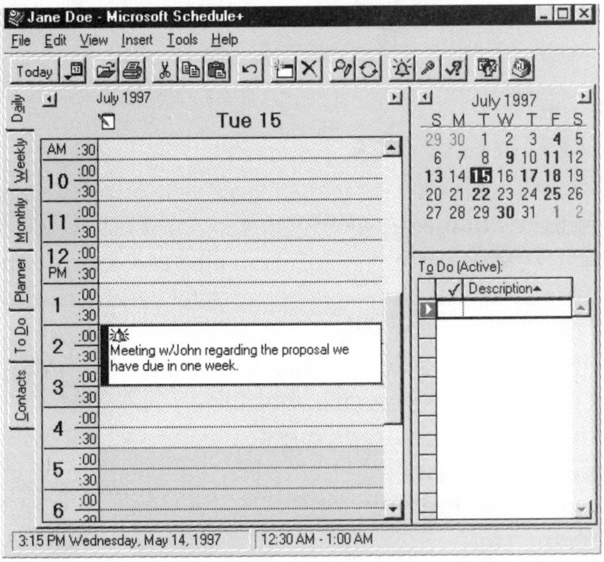

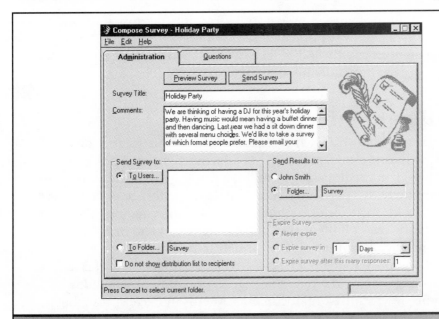

Figure 1-3. *A view of a day's schedule*

Figure 1-4. *Using forms to invoke and require specific information from an individual*

fields that other users must complete in order to submit the request, or else the form cannot be sent.

What is Groupware?

Groupware is the latest innovation in electronic communications. Groupware retains the basic features of electronic messaging and adds in extended functions that improve workgroup communications. Groupware can include functions such as group appointment scheduling, document management, and discussion group communications.

As outlined earlier in this chapter, Microsoft Exchange includes groupware functions such as group and personal appointment scheduling, forms creation for discussion groups and structured communications, and public and private folders for document management. However, in addition to these very important groupware functions, one of the biggest strengths of Microsoft Exchange has been the support by third-party software developers to create add-in applications for Exchange. Some of these add-ins include network faxing, voicemail integration, document routing, and Internet and intranet integration. Many of these add-in applications will be detailed in Part Four of this book.

So why has groupware become so popular? Mainly because groupware is exactly what organizations want, which is the ability for their employees to communicate more efficiently and quickly within a workgroup. Some of the benefits of groupware functionality are discussed in this chapter.

Centralization of Information

Through the use of Microsoft Exchange public and private folders, any information (including e-mail messages, fax documents, word processing files, spreadsheet files, voicemail messages, and the like) can be easily stored together for future reference. Unlike older database or storage systems that require special fields to include anything but textual information, Microsoft Exchange supports object linking and embedding (OLE) and drag-and-drop technologies, which allow multiple file formats to be stored in their native formats directly into a public folder. As shown in Figure 1-5, a folder within Microsoft Exchange can hold e-mail messages, appointment schedules, electronic forms, Microsoft Word documents, Microsoft Excel spreadsheets, and graphic files all in their native format (dragged and dropped into the folder).

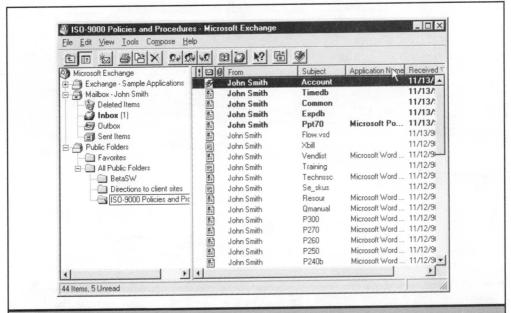

Figure 1-5.   *A sample Exchange folder containing a variety of files saved in their native format*

Demand-Pull, Not Demand-Push

Because information can be centrally stored in public folders and shared by selected workgroup users or all company employees, the need to e-mail every recipient each time something needs to be communicated is eliminated. This functionality is called *demand-pull*: information can be "pulled" or searched when it is needed, rather than "pushed" to every desktop in an e-mail message whether the user needs or wants the information or not. Figure 1-6 shows how a company has stored notices of information for their staff for common access and reference, minimizing the number of electronic messages e-mailed to every employee in the organization.

Easy Information Reference

As information is stored in public and shared private folders, the ability to search the folders on the Exchange Server becomes important in order to find the information when it is needed. Microsoft Exchange has a basic "find" utility, as shown in Figure 1-7, that searches messages stored in a folder, and there are also a number of third-party companies (a few outlined in Part Four

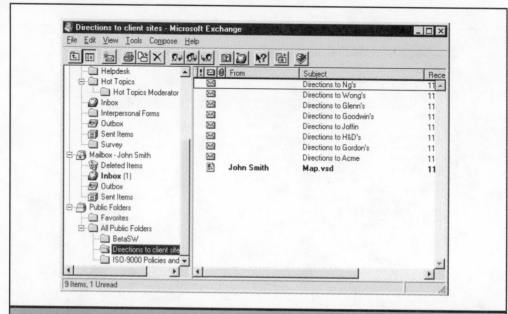

Figure 1-6. *Centralizing information so that e-mails are not sent to every user, every single time*

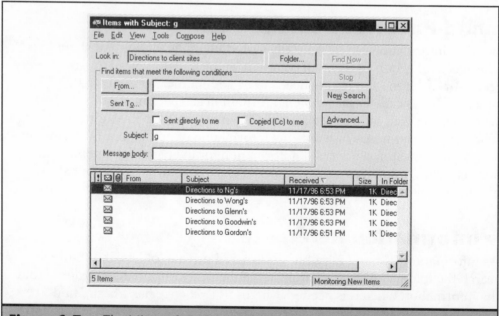

Figure 1-7. *The Microsoft Exchange find utility can look up information*

later in this book) that make sophisticated search engines that can find information in a text format, in attachments, or in native file formats in the folders within seconds.

Interactive Discussion Groups

Through the use of shared information storage locations in Microsoft Exchange, groups of users can carry on discussion sessions by posting messages or discussion topics with common response forms. As shown in Figure 1-8, discussion topics can be initiated with responses to the initial topic indented below the primary topic. Groupware discussion groups can take the place of conference calls or meetings while keeping rebuttals and responses to discussions documented and accessible for many users to review.

Management of Information and Discussions Through Forms

With the use of structured forms, information such as discussion topics and conversations can be routed through the groupware environment to ensure pertinent topic information is acquired and properly sent within the organization. Communications will improve any time you can centralize information and direct a workgroup of users toward that information easily or collaborate on a discussion topic. Creating a specific form like the one in Figure 1-9 helps to keep discussions or the distribution of information structured and focused. Instead of carrying on disjointed e-mail discussions (one-on-one, or limited to a small e-mail distribution group), complete discussion topics can be shared among a group of users, which can in turn invoke the participation of more users. Even if the discussion and consensus is made by a limited group, the contents of the discussions (better known as the *thread* of the discussion) can be reviewed for future reference.

Why Does Groupware Fit So Well into Enterprise Networks?

As more and more people are connected to local area networks, wide area networks, or to the Internet, the ability to carry on group discussions or to function as a distributed workgroup becomes a possibility. Prior to workgroup connectivity, there was no infrastructure in place to facilitate easy group

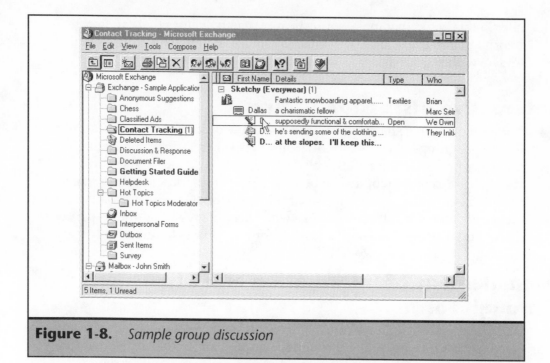

Figure 1-8. *Sample group discussion*

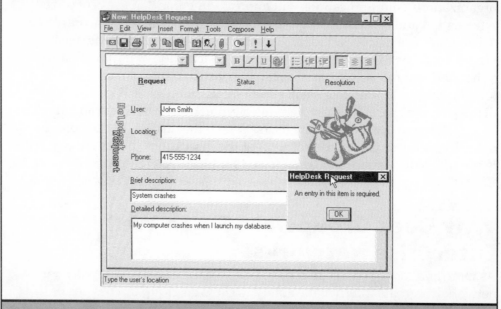

Figure 1-9. *A form tells users what they must complete before they send the message*

communication. Whether it was the advent of interconnectivity that made it easier for people to work in more distributed work environments, or that distributed work environments created the need for improved interconnectivity, the end result is that many corporations and organizations have geographically disbursed employees that need to work together. This distributed workgroup environment takes a group of talented individuals (regardless of their geographic locality) and allows them to work together on projects, processes, or operational systems. Through the use of improved communications systems like Microsoft Exchange, these distributed workgroup users can carry on discussions, share files, exchange information, or post work in a centralized location in a collaborative effort on a common project or task.

Microsoft Exchange can replicate information, either from one server to another server or from a remote client to a server. This allows information to be stored in one location and then distributed in a background process to another location. This is how information is stored and replicated for access by other users within the workgroup.

What Are the Business and Technical Benefits of Groupware?

Since information is replicated between locations and only one set of information is commonly stored and shared, this minimizes the number of e-mail messages that would typically be sent to a large distribution group of users any time communication needs to occur. Quite frequently in a non-groupware environment, a copy of a document (word processing document, or spreadsheet file) will be e-mailed to a group of users. If the file is large, it will be sent throughout the network to all recipients. The groupware function of storing one copy of the file in a central location minimizes the need to electronically transport the large file to a distributed number of users. Also, the storage space that would be required to store multiple copies of the same document is eliminated. Additionally, since there is only one copy of the file in a groupware environment, the chance of multiple copies of the same document (in various states and forms of edits and revisions) is minimized. The centralization of master documents assists in document revision control.

Why Has Exchange Become the Most Popular Groupware Application?

As described earlier in this chapter, groupware improves workgroup and corporate communications, which subsequently improves worker productivity. Microsoft Exchange was the right product at the right time to provide this functionality. Microsoft had the significant advantage of an existing e-mail customer base in excess of seven million users of Microsoft Mail, who are considering or have already begun upgrading their standard e-mail to the new Microsoft Exchange groupware environment. Additionally, because Microsoft has such a significant share of the standard office application market with their Microsoft Office and Office 97 products (which includes Microsoft Word, Microsoft Excel, Microsoft PowerPoint, and Microsoft Access), the integration between these Microsoft products as well as other Windows and Windows 95 applications makes it easy for an organization to leverage their existing office automation tools into the new Microsoft Exchange messaging and groupware environment.

Some key examples of integrating Windows products like Microsoft Office, Visio, or Microsoft Project are described in detail in Part Four of this book.

Microsoft Exchange as an Environment, Not an Application

Microsoft Exchange is not just an e-mail program with scheduling and forms functions, but rather it is an entire messaging and information management environment that provides the infrastructure for a variety of workgroup communications add-in applications. Some of the popular add-ins include network faxing, document routing, and document management. Microsoft developed the Exchange Server product to provide an operating and communications environment that supports the addition of these new capabilities without the replication of administration, operation, or management of the add-in product. The global environment approach of Exchange minimizes administration and support, improves the efficiency in routing messages, and in turn maximizes the overall reliability of information management.

How Messages Flow Within Microsoft Exchange

Much of the core message handling capability of the Microsoft Exchange Server is integrated into four components of the Exchange Server software. They are the information store, the directory store, the messaging transfer agent, and the system attendant, as shown here:

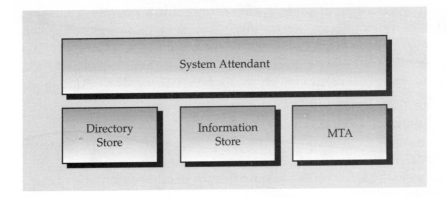

Understanding how these components work is the key to understanding how Exchange routes messages from one Exchange user to another. These exact same components route messages to external message systems like the Internet. Within these four core components are the mechanisms that provide the administrator of the Exchange system with the ability to track the location of messages if they get lost, confirm that all internal and external message routing components are working properly, and verify that they are the components that allow for the easy integration of third-party add-in products and utilities.

Information Store

The information store in Microsoft Exchange includes the private information store that contains information about the users' mailboxes, and the public information store that contains information about the public folders. The information store is similar to the table of contents of a book. The information store has a list of all mail messages in each user's inbox and personal folders that point to messages residing in the message database. The message database is separate from the information store and is the depository for all messages on the Exchange server. When a message is created, deleted, or modified, the information store maintains a log of the transaction and updates or modifies its link to the message database and the data in the message database.

Directory Store

The directory store in Microsoft Exchange keeps track of the users on the Exchange server, monitors the security rights of the users in regard to their access to information in public folders or individual messages, and maintains all of the address information for internal and external users on the network. The directory store is queried any time there is a transaction on the Exchange server to verify whether a user, resource, or folder store resides on the current server or another server in which the Exchange server has information.

Messaging Transfer Agent

The messaging transfer agent is the component that routes a message between other Exchange servers or to other agents that may manage routing of messages to the Internet, to a fax modem, or to other external services. The messaging transfer agent handles all message routing internal and external to the Exchange server.

System Attendant

The system attendant is the management component that directs messages through the information store, the directory store, and the messaging transfer agent, and rebuilds the routing tables as information is changed in the directory store. The system attendant also manages the server and link monitors that track message logging.

Messages from an Exchange Client to a Client on the Same Exchange Server

When an Exchange client sends a message to another Exchange client on the same Exchange server, the message takes the following path:

- Checks the information store to see if the message is already in the message database

- Checks the directory store to determine where the message should be sent

- When the recipient is determined to be on the same Exchange server, the system attendant updates the information store record for the recipient to point to the information store ID of the new message

- The recipient's inbox is refreshed and the Exchange client is notified

- Server-based rules are run on the message (if rules have been enabled and are applicable)

- All logs are updated at each step of the message route

Messages from an Exchange Client to an Exchange Client on Another Exchange Server

When an Exchange client sends a message to an Exchange client on a different Exchange server, the message takes the following path:

- Checks the information store to see if the message is already in the message database

- Checks the directory store to determine where the message should be sent

- When the recipient is determined to be on another Exchange server, the message is then passed through the messaging transfer agent to the messaging transfer agent of the Exchange server where the recipient resides

- The system attendant on the recipient server checks the information store and directory store of that server, and then the recipient's inbox is refreshed and the Exchange client of the recipient is notified

- Server-based rules are run on the message (if rules have been enabled and are applicable)

- All logs are updated at each step of the message route

Messages from an Exchange Client to an External System (like the Internet or Fax)

When an Exchange client sends a message to an external system like the Internet or a fax destination, the message takes the following path:

- Checks the information store to see if the message is already in the message database

- Checks the directory store to determine where the message should be sent

- When the recipient is determined to be external to the network, the message is then passed through the messaging transfer agent to the external connector (Internet connector, fax connector, X.400 connector, etc.)

- The external connector transfers the message to the mail host of the recipient or transfer device

- All logs are updated at each step of the message route

Logging Message Transfers

Because the messages are managed by the system attendant throughout the route, the message route is logged throughout the entire transaction. In a Microsoft Exchange environment, messages are no longer lost without a trace. With the built-in robust messaging processes in Exchange, messages can be easily tracked and logged all the way to their intended recipient.

Rollback of Messages

Because messages are tracked within their route on the Exchange server, any time that there is an interruption of the message transfer (server failure, incomplete message header to complete a message route, corrupt message), the message is completely rolled back to the last full transaction. The rollback function of Exchange is automatic and is intended to minimize the chance of a message that appears to have been received but did not necessarily complete the transaction due to some routing error. Within Microsoft Exchange, a transaction is either completed successfully or the message is rolled back and the sender is notified of the error.

Add-in Versus Add-on

In early versions of e-mail applications, the third-party groupware application provided some core capabilities and functions and would share some of the functional resources of the core messaging product. However, the groupware product was still an add-on to the original product and was not tightly integrated for administration or operation. With the open architecture of Microsoft Exchange, additional functionality is integrated directly into the Microsoft Exchange program as a connector or add-in. This allows a Microsoft

Exchange-aware add-in application to share critical management and administration functions with all third-party add-in products.

For example, a fax application in an older messaging system would allow users to send and receive faxes from within their e-mail client software; however, the administration and management functions of the application would export the authorized user list for the application out of the electronic mail system into the separate fax administration program. Since the fax software has a completely separate administration and management program, as users are added to the network and the e-mail administration program, they must be added separately to the fax administration program. Other administration functions of the older messaging and fax application would also be distinct, such as error logging, fax queue lookup, or least cost fax routing administration. However, within the Microsoft Exchange environment, a Microsoft Exchange-aware fax application would be integrated directly into Microsoft Exchange as an Exchange Connector. As an Exchange Connector, the third-party fax application shares the same user administration tool, the same error log manager, and the same information management tools as the core Microsoft Exchange application. Thus, when users are added to Microsoft Exchange with a third-party fax application installed, they immediately have inbound and outbound faxing capabilities. The same utility that logs inbound and outbound e-mail messages, Internet messages, or schedule updates is the same utility that logs inbound and outbound fax messages and errors.

In addition to minimizing the administrative overhead of third-party add-ins in a Microsoft Exchange environment, this tight integration of add-in products also minimizes the potential for integration problems created by add-on products such as memory management problems or software incompatibility. Since the third-party Microsoft Exchange add-in becomes a part of the core Exchange application, the client workstation just has a pull-down option within their Exchange client software, or another option in the send and receive option, instead of an entirely new executable or memory resident add-on competing for workstation memory or application environment workspace. As a tightly integrated add-in to Exchange, the creation of a fax message should be as simple as creating a regular e-mail message, as shown next:

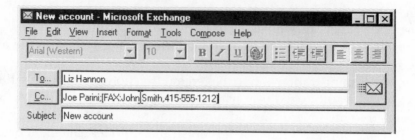

The Benefits of an Object Oriented Client/Server Application

Few people realize that a significant aspect of making Microsoft Exchange a very reliable message and information storage system is the fact that Microsoft Exchange stores information as objects rather than as files or within a file system. The storage and management of information as objects improves how information is stored, managed, and maintained in a Microsoft Exchange environment.

The Problem with Older File-Based Message Stores

Most e-mail programs store information as data appended to a file (Microsoft Mail stores its information in an MMF file as appended text and data). The problem with a file storage system is the dependence on the operating systems that read, write, modify, and append information to the data file. As a file system data file gets larger, the ability to manage and maintain the integrity of the data within the file diminishes. Every message that the user sends and receives and then stores is appended to the user's message file. In the Microsoft Mail program, this personal file store is the user's MMF file. An average user who sends and receives a few messages a day and has a few hundred messages stored has an MMF file that is 1-2MB in size. However, active e-mail users who send and receive dozens of messages a day and store hundreds or thousands of messages have very large MMF message storage files commonly averaging 30-60MB in size or larger. Most administrators who use Microsoft Mail are familiar with MMF file corruption and the need to reorganize MMF files for users with very large message storage files. The frequency of message file corruption on large message files increases because the e-mail program has to communicate with the operating system (DOS, Windows 95, NetWare, Windows NT) to manage the large file(s) and lacks the ability to manage the file(s) in any other way than through the user's core operating system.

Information Stored as Objects in Microsoft Exchange

Within the Microsoft Exchange environment, information is stored as objects in the Microsoft Exchange message database. Since the message database resides on the Microsoft Exchange Server, the Microsoft Exchange Server program manages the information, the allocation of disk storage, and the saving and retrieving of information from the message database. Also within the object storage system of Microsoft Exchange is the fact that Microsoft Exchange looks at information as an object, not as a text file, attachment, binary Word document, TIF or GIF graphic file, or AVI video file. Thus, when Microsoft Exchange stores attachments or other file information, it views all information as the same (as shown in Figure 1-10), and treats all information as the same. The benefit of equal treatment of information is the flexibility Microsoft Exchange has in its ability to manage anything from text electronic

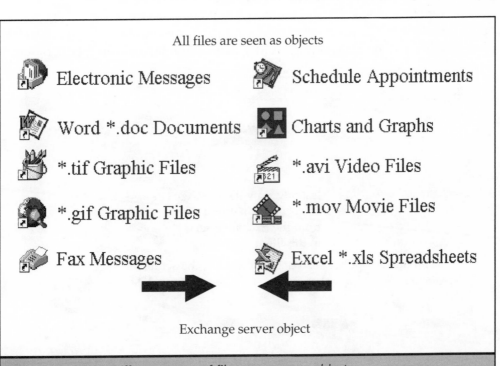

Figure 1-10.   *Different types of files are seen as objects*

messages, to voicemail messages, to graphic files in the public and private folder storage system.

The Efficiency of Objects in Information Access

As information in a Microsoft Exchange client/server environment is managed as an independent object by the Exchange server, only the individual object is transferred from the server to the client workstation. The Exchange client sees a list of messages on the screen, similar to a table of contents in a book. When the user selects a message to view, the Exchange server sends only that individual message, as shown in Figure 1-11. This object management minimizes the traffic between the client and the server only to the object (electronic message, attachment, graphic file, fax message, etc.) immediately being accessed, and not the entire user's message storage file. Efficiency and reliability are gained in an information management system such as this that does not need to either send or receive a large file over a LAN or WAN.

Single Object, Multiple Message Pointers

In older e-mail systems that are file-based, not object-based, when each user opens a message or attachment, that information is replicated and stored in the user's individual message storage folder. Many companies using these older

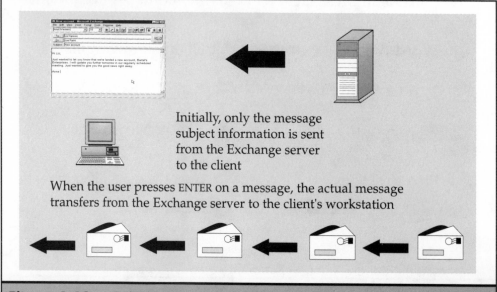

Initially, only the message subject information is sent from the Exchange server to the client

When the user presses ENTER on a message, the actual message transfers from the Exchange server to the client's workstation

Figure 1-11. *Only the message being accessed goes from the Exchange server to the client*

e-mail systems are familiar with a scenario in which a user would send a
1/2MB attachment to a group of dozens or hundreds of users, and by the end
of the day the company's mail server runs out of disk space as each user has a
separate copy of the attachment in the user's personal file store. However,
since message files, attachments, and content information in an Exchange
server environment are stored as objects, each object is assigned an object ID. If
multiple users receive an electronic mail message or attachment, only one
copy of that message or attachment is stored on the Exchange server. Each
recipient of the message or attachment has a reference to the single object ID.
When the attachment is opened, that single copy of the attachment (object) is
opened and viewed for the individual, but an entire copy of that message or
attachment is not individually stored for each user. This one object, multiple
pointers framework, is depicted in Figure 1-12. This significantly reduces the
rate at which a Microsoft Exchange Server network storage system grows
compared to a standard file-based messaging system.

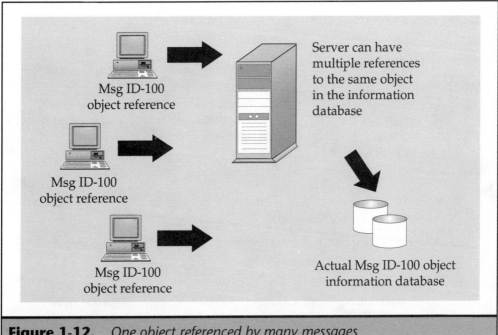

Figure 1-12. *One object referenced by many messages*

Industry Standards in Exchange

Microsoft Exchange incorporates industry standards such as X.400, X.500, SMTP, and MAPI. Through the implementation of these standards, Microsoft Exchange provides better compatibility with other messaging systems and integrated applications. The benefits of native transport of messages in industry-standard messaging formats is best seen when the Microsoft Exchange message system needs to communicate with other electronic messaging systems. When an e-mail system communicates as a proprietary messaging format and then needs to communicate outside of its message system (such as to the Internet), messages need to go through a gateway to convert the message from the proprietary format to one that the Internet understands. Since both the Internet and Microsoft Exchange natively communicate over SMTP, the communication between Microsoft Exchange and the Internet becomes a native connector rather than the conversion process of a gateway. Any time a message can transfer from one system to another without conversion, the chance of losing information in a conversion is minimized. This minimization of conversion also translates to minimization of the overhead to convert the message and information.

X.400

What is X.400? X.400 is a widely recognized and accepted set of standards for electronic messaging and communications. Microsoft Exchange has built-in support for X.400 and is U.S. GOSIP-certified for both the 1988 and the 1984 standards. Microsoft Exchange's support for X.400 means that information from Microsoft Exchange:

■ Can communicate better with other messaging systems because of standard industry transports such as X.25, TCP/IP, and TP4.

■ The parts of an Exchange message (from the textual body part through attachments) are of standard definitions.

■ The addressing of the sender and recipient use X.400 naming schemes such as Country Code, ADMD, PRMD, Organization Name, and Common User Name.

Microsoft Exchange can connect directly into an existing X.400 backbone, or the Exchange server can serve as an X.400 backbone itself (since the Exchange server is a full relay host or Message Transfer Agent (MTA)).

X.500

X.500 is a series of definitions of how directory services are to be designed to provide a global directory structure. Microsoft Exchange supports the X.500 object schema for directory querying and replication. Just as X.400 defines the parts of a sender's or recipient's name, X.500 defines the parts of a directory. The classes include country, organization, organization unit, and common name. Microsoft Exchange matches these classes as an Exchange server country, organization, site name, Exchange server recipient container, and the Exchange server recipient.

SMTP, UUENCODE, and MIME

Simple Message Transfer Protocol (SMTP) is defined in RFC 821 on how an Internet mail message is transferred. The Internet Connector for Microsoft Exchange utilizes RFC 821 as messages are passed between the Exchange server and another mail message server. Exchange also supports RFC 822, which defines how the message content is defined, including the message format, headers, and text-based content. When a message includes a non-text attachment, the non-text information must be converted to a 7-bit ASCII standard before it can be transported over SMTP. The most common way of handling this non-text information is by encoding and decoding the information (UUENCODE/ UUDECODE). More recently, the multipurpose Internet mail extension (MIME) under RFC 1521 defined how actual message body parts and their contents should be managed in a message transfer. MIME allows different kinds of data to be sent as different body parts; thus text, word processing document attachments, audio files, and graphical images are independently tagged, separated, converted, sent, and reassembled. UUENCODE and MIME are the two most common conversion methods, and SMTP is the standard for Internet message transport. As messages are transferred from Microsoft Exchange to other messaging systems, these standards provide better compatibility and assurance that the information will be received by the recipient in a readable format.

MAPI

Messaging application program interface (MAPI) is the key industry standard for message transports because it enables applications with a Microsoft Windows environment to interact with many messaging services using a single method of communications. The MAPI architecture in a Microsoft Exchange environment, as shown in Figure 1-13, starts with the Exchange client software that communicates with the MAPI subsystem, which in turn communicates with the MAPI Service Provider such as the message store, address book, and message transport providers, and then ultimately to the Microsoft Exchange Server.

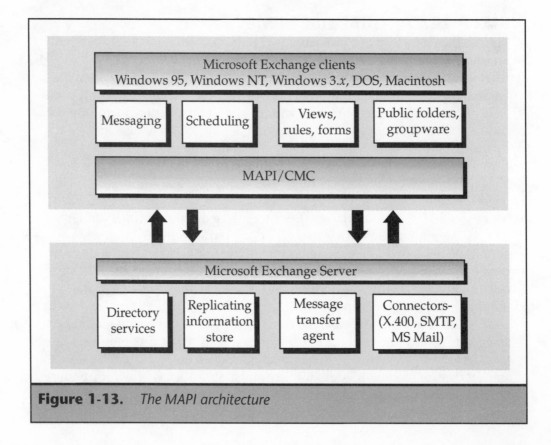

Figure 1-13. *The MAPI architecture*

Communicating with the Rest of the World

With integrated support for X.400 and SMTP/Internet, Microsoft Exchange has integrated connectors for the two most common external communication systems. Additionally, Microsoft provides native support to communicate with Microsoft Mail and IBM/Lotus cc:Mail. However, other messaging systems that communicate with Microsoft Exchange are available for systems such as MCI Mail, IBM Profs, DEC All-in-One, Lotus Notes, and Novell Groupwise. Because of the third-party market support for Microsoft Exchange, connectors and gateways to these other messaging systems are readily available. There are three strategies for gateways to these environments:

- **Common Message Transport (X.400 or SMTP)** Because Microsoft Exchange has X.400 and SMTP message transport capabilities, having the other messaging environment communicate with Exchange through either X.400 or SMTP can facilitate communications between the two systems in one of these common message transfer processes.

- **Standalone Gateway** Many third-party companies make standalone gateways that allow for inbound and outbound message conversion and transfers from Microsoft Exchange to other e-mail systems.

- **Consolidated MultiTransport Gateways** Other third-party companies make single gateways that support multiple different transports for the conversion and transfer of messages from a Microsoft Exchange network to a number of other e-mail systems simultaneously.

How Does Exchange Compare with Other E-mail and Groupware Packages?

Microsoft Exchange can be best compared to other e-mail and groupware packages by grouping the other applications into common categories. While this is not a direct comparison of every feature and function of the other application packages, the following comparison is intended to provide the reader with a basis for understanding the features and functions of Microsoft Exchange that will be outlined throughout this book.

Exchange Compared to Other E-mail Systems

Microsoft Exchange typically includes all of the features, functions, and capabilities of standard electronic messaging systems, such as sending messages, receiving messages, replying to messages, and individual user mail stores. As a groupware application, Microsoft Exchange includes a family of interconnected applications, such as personal and group scheduling, discussion groups, public folder replication between multiple sites, and an open architecture environment that allows for tight integration with third-party applications such as faxing, document routing, and document management. These e-mail packages do not have the same robust, integrated groupware capabilities as Microsoft Exchange.

Exchange Compared to Other Groupware Applications

In addition to having what is said to be a better e-mail and group scheduling environment than other groupware applications, Microsoft Exchange is best known for its extremely tight integration with Microsoft Windows 95 and Windows NT Workstation, as well as with Microsoft Office and other Windows-based applications (such as Microsoft Project or Visio).

The Chapter in Review

- A local area network (LAN) is a communications network used within an organization locally that allows users to share information and resources.

- Electronic messaging is the means by which users on a LAN can exchange messages over the network electronically. These electronic messages are known as e-mail. Because there are so many networks, e-mail has evolved to the next step, groupware. Groupware allows for the centralized storage of information and collaborative computing within a workgroup. This is the centralized storage of documents and information. If a single message is sent to multiple users, only one copy of the original document is stored. Conversation threads can be easily traced and documented. Search engines help find information. Groupware is a key tool for distributed work environments.

■ The four messaging handling components of Exchange are the information store, the directory store, the messaging transfer agent, and the system attendant. The information store is like a table of contents in a book. The directory store tracks users and their security access rights. The messaging transfer agent routes messages between servers and services. The system attendant directs and tracks messages. Exchange works more seamlessly with third-party products than earlier messaging systems because its open architecture allows developers greater access to its internal workings.

■ The benefits of Exchange being an object-oriented client/server application are many. Message files are much less likely to get corrupted, thereby causing a server to crash. This type of application also allows Exchange to manage a vast array of files in many different file formats, which provides for the integration of audio and image files like never before. Exchange supports the broadest industry standards to have the greatest degree of compatibility with existing messaging systems, all while requiring as few gateways as possible.

Review Questions

Q. Why is e-mail such a popular method of communicating?
A. Communications are expedited and can be delivered quickly; it's a method of communicating that does not require people to be speaking at the same time to each other; it is an easy way to communicate over wide distances; it allows for group conversations; it allows for conversations to be documented, complete with a date and time stamp; and it is relatively reliable and inexpensive for such a quick communications method.

Q. Name some of the inherent added features of Exchange besides e-mail. What are additional, third-party options?
A. Scheduling, forms, intranet information management, document management, discussion groups. Add-ins available for an additional cost include network faxing, voicemail integration, document routing, document tracking, workgroup collaborations, and search engines.

Q. Why are forms sometimes more efficient than e-mail?
A. They can force a user to fill in certain fields that they might otherwise forget. For example, the quantity of items requested for purchase can be a mandatory field. The message will not be sent without that information.

Q. Name some benefits of centrally storing master documents.

A. Centralized storage of master documents greatly improve a company's document revision control. Rather than having, for example, a word-processed document e-mailed to multiple users as an attachment, the original document can be stored in a folder for people to comment on. This allows the group to reach each other's comments, to know who made them and when, and to keep one master copy of the document to ensure all revisions are incorporated.

Q. When is a server-based rule run on a message being sent to an Exchange client? Does the message have to be from another Exchange client for the server-based rule to run?

A. A server-based rule is run on any Exchange user's message that has one set, regardless of whether or not it is from another Exchange user. The rule is run after the recipient's inbox is refreshed and before all logs are updated.

Q. What are the benefits of an object-oriented client/server application?

A. The object management minimizes the traffic between the client and the server to only the object immediately being accessed and not the user's entire message store. This significantly minimizes the problem of message file corruption.

Q. Name four industry standards for messaging that Exchange supports.

A. X.400, X.500, SMTP, and MAPI. (See Glossary for definitions.)

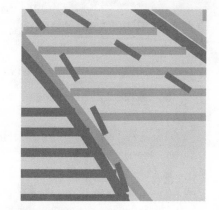

CHAPTER 2

The Microsoft Exchange Client

As a client/server application environment, the client component of Microsoft Exchange includes the features and functions that users of Microsoft Exchange access, such as sending and replying to messages, saving message files, and printing messages. However, in addition to these basic e-mail features, the client software for Microsoft Exchange includes advanced message formatting and message management features, such as server-based rules, message filtering, digital encryption and digital authentication, and integrated Internet Web URL support. These client components are what make Microsoft Exchange user-friendly as well as extremely feature-rich. This chapter will provide an overview of the major features and functions of the client component of the Microsoft Exchange Server product.

Features and Functions of the Microsoft Exchange Messaging Client

The Microsoft Exchange Server includes client software for a variety of operating system formats, including DOS, Windows v3.x/Windows for Workgroups, Windows 95, Windows NT, and the Apple Macintosh. The client software is so similar, a user sending a mail message from a Macintosh to a Windows workstation will retain the same fonts and formatting even though the two computers have different core desktop operating systems.

The Microsoft Exchange client software includes dozens of features that can be broken down into four separate categories to help you better understand the feature sets of the Exchange software. The categories include:

- The basic features of the Exchange client (including sending, receiving, sending attachments)

- The message formatting features (including rich text formatting, embedding graphics into a mail message, and automatic signatures)

- Message management (including intelligent message rules, filtering, and folder views)

- Enhanced features (including digital message encryption, integration with other Windows applications, and Web hotlinks)

All of these features in electronic messaging systems have evolved over time and are included as part of the Microsoft Exchange client application.

Basic Features

Microsoft Exchange, like most electronic messaging programs, allows users to send, receive, reply to, forward, and print messages. Unlike other programs, however, Microsoft Exchange has enhanced these features in its fully integrated groupware Exchange Server environment, providing users with a centralized message storage system with its Universal Inbox, better compatibility for the sending and receiving of attachments by supporting the two most common file attachment translation formats, and easier reference and creation of message recipients with an improved address book. These features form the core to workgroup communications and information management.

The Universal Inbox

One of the most innovative new functions of the Microsoft Exchange client is the concept of the Universal Inbox. As described in Chapter 1, all information is stored on a Microsoft Exchange Server as objects, which enables it to centralize all forms of information in a single message folder. Information can consist of text messages, graphic files, word processing documents, fax documents, voicemail messages, specialized forms, and posted message information. Thanks to this capability, many organizations have replaced databases and shared subdirectories with Exchange folders. Since an Exchange folder can hold more than just text information, and the information can be searched for future reference, the Exchange folder has become the universal information depository. Figure 2-1 shows a Microsoft Exchange client screen with various types of items stored, including basic electronic mail messages, mail messages with attachments, discussion group forms, Microsoft Word documents, Microsoft Excel spreadsheets, and appointment schedule confirmations.

Send, Receive, Reply to, Forward, and Print Messages

These essential features allow users to create electronic messages, respond or reply to messages, forward messages to another recipient, and send messages to a printer. In Microsoft Exchange, these options are selected either as pull-down options or as button bar options.

- To compose a new message, select Compose | New Message or click on the Compose icon on the toolbar.

- To print a message, select File | Print or click on the Print icon on the toolbar.

- To reply to a message, select Compose | Reply to Sender, or click on the Reply icon on the toolbar.

- To reply to a message and include all carbon copy recipients, select Compose | Reply to All, or click on the Reply All icon on the toolbar.

- To forward a message, select Compose | Forward, or click on the Forward icon on the toolbar.

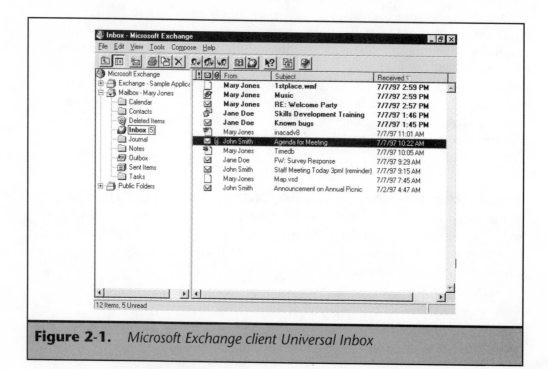

Figure 2-1. *Microsoft Exchange client Universal Inbox*

Attachments

Microsoft Exchange allows users to easily attach files to their outgoing e-mail messages. The file(s) can be a word processing document, a spreadsheet file, a graphics image file, or any other application or data file. Files can be attached to a mail message by selecting Insert | File as shown in Figure 2-2, or by dragging and dropping the file from the Windows File Manager utility or the Windows 95 Explorer utility directly into the message. The Microsoft Exchange Server will automatically convert attachments in either a MIME or UUENCODE format which are the two most common file translation formats in Internet attachment interchange.

Global and Personal Address Books

Microsoft Exchange provides users with a Global Address Book that contains the addresses of all of the e-mail recipients in the organization. In addition, individual users each have their own personal address book in which they can insert their personal e-mail address list. Addresses are created by selecting the type of address (Internet, X.400, fax, MS Mail, etc.) and entering the correct information into the necessary fields. The available address options are shown

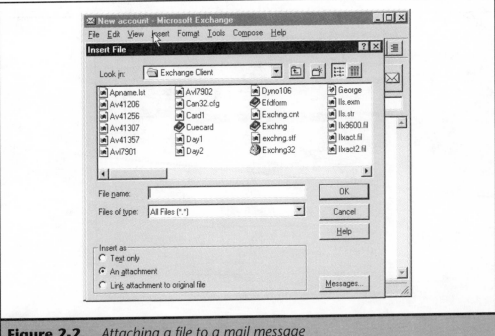

Figure 2-2.   *Attaching a file to a mail message*

in Figure 2-3. To enter a new recipient into the personal address book, do the following:

1. Choose Tools | Address Book from the main menu.
2. Select File | New Entry from the address book submenu.
3. Select the type of recipient format (fax, Internet, X.400, etc.).
4. Enter the recipient's information.

cc:s and bcc:s

Carbon copies (cc:) and blind carbon copies (bcc:) are ways for users to send a copy of a message to someone other than the intended recipient. The message may be sent to invoke a response, or it may simply be sent for the recipient's reference. If the recipient resides in the sender's address book, the name can be pulled from the address book as shown in Figure 2-4, or the e-mail address can be manually added when the message is sent by typing the user's e-mail address.

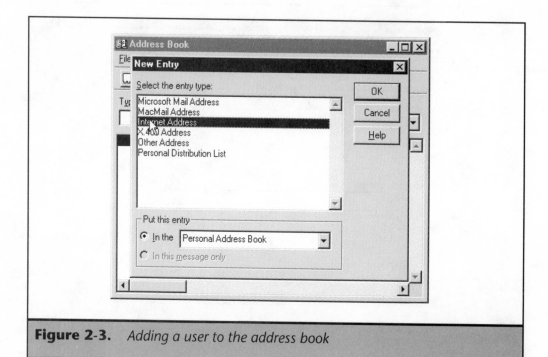

Figure 2-3.   *Adding a user to the address book*

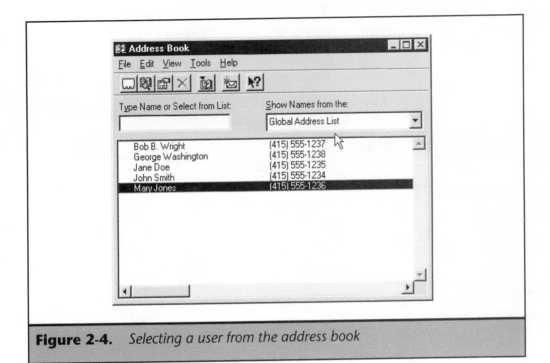

Figure 2-4. *Selecting a user from the address book*

Message Formatting

As electronic mail messaging has evolved, users have become more sensitive to how their mail message looks, so the need to improve the way messages are created and formatted became an important focus of the Microsoft Exchange client software. Rather than creating completely new tools for the message format enhancements in the Exchange Server software, Microsoft built on the existing message formatting tools and borrowed from standards such as OLE 2.0 and Microsoft Word.

Rich Text Formatting

Microsoft Exchange supports rich text formatting or *WYSIWYG* (what you see is what you get), which allows for the intermixing of text, variable font styles and sizes, boldface and underlining, bulleted text, color text, graphics, and image files. Rich text formatting similar to the text in the sample mail message in Figure 2-5 provides users with the ability to line up columns, highlight information through font sizes or colors, and integrate graphics and images to improve the message content.

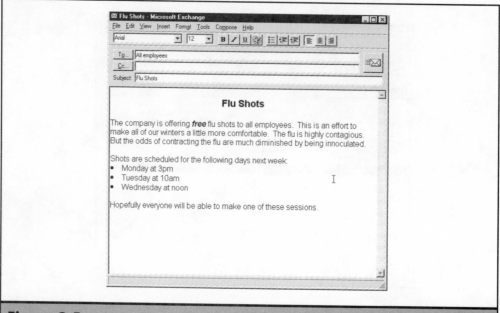

Figure 2-5. *An Exchange document utilizing rich text formatting*

WordMail Formatting

WordMail Formatting allows a user that is using the Exchange client as well as Microsoft Word to use Microsoft Word as the editor for mail messages. Because Microsoft Word has many more editing features and document management utilities than the standard Exchange client, the options available for the WordMail user include thesaurus look-up, .dot document templates, form fill, borders and shading, paragraph management, tables, and macros. An example of an e-mail message generated with WordMail and containing a table, borders, shading, and form fill is shown in Figure 2-6. The WordMail feature gives Exchange users more flexibility and control in generating the look and setup of their messages than ever before.

OLE 2.0 Support

The Microsoft Exchange client supports the linking and the embedding of information directly into the body of the electronic message. Rather than attaching the entire contents of a file to an e-mail message, Exchange allows

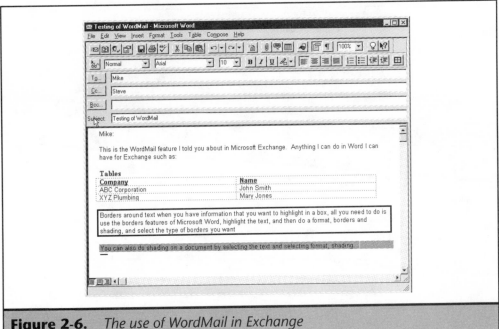

Figure 2-6. *The use of WordMail in Exchange*

users to insert a link to a document in the e-mail message that points to a common storage location of the document. This function significantly minimizes the amount of messaging traffic on the network, the storage space that multiple copies of the same file would take up, and eliminates the multiple versions of a file that would exist on the network. An object can be linked by choosing Insert | File from the main menu and selecting Link Attachment to Original File instead of Attachment. Object embedding allows a selected portion of a document to be visually stored in an Exchange message, similar to the embedded graphics file shown in Figure 2-7. The portion of the embedded document can be double-clicked to open the full document for editing, viewing, or printing.

Automatic Signature

At the end of each e-mail message, a signature can be added (either manually or automatically). Typically the signature would be text-based, such as the

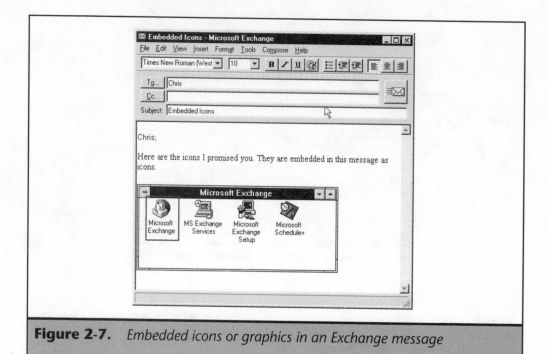

Figure 2-7. *Embedded icons or graphics in an Exchange message*

sender's name, address, phone number, or other pertinent information, similar to the electronic signature shown here.

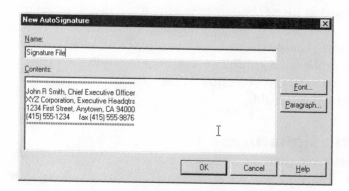

The signature could also include information such as the fact that the sender is sending the message from a remote location or from a different time zone. Multiple signatures can be created and manually invoked at any time. To create an automatic signature, do the following:

1. Choose Tools | AutoSignature from the main menu.

2. Select New.

3. Give this new signature a name and enter in the text of the signature.

When you are ready to insert the signature in your document, do the following:

1. Choose Tools | AutoSignature from the main menu.

2. Select the signature you want.

3. Select Insert.

To have a signature added to the end of every e-mail message that is sent:

1. Choose Tools | AutoSignature from the main menu.

2. Select the "Add the default selection to the end of outgoing messages" checkbox.

Message Management

Now that the e-mail user can create—and receive—sophisticated mail messages with embedded graphics, colors, variable fonts, and attachments, the need to manage all of these messages becomes very important. The Exchange client software contains message management features that help users sort their messages, view messages by user-definable groupings, or automatically respond to or act on incoming messages based on their characteristics. These features, which are the basics of workgroup and groupware information management, allow Microsoft Exchange users to easily find and categorize their messaging information.

Out of Office Assistant

The Out of Office Assistant is a server-based rule supported by Microsoft Exchange that allows e-mail message recipients to automatically reply to messages if a particular event occurs. The event may be a vacation (in which case the vacationing recipient would want to notify the sender that he or she will be gone until a specific date), as shown in Figure 2-8. There are a variety of options and triggers for the out of office response. An out of office trigger

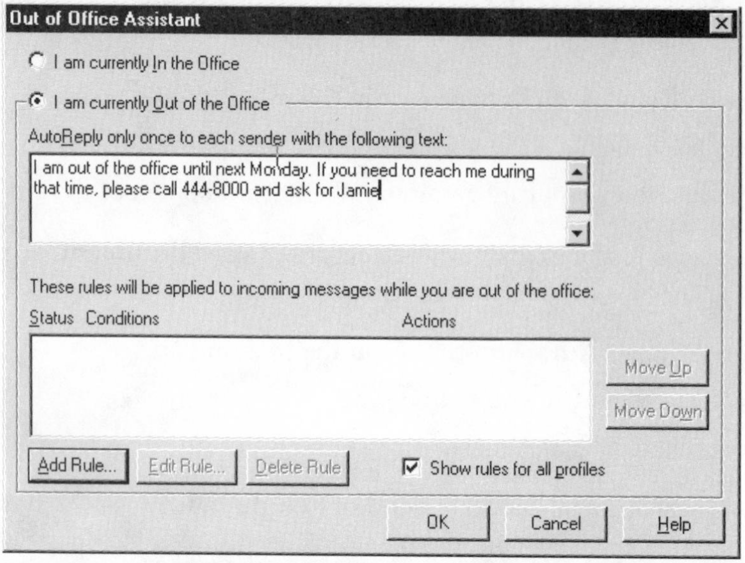

Figure 2-8. *Creating an out of office notice*

can be created by choosing Tools | Out of Office Assistant from the main menu of the Exchange client and then selecting the options and events the user desires to occur when a message is received.

When a message is sent to a user with an out of office rule set for his or her system, the sender of the message will receive the notice created by the intended recipient. These rules in Microsoft Exchange are server-based, so they remain active even if the creator of the rule is not logged in to the system. The Exchange Server manages these rules and applies them when the condition of the rule is triggered. In addition, Microsoft Exchange rules are intelligent: when a sender receives a copy of a notification that the recipient is out of the office for a period of time, any subsequent messages to that recipient will not invoke additional out of office notices. The sender will only receive one out of office notice from that recipient, thus minimizing the number of spurious message responses distributed.

Inbox Assistant

The inbox assistant enables a series of triggers to invoke a specific result. The trigger may include automatically moving all e-mail messages received from a specific sender to a specific user folder. The rule shown in Figure 2-9 shows

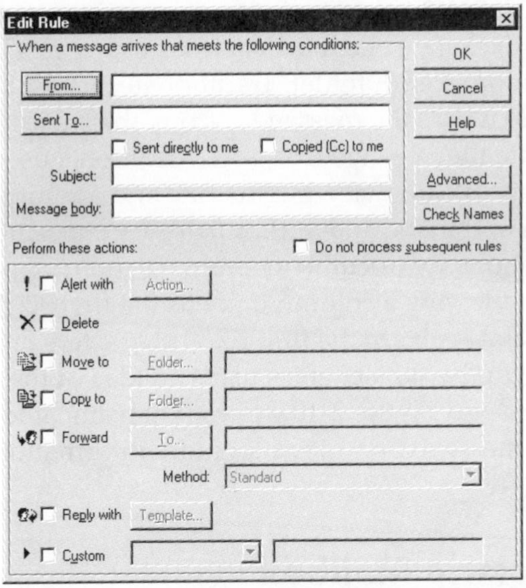

Figure 2-9. *An inbox assistant rule to move specific messages to a folder upon receipt*

how the inbox assistant can be configured to perform this automated procedure. The trigger may also induce a pager to notify the recipient of an incoming urgent e-mail message, or cause a message to be marked with priority status. The inbox assistant will function whether users are logged in or not, as it is also a server-based rule.

Client-Based Filtering

Users can select which e-mail messages they would like to filter to see (or to not see) within a folder. By selecting from a series of options, a user can choose to filter by recipient name for messages the user sent, or filter by a sender's name for messages the user received. This is done by selecting View I Filter in the main menu of the Exchange client and then selecting the desired filtration options. Users can also choose to filter by the size of the file or by the date range of the receipt of the message. This option is frequently used by individuals who have dozens of mail messages in a folder and only want to see the messages from a particular sender, messages related to a particular subject topic, or messages received during a one-week period. Filters can be invoked on any folder in Microsoft Exchange.

Client-Based Views

Within a folder, the Exchange client user can select any of 45 plus different columns of information in each folder. Traditionally, users' mailboxes have columns that include where the message is from, the subject of the message, and the time and date the message was sent. Additional user-definable options in Microsoft Exchange include viewing the title and author of the message (which corresponds to the title and author fields by choosing File | Properties in Windows applications for documents dragged and dropped into an Exchange folder), or viewing a column that has the first 30 characters of the message itself. The ability to see the first 20-30 characters of an electronic message in addition to the subject gives users an idea of the content of an incoming e-mail message. Figure 2-10 shows that being able to view the first 25 characters of the message provides a lot more information than just the subject.

Delegate Access to Mailbox

Microsoft Exchange allows a user to delegate message replies or the initiation of messages to another user. This other user may be a secretary, an associate, or

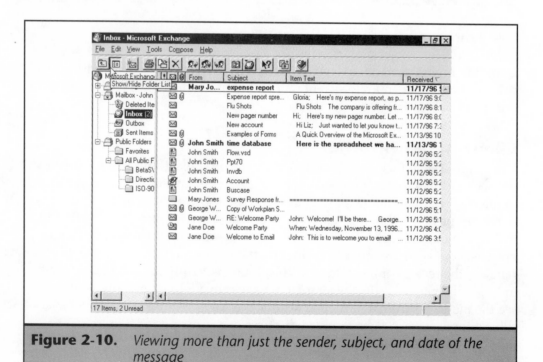

Figure 2-10. *Viewing more than just the sender, subject, and date of the message*

a business partner in charge of correspondence during the user's absence.
When a user delegates his or her mailbox functions, as shown here,

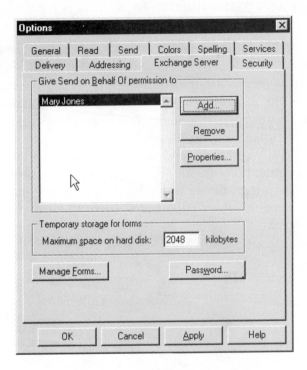

recipients of e-mail messages from the designated user will notice a line in the
message telling them that the e-mail message was sent on behalf of the
original user. The original user retains the ability to prevent the designated
correspondent from viewing personal messages or confidential information. A
user can delegate rights to another user by doing the following:

1. Choose Tools | Options from the main menu.

2. Select the Exchange Server tab.

3. Enter the name of the person to whom you want to give privileges in
   the Give Send on Behalf Of permission to box.

Enhanced Functionality

Now that users can send and receive fancy e-mail messages, as well as manage
these messages, it's time to look at the additional features that have been

included in the Exchange Server software. The additions make Microsoft Exchange more compatible with other applications (including the Internet) as well as more secure in its confirmation and authentication enhancements.

Integration with Other Microsoft Applications

Microsoft Exchange provides integration with other Microsoft Office applications as well as other Windows-based applications. The integration may be as simple as enabling a document to be selected and sent via e-mail from within the application, or it could involve integrating complete information (such as project schedules) directly into Exchange schedules. The amount of integrated support is dependent upon the application (detailed application integration options are highlighted in Part Four of this book). A simple example of the integration of a Windows application into Exchange is the ability to send and post information from Microsoft Word directly into Microsoft Exchange mail and folders, as shown here.

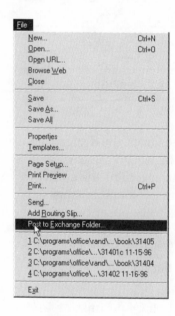

Many users of Microsoft Exchange are no longer storing documents on their C or F drives, but rather posting information into Microsoft Exchange folders. The main benefit of posting information to an Exchange folder is that it centralizes e-mail messages, Word documents, faxes, voicemail messages, or any other Exchange information into a central folder similar to a contact management software or tightly integrated information store.

Integrated Spell Checker

Microsoft Exchange uses the same Spell Checker that Microsoft Office uses. Spell checking can be selected by the user at any time by choosing Tools | Spelling, or it can be configured to spell check the document every time before sending a message.

Integrated Remote Connectivity via Point-to-Point Protocol (PPP) and RAS

Unlike most e-mail programs that have a separate LAN version of the mail client software and a separate remote version of the mail client, the Microsoft Exchange client software supports messaging within an office for sending and receiving electronic messages as well as remote access to Exchange, all in the same client program. When the Microsoft Exchange client is launched and an individual uses his or her computer for both LAN-based and remote-based message access, an option will appear on the user's screen allowing him or her to select an Exchange Server on a LAN or to use dial-up remote access, as shown in this dialog box:

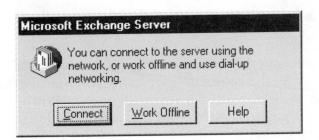

When users are remotely connected to the Exchange Server, they use the Remote Mail options of the Exchange client, as shown next. Remote access configuration and operation is detailed in Part Four of this book.

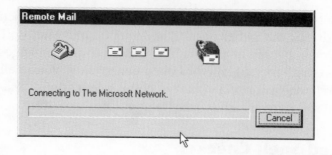

Digital Signatures and Public and Private Key Encryption

To ensure security between users or from a user to the server, Microsoft Exchange supports a number of security systems including digital signatures, which verifies that the true respondent is actually the originator of the reply, and public and private key encryption, which ensures the link between the client and the server are authenticated. Digital signatures and encryption need to be configured by the Microsoft Exchange administrator for the entire network. If the network has digital signatures and encryption enabled, a user can invoke these options by doing the following:

1. When composing a message, choose File I Properties.
2. Select the Security tab.
3. Select Encrypt message contents and attachments or add digital signature to message.

Automatic Hotlinks to Web URL Addresses in Messages

Microsoft Exchange supports automatic hotlinks between URL listings in a message to automatically launch the user's browser. With just one key click, the user can access a Web site listed on a mail message. When a user receives anything containing *http://*, the Microsoft Exchange client highlights this Web URL as an embedded link to a message, similar to the link shown in Figure 2-11. When users click on that link, their browser software is automatically loaded and brought up onscreen for the URL link specified.

Figure 2-11.   *A Web URL automatically highlighted in a message*

Features and Functions of the Microsoft Outlook Client

The Microsoft Outlook client began shipping with Microsoft Office 97 and is compatible with Windows 95, Windows NT v3.51 (Service Pack 5), and Windows NT v4.0. The Microsoft Outlook client does not replace the Microsoft Exchange client in all instances. Because of the limited operating system support for the Outlook client (Windows 95 and NT v4.0), and some issues of cross-compatibility between the standard Exchange client and the Outlook client (detailed later in this chapter), the Exchange client may be more appropriate as the standard for many environments.

The Exchange Outlook client supports all of the features and functions of the original Exchange client described earlier in this chapter. The main Outlook client screen is shown in Figure 2-12.

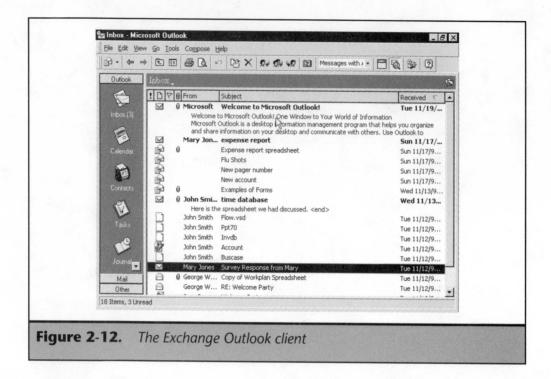

Figure 2-12. *The Exchange Outlook client*

Message Recall and Message Replacement

The message recall and message replacement features of the Exchange Outlook client, as shown next, allow users to recall messages they have already sent as long as the recipient has not already viewed the message. The user has the option of either deleting the sent message or replacing the sent message with an updated or modified version of the message.

Locking Message Reply Text

The Outlook client presents users with the option of locking the content of the messages they are sending in order to prevent recipients from changing the content of the information and forwarding it on to another e-mail user. Although this option was enabled in the Exchange client by setting the message sensitivity to "private," the Outlook client has a specific lockout option It is important to remember that although message locking can significantly minimize the chance that a message will be altered and forwarded, the only way to ensure a message is locked and authentic is to use the digital signatures features of Microsoft Exchange.

Individual Message Tracking

Although most e-mail programs allow users to receive notification of whether a recipient has received or read a message, the Outlook client takes that function one step further by allowing the sender to track the message status in the original sent mail copy of the message. Now a user can easily verify that a particular message was received and read by the intended recipients all in one message location rather than receiving individual message confirmation of receipts. Figure 2-13 shows a message tracking summary viewed by opening the message in the Sent Mail folder and selecting the Tracking Message tab.

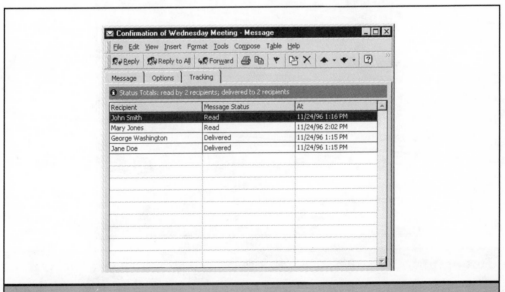

Figure 2-13. *Message tracking summary*

Expanded Hyperlinks

The original Exchange client automatically highlighted all http:// Web links in a message. The Outlook client adds mailto: links as well as file: links to highlight e-mail names as well as file names and file locations. A recipient can simply click on the highlighted link and immediately access the highlighted Web page, compose a message to send to the highlighted name, or open the highlighted file.

Message Voting

The Outlook client includes an options button on the message that allows the user to create a simple voting function for the message recipient. To create the voting options, the sender of the message would select the Options tab on the mail message and fill in the information as shown in Figure 2-14. The vote could be something as simple as "yes, I agree with the message" or "no, I disagree with the message." With a single keystroke, the recipient of the mail

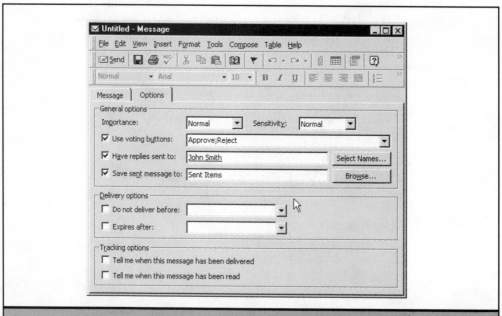

Figure 2-14.   *The voting screen that simplifies a user response to a message*

message can automatically respond with a vote without having to type a response. The text of a vote is user-definable and can be one of many options in a list.

Relative Date Fields

The Microsoft Outlook client allows users to search, sort, or filter information based on relative dates, such as in the last four weeks, past six months, or last seven days (as shown here), rather than confining them to actual dates.

Redirected Replies

The sender of a message can specify a different user as the intended recipient of message replies. Rather than automatically sending the reply to a message back to the sender, the reply can be confirmed and sent to an assistant, or automatically posted to a message folder. This feature helps users redirect information to another individual or centralized location of their choosing. The redirected reply option is chosen when the user is creating a message by selecting the Options tab on the message and entering the name of a recipient or folder in the Have replies sent to section.

Single Step Off-line Synchronization of E-mail, Calendar, Contracts, Tasks, Journal, and Notes

Because the client components of the original Microsoft Exchange client software were separate programs, whenever users wanted to replicate their e-mail messages, schedule, or public folders, they needed to load the separate programs and run through a complicated procedure to replicate the information. The Outlook client consolidates this process. When a replication is initiated, everything from e-mail messages, appointment schedules, public folder information, contract information, tasks, journal, and notes are all replicated in a single procedure.

The Exchange Client Versus the Outlook Client

The question many people ask is "if the Outlook client is the new version of the Exchange client, why wouldn't I want to use the most recent Outlook client version?" The deciding factor for many organizations is cross-platform compatibility. The Outlook client is only available for Windows 95, Windows NT v3.51 (Service Pack 5), and Windows NT v4.0. For organizations that need to communicate with users on other platforms such as DOS, Windows v3.*x*, or Macintosh that must use the original Exchange client, it may be desirable to maintain the same client software on all desktops.

As for e-mail capabilities in a mixed Exchange client and Outlook client environment, the two client applications can interchange e-mail messages, reply, forward, and manage messages between the platforms without a problem. There are hitches, however; feature set incompatibilities within a workgroup of mixed Exchange and Outlook client users include a lack of response to or interaction of the original Exchange client user and the new Outlook features such as message voting or hyperlink connections. The more significant incompatibilities between the two different client applications are those that affect the groupware interactions of a workgroup, such as scheduling, discussion groups, and forms management (these are detailed at the end of Chapter 3). It is the extension of these groupware capabilities that need to be reviewed to determine if the impact of cross-organizational interaction between the Exchange client and the Outlook client are of significance for the workgroup.

The Chapter in Review

- Exchange has rich features that make it more user-friendly and useable than most e-mail appliciations. Exchange has basic mail features, as well as advanced message formatting, server-based rules, message filtering, digital encryption, and digital authentication (integrated support for Internet home page addresses). Server-based rules are better than client-based rules in that they allow the rules to be run even if users are not in the office and have the PC turned off. This ensures that the rules get applied as often as needed without jeopardizing the security of the network by having a user's PC left on.

■ Exchange is also more user-friendly by having a consistant interface between platforms. This helps users to leverage their knowledge of this application, even if they work on a Macintosh at home and a PC at work.

■ Exchange has four feature categories: basic features, message formatting features, message management, and enhanced features. Because of the universal inbox, Exchange has become the universal information depository. Toolbars can be used to create, respond to, or move a message. The bcc: (blind carbon copy) field allows some users to receive a message without the original recipient being aware of everyone else on the distribution list. Rich text formatting allows e-mail to have the same benefits of formatting options available in word processing documents. Exchange supports linking a document that needs routing rather than inserting an attachment. This minimizes network traffic, hard drive storage space usage, and message size. Graphics can be embedded so that users can see graphics in e-mail as they have with text documents. A signature can be added manually or automatically, along with messages such as business card information, the user's current physical location, and time zone.

■ The Out of Office Assistant is a server-based rule supported by Exchange that allows messages to receive automatic replies if a particular event occurs. An inbox assistant enables a series of e-mail events to trigger a specific result. Filters are used to limit the number of messages listed based on a certain set of criteria. A user can delegate rights to another user to respond to e-mails while out of the office. Remote access users utilize the same software as network users. The Outlook client supports message recall and message replacement. Outlook enables users to track the status of a message within a summary folder.

Review Questions

Q. What are the benefits of Exchange's wide variety of features?

A. Ease of use leads to fewer support calls, greater excitement about the product means greater product utilization by end users, greater message management means more sophisticated storage and retrieval of messages, and enhanced features provide benefits to end users in areas they don't even realize they might need.

Q. Name five basic features of all messaging applications.

A. Send, receive, reply, forward, and print.

Q. Name seven information formats Exchange can accept.

A. Text messages, graphic files, word processing, fax documents, voicemail messages, specialized forms, and posted messages.

Q. How can a user set up Exchange to insert an electronic signature each time a message is sent?

A. From the main menu, choose Tools | AutoSignature. Select Add.

Q. Why is message management such an important feature to Exchange users?

A. With the added capabilities of Exchange, users have an increase of documents stored within Exchange. That makes document management features all the more important.

Q. How many Out of Office notifications will colleagues receive before the Automatic Assistant quits triggering them?

A. One.

Q. Can Exchange work with external user notification systems?

A. Yes; for example, it can page you via the inbox assistant.

Q. Name three security features of Exchange.

A. Digital signatures, encryption, and message locking.

Q. Name two clients that Microsoft Exchange Server can be used with, and their differences.

A. Outlook 97 and Exchange. Outlook is 32 bit and is supported on Windows 95 and NT 4.0 workstations. The Exchange client supports other platforms.

Q. Name additional benefits in using the Outlook client over Exchange.
A. Message recall, message tracking, extended hyperlinks, voting, relative fields, and all Exchange-related data is replicated at the same time.

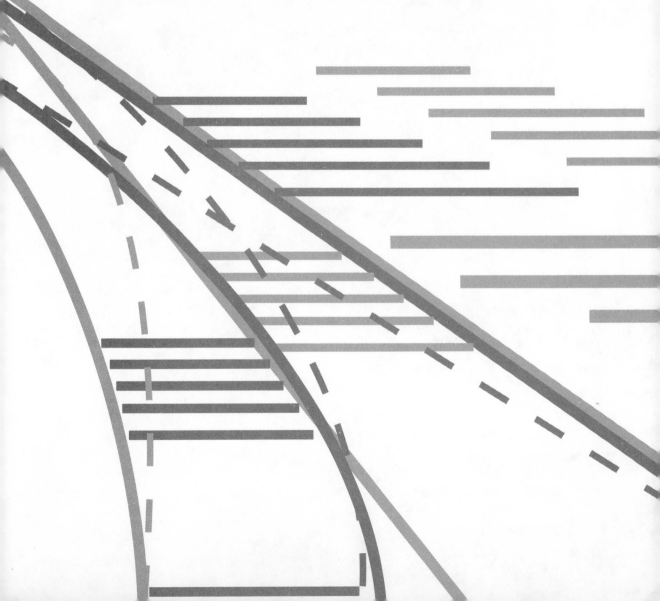

CHAPTER 3

The Groupware Capabilities of Microsoft Exchange

As you saw in Chapter 2, Microsoft Exchange contains a very robust set of features that have made it stand out as one of the best e-mail systems ever developed. However, it is the groupware capabilities discussed in this chapter that utilize Microsoft Exchange's extensive e-mail features that make Microsoft Exchange a full-featured intranet, workflow, and workgroup information manager. At a time when organizations around the world are attempting to increase workforce efficiency by providing systems to improve corporate communications and easier access to information regardless of its source (Internet, mainframe, local area network, text, graphics, or database), Microsoft Exchange Server is available to provide the information and communications infrastructure to facilitate these services.

This chapter will highlight the major groupware features of both the Microsoft Exchange client as well as the Outlook client, and will provide examples of how organizations are leveraging these capabilities to improve the way they communicate and do business.

Groupware Features and Functions of the Microsoft Exchange Client

The groupware functions of group scheduling, forms creation, and centralized information storage and management are all included in Microsoft Exchange. All of these features provide workgroups with an infrastructure that allows them to streamline their means of communication. A group of individuals gains workgroup capability when they specify a shared method of communication in addition to a centralized location in which to store and retrieve information. Since all of these processes in Microsoft Exchange are electronic, the workgroup can become virtual, spanning a group of cubicles, multiple floors in a building, or multiple dispersed locations around the globe.

The Microsoft Scheduler Program

The Microsoft Scheduler program (known as version 7.5 with the release of Microsoft Exchange v5.) is typically the initial groupware application from the Microsoft Exchange Server environment that organizations use. The Scheduler component of Microsoft Exchange allows an individual to enter and keep track of personal appointments, such as meeting dates, scheduled reminders, vacations, and holidays. Since users are integrated into the Microsoft Exchange Server enterprise-wide environment, they have the ability to make their personal schedules available to view by others in Microsoft Exchange. The ability for users to share their schedules forms the first workgroup-enabled process. The Exchange Scheduler facilitates this process by providing a number of calendar features and capabilities.

Personal Appointment Scheduling

Microsoft Exchange users can easily create and maintain a personal appointment calendar or schedule. Users have the option of entering one-time appointments or events or recurring events (such as weekly Friday meetings, or a first-Tuesday-of-the-month conference call). The procedure for inserting appointments is similar whether it is a single or recurring event. To add an appointment:

1. Choose Insert I Appointment from the main menu of the Schedule client software.

2. Enter the date, time, and description of the appointment, as shown here:

3. If the appointment is recurring, select the Make Recurring option and enter the characteristics of the recurring appointment, as shown here:

The main appointment screen has a few options to choose from. By selecting the Set Reminder for option, users will be notified on their desktop screens of an upcoming appointment. If the user selects the Private option, the appointment will be marked as private and the appointment description will become unavailable to other workgroup members. This function allows users to enter private notations or appointments without worrying that the entire organization will know about personal events entered into their calendars.

Setting Privileges for Appointment Calendar Access by Others

Once users enter their personal appointments into their personal calendars, they can make their calendars available to be viewed by others within the organization. By default, an individual's calendar is inaccessible to anyone in the Microsoft Exchange organization. In order to grant other users with access to their calendars, users must configure the access permission. The available permissions are as follows:

- **None** No access to the user's calendar
- **Read** Ability to read appointments (non-private appointments only)
- **Create** Ability to read non-private appointments and create appointments for the user
- **Modify** Ability to read non-private appointments, create appointments, and modify existing appointments in a user's calendar

- **Delegate** Ability to read non-private appointments, create and modify existing appointments, to invite others to appointments on behalf of the user

- **Owner** Full rights to read, create, modify, and invite users to appointments

- **Delegate Owner** Full rights to a delegated user(s) to read, create, modify, and invite people to appointments on behalf of the individual

To allocate these rights to others, users would need to determine which privileges they would want to give to others in the workgroup, and then set those privileges in their schedule. To do so:

1. Choose Tools | Set Access Permissions from the main menu of the Scheduler program.

2. Select Add and select the individual(s) or group(s) to be defined for special privileges.

3. Select the user role of none, read, create, modify, delegate, owner, or delegate owner.

Once the privileges are assigned for an individual's calendar, other users that have been given access privileges will be able to read, create, or modify appointments according to the access permission designation.

Group Scheduling

Regardless of whether a user has been given the right to read, create, or modify appointments, all users have the ability to invite others to appointments. The Scheduler software does not automatically book an individual to an appointment unless that individual has the right to create appointments for the attendees; however, the attendees will, at minimum, receive an invitation to an appointment that they can either accept or deny.

To invite others to an appointment, the user would follow the procedure for creating a personal appointment (Insert | Appointment), and enter in the time, date, and description of the appointment. In order to invite others to the appointment, the individual would now select the Attendees tab and include those to be invited. The individual can select required attendees as well as optional attendees. The designation of required and optional attendee is not enforced by Microsoft Exchange, but it does allow the invitee to know how urgently his or her presence is requested at the meeting.

Another way to invite a group of users to attend an appointment is to use the Planner option in the Scheduler software. By showing both the available and busy schedules of potential invitees in a graphical format, the Planner option can help determine an appointment time that won't conflict with anyone's prior engagements. You can use the Planner option when you create an appointment using the Insert | Appointment option. Before entering the time and date, select the Planner tab on the Appointment option screen. Click on the Invite button and select the desired attendee(s) to the appointment. All attendees' available and busy schedules are shown onscreen:

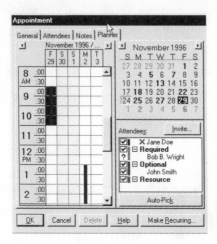

The user can now select an open appointment time for all attendees. By highlighting a time and date range on the planner and then clicking the right button on the mouse, the other attendees' schedule conflicts will be displayed as long as the user has at least read privileges on the attendees' calendars. This option allows a user to determine if an attendee's schedule conflict is actually due to another appointment, or if the time is blocked off simply as a reminder or notation to return a phone call at some time during the day.

Once a Planner-defined appointment is selected and the user selects OK, an e-mail message is created that invites all attendees to the appointment. When the user selects the Send button, the invitations are distributed.

Resource Scheduling

In addition to scheduling appointments for individuals and groups of individuals, Microsoft Exchange also supports the scheduling of resources that may be necessary for the appointment (such as a conference room), or for an individual user (such as use of a company vehicle). Resources are created by the Microsoft Exchange administrator just like an electronic mail user is created. The difference between a resource and a user is that a resource does not have an e-mail message box to receive invitations to appointments. The resource has a schedule that is viewable by users of the workgroup who have been granted permission to schedule the resource (read, create, or modify the resource availability).

When users are booking an appointment using the Insert | Appointment option from the main Scheduler menu, they would select the resource exactly like they would select other attendees to the appointment: straight from the organization's Global Address List.

Integrated Task and Contact Management

In addition to standard appointment scheduling, Microsoft Exchange also has an integrated task and contact management utility. To enter either a task or a contact, users select the Insert | Task or the Insert | Contact options from the main Scheduler menu. An entered task shows up in the user's To-Do list, which is a tab on the left side of the user's schedule list. Instead of seeing a daily view of the appointment calendar, an individual can click on the To-Do tab to see any of the tasks they have outlined. A task can be specified with an end day (like a due date by which the task must be completed), and can be tracked with a status, such as percentage completed of the task, as well as a rolling history of notes on the task.

The contact component allows an individual to enter in the names, addresses, phone numbers, and notes on other individuals. This information becomes a mini-contact database for the individual.

Multiple Calendar Views

Microsoft Exchange provides the ability to view and print calendars in any of a few dozen different ways. A few of the options include viewing/printing based on:

- A daily view of appointments (including or excluding private appointments)
- A weekly view of appointments (5-day week, 7-day week, including or excluding private appointments), as shown in Figure 3-1
- A monthly view of appointments
- Appointments and To-Do lists

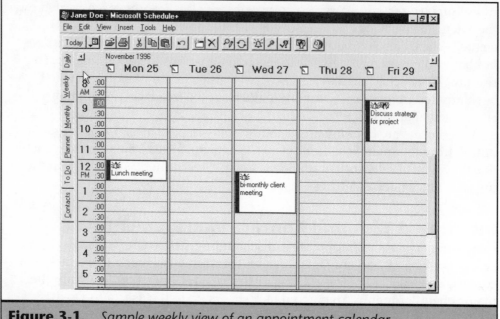

Figure 3-1. *Sample weekly view of an appointment calendar*

- Contacts and To-Do lists
- A daily or weekly view based on a user-defined length of day (such as an 8 a.m.-5 p.m. day, or 6 a.m.-6 p.m. day, etc.)

Viewing or printing a calendar, contact list, or To-Do list enables a simple view at-a-glance method of seeing information entered into the Scheduler application.

Public Folders and Folder Replication

The public folders and folder replication of Microsoft Exchange comprise the heart of its group communications infrastructure. The public folders in Microsoft Exchange are storage folders available to a defined group of Microsoft Exchange users. Users can drag and drop e-mail messages, word processing documents, and graphic files into public folders designed for a number of users just as they can drag and drop similar files to universal private folders (as described in Chapter 2).

Creating Public Folders and Public Folder Security

A public folder is created by the Microsoft Exchange administrator or by any user who has been given the right to create public folders for the organization. The security and access to these folders are also created by the Microsoft Exchange administrator or by the original creator of the folder. An individual who creates a public folder can click on the right mouse button and select Properties | Permissions and identify the individual(s) or group(s) of users that should have access to the folder as well as the level of their rights to the folder (to read, create, or modify information stored in the folder).

Managing Information Within a Public Folder

As long as a user has privileges to the public folder, he or she can drag and drop information into the folder such as e-mail messages, documents, and graphic files. A core functionality of public folders is the ability to share information across a workgroup of users. This may include a folder full of common document templates used by the organization, a clustering of company policies and procedures, or a consolidation of e-mail message information like a common newsgroup store.

Because the information in any folder in Microsoft Exchange can be a variety of types of information shared by a defined group of users, the possibilities of this capability is extensive, and is the core to intranet and workgroup communications that will be highlighted throughout this book. One of the first tools provided in the Microsoft Exchange Server software to help manage this workgroup information is the Exchange Forms Designer.

Exchange Forms Designer

The Microsoft Exchange Forms Designer is a utility that allows users to create electronic forms with fill-in fields for an individual to enter text, graphics, or other structured information. Rather than allowing information to be disseminated across a workgroup that has the potential of invoking a variety of free form responses, a form targets specific information being requested in a structured format to enable a more efficient method of directed reply. For example, a form can be a series of questions for an office supplies order request that can include queries to users about what office supplies they need, the quantity of supplies they need, and when they need the item(s). Or, a similar form can actually have the type of items already listed in a checkbox format so that an individual filling out the form can select items from the list that they need such as staples, pens, notepads, or paper clips.

Graphical Drag-and-Drop Forms Development

The Microsoft Exchange Forms Designer is built on the Microsoft E-Forms product, which allows for a graphical drag and drop of the form components. The form components may be a box for a name, a checkbox or button that a user selects or deselects, or a text box with a scroll bar in which to fill in a paragraph of information. The Forms Designer comes with a tutorial that introduces users to sample forms and helps them to start creating their own basic forms. The tutorial can be easily completed in one to two hours. Many users take one or more of the handful of sample forms provided free with the Microsoft Exchange product, like the one shown in Figure 3-2, and modify them to meet their needs.

More sophisticated users and programmers familiar with Visual Basic can modify and edit the basic drag-and-drop Forms Designer templates since the forms are stored in a standard Visual Basic project format. This can allow a programmer to add in links to SQL databases, open existing database files from Microsoft Access or other databases, and integrate simple forms information with live database information.

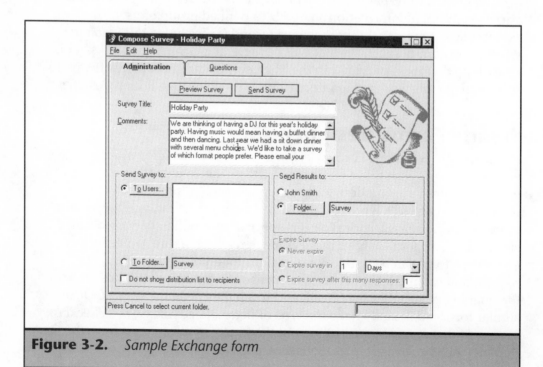

Figure 3-2. *Sample Exchange form*

Forms Designer Wizard

To assist in the creation of forms, Microsoft Exchange includes a forms designer wizard that walks a user through the creation of a basic form. The forms designer wizard asks users if they want the form to be a posting form (used to fill in information and post the information to a folder), or a form that is part of a discussion and response (used to start a discussion and then invoke a response form for a reply). The fields, names, and storage functions of the form creation are all outlined so that users enter all of the required information to successfully create an Exchange form. The forms designer wizard also walks the individual directly through posting the form on the Exchange server so that other users will have access to the form when they are required to post information to a public folder.

Compose and Response Forms

One of the options for forms is a Compose and Response form. These forms are used to create discussions in which the compose form invokes a discussion topic, and users who wish to reply to the discussion topic can do so with a response form. If a new, separate topic is created, a new compose form is filled out with linked response forms to that discussion topic. When a compose form is created, the designer of the form will typically create a response form that is linked to the compose form. This tight linkage of information between the compose and response keep the thread of the discussion topic in sequence. Also, responses to initial topics are indented so a link between the creation of and response to a discussion can be visually tracked.

Built-in Forms Runtime

The Microsoft Exchange Forms Designer includes a Forms Runtime so that users that will not be creating forms and have no need for the full Forms Designer program can launch and run a form within a public folder using the included runtime module. This minimizes the amount of disk space required by each user to run group forms, and it also limits who has access to creating forms and adding them to the Exchange forms library.

Organizational and Personal Forms Library

Forms can be posted either globally on the Microsoft Exchange Server for all users with the appropriate rights to access the public folder and run the form to use, or they can be personal forms that are installed only on selected workstations. Most forms are typically global forms with access restrictions governed by the user's rights to access the public folder to which the form is linked. Global organizational forms are not automatically installed on every user's workstation. Organizational forms are stored on the Exchange server, and when a user with the appropriate folder rights wants to create or post a form, it is transferred from the server to the user's workstation and is run by the Forms Designer runtime module. Only a fraction of the form is loaded onto the user's workstation; the balance of the form continues to reside on the server. This ability to load and launch forms as they are needed helps an organization minimize the amount of desktop-to-desktop maintenance required to install or set up forms every time one is created. Personal forms are installed only on local workstations specific to a user. An example of a personal form may be one that is part of a message creation form (not a Compose and Response form) in which a user will fill in information to send to another recipient in a mail message (not posted to a public folder). Since the form only transfers over e-mail from one user to another, it only needs to be on the workstations of the sender and the receiver. A user may also use personal forms to create and test various forms prior to posting them as global organizational forms.

Updating Forms

As forms are updated within the organization, the global organizational forms can be replaced or updated at any time. When a user accesses the public folder with the organizational form attached, if the form was updated since the last time the user accessed it, the user's client software will automatically install and load the new or updated version of the form. This automatic forms update process helps the organization to create and modify forms without ever having to install or update software on every user's desktop.

Groupware Features and Functions of the Microsoft Outlook Client

Just as the Microsoft Exchange client was updated by the Microsoft Outlook client for e-mail, the Outlook client has updated the features and functions of the groupware portion of Microsoft Exchange. These groupware components include the scheduling, folder management, and electronic forms capabilities of Microsoft Exchange.

The overall improvement made in the Outlook client components affecting the groupware capabilities of Microsoft Exchange is the centralization of the groupware components into a single user application and interface. Rather than having a separate Microsoft Exchange e-mail client, a Microsoft Exchange Scheduler client, and a Microsoft Exchange Forms Runtime client, the Outlook client is one application that has all of these functions built into the single client software.

By centralizing all of the e-mail and groupware capabilities into one application, information can be linked, searched, and updated all at the same time, all from a single reference and edit process. An example of unified reference is the ability to search for all mentions of a client's company name. Under the original Exchange client, users can look up information based on the client's company name for any folder or group of folders (private or public) for any reference to the company. The information could be e-mail messages, word processing documents, spreadsheet files, or other information stored in a user's folder. With the Outlook client and the integration of groupware information along with mail message and folder information, that same reference in the Outlook client will additionally find calendar appointments, forms information, journal entries, and notes relative to the client's company name.

The option of switching between the mailbox, scheduler, contact names, journal entries, and notes are selected by choosing an option on the Outlook bar, as shown here:

The Outlook Calendar Program

The Outlook Calendar (or Scheduler) component has all of the same functions and features found in the Exchange Scheduler described earlier in this chapter, including creating personal appointments, inviting groups of individuals to a group appointment, scheduling resources, and viewing and printing in a variety of formats. The Outlook Calendar includes a number of new features that make the calendar easier to use, easier to manage, and provide enhanced scheduling functionality.

Selection of Discontinuous Days

While viewing calendars, if users want to view a series of days that are not continuous, the Outlook client now allows them to select a series of discontinuous days to view by simply holding down the CTRL key and clicking on the individual dates. Each of the dates show up onscreen as shown in Figure 3-3. This can be helpful if individuals are trying to book themselves for any three days over the next two weeks.

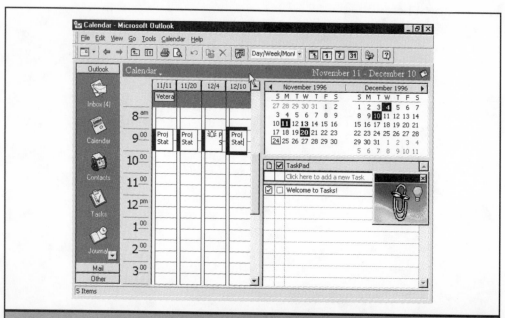

Figure 3-3.   *Selecting discontinuous days to view a schedule*

Shared Calendars

A shared calendar in the Outlook client is similar to a resource calendar in the Exchange client that is used by a number of individuals. However, a resource calendar is available for the entire workgroup to access, whereas a shared calendar may be created by one user who subsequently makes it available to another user. These two individuals can share this calendar without having to ask the Exchange administrator to create a resource, lock the security so that only they have access to the calendar, and then delete the resource upon completion. Shared calendars can be created at any time by any users with the right to create shared calendars.

Compressed Weekends

When viewing or printing schedules, weekends can be flagged to be compressed so that the displayed portion of the calendar can focus on the five days from Monday through Friday, giving more screen or print space to weekday schedules. Gaining back almost a quarter of the width of a schedule allows for more information and details to be displayed using the Outlook compressed weekend option than the original Exchange client is capable of showing.

Built-in Holidays

The Microsoft Outlook client includes a list of thousands of holidays from around the world that can be inserted into an Exchange calendar. This feature allows users to automatically insert all standard U.S. holidays such as Presidents' Day, Fourth of July, Labor Day, and Thanksgiving into their calendars. The Outlook client includes a series of standard holidays for different countries or religions that can be inserted and embedded into users' calendars, as shown here:

Contacts, Task Management, and Outlook Journals

The Microsoft Outlook client has enhanced and added features such as contact and task management as well as journal entry tracking of information. These features help users organize information more efficiently and quickly, and are similar to the capabilities of a personal information manager (PIM). Because these features are embedded into the Microsoft Outlook software as part of the Exchange Server enterprise application environment, any information stored in these modules can be integrated as part of the groupware and workflow of an enterprise workgroup.

View and View Switching for Contact Look Up

The contact component of the Outlook client allows an individual to enter names, addresses, phone numbers, and notes on individuals just like the contact information in the original Exchange client. The added functions in the Outlook client include the ability to view and switch the views of the contact information (similar to the view in Figure 3-4) to simplify the reference and printing of the stored information. By making this information easier to search and print, an individual can use the contact section of the Outlook client to link private and public folders to contacts similar to a full contact management software program.

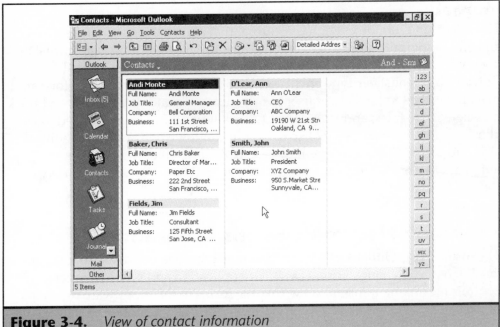

Figure 3-4. *View of contact information*

Shared Contacts

Just as calendars in the Outlook client can be shared between multiple users, contact names and folders can be shared between multiple users. A workgroup of users may create a workgroup contact list that can be viewed and accessed by a number of its members. This can minimize the entry and multiple entry of client or vendor information within a workgroup, as all of the individuals have access to a centralized store of information.

Task Request and Tracking Tasks

Tasks can be assigned using a request and reply system similar to the way users are invited to appointments and requested to confirm their attendance. A task can be created using the task option of Outlook and then assigned to a user, asking if he or she accepts the task. Once the task is accepted, it is tracked by the originator of the task. The recipient of the task can annotate the task, noting his or her completion percentage, which then updates the list. Any time information is updated on the status of any tasks, the originator will see the updates in his or her task summary. The Outlook tasks are integrated with Microsoft Project and are highlighted in detail in Part Four of this book.

Journals

The Microsoft Outlook client has a journal that allows the user to take notes and chronologically store information. The journal can be a private journal or one that can share information with other Outlook clients. The journal provides a spreadsheet-type entry as shown in Figure 3-5, and is in a format that allows the Outlook client user to organize ideas and discussions, and track messages, schedules, and tasks. The Outlook Journal can be automated to allow for automatic tracking of specific information (such as information keyed to a specific mail recipient or task manager). All of the information automatically or manually tracked can be entered and viewed in a variety of Journal formats.

The Outlook Electronic Forms Program

The forms in the Outlook client for Exchange have been updated to a 32-bit version of the Exchange Forms Designer application and provide better controls for linking information within the forms to the groupware functions of Exchange. The new Outlook Forms application can be linked so that

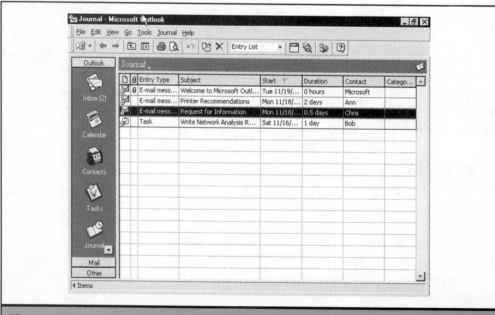

Figure 3-5.   *Sample use of the Outlook Journal*

calendar views can be inserted or retrieved from a form, Web links and Active-X controls can be integrated into a form, a users' journal can track inbound and outbound entry into a form, or a form can interlink contact, task, and journal entries in a contact management application process to track customers and revenues.

Outlook Views

The new Outlook Forms application allows users to calculate columns as well as control text, number, and font formatting within the form. Users create views by dragging and dropping column names and groups of items, or by selecting fields of information. Fields on an Outlook form can include calculated expressions, number and text formatting, and validation formulas. Forms can also support digital signatures and encryption.

Users can embed layouts or form definitions in a message and send them internally or externally to their organization to other users that may not have the form on their system.

Active X and Visual Basic Scripting

The Outlook Forms can be extended by integrating Active X controls to bring the power of development tools and controls into a workgroup form. Between Active X controls and Visual Basic scripting, basic Outlook Forms can be used for major implementation of information and forms management.

Replicating Information from One Workgroup to Another

As organizations begin to deploy public folder shares, share schedules, and electronically route information throughout the organization, the need to communicate outside of a single Microsoft Exchange Server to other Exchange servers in different business units becomes extremely critical. Microsoft Exchange provides the mechanism to replicate selected information from one Exchange server to another.

Identifying the Information to Replicate

The replication of information can be anything from a single folder all the way through the entire public folder structure of the entire organization. It all depends on whether the users on other Exchange servers or in different sites need to access the shared information. An example of sharing an entire public folder structure is an organization that is storing only corporate policies, marketing documents, and global client information in public folders. This information is valuable to all members of the organization and should be readily available to all employees regardless of their locality.

However, for an organization that may split their public information storage into global information and regional information, the organization may have folders on their servers that are corporate-wide and should be replicated, and some folders that have local business information that do not need to be replicated, as shown in Figure 3-6. In this case, the organization will designate only those folders that have global corporate information to be replicated, and leave the rest of the folders as locally accessible with no replication to other sites.

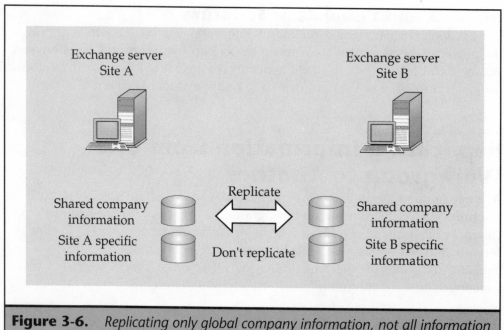

Figure 3-6.   *Replicating only global company information, not all information*

Configuring, Securing, and Managing Replications

Once the organization determines which information they are storing and which information needs to be replicated from site to site, they need to configure their Microsoft Exchange Servers to replicate the information, set up a security system to prevent users from accidentally or purposely deleting or modifying information, and finally manage the information that is replicated throughout their organization.

Setting up the Exchange Server to Replicate Information

On the Microsoft Exchange Server, the Exchange administrator has the ability to identify which folders should be replicated with other Exchange servers and how often the information should be replicated. During the replication process, the Exchange servers communicate with each other and compare the information to be replicated. The servers then determine which information is not identical and needs to be copied. The information could be different because something was added to the folder that needs to be replicated, something has been deleted from the folder, or the content of a message or object within the folder has been modified. The Exchange servers then determine what information needs to be sent and what information needs to be received between the two servers and begin the process of updating files, objects, and stored information.

The replication process can be configured to run continuously throughout the day whenever information is found to be out-of-sync and requires updating, or the Exchange server replication can be updated at a specific time (or at specific times) during the day.

The frequency of replication is dependent on the administrator of the network based on the bandwidth capability between the Exchange servers and the requirement to have updated information on both servers. If an organization requires up-to-date information, but the Exchange server only updates information once a night, the users potentially are using information that is an entire day old and may be of little value. The organization may have a requirement to update information on a regular (hourly) basis; however, the bandwidth between the two Exchange servers is an old and very slow 19.2K data line. During a full replication process, the Exchange servers can potentially tie up the entire bandwidth of the slow data line, leaving no available communication link bandwidth for other business purposes.

The actual configuration and sizing of the link lines between Exchange servers will be discussed in the planning, configuration, and implementation portions of Part Two of this book.

Securing Shared Information

Once the categories of information and the frequency of information updates has been determined, the organization needs to decide which users should have access to this information to read, create new, modify, or delete information on either side of the replication link. If the organization has one person at Site A creating information and storing it on the Exchange server, and a user at Site B doesn't know what the information is and begins to delete the information, the deletion will be replicated back over the link connection. Obviously, the ability to secure information in various locations is extremely critical. Most organizations limit replicated information to read-only, so that individuals can access and read shared information, but cannot modify or delete the information. By default, this is the easiest way to prevent accidental deletions of organization-wide information.

Managing Replicated Information

Once the information is secured, someone within the organization needs to determine how often the information should be examined and maintained on a regular basis. If the information is relatively static (like company policies or procedures), it may only need to be reviewed once a quarter or once a year. However, if the information needs to be updated weekly or monthly, like company marketing information or company product information, then the old information needs to be deleted so that it is not accidentally used or accessed (or unnecessarily taking up disk storage space). New information can then be updated on the server.

As organizations start to leverage the capabilities of a groupware environment and more and more users are sharing large sets of information, it becomes more and more important for organizations to have an efficient and specific process to identify unused information and conduct periodic reviews of the information. The topics of maintenance and tuning the Exchange server are detailed in Part Three of this book.

Using Microsoft Exchange for Basic Workgroup Communications

As a Microsoft Exchange client or Outlook client has access to some of the most sophisticated e-mail features available, including the capabilities of the groupware functions of group and personal scheduling, forms management, and public and private information stores, Microsoft Exchange has developed the infrastructure of a very sophisticated intranet communications system.

By utilizing the workgroup capabilities of Exchange in document management and discussion groups, organizations can improve the way they work as well as the way they communicate.

Document Management and Message Management Through Public Folders

As an example of using public folders for managing documents and information, the following description shows how a company is using Microsoft Exchange to manage their ISO-9000 policies and procedures across an enterprise domain. The organization went through the following procedures to organize this information:

1. The organization gathered all of their policy and procedure documents, placed them in a consistent document format, and stored them in a central location for later retrieval.

2. The organization created a public folder in Microsoft Exchange called ISO-9000 Procedures and set the security on the folder so that everyone in the organization has the right to open and view any of its documents; however, the ability to read, create, modify, and save files into the folder was limited only to the ISO-9000 Procedures committee members.

3. Because the information was being shared across three separate corporate regional offices and each office had their own Microsoft Exchange Server, the information needed to be replicated across all three organization units for common information access.

4. Once the folder was created and the appropriate security implemented, the document files were dragged and dropped directly into the folder on the Exchange server. This centralized all documents for enterprise access.

5. On a nightly basis, the information stored in the ISO-9000 policies and procedures folder is replicated to the other sites of the organization. Since the information is modified only on certain occasions, the amount of information replicated nightly is very minimal.

6. Users anywhere in the organization can use the Find utility in the Exchange and Outlook client software and they have the ability to find information about a specific policy or procedure.

A sample of one of the screens that holds the ISO-9000 information is shown in Figure 3-7.

Discussion Groups Through Exchange Forms

With the discussion group capability of Exchange Forms and public folders, workgroups of users can carry on discussions and share information. Rather than using e-mail messages to transfer information from one individual to many users of a workgroup, by posting a single discussion topic, the results or responses of the discussion topic are centralized in one location. As shown in

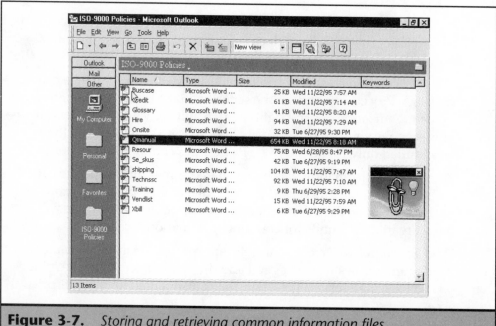

Figure 3-7. *Storing and retrieving common information files*

Figure 3-8, weekend activities are the main topic of the discussions. For the topic on golf, rather than e-mailing a request to a number of workgroup users to see if anyone wants to play golf on Saturday, the user posted his discussion topic. This posting may invoke one or many responses. Since the body of the message noted that the user wanted to organize a group of four to golf on the weekend, by the time four people respond to this discussion topic, the rest of the users interested could elect to not post their response and wait until the next golf outing. Or, if a user waits until the last day to respond and would normally think that a foursome had already been selected, by checking this discussion group session, he or she can find out that they have been looking for a fourth person all week.

The discussion topics and responses can be put into formal Exchange Forms Designer forms, or they can be simple message postings from an Exchange or Outlook client. The main goal is to centralize communications and responses so that there is one place to find information, and one place to respond to the information.

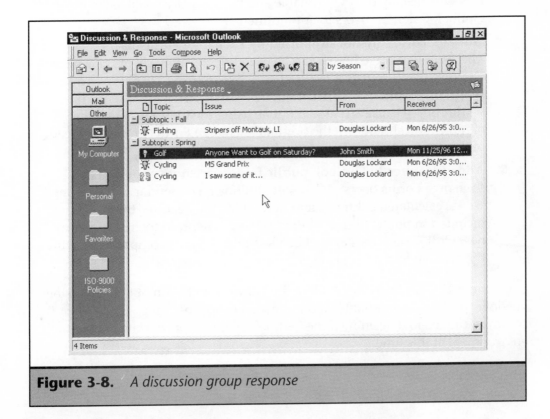

Figure 3-8.   *A discussion group response*

Intermixing the Exchange Client and the Outlook Client for Groupware Activities

As summarized in Chapter 2, deciding whether the Outlook client versus the original Exchange client is appropriate for the workgroup is dependent upon whether the workstations in the workgroup are running Windows 95, Windows NT v3.5l, or Windows NT Workstation v4.0, with users wanting to run the Outlook client. The intermixing of the Exchange client and the Outlook client have very little impact on the interaction of electronic messaging between the two application platforms, but the problems arise in the use of the groupware features between the two client applications. The problems include:

- **Cross-platform schedule viewing**   The Microsoft Outlook Calendar can view and edit any Scheduler 1.0 (MS Mail version), Scheduler 7.5 (MS Exchange version), and Outlook Calendar (Office 97 version); however, the Schedulers in v1.0 and v7.5 cannot view or edit details of an Outlook client calendar. The individual using the Scheduler v1.0 and v7.5 will be able to view available and busy times as well as invite Outlook Calendar users to appointments.

- **Outlook Forms are not supported by Exchange Forms users** Microsoft Exchange Forms can be used by Exchange clients as well as Outlook clients, but as a result of added features to the Outlook Forms program, an Outlook form cannot be used by Exchange clients. If a workgroup has users that will not be using the Outlook client, the organization should use the original Exchange Forms product instead of the newer Outlook Forms product.

- **Added features in Outlook public folders are not supported by Exchange Forms users**   Microsoft Outlook has calendar and timeline views, calculated columns, and non-table view features that were not included in public folders of the Exchange client, so the use of these new Outlook features cannot be used if backwards compatibility with the original Exchange client is necessary.

An organization needs to weigh all of the variables between operating system versions, product functionality, and impact on cross-operating communications to determine if the Outlook client is appropriate for their environment at this time.

The Chapter in Review

- Microsoft Exchange is more than just an e-mail package; it also serves as the engine for groupware applications such as scheduling, form flow, and centralized data storage. The scheduling module allows for multiple users to share schedule information, for users to schedule a single appointment or recurring appointments, or for scheduling the usage of shared resources. It also allows for the management of tasks and contacts. Public folders are created by the network administrator and others with the specific security rights to create folders.

- Forms Designer helps users create forms that target the type of response desired. Forms can provide respondents with a menu of response options or with a blank field where they choose how to respond. More complicated forms can be created by using Visual Basic and can have links to SQL databases, Access databases, etc. A designer wizard assists users with creating forms. Exchange includes a runtime copy of Forms so that all users can respond to forms, but not necessarily create them. Forms are automatically updated to the latest revision when a user requests access to that form.

- A search within Exchange using the Outlook client will reveal instances of a word or phrase within e-mails, word processing documents, spreadsheet files, mail messages, folders, calendar appointments, forms, journal entries, and notes. The Outlook Calendar client has the additional ability to select discontinuous days in the calendar, create a shared calendar for a group of end users, print compressed weekend schedules, and also has built-in holidays with many options from cultures around the world.

- The Outlook client contacts can be shared with public and private folders for full contact management. Tasks can be assigned and managed within Exchange. Journals can be used to track tasks, messages, schedules, and ideas.

- Replication is the process by which two Exchange servers determine which information needs to be updated between them, and then transfer data until both have the most current information of folders relevant to them. The administrator determines who has access to which data, which data gets replicated and which doesn't, how frequently data is replicated, and at which times of day. An organization can implement mixed platforms of Exchange and Outlook clients. But Exchange users will not have access and views to the new Outlook features.

Review Questions

Q. When setting access rights, what is the difference between delegate and delegate owner?
A. The delegate has access to non-private appointments. The delegate owner has access to all appointments, public and private.

Q. How can users see an overview of their Scheduler activities?
A. By viewing the calendar, contact, and To-Do list within Scheduler.

Q. What is the heart, the engine, of Microsoft Exchange?
A. Folders and folder replication.

Q. Who uses folders and what information can be stored in them?
A. Folders are accessed by a defined group of users who have access privileges. Exchange can accept documents created by any type of application, such as word processing, spreadsheet, and graphics applications. This is the core to intranet and workgroup communications.

Q. What is Forms Designer?
A. A utility allowing the creation of electronic forms with blank fields that the respondents fill in.

Q. Name the components of the Outlook client.
A. The Outlook client consists of the E-mail client, the Scheduler client, and the Forms client of Exchange.

Q. Name the features of the Outlook client that function similarly to the personal information manager.
A. Contact management, task management, journal entry tracking.

Q. What additional features are available within the updated 32-bit version of Exchange Forms?
A. Calendar views can be accessed from a form, Active X and Web links can be integrated into a form, the personal journal can be used to track form entries, and contacts can be managed by utilizing entries from contact lists, task lists, and journal entries.

Q. Which does Exchange Forms support, digital signatures or encryption?

A. Both.

Q. How does one Exchange server share information with another Exchange server?

A. Via replication.

Q. What is the best way to secure against accidental deletions of data within Exchange?

A. The best way to secure against accidental deletions of data is by giving remote administrators read-only access to data originating on their server. That way the only person with delete rights is the creator of the information.

Q. Why might an organization choose to have a mixed platform of Exchange and Outlook clients? What are the implications of doing this?

A. Outlook requires a 32-bit desktop operating system such as Windows 95 or Windows NT. Some problems that may arise in a mixed platform environment include those related to different views of the calendar; Outlook Forms cannot be used on an Exchange client, and Exchange clients do not see all the public folder views that Outlook clients see.

PART TWO

Designing, Planning, and Installing or Migrating to Microsoft Exchange

In Part One, the Microsoft Exchange Server product and its general capabilities were outlined in order to provide an introduction to and background of the Exchange environment. In Part Two, we will examine the conceptual framework of Microsoft Exchange and evaluate its capabilities and components in order to design and build a full messaging and groupware environment tailored to your organization's needs.

Chapter 4 covers the background concepts of Microsoft NT such as domain structure, and the concepts of Microsoft Exchange's organization and site naming. Chapter 5 assesses the current networking infrastructure and business goals of a messaging and groupware environment and how it applies to a Microsoft Exchange environment design. Chapter 6 addresses the integration or migration to a Windows NT network environment. Chapter 7 takes these designs and begins to match hardware and software, and develop the step-by-step processes for the implementation plan. Chapter 8 addresses communicating with other mail messaging systems such as the Internet, and Chapter 9 continues the mail messaging systems to Microsoft Exchange. Chapters 10 and 11 summarize the installation and implementation of a Microsoft environment.

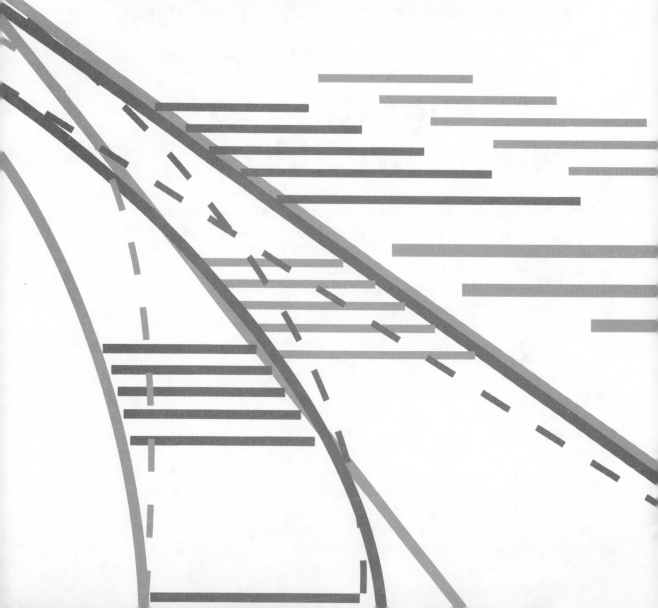

CHAPTER 4

Designing a Microsoft Exchange Environment

The first step in developing the design of the Exchange environment is to arrive at an understanding of the Microsoft Windows NT domain structure on which Microsoft Exchange is developed, and to then fit the NT domain structure into the site and organization components of Microsoft Exchange. Learning about how Microsoft Windows NT and Microsoft Exchange treat these various components and how they interact is crucial to the maintenance of security and the minimization of unnecessary administration and messaging management once the Microsoft Exchange environment is fully implemented.

Understanding Windows NT Domain Models

Because Microsoft Exchange is built on Microsoft Windows NT, much of its user creation, resource security access, and Exchange Server implementation is based on Windows NT domains. Although there has been a lot of discussion about the fact that Windows NT lacks a domain or directory services infrastructure, Windows NT has been successfully deployed in companies with fewer than 20 employees as well as those with over 20,000 employees. Knowing which domain model to implement can mean the difference between a successful Windows NT environment and one that is difficult or cumbersome to manage. Domain models are selected on the basis of a company's structure and administration, not necessarily on its size.

A Microsoft NT domain is a logical grouping of one or more Windows NT servers that need to be or should be managed as a single entity. By grouping users and servers into domains, an administrator of the domain only needs to add a user to the domain once in order to grant the user access to all its resources. For example, an organization with three servers and five printers that chose not to use domains would need to give each user on the network individual rights to each device. In addition, as part of a single grouping, users only need to provide a single logon name and password to gain access to all of the resources within the domain, instead of supplying a separate logon name and password in order to access each device.

The Components of an NT Domain

A Windows NT domain is comprised of domain controllers and servers. The domain controllers maintain the security account information for the domain—stored in the security account managers (SAM)—which is used to authenticate the logon and access requests of the users. Servers, as well as other resources such as printers, modem pools, and gateways, are manageable devices that the administrator of the domain identifies and allows entry or utilization to users with full or limited access rights.

Primary Domain Controller

Each domain has one—and only one—primary domain controller (PDC). The primary domain controller holds the master copy of the domain security information database. When new users or resources are added to the domain, the primary domain controller is always updated as the central source for all domain security access information. Additionally, if users log in to the domain, their security access is authenticated and their privileges to the resources of the domain are granted.

The primary domain controller system is typically a dedicated server for a domain of over 100 users; otherwise, the primary domain controller functions can be activated on any Windows NT file server in the domain.

Backup Domain Controller

The backup domain controller (BDC) also stores a copy of the domain's security database and is used to distribute the load of network security authentication to more than just the primary domain controller. The backup domain controller is also a fault tolerance replication of the primary domain controller in the event of a PDC failure. When a user logs on and requests security authentication to the domain, a backup domain controller can authenticate the user just as if the authentication was granted from the primary domain controller itself. There can be more than one backup domain controller in a domain. In the event of a PDC failure, one of the backup domain controllers can be promoted to the function of the primary domain controller.

Strategic placement of the backup domain controllers can minimize the security authentication traffic on the domain. For example, if an organization has a domain that spans two sites across a T1 lease line, placing a server configured as a backup domain controller in the site on the other side of the lease line will greatly minimize the amount of network traffic across the lease line required to authenticate a user's security access to the domain. Users will authenticate to the domain controller on their side of the lease line, and the domain controllers will periodically update themselves over the lease line to synchronize the security database.

Any server in the domain can be a backup domain controller; however, the server must be identified as a backup domain controller server at the time of the installation of the Windows NT Server software. If a system is not configured to be a primary or backup domain controller at the time of the NT software installation, it will require backing up all of the programs and data information on the server, reformatting the server hard drive, reinstalling the NT Server software (this time specifying that this server will either be a primary domain controller or a backup domain controller), and then restoring the programs and data to the server.

The function of the backup domain controller is not as taxing as that of the primary domain controller; however, in a fully performance-optimized network, the backup domain controller would be a completely dedicated server system. The performance lost in making a file server into a backup domain controller is offset by the creation of a redundant security database replicated across multiple systems in the domain. This is crucial since the domain controllers maintain the list of all users and user security access to the entire domain.

Windows NT Servers

The Windows NT Server is solely a resource server in the domain. The NT Server may manage file services as a file storage system in the domain, or the NT Server may be an application server, like a Microsoft Exchange Server that manages electronic message and groupware communications. An NT Server acts only as a resource on the network and does not participate in the authentication or security management as would a domain controller.

Windows NT Domain Models

There are four commonly identified Microsoft Windows NT domain models. The four different domain models vary, not necessarily due to the size of the organization, but rather based on the way the business is organized and administered from an information system standpoint. The organization can be large and dispersed around the world, but if it is centrally administered from a central office, that makes it different from a large organization that is

regionally administered by departments or divisions. The four different
Windows NT domain models are outlined as follows.

Single Domain

The simplest of all of the domain models is the single domain model. As the
name suggests, there is only one domain in this configuration. All users, file
servers, printers, and domain resources belong to the single domain, as shown
in Figure 4-1. When users log in to the domain, their access rights are centrally
managed and administered. Their privileges to resources in the domain (such
as printers or file directory shares) are also centrally administered and
allocated. This domain will have only one primary domain controller, but it
can have multiple backup domain controllers, file servers, printers, and other
resources. Adding a user to the domain gives that user rights to all resources
in the domain as long as the user has been granted the central rights to access
the resources.

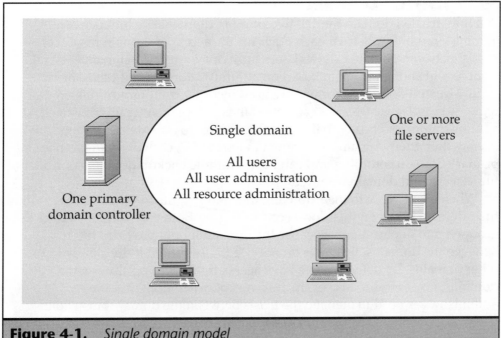

Figure 4-1.   *Single domain model*

This model is the easiest to administer since all users and domain resources remain in a single domain list. However, because all users and resources reside in a single security database, this database can be slowed significantly if the number of users or resources grows substantially. In addition, because of a single flat domain hierarchy, the ability to distribute administration to others is difficult since the domain is expected to have a single, central location for administration.

How the single domain is designed:

- One domain
- One administration level
- One set of users, file servers, and resources
- Best for small- to medium-sized organizations
- Best for relatively flat, centrally administered organizations

Fully Trusted Domain

In a fully trusted domain model, two or more domains are independently administered but fully trust each other for the access of domain resources. A *trust* between domains allows users from one domain to gain access to resources in another domain based on administrator-defined parameters. A fully trusted domain is commonly used by organizations administered in regions or divisions. Because each domain is independently administered, the administrators for each domain have full control to add, delete, and modify users within their domains. As shown in Figure 4-2, each domain has one primary domain controller and can have multiple backup domain controllers, file servers, and domain resources.

When users log in to their domain, they have rights to the resources within their domain based on their local security rights. Both users and resources are grouped into departments. Because the domain model provides full trust between the domains, the users do not need to be added individually to the other domains. By default, users have access rights across fully trusted domains; however, because of the full trust between domains, the administrators need to manage the trusts between the domains instead of users or group rights across the domain. A fully trusted domain is well-suited for an organization that has distributed administration of users and resources with the need to share resources in other organizational units.

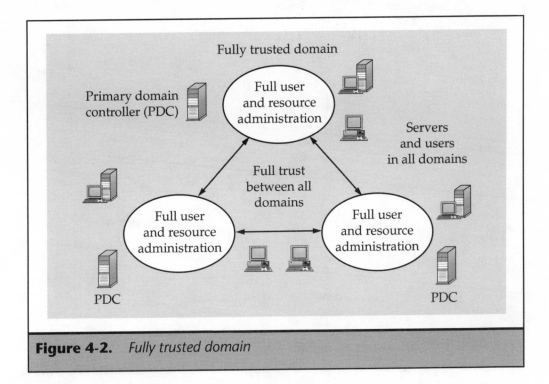

Figure 4-2.   *Fully trusted domain*

How the fully trusted domain is designed:

- Two or more domains
- As many administration levels as there are domains
- As many sets of users, file servers, and resources as there are domains
- Best for organizations that are regionally or departmentally administered

Single Master Domain

The single master domain model has two or more separate domains that are all centrally administered for users but have distributed administration for file servers and domain resources. The single master domain has one domain that maintains all user names and user security for the entire domain, as shown in Figure 4-3. The centralized administration of the users allows an organization to maintain a single security system. Resources have distributed administration so file servers, printers, and domain resources can be administered by local administrators within the organization.

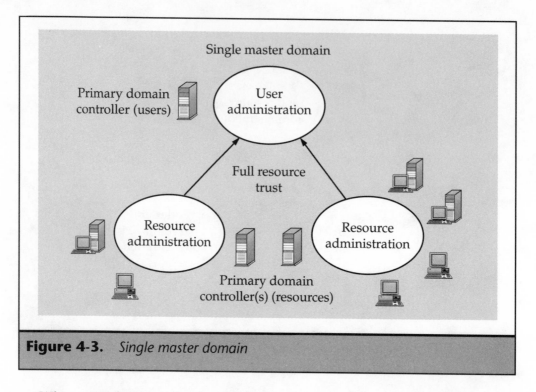

Figure 4-3. *Single master domain*

When users log in to the domain, they are authenticated by the centralized user domain and are then given access to the file servers, printers, and other domain resources within their local domain.

The single master domain allows resources to be grouped and managed locally. However, because resources are distributed, access to the resources needs to be specifically identified for each domain group.

How the single master domain is designed:

- Two or more domains
- Single centralized user domain administration
- Multiple distributed resource domain administration
- Best for organizations that are centrally administered for users, but regionally or departmentally administered for resources

Multiple Master Domain

The multiple master domain model, as shown in Figure 4-4, consists of two or more single master domains that have centralized user security management

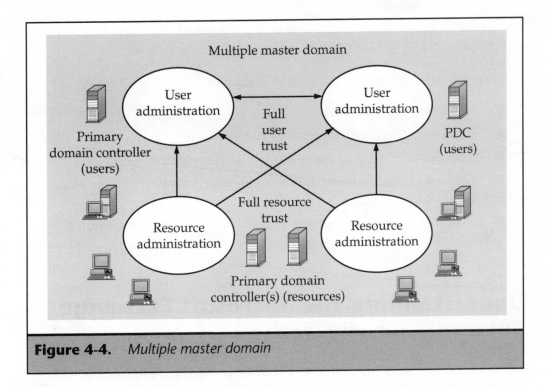

Figure 4-4. *Multiple master domain*

in each of the single master domains. Every user is created and maintained in one of these first-tier master domains. The other domains in the second tier of the multiple master domain are resource domains that manage file servers, printers, and other domain resources. In this model, the first-tier master domains are connected to every other master domain in a two-way trust relationship. The second-tier resource domains trust the first-tier master domains as well as they can trust other resource domains, but the first-tier master domains do not trust the second-tier resource domains.

Because every user belongs to one of the master domains and the master domains have full trust between each other, each user can have access to resources throughout the domain. The administrative requirements for this model are greater than those of the other models because local and global groups may have to be defined several times depending on the required level of security between the resources.

The multiple master domain works well for companies that have centralized administration but need the scalability to support a large number of users. Centralized user administration provides uniformity in user security while preserving the ability of regions or departments to manage their own local resources.

How the multiple master domain is designed:

- Two or more master domains
- Single centralized user domain administration
- Multiple distributed resource domain administration
- Full trust between master domains, one-way trust between the resource and master domain
- Best for organizations that are centrally administered for users, but regionally or departmentally administered for resources that need scalability of their domain

Understanding the Microsoft Exchange Environment Hierarchy

The Microsoft Exchange environment topology differs from the Microsoft Windows NT domain. The Windows NT domains are the basic units of security and administration for the organization, whereas the Microsoft Exchange sites are the user communications and messaging methodology for the organization. The Microsoft Exchange environment is divided into the categories of organization, sites, servers, and users, and is based around the X.400 naming scheme shown in Table 4-1.

X.400	Microsoft Exchange	Example
Country	Country	c=us
Primary Administrative Domain (PRMD)	Organization	o=XYZCorp
Organization	Site Name	ou=SF
Surname/Given Name (Common Name)	Recipient	cn=Jsmith

Table 4-1. *Mapping X.400 to Exchange Designations*

Within Microsoft Exchange, users can be addressed by their X.400 name or by their common name. If a user is addressed by his or her common name, Microsoft Exchange matches the user's name with the corresponding name in the address book, which links back to the user's X.400 name.

Organization

The topmost component in the Microsoft Exchange hierarchy is the Microsoft Exchange organization name. The organization name is typically some level or representation of the company name (like XYZCorp). The organization is the largest grouping for an Exchange enterprise. When selecting the name of the organization, it is critical to select a distinctive name that won't create a compatibility problem with external mail systems or even versions of the Microsoft Exchange client software (see "A Note on Name Lengths and Special Characters," next). Once selected, the organization name cannot be changed without completely reinstalling the entire Microsoft Exchange Server software. However, the organization name has no direct bearing on the organization's Internet domain name (like @xyzcorp.com), as the Internet domain name for the organization can be defined separately.

A Note on Name Lengths and Special Characters

Although Microsoft Exchange will allow an organization and site name with up to 64 characters including spaces and special characters (like &, +, =), it is suggested that the organization name contain no spaces and only use the characters A-Z, zero through nine, and the hyphen (-), if possible. While almost everyone will agree on the appropriate characters to be used (or not used), some will argue about the maximum number of characters to use in the organization name. Many legacy messaging systems only allocate an 8-bit naming system for the components of the message name, and some older legacy messaging systems run on a 7-bit data system, limiting the naming scheme even further. Additionally, some client software applications (like MS-DOS) do not have the ability to manage spaces within device names, so the ability to identify an Exchange organization, site, or server based on a name with a space or non-DOS-supported character can be a problem. Although problems with name lengths and included characters are limited, because Microsoft Exchange does not have a warning of the potential impact of a particular name configuration, it is a problem worth noting.

Sites

The second component in Microsoft Exchange hierarchy is the Microsoft Exchange site name. The site name is typically some level or representation of a geographic designation for the company, like a region (Western, Northeast, Europe), a city (San Francisco, London, Tokyo), or a building (Bldg. 1A, 5-East), or by a function or department name (like Marketing or Finance). Similar to selecting the name of the organization, choosing a distinctive name for the site without creating a problem of compatibility with external mail systems or even versions of the Microsoft Exchange client software is critical. Once selected, the site name cannot be changed without completely reinstalling the entire Microsoft Exchange software. Like the organization name, the site name has no direct bearing on the organization's Internet domain name (for example, @xyzcorp.com), as the Internet domain name for the organization can be defined separately.

Servers

The name of the Microsoft Exchange Server is derived from the name of the Windows NT Server defined at the time that Microsoft Windows NT was installed on the system. This name is important to plan and select since each server name must be unique and can be easily changed from the NT Server software (Settings | Control Panel | Networks), but cannot be changed once Microsoft Exchange is installed without completely reinstalling the Exchange Server software. The Exchange Server name is the name that is referred to by each client as the location and store of its mailbox.

Users

The user name is extremely important to plan because it typically becomes the logon name of the user to the network as well as the name portion of the user's Internet address. Although a user's name can be independently defined (logon name as John, Internet address as jsmith@xyzcorp.com, and Microsoft Exchange name as JohnS), administration is drastically simplified when the user's name is the same for all components of network security. It is suggested that the user name be kept to seven characters or less for the same reasons cited for keeping the organization and site names to seven characters or less. Many organizations choose to use the first initial and the balance of the user's last name for the naming scheme (John Smith becomes jsmith; Roberta

Montgomery becomes rmontgo). Other variations include combining the user's first and middle initials plus a portion of his or her last name (John A. Smith becomes jasmith). For smaller organizations, using more of the first name instead of the last name makes it easier for other users, as more people would know the individuals by their first name and some last names are difficult to spell or remember (for a user like Joan Quiesta, joan or joanq is a lot easier than jquiesta). Be careful about simplifying names too much for a large or growing organization that may end up with multiple users with potentially similar—and confusing—names (for example, John Smith, John Stone, John St. James and John St. John could end up with user names johns, johnst, johnstj, and johnstjo). The naming scheme chosen by the network and Exchange administrator creates the user names for the individuals in the organization. So, the more universal the naming scheme, the easier it is for the users of the network to describe their user names as well as for the administrator to administer the names on the network.

Mapping the Windows NT Domain and Microsoft Exchange Hierarchy

Given the Windows NT domain scheme and the Microsoft Exchange naming scheme, the next step is deciding how to organize the administration and the messaging system for the organization. This is accomplished by matching the appropriate Windows NT domain security infrastructure with the Microsoft Exchange messaging organization and site topology.

The design of the security and communications system in a Microsoft Exchange environment is based not only around the organization infrastructure hierarchy (placement of servers, departmentalization of the company's organization structure, or information systems administration structure), but also the bandwidth between sites, security needs and requirements, how the organization wants to share information, the redundancy of the information being stored, and the replication of public folder information across the domain.

Windows NT Domain Administration

As mentioned at the beginning of this chapter, the Windows NT domain administration plays an important role in a Microsoft Exchange messaging environment. Microsoft NT domains manage and implement security by:

- Authenticating a user's logon privileges to the domain
- Controlling the user's access to a personal mailbox and the messages within the mailbox
- Authenticating servers within the domain
- Providing centralized error logging (through NT Event Viewer)

Without this level of centralized domain administration capabilities, it would be very difficult to manage the users' basic security rights within the organization. It is important to take into consideration how the users' domain security as well as the network administrator's security privileges affect how the user is managed and administered within the Microsoft Exchange site and organization.

Requirement for Permanent Connections Within a Site

By definition, an Exchange site requires permanent connections between all of the Exchange servers within the site. A permanent connection would be a LAN connection or a fixed lease line between locations. This is necessary because the administration of an Exchange site is conducted through synchronous remote procedure calls (RPCs). Exchange servers within a site exchange messages and directory information to each other using synchronous RPCs. As a site grows beyond the capabilities of the permanent physical connection of its servers, an organization would need to consider either splitting the site into a new site, or establishing a permanent high-speed connection to the new server to maintain a permanent connection.

Cost and Performance/Bandwidth

One of the biggest reasons a domain is split into multiple Exchange sites is because either the cost to interconnect the domains is prohibitively high or the bandwidth to interconnect the sites is too slow. The interconnection of servers within a site usually assumes that the bandwidth between the Exchange servers is at least half-T1 (768K) or full-T1 (1.54MB) speed (a normal Ethernet LAN connection is 10MB). The speed of the connection between Exchange servers within a site is crucial because all messages and administration instruction sets are communicated to each of the Exchange servers within the site. As an NT user is added to the site, all servers within the site recognize the user as a member of that site. Additionally, as messages are directed to the site, the message is confirmed and forwarded to the appropriate user based on a process that is dictated by the Exchange server site itself. If the bandwidth between the Exchange servers is slow, any updates to the site for messages or administration will be sluggish. This is typically not a problem for an organization that does not have a high volume of message communications or administration changes; however, most organizations with multiple sites typically need to communicate through electronic messaging or groupware communications on a frequent basis.

Bottlenecks can be minimized by either adding in more bandwidth, such as a faster dial-up or lease line connection, or possibly through the implementation of folder replication instead of mail messaging. If the traffic within a workgroup is very high but users are chiefly sending mail messages to each other with attachments, the workgroup would benefit from using replicated public folders in which one copy of the information in question is replicated between sites rather than repeatedly transferring the entire content of the message as a message attachment.

As the bandwidth of the link between sites increases, so does the monthly cost to maintain the data communications link. In most cases, the bandwidth is dictated by the budget and cost justification of the communication between the multiple sites.

Replication Between Servers

Part of Microsoft Exchange's enterprise view of messaging and communications is the ability to replicate information from server to server. The replication of information may be for the purpose of providing the information across a wide area link so that the users on the other side of the link do not have to go across a slow data communication link to access information. The replication of information may also be a form of information load balancing, in which high demand information is replicated to multiple servers within a site so that users can access the same information from different servers without the degradation caused by too many users accessing the same common information resource depository. Lastly, replication could be a component of a data information fault tolerance system in which high-profile information may be required to be distributed to another location within the same site (or to a different site) so that the information can be made available even in the event of a primary Exchange server failure.

In any of these cases, the need to map the organization's replication process and demands must be acknowledged so that the appropriate disk space and server-to-server bandwidth is adequate to handle the replication needs of the organization. This would include mail messages sent and received by users (quantity and frequency) and the estimated user transactions with groupware applications such as document management, faxing, and resource sharing within and throughout the environment.

While e-mail message transport has relatively low bandwidth requirements, messages with large attachments or workgroup groupware interaction with large sets of data can cause heavy traffic between multiple points within the Exchange environment. When there is a very heavy communications load with other groups of users within the organization, it may be appropriate to ensure that the communication link between the locations is of sufficient bandwidth to manage the traffic.

Exchange Administration

While the administration of an Exchange organization takes the core security information set from the Windows NT domain security database, the Exchange administrator has additional privileges to the messages and public folders that users access. In many cases, when the NT domain administration and security is developed in accordance with the organizational structure of the company (such as by department or division), the Microsoft Exchange site creation and administration may be more appropriately split based on the physical geographic location of the users. The Exchange site may need to be split on the city or even building level if the users within that city or building belong to separate logical Windows NT domains because the communication from site-to-site is over slower data communication lines. An Exchange administrator needs to have a high-speed connection to the entire Exchange site or domain to properly manage and maintain users within the organization.

Organizational Structure

Because an organization may be administered differently than the geographic distribution of the user community, the variation of the Windows NT domain structure and the Microsoft Exchange site topology can also differ. The organization may have the same domain and site topology, multiple domains for a single site, and multiple sites for a single domain.

Domain and Site Topology Are the Same

In a simple site and domain topology, there is only one NT domain and one Exchange site, similar to the organization shown in Figure 4-5. This is common

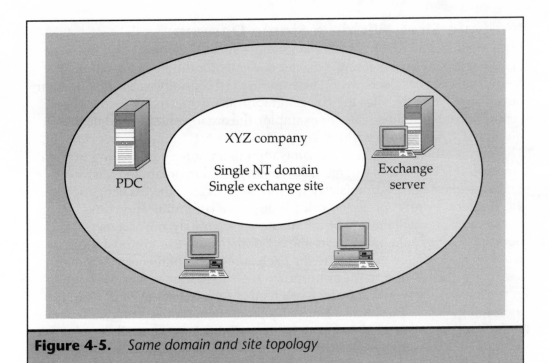

Figure 4-5. *Same domain and site topology*

for small organizations or highly departmentalized and administered organizations in which the Windows NT domain for user security and resource management is the same as the workgroup for electronic messaging and groupware communications. In this model, when users are added to the domain and given domain security rights, they are also added to the Microsoft Exchange messaging site for access to shared folders and groupware information with the same workgroup of users as the NT domain. The network administrator who adds users to the domain is the same administrator who manages the Exchange user permissions and security. This model could work for an organization that either has a single domain or a fully trusted domain in which each domain is a separate site. It probably would not be appropriate for a single master domain or multiple master domain—not that a single site could not encompass the entire domain—but rather that the distribution of users across multiple locations typically would not have the bandwidth of LAN/WAN communication with fast enough permanent connections between the sites. In the case where the organization is split across multiple locations, establishing multiple Exchange sites and communicating via e-mail would be more appropriate.

Multiple Sites Within a Single Domain

In an organization that has multiple locations that are centrally administered (and that probably uses a single master domain or multiple master domain model), all network users would be administered centrally as a single domain; however, because the sites may be geographically dispersed with low-speed connections (56K frame relay for example), the organization would have multiple Exchange sites within a single Windows NT administrative domain. This organization could have the same administrator (or administration team) who adds users to the NT domain also manage and maintain the Microsoft Exchange messaging administration. However, because the Exchange servers are not permanently connected using high-speed communication links, each Exchange server will have to be administered separately, not as a messaging domain. A user could be added to the NT domain, but the administrator would have to dial in or log on to the Exchange server of the user's primary site to link the NT user to the appropriate site's Exchange server. Messages between each site would transfer to each other over X.400 or SMTP mail messaging. Figure 4-6 shows a single master domain model with two separate sites (San Francisco and New York) that are administered centrally for the addition of users and user security. However, because there is a 56K link between the two divisions, they are separated as sites within Exchange.

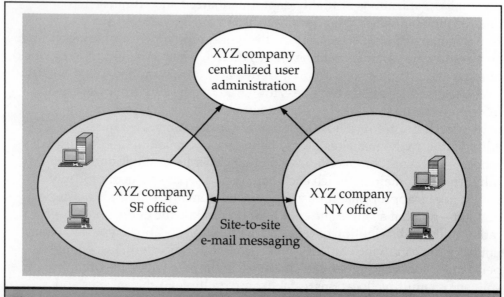

Figure 4-6.   *Multiple sites within a single domain*

Multiple Domains Within a Single Site

A single Microsoft Exchange site can span multiple Microsoft Exchange domains. This may be common in an organization that has multiple departments in multiple locations in which each department is managed and administered as a department; however, the communication between the sites is done over low-speed lease lines. As shown in Figure 4-7, the organization has a marketing, finance, and production department in each of the three cities. Each department is administrated by the department administrator across the entire company (marketing administered by the marketing administrator, finance administered by the finance administrator, production administered by the production administrator), thus each department is configured as a separate Windows NT domain. However, because the communication links between the three cities are 56K lease lines, each of the three cities is considered a separate site within Microsoft Exchange so that messages transfer from site-to-site over X.400 messaging.

In this configuration, there must be a two-way trust between all of the domains because Microsoft Exchange assumes that a site is part of the same security context. Microsoft Exchange specifies the same service account for

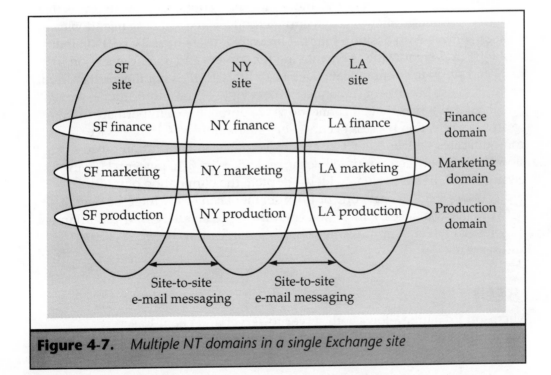

Figure 4-7. *Multiple NT domains in a single Exchange site*

every Microsoft Exchange computer by default. This allows the Exchange administrator to log on to the network once, run the Exchange Administrator program, and manage all users, groups, resources, and servers within the site.

Determining Which Transport Protocol(s) to Use

When connecting multiple Microsoft Exchange servers, administrators must choose a transport protocol to use during server-to-server communications. Although typically the Exchange server would communicate over the company-standard communication transport, Microsoft Exchange servers can communicate with each other over whatever standard is requested. Many organizations take this opportunity to implement their future standard (such as an all-TCP/IP environment) by first configuring the Exchange servers as only TCP/IP transport server systems.

TCP/IP

TCP/IP has become the *de facto* standard for many organizations to use as their preferred communications system and method. Since many organizations are providing users with desktop Internet browsing, users have TCP/IP on their desktops, and organizations are moving file servers and other devices on the LAN and WAN to communicate over TCP/IP. TCP/IP is not the most efficient protocol to use because of its connectionless view of communications (in which it assumes that all connections are unreliable or impermanent, so an authentication process occurs every single time a TCP/IP device communicates with another TCP/IP device). This authentication process can slow the link between multiple Exchange devices by 5-10 percent. However, because TCP/IP has become widely adopted, the elimination of multiple protocols on a single backbone or LAN segment can easily increase overall network performance by 10-20 percent. Moving to an all-TCP/IP environment may result in overall improvements in communications between clients and servers.

NetBEUI

Microsoft Exchange allows both server-to-server and client-to-server communication over NetBEUI. NetBEUI is more efficient than other mediums because the query and request are handled at the core server-to-server level of communications. In a small network or in a relatively closed single site/single domain environment, NetBEUI is more efficient than something like TCP/IP for server-to-server or client-to-server communication, and can provide the fastest Exchange communications performance of any of the various options.

IPX/SPX

Many organizations still have a large install base of Novell NetWare servers. Novell communicates over IPX/SPX as its primary method of communication. The servers within Microsoft Exchange and the clients within an Exchange environment can also communicate over IPX/SPX. Although the clients can communicate over IPX/SPX, many organizations that are adding in desktop Internet browser access are also adding TCP/IP to every desktop, and are frequently migrating their standard transports from IPX/SPX to TCP/IP. A NetWare client, however, can still use IPX/SPX for its LAN access and TCP/IP for its Exchange messaging access. In addition, server-to-server communications do not need to be drastically changed.

Securing the Exchange Environment Internally and Externally

For every connection that goes outside of the LAN/WAN internal network environment (such as to the Internet, to a public administration manager (like an X.400 message transport provider), to remote users, or to a replication share public folder provider, security of the network and the Exchange environment becomes very important. When a network is connected to the Internet or other transport provider, the intent may be to solely send and receive e-mail messages, but the fact that a connection exists for the transport of messages does not necessarily mean that the connection cannot handle other forms of communications, such as unwanted network intrusion. There are a number of ways to secure the network against undesired access.

Password Security

The easiest (and the most commonly breached) form of security is the acquisition of a logon name and password strategy to gain access to the network. At minimum, passwords should be placed on all logon names on the network, and the administrator logon password should be unique (not something like *password*) and even changed every 30 days to prevent accidental or deliberate access to the administration of the network.

Key to a Microsoft Windows NT network are particular "services" that run on the network, such as fax server queues, tape backup background tasks, Exchange service managers, or other administrative tasks that automatically run in the background of the network and automatically log on to the network upon boot-up of the server. In many cases, when a server service is being installed and the network administrator is asked to enter the name of a logon user, the administrator chooses the user "administrator" for this function and enters the password for the service. If the password for the administrator is ever changed and the server is rebooted, any services keyed to the administrator logon will fail to restart. It is important to identify all services that are automatically being logged on to the network to ensure the appropriate service logons are not dependent on the administrator's logon and password. Services logons can be verified by going in to Settings | Control Panel | Services | (select each service individually) | Startup and see if there is a service account attached to the service. If there are any service accounts that are designated "administrator," change them to a different network user with the appropriate security rights (at a minimum, "Allow to Logon as Service"). (See your application's administration manual for information specific to the program.)

Protocols Used in the Environment

In addition to passwords, the protocols used in the environment (TCP/IP, IPX/SPX, NetBEUI) should be blocked at all routers and on all network server adapters when not needed to minimize the potential for information access from a resource that does not need to have access to the system. Filters on a router can be easily enabled to filter any unnecessary protocols from going beyond the router. If an e-mail connector to the Internet is using TCP/IP to send and receive mail messages with the Internet, there is no need for IPX/SPX, NetBEUI, or other protocols to be configured on the adapter or port going to the Internet.

Most organizations have two network adapters in an Exchange server that communicate with the Internet. One adapter goes to the "trusted" local area network where all of the network users reside. The other network adapter goes to the "untrusted" network that leads to the Internet. Since communications with the Internet use TCP/IP as the transport method, the administrator can go into Settings | Control Panel | Networks | Bindings (for the adapter going to the Internet) and disable all protocols (such as NetBIOS, IPX/SPX, NetBEUI) except for the TCP/IP, similar to the diagram shown in Figure 4-8.

Adding Firewalls for Advanced Security

Lastly, the best security method is the implementation of a firewall. Firewalls should be set up to limit both inbound as well as outbound communications transfer of information from the NT and Exchange environment with the rest of the disparate components of the messaging organization. Whereas a router or network bindings in NT will disable entire protocols from communicating from the local area network to the external network, a firewall can be configured to filter parts of a protocol information stream from passing between the Exchange server and the external network. With TCP/IP as the only protocol enabled to the external network in an Internet connection, the intent would be to only enable the portion of the TCP/IP protocol stream specific to inbound and outbound electronic messaging (and disabling the components of TCP/IP that handle FTP file transfers, http Web access, telnet

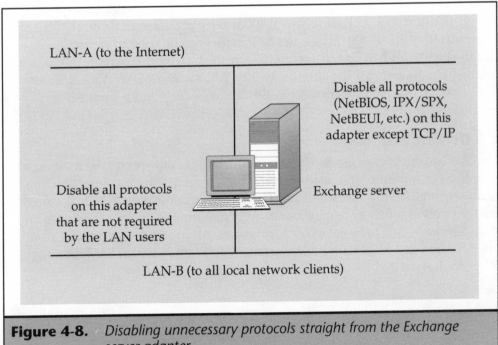

LAN-A (to the Internet)

Disable all protocols (NetBIOS, IPX/SPX, NetBEUI, etc.) on this adapter except TCP/IP

Exchange server

Disable all protocols on this adapter that are not required by the LAN users

LAN-B (to all local network clients)

Figure 4-8. *Disabling unnecessary protocols straight from the Exchange server adapter*

login access, or other services that are not necessary in an inbound/outbound e-mail messaging configuration).

The filtering configuration of a firewall should be conducted by an expert who knows what is appropriate to set and not set on the firewall and how the total effect will impact the rest of the network. Filtering solely for electronic messages through the Internet (Port 25, SMTP message stream) is fine for Microsoft Exchange, but there may be other services that are required for other servers within the environment such as Web servers, FTP servers, and the like.

The end result of configuring a firewall is that specific TCP/IP ports should be enabled on a well-thought-out plan to only permit communications to and from an untrusted network into the Exchange environment based on the design and understanding that specific access is being permitted (or purposely blocked).

Linking Sites Together

When linking multiple sites together, there are three different methods of interconnecting the sites. When bandwidth permits (high-speed permanent connections), using the Microsoft Exchange Connector provides the most comprehensive connection between servers. When linking sites through a public medium such as through an X.400 service provider or through the Internet, either the X.400 or Internet connectors can be used to create the site-to-site link. When cost is prohibitive, or the bandwidth of a dial-up line is minimally adequate for the site-to-site link, Microsoft Remote Access Server (RAS) can be used to interconnect multiple sites over dial-up phone lines.

Site Connector

The Site Connector for site-to-site communications is the preferred method to interconnect multiple sites as long as the link is a permanent connection of a relatively high bandwidth medium. The Site Connector uses RPC to connect the two sites together and to exchange information. RPC does not require any transport protocols to be set up or configured. All messages go directly from one server to the other without being translated into X.400, or SMTP, or any other format.

X.400 Connector

In some instances, two or more Exchange servers are interconnected through a public service provider like X.400. The connection may still be a high-speed, permanent connection, or possibly a slower frame relay link. The big difference between a native Site Connector linkup of sites and an X.400 Connector link is that messages are converted to X.400 before being transported. This conversion allows for the transfer of Microsoft Exchange public folder or message information over universal public networks. Additionally, since the information is being filtered through X.400, the administrator has the option of controlling the message size and routing path between sites. Thus, if the administrator wants only public folder information smaller than 500K per message to pass, only that information will be transported over the service provider. The routing path can be defined using least-cost routing to determine the best route for a message or sync to be conducted. However, the drawback is that all messages must be converted to X.400 and then transported over an established protocol like TCP/IP, which takes time, requires translation (which is not always 100 percent), and adds in more complexity and room for error. The preferred method of transportation is to go directly from a public folder to a public folder over RPCs.

Remote Access Server (RAS)

When a permanent high-speed connection cannot be established between multiple sites, the Windows NT Remote Access Server (RAS) service can be used to create a dial-up connector between Exchange servers. A RAS connection can be set up as a fallback option in the event of a primary lease line connection failure, or the RAS connection can be part of the primary site-to-site strategy in locations where cost may be prohibitively high or where performance of the link is not an issue.

Validating the Design

Once the organization has chosen a type of Windows NT domain structure that is appropriate for its user administration needs, and the suitable Microsoft

Exchange site topology is determined for the physical layout of the users, the initial design plan needs to be validated.

The first thing to validate is the administration of the organizational structure. Follow the steps here:

1. Draw a map of the domain structure of the organization.

2. Identify on the map the users, the groups, and the administrator(s) of the domain. The administrator(s) should have the ability to add users, delete users, and modify users' access privileges to files, directories, and objects within the domain. The users should be grouped by organizational roles parallel to security access and data access within the domain.

   Questions:

   - Do the users have access to the files and shared directories appropriate to their needs?

   - Are the groups designed in such a way that if a privilege is given to a group (eg., to access a message or a folder of messages), all the members of that group are appropriate and are receiving the privilege?

3. Draw a diagram of the Exchange site topology for the organization. The Exchange site diagram should note physical boundaries of the Exchange organization, such as divisions, cities, departments, or building designations. A site will note the differentiator based on locality, cost, or bandwidth where permanent high-speed data communications are not available and need to be considered as a separate site.

4. Identify on this map the users, departments, or organizational roles of all users as they apply to the appropriate portion of the site diagram.

   Questions:

   - Are the users within a site communicating over a high-speed LAN or WAN connection (half-T1 or faster)?

   - Do the users across sites communicate over dial-up or slower speed connection lines or are part of a completely separate operational business unit?

5. Superimpose a copy of the Exchange site diagram over the domain diagram.

6. Match up users, groups, and sites.

Questions:

■ Do all the users within the organization match up within a domain as well as a site on the diagrams?

■ Is it clear which administrator (NT domain or Exchange administrator) has the responsibility to add/modify the user as well as modify/manage messaging privileges and security?

If you can answer yes to all of these questions, then the design plan on paper is valid for the organization. If there are any problems with the design plan, further review may be necessary to ensure that a solid plan will lead to a successful implementation.

The Chapter in Review

■ The Microsoft NT network operating system is the foundation of the Exchange messaging system, and the NT domain structure has a tremendous impact on how Exchange is administered. An NT domain is comprised of a primary domain controller and backup domain controllers. The primary domain controller maintains the master copy of the domain security information database. A backup domain controller stores a copy of the domain security database, shares the task of authentications with the primary domain controller, and functions as an online backup should the primary domain controller fail. Ideally, at least one backup domain controller would exist at each physical site within the WAN. Possible exceptions include single user sites.

■ An organization should choose its NT domain model based on the way the network is administered rather than solely on its degree of geographic dispersion. There are four domain models that organizations can choose from based on their size, geographic dispersion, and degree of centralized network management. A key component of the network installation plan is to develop naming structures. Naming structures impact the organization for the duration of the network's usage, and thus must be chosen carefully. The organization name and site name have no direct relation to the organization's Internet domain name.

- Exchange sites must have a permanent data communication connection between them because the Exchange administration is dependent upon remote procedure calls. This need affects the maintenance cost of the network and thus influences what type of domain structure an organization chooses to implement. Information is replicated between sites based on the conditions that the network administrator sets. Replication allows a greater number of users to access information without overtaxing a single server. Organizations need to map out how they plan for data to be replicated to ensure that sufficient resources are available.

- A company's organizational structure influences domain and site topology. The NT domain and Exchange sites do not necessarily have to be identical, but there must be a two-way trust between the domains. This allows each Exchange administrator to log on to the network once and access all Exchange servers. Exchange can use multiple transport protocols, some options of which include TCP/IP, NetBEUI, and IPX/SPX.

- Network security is required for every external network connection and needs to be considered with internal connections as well. Password security is one of the easiest security barriers to implement and one of the most frequently skipped steps. Protocols not used in a specific segment of a network should be blocked by routers. The most advanced security system currently available is a firewall, which is used to filter inbound and outbound messages.

- Three different connectors are available for linking sites together. The Site Connector is a high-speed permanent connection, the X.400 Connector is used to link multiple sites via a public service provider, and Remote Access Server (RAS) is a nonpermanent, low-speed link that can be used as a backup alternative to permanent links. When validating the network design, first draw a diagram of the network, then ask questions about access and administration from each person's perspective.

Review Questions

Q. Where are much of the security access rights, user creation, and server management performed?
A. Within the NT domain.

Q. What additional steps would be required without the use of domains?
A. Each user would need to be given access rights to file servers, printers, and other network resources individually. Also, users would have to log on to each secured network resource individually.

Q. Define a domain controller.
A. A domain controller is a server that also maintains security account information. That information is used to authenticate users' logon and access rights, as well as access rights to resources.

Q. What happens if the primary domain controller fails?
A. One of the backup domain controllers can be promoted to primary domain controller.

Q. What is the function of an NT server within an Exchange domain?
A. An NT server functions as a resource server within the domain.

Q. Name the four domain models.
A. Single domain, fully trusted domain, single master domain, and multiple master domain.

Q. How many administration levels are there in a fully trusted domain?
A. There are as many administration levels as there are domains.

Q. Describe a single master domain.
A. A single master domain has multiple separate domains with a central user administration and a distributed resource administration.

Q. Describe a multiple master domain.
A. A multiple master domain is a collection of several single master domains.

Q. Describe the trust relationships in a multiple master domain.
A. Multiple master domains have a full trust relationship between master domains, and a one-way trust from resource domains to master domains.

Q. How do you change the organization name or site name within NT and Exchange?

A. By reinstalling the software. The further along in the installation process, the more difficult it is to throw away all the previous efforts and restart from the beginning.

Q. List the securities that access control domains have.
A. Domains determine the security to authenticate users and manage user mailboxes, and to authenticate servers and provide centralized error logging.

Q. Name three network transport protocols that Exchange supports.
A. Exchange supports TCP/IP, NetBEUI, and IPX/SPX.

Q. Name steps that should be taken to ensure password security is properly utilized.
A. Passwords should be on all network logon names, and they should be unique and set to be changed every 30 days to a different password.

Q. What is the next step after choosing an NT domain structure and Exchange site topology?
A. Validate the design.

Q. If you have a hesitation about one aspect of the network design, what should you not do?
A. You should not move forward with the network implementation until you are completely confident of all aspects of the network plan.

CHAPTER 5

Assessing the Infrastructure and Goals of the Business to Establish Electronic Workgroup Practices

In Chapter 4, we explored the components that made up the infrastructure of Microsoft Exchange and the Windows NT operating system upon which Exchange is built. In this chapter, we will continue to develop the design of an Exchange environment by analyzing the business and information technology goals of the organization, and gain an understanding of the components within Microsoft Exchange that will assist in the development of electronic workflow and workgroup processes.

Unlike any other software program installed on a network in the past where the program served a specific function and purpose, Microsoft Exchange has the ability to improve how organizations communicate and how workgroups interact. One of the critical steps in the design of the Microsoft Exchange environment is to assess the current operational processes and the future operational goals of the organization so that Microsoft Exchange can improve the ways that the organization will communicate and conduct business in the future.

In this chapter, business goals, organizational structures, and existing local area and wide area network infrastructure designs will be evaluated, and future goals and procedural expectations will be assessed, in order to begin to structure the organization's workgroup and workflow processes. From this foundation will evolve a strategy for the implementation of the Microsoft Exchange environment, which will combine the best in computer software technology with strategic organizational processes.

Analyzing the Organization's Business Goals

An analysis of the organization's business goals is absolutely critical to the preparation of its design plan. Microsoft Exchange can serve two distinct roles for an organization:

- Microsoft Exchange can serve as a tool to help organizations communicate better through e-mail and group scheduling.

- Microsoft Exchange can be a catalyst to improve the way organizations do business through groupware and workflow processes.

Many organizations upgrade to a newer version of the software they have been using because of a handful of new features in the new product, or to retain support from the manufacturer or compatibility with third-party add-ins to the application. Although many organizations are electing to upgrade from MS Mail to Microsoft Exchange (basically a version upgrade in mail messaging), Microsoft Exchange offers such core strategic business features that organizations are adopting Microsoft Exchange as a full-featured solution, not simply as a revision update.

What Role Does Messaging Play in the Organization?

The two distinct categories of electronic communications that can be identified are those that are demand-push communications and those that are demand-pull model communications (see Figure 5-1).

Typical electronic mail is a demand-push method of communications. When a user wants to get a message to several other users, he or she sends an electronic message to the targeted recipients, whether they want the information or not. E-mail allows users to disseminate information throughout an organization more quickly and easily than ever before. Within seconds of a

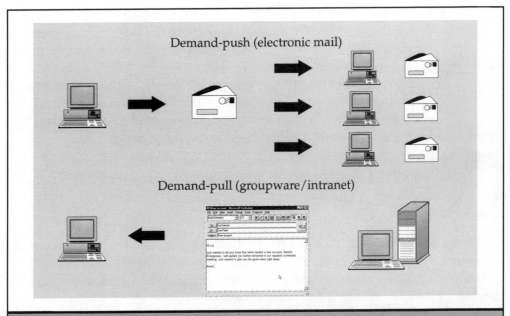

Figure 5-1. *Demand-push versus demand-pull*

memo or a message's creation, the user can press the send button to distribute the message to one, ten, one hundred, or thousands of recipients.

Companies that have been using e-mail for some time have seen how it facilitates and improves business communications, as employees now have a quick and efficient method to transmit information to others. However, e-mail can also be extremely detrimental to worker productivity. The abuses of e-mail can include:

- Users who type slowly and ultimately spend more time composing an electronic message than a simple phone call or jotted-down memo would take. Additionally, some users get so involved in writing their e-mail messages and formatting them perfectly (with the right colors, the right font, and clever embedded images) that they negate the efficiency of electronic messaging.

- Users who feel that it is necessary to carbon copy (cc:) a large workgroup of users on any and all communications. Although every detail of every e-mail message may be important, once users join a few group distribution lists and start to receive 50-100 cc:s a day, the details of each conversation begin to lose their impact and value.

- Users who find e-mail so attractive that they send either a large number of messages or very lengthy messages, without considering that their messaging could benefit from conciseness. When users are limited to 60 seconds when leaving a voicemail message, they are forced to make their point very quickly and very clearly. When e-mail users are given an empty (and unlimited) canvas to write on, they can end up spending all day or a span of a few days composing one e-mail message. Clearly, when it comes to e-mail, quality does not equal quantity.

- Users who continually forward amusing stories, jokes, or relatively random information to all of their friends. Inevitably, the same tired jokes and stories find their way to everyone's mailbox over and over and over.

After a while, the abuses of an openly demand-push model of communications numb e-mail recipients and prevent them from differentiating between important versus unimportant messages, and soon all messages lose their meaning and urgency.

As organizational messaging matures, the request for a demand-pull (more recently equated with an intranet) model becomes the communications ideal.

In a demand-pull model, individuals within the organization know where to find and search for the information they desire when they need it.

Organizations that are implementing demand-pull communications systems like an intranet or groupware environment create message stores where topics are categorized and available in order to allow users to post information easily and quickly. A simple example of how an organization can minimize unnecessary e-mail distribution (which in turn requires recipients to spend time viewing every single message they receive) is the creation of a publicly-accessible message store or folder for the posting of the latest jokes and humorous stories. Users who may be interested in distributing or viewing this information can easily access this public storage area. However, users who do not want to be disturbed by "junk e-mail" can elect not to view the storage area for this type of information. The person who posts information to this folder knows that users can access this information and benefit from it, while users who do not want the information are spared the burden of receiving it. Companies are starting to realize how much productivity they gain back by implementing a system that allows individuals on the network to access only the information they want, when they want, and also allows users to ignore irrelevant information.

Many managers and users of a demand-pull system of communications worry that users given the responsibility to check for messages in specific public folder areas will not access the information and will miss out on important conversation topics. This concern is legitimate; however, when a demand-push method of communications is abused and users receive dozens of e-mail messages daily that they end up ignoring, they obviously aren't reading the information sent to them anyway. If a demand-pull process of public folders is properly implemented, an organization can denote the priority of posted messages within a public folder or set up public folders in such a way that users can be made aware of priority messages and read them at their convenience. When users have the ability to access urgent information at their convenience and have messages prioritized for them, they are far more likely to be attentive to the information available to them.

The goal of this methodology of organizational communications is to maintain the value of important message communications while providing a system to foster open communications. The faster an organization can move from a demand-push to a demand-pull method of communications, the faster the organization will be able to value from the benefits of true groupware and workgroup interactive communications.

Analyzing Your Organization's Current Process of Sharing Information

A problem that many information system managers and designers of electronic communications systems face is designing and implementing an electronic process of communications without understanding the manual process for communications. An automated, electronic system cannot be effective unless there is a competent manual system at work within the organization. If an efficient manual communications system is not in place prior to the implementation of an automated electronic system, the new electronic system may not work, may not be understood by the individuals using the system, or may be designed improperly.

An understanding of the process of electronic communications within the organization requires an understanding of which information is shared, where it is stored, and how users can search and access the stored information.

Which Information Is Shared?

What an organization determines to be important or appropriate to share varies from organization to organization. A law firm may save and share word processing documents, an architectural company may do the same for CAD drawings, an advertising firm would value photos and articles, and a maintenance company may want to save and share service records. When asked the question "what information do you need to access?," the response is usually "everything." Before the designer can begin to determine the extent of the needs of the organization's groupware environment, there must be a limit on the amount of required information to be shared.

Where Is Information Stored?

Once the type of information designated to be shared has been identified, knowing where the information is stored is the next step. Sometimes organizations store information on a shared network file server hard drive, some organizations store information on local hard drives, and sometimes information is stored on removal cartridge hard drives. Or the information to be accessed is photos and articles that may actually be film, negatives, or printed information stored in filing cabinets (see Figure 5-2). Prior to the implementation of a groupware application like Microsoft Exchange, the organization would have to convert the information to an electronic format in order to share it electronically. Likewise, if the information the organization

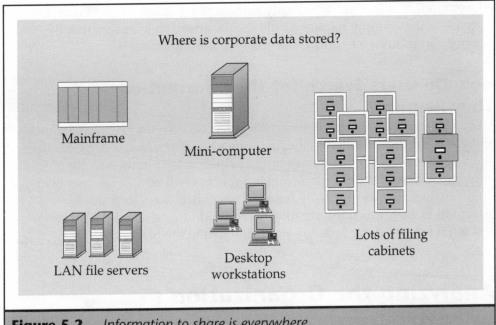

Figure 5-2. *Information to share is everywhere*

wants to share is service records that reside in a database on a mainframe computer, that information would need to be linked and made accessible in the Microsoft Exchange environment. It is important to identify where the information is stored to ensure that all steps are taken that are necessary to convert the information into a format that can be accessible from Microsoft Exchange.

Who Needs Access to the Information?

Once the information to be shared has been identified and located, it needs to be reviewed for authority and security access. When information was stored in a locked filing cabinet in the executive office, the organization had a built-in security access system. However, information sitting on a shared location on the network needs to have an even more automated method of identifying user access and limiting access to and control of the information. Although it would be convenient for it to be available to share, some information may not be appropriate for network storage if the potential for access may constitute a security threat (such as sensitive human resources information, or legal information). Rather than summarily eliminating this information from the network, it may simply require a little special attention to ensure that the information is limited to only those with the need to access it.

How Do Users Search for the Information They Require?

Most organizations already have a designated way for users to search quickly and easily for the information they require. Knowing which tools users share and utilize to search for information can help in determining how the implementation of the electronic look up process will benefit the user over their existing manual process in terms of how often users look up information, how much information is acquired through the look-up process, and what information needs to be consolidated in the process.

Analyzing the Organization's Infrastructure

Key to assessing the needs of an organization is the ability to understand the existing infrastructure of both the organization and its information technology infrastructure. This includes the number of users within the organization, the breakdown of its workgroup infrastructure, the management and communications hierarchy, and the workflow processes of the workgroups and organization.

The Business Organizational Infrastructure

The business organizational infrastructure essentially constitutes the size and physical and logical make up of the organization. These are the components that dictate the scalability of the Exchange server equipment and the need for interconnectivity within the organization. An organization's complexity is not necessarily measured by the sheer number of users within the organization, but also by the distribution of the users, resources, and logical workgroups across multiple locations of the organization.

Size and Physical Organizational Layout

The size of the organization will help to decide the scope of the installation of the Exchange Server environment. Obviously, an organization with less than

50 employees is not going to have as complex a domain, site, and organizational structure as an organization with 10,000 employees. As we explore the sizing of the Microsoft Exchange servers in Chapter 7 of this book, the variation in organizational size will play an important role in determining the distribution of servers and Exchange resources within the organization.

More important, however, than the sheer size of the organization is the physical layout of the environment. This includes divisional offices, branch offices, job sites, and remote and mobile individuals of the Microsoft Exchange organization. As an organization's user base becomes more distributed and dispersed, the need to take sites, servers, replication shares, and access points into account increases in order for users to access information efficiently within the Microsoft Exchange environment.

For example, if a user is a crucial member of a workgroup workflow, but he or she has a very slow dial-up connection, the ability of the user to actively participate as a member of the workgroup is hindered. Similarly, if a large portion of a workgroup resides in a completely different division or Exchange site and is required to share information with another division or site, the need to replicate critical information from site to site can drastically decrease the overhead placed on the wide area connection link and improve communications and information access through Microsoft Exchange.

Diagramming the organizational structure as well as the distribution of users throughout the physical organization, as shown in Figure 5-3, will help to determine the appropriate server size required, evaluate the adequacy of access links between locations, and provide the basis from which server-to-server replications will be planned.

The Organization's Physical and Logical Workgroups

Workgroups generally take on two separate designations within an organization. The *physical workgroup* in an organization is typically based on its physical geographic configuration (see top of Figure 5-4). A traditional workgroup typically resides in cubicles tightly clustered on a single floor work area. The *logical workgroup* in an organization is one that outlines the actual interactions between its members on projects, processes, sales, or other functional tasks or procedures (see bottom of Figure 5-4). A logical workgroup may involve the interaction between multiple individuals from various departments, such as a capital purchase process that requires input from a department planner, a department manager, a finance approval manager, a purchasing agent, etc. In cases where the organization has its users predominantly within a single office, the logical and physical workgroup may

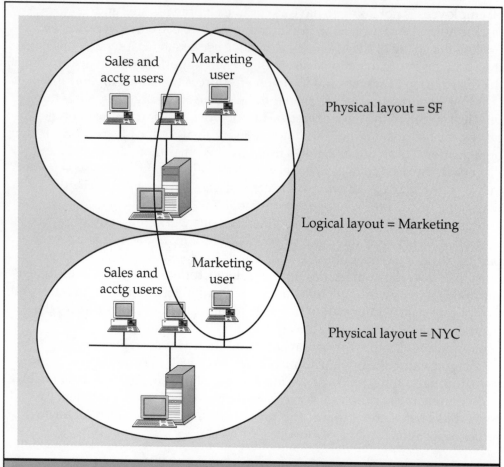

Sales and
acctg users

Marketing
user

Physical layout = SF

Logical layout = Marketing

Sales and
acctg users

Marketing
user

Physical layout = NYC

Figure 5-3. *Physical versus logical layout of an organization*

be one and the same. An organization with a number of users in several different offices may have separate divisions or regional locations, which would then be divided into separate operational sites. Each site would be broken down based on servers assigned to workgroups in each regional location.

The logical organizational structure of a larger location may differ drastically from the physical configuration design layout for the organization as responsibilities for processes become more departmentalized.

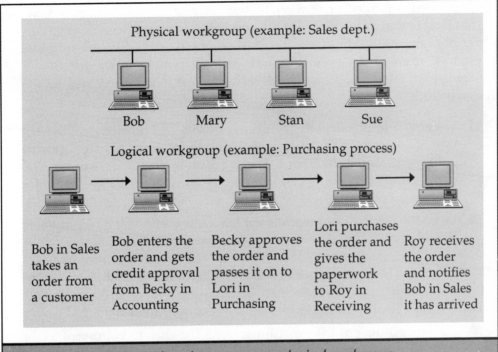

Figure 5-4. *A physical workgroup versus a logical workgroup*

The Organization's Information Technology Infrastructure

In addition to evaluating the business organizational structure, an evaluation of the information technology infrastructure needs to be conducted. The information technology infrastructure is simply an organization's current design and implementation of local area networks, wide area networks, and other communications systems. In many cases, existing information technology infrastructures have already taken into account business organization structures (with both physical and logical groupings) to assist with the implementation of a workgroup and workflow electronic system. However, in other cases, the existing information technology infrastructure is designed for an older method of organizational communications and would require restructuring to meet the needs of the new virtual workgroup procedure and implementation.

The organization needs to determine the appropriate layout of the computer network infrastructure, but instead of an infrastructure plan that involves the distribution of network file servers and workstations based on the physical layout of the building (like one file server per floor, or one file server per campus building), the distribution of servers and systems should be planned around how workflows and workgroup information dictate the demand of these resources. The deciding factors in infrastructure design include:

- **Number and physical distribution of users**   A knowledge of the number of users in the organization and their physical distribution by both site as well as by floor will assist in an understanding of user density and in planning physical user access to information technology resources.

- **Logical workflow of information between users**   Assigning users to a logical distribution scheme based on workgroup practices and workflow will focus attention on users' physical distribution and location. The logical workflow and workgroup information will show which individuals need to share information with other individuals, and how logical sites, groups, and servers need to be managed.

- **Current volume of information access**   The current volume of information access would be the amount of information (in stored files, or database or information queried access) that each individual or groups of individuals need on a daily basis. On average, how much information is accessed daily, weekly, and monthly? Where is the information currently stored (on a network file server or on a local hard drive)? How much information does an individual or workgroup need to have available for archival information access (for example, up to seven years of historical records, or two years of active project information)?

- **Centralized or decentralized information system administration**   Information systems administration plays an important role in how the organization's infrastructure is designed and deployed. In a centralized administration structure, servers and primary resources will typically be located in a single location, whereas in a decentralized administration structure, there would tend to be a greater distribution of servers and resources throughout the organization. Priority must be given to determining the value of centralizing servers in contrast to placing servers in a location that can most efficiently serve users. Obviously, if users are physically closer to the servers they access, they will benefit from faster performance and experience a minimum of long-distance communications and infrastructure bottlenecks. However, if fault tolerance and system redundancy are compromised by the distribution of resources, then centralizing the resources may be more appropriate for the organization.

- **Number and distribution of remote users** Dial-up remote users play an entirely new role in organizations and present new challenges. As remote users begin to gain access to servers and network information just as if they were physically in the office, the need to provide them with a well-planned communications strategy becomes even more important.

No Existing Computer Network

An organization that has no existing computer network or that wants to replace an existing network infrastructure has the luxury of designing, planning, and implementing a network infrastructure based on the best physical and logical design for its current and planned workflow processes.

Starting with a clean slate, the organization can begin with a physical and logical business organization structure, overlay a workgroup and workflow infrastructure, design the NT domain structure, and finally match up sites and servers within the organization to balance the workload and interconnect the systems into a complete communications infrastructure.

Existing Windows NT Local Area Network

If the organization has an existing Microsoft Windows NT network, the domain design, infrastructure layout, and load balancing of the NT network needs to be evaluated.

The existing NT network domain design needs to be reviewed to ensure that the NT domain model originally deployed is appropriate for the current and future implementation of the Microsoft Exchange environment. The domain model needs to properly account for all users, all logical groups, and the planned resource access by the users within the organization.

The existing infrastructure layout of servers and resources needs to be reviewed to ensure users are located near and attached to servers that most appropriately match their access needs when the new Microsoft Exchange environment is deployed. This would include connection to servers for file sharing, relaying messages, and public folder access to information stored on the network.

Lastly, load balancing needs to be taken into account to ensure that current infrastructure of servers, domain controllers, LAN topology and WAN connections have adequate bandwidth to support the demands of the new Exchange infrastructure. The load balance analysis may be something as simple as verifying that the servers have enough disk space to handle the storage of workflow information, or it may be as extensive as running actual load simulations on the existing infrastructure to ensure that current servers, LAN and WAN connections are adequate for the planned needs of the organization. Load simulation is covered in-depth in Chapter 7 of this book.

Existing Non-Windows NT Local Area Network

For an organization that has an existing local area or wide area network, similar considerations of design, layout, and load balancing need to be reviewed. In addition, the organization needs to understand how Microsoft Exchange interacts with other operating systems. Some organizations want to keep their existing network infrastructures, while others take the opportunity to migrate completely to a Windows NT environment. The issue of migrating to or having an existing operating environment coexist with Microsoft Exchange is covered in detail in Chapter 6 of this book.

Components that Will Improve Groupware Communications

Before going in-depth on establishing the workflow processes of an organization, it is important to understand some of the key components of Microsoft Exchange that will be used to implement the workgroup communications system. The three main capabilities of Microsoft Exchange that organizations use to accomplish their goal for improved groupware communications are centralized file and information storage, discussion groups, and replication shares.

Posting Information to an Exchange Folder Rather than Saving Files to a Directory Share

A method that most organizations use to share information is to set up subdirectories on a network where the users of a workgroup or the organization can store common information. These subdirectories form the centralized storage system for the workgroup. One way to leverage the capabilities of Microsoft Exchange is to set up a similar common storage tree system, but use Microsoft Exchange public folders as the medium for centralized information storage instead of a file subdirectory storage system.

By using Microsoft Exchange public folders, information is similarly structured for common storage and retrieval and the public folders can be configured for various levels of security to provide access to specific individuals, to many users, to groups of users, or to all users in the organization.

The advantages of using Microsoft Exchange public folders instead of standard network file server subdirectories include:

- **Centralized information store**   Unlike a file server subdirectory that is common only to users with security rights to the single location server, Exchange public folders can be set up to be viewed by any user in a Microsoft Exchange site as well as a Microsoft Exchange organization.

- **Automated information replication**   Through site-to-site replication, information in a Microsoft Exchange public folder can be replicated beyond a site or organization to other workgroups or locations. Since file server replication is automatic, any information stored in one public folder can be replicated without user or administrator intervention to other Exchange server locations.

- **Integrated information portability**   Through the use of Microsoft Exchange remote access replication to remote and mobile Exchange clients, information that is stored in public folders can be automatically replicated to remote users just as easily as the information can be replicated across multiple locations and sites.

- **Multi-platform file interchangeability**   Since information is stored in Microsoft Exchange folders as objects and the Exchange client comes in multiple operating system formats (DOS, Windows, Macintosh, UNIX), information stored in an Exchange public folder can be accessible to any user regardless of his or her operating system format (as long as the client has a browser, viewer, or application that can view or retrieve the native file formats of the information stored).

- **Quick and simple file look up**   Through the use of the Microsoft Exchange FIND function or third-party search engines, core message header information in public folders can be quickly and simply searched.

■ **Ability to search across multiple file types and formats** In addition to searching for stored mail message headers, third-party search engines can actually look inside attachments and native file formats within public folders and create an index of information stored in native formats for extremely fast information reference.

The ability to reference information quickly and easily across multiple operating system formats, as well as both in the office and a remote location, makes Microsoft Exchange public folder storage an extremely valuable reason to use Exchange folders instead of file server directories for common information storage.

Sharing Ideas and Information Within the Company or a Workgroup

Through the use of discussion groups linked to common public folders, organizations can carry on discussions with LAN and remote users within Microsoft Exchange. Now, not only can users store common information within Microsoft Exchange public folders, they can notify other users of the existence of information stored in a public folder in a common discussion area without having to e-mail all of the users. Additionally, the virtual workgroup can use discussion groups to share thoughts and ideas about workgroup information without ever having to get together physically for meetings or conferences. The ability to share information and communicate in the virtual workgroup (whether the user is on the LAN, on the WAN, or a remote mobile user) can provide the diversity an organization may need to communicate with team members in geographically dispersed areas, as well as improve communications among workgroup members that may all work in a common area.

Reaching Beyond the Traditional Organization to Include Strategic Business Partners

As organizations expand their use of Microsoft Exchange shared resources, individual user information storage is supplemented by workgroup information storage and sharing, which then provides an avenue for sharing information across multiple organizations. The ability to interconnect an organization's clients and vendors to common public folders greatly enhances the ability of the organization to expand the scope of workgroup or organizational communications.

As an organization allows its clients to participate in shared information stores, document routes, and discussion groups, the ability to communicate the status of projects, product orders, promotions, service requests, or customer service follow-ups provides a very strong communication link between client and vendor. As more and more organizations use the demand-push functions of e-mail to communicate information, the need to carbon copy messages to all members involved in the client/vendor relationship (including account reps, department managers, account assistants, support personnel, main client contact, secretaries, administrators, and assistants) creates a lot of demand-push e-mail messages. As organizations interlink their Microsoft Exchange communication systems, workgroup discussions and workflow processes can be commonly shared in a more productive demand-pull method of communications.

Leveraging the Components of Exchange to Establish Electronic Workgroup Practices

The challenge that the designers of electronic communications systems face is that many organizations do not even have a strategy for general workgroup communications, so the preparation of an electronic groupware system not only becomes an information systems task, but also a mandate for the installation of a new organizational and operational method of doing business. This is called *business process re-engineering* (BPR).

Gradual Development of Workflow and Workgroup Practices

Spending time to review the existing processes and practices of an organization before deploying Exchange will result in a more successful groupware implementation. Although every organization does not have to spend hours, days, weeks, or months redesigning its procedures in order to install a groupware environment like Microsoft Exchange, reviewing the organization's procedures and functions will greatly increase the odds of a successful Microsoft Exchange implementation and efficient and effective end result.

The first thing the designer of the Exchange implementation system needs to understand is how the organization currently communicates, what processes are used to gather information within the organization or external to the organization, and what various flow processes are in practice within the organization. This is typically done by attaining copies of organization procedures, flow charts, or other process documents of the workgroup. If written copies do not exist, interviews with individuals within the workgroup or even physically overseeing the process can provide the designer with extremely valuable information about the processes currently in place. The information that should be collected in the initial interview or analysis process should include:

- The name of this process (i.e.: submitting an office supply order request)

- Who initiates this process and/or when the process is initiated (i.e.: anyone requiring an office supply)

- How the process is initiated (i.e.: individual fills out an office supply request form)

- What happens next in the process (i.e.: form is put in the mailbox of the office manager, office manager calls the office supply company every Friday to place orders, office supply company delivers the ordered items on Monday, items are distributed to the individuals who submitted the requests)

- What are the end results of the process (i.e.: individual receives requested item(s) within one week of order)

 NOTE: Gather all copies of forms, written documents, and procedures.

Through the gradual development of workflow and workgroup practices, the organization can isolate a procedure, analyze it as explained in the previous procedural analysis, and then implement the workflow procedure electronically. Depending on the size of the workgroup and the number of procedures, it could take days, weeks, or even months or years to completely convert from manual (or ad hoc) to structured electronic processes. Although the implementation of an electronic workflow within an organization may take time, the benefits and results of the effort will be evident in user productivity, enhanced communications, and process tracking and workflow management.

Streamlining Processes in an Electronic Workflow

What many organizations realize when they convert processes from manual systems to electronic workflow systems is that many steps within the manual process are only in place because the system requires structured checks and balances. Steps need to be added to the manual system to ensure the end-to-end success of the process. In an electronic workflow process, however, because the flow is electronically tracked and logged, certain manual tracking steps are no longer necessary.

An example of a procedural step that was converted from a manual system to an electronic system is a company that dispatched repair technicians on a manual process, multipart work order ticket system. When the work order was submitted, one copy would go to the dispatch administrator (to schedule the repair technician to do the work), one copy would go to the billing administrator (to make sure that when the work was completed that the service would be billed), one copy would go to the parts manager (to allocate necessary repair parts for the service), one copy would be filed chronologically in a filing cabinet noting all work orders based on the date of submittal, and one copy would go to the process administrator who keeps track of all repair orders in process. Supposedly, at the end of the manual process the various parts of the work order would be matched up and filed in work order number sequence. Inevitably, 20-30 percent of all work order pieces never matched up at the end of the process because the paperwork would get lost or the manual process was too tedious to maintain, manage, and oversee.

When this process was converted into an electronic workflow, a number of the steps were eliminated. Since the information in a workflow is stored electronically on the network in a searchable format, the information did not need to be separately "filed" chronologically, nor did the information need to be separately filed by work order sequence, and the administrator of the department did not need a copy of each and every work order to keep track of all orders for end-to-end completion. When users need to reference information chronologically, they can sort the information by date. When they need to look up information by work order number, they can use the same information and sort it by work order number. Whenever a work order was scheduled for completion but did not show up in the system as completed, the administrator would be automatically notified of all such past-due order completions. This workflow procedure cut a five-step process down to a three-step process, and minimized the administrator's responsibility to manually check the status of all work orders in process to one in which the system automatically informs the administrator of the outstanding orders that require immediate attention.

Thus, when converting a manual system into an electronic workflow system, the entire process must be evaluated and analyzed to ensure that all procedures are appropriate for electronic implementation.

Business Process Re-Engineering

Business process re-engineering is a fundamental change in how an organization does business and, in many cases, a prerequisite for new workgroup, workflow, and full groupware environment implementation. In cases where an entire workflow is inappropriate for the organization (possibly developed long ago when the criteria for the workflow was different), a new process may need to be developed. Often, the simple fact that the organization must rethink procedures and implement the new system will improve worker efficiency.

Processes that typically need to be re-engineered are those that have been dependent on the flow of paperwork within an office. For many companies, most projects and processes were developed at a time when office-to-office communications was typically done by phone or by U.S. Mail. Today, with faxes, voicemail, and e-mail, a whole new range of communication tools is available. It is within these processes that global workgroup communication systems like Microsoft Exchange can be the instruments that assist in the implementation of a new business workgroup, restructuring how an organization does business.

The end result in performing a conversion from manual processes to electronic processes is to prevent the inclusion of a manual step that is no longer necessary in an electronic process, and to avoid implementing the same inefficient system in electronic form. Restructuring the process can save time, which in turn improves the efficiency and effectiveness of procedures in an organization.

The Emergence of the Virtual Workgroup

When rethinking processes in a completely new manner, organizations begin to realize that not only can they delete ancillary steps in the process because they are no longer necessary, but the designers of the new processes now understand that workgroups are no longer restricted to a physical locality where paper documents flow from mailslot to mailslot. This is a paradigm shift, in which a workgroup can be a virtual workgroup anywhere electronic workflows and communications can reside, rather than a physical group of users on a single floor in a building.

How an Organization Leveraged the Capability of the Exchange Environment

An example of a business that leveraged the capability of Microsoft Exchange in a process restructuring is an organization with multiple offices across the country that used to do its company marketing and advertising on an office-by-office basis. Because marketing and advertising typically involves artwork, ad layouts, and structured textual information, the best way to manage these functions when the organization was founded 50 years ago was on a location-by-location basis. Additionally, the firm had also established clients on a local or regional basis on an office-by-office basis. However, over the past five years, the company needed to attract larger, nationwide clients, but its ability to do so was hampered by its business infrastructure and implementation of computer infrastructure technology. Even if the organization implemented a groupware system across its entire national domain, the simple fact that each office still independently did its own advertising and marketing put a limit on the national organization's ability to make changes in the way they did business. Clearly, this organization required a complete business process re-engineering to change the way it planned, developed, and managed its internal marketing and communications. The company additionally has excellent talent across the country and did not need to dismantle the entire marketing and advertising infrastructure in order to centralize it.

The company re-engineered its business procedures by structurally evaluating a workgroup process that involved creating a virtual workgroup spanning all of the offices in the organization. Through the implementation of the groupware document sharing and collaborative computing capabilities of Microsoft Exchange, the organization was able to have members of the entire national marketing and advertising operation work together to share ideas, distribute work, and track and manage the work over a national corporate wide area network. Although they are hundreds if not thousands of miles apart, users are now able to view, annotate and update information on various marketing and advertising projects by sharing and storing information in publicly-shared message and workflow folders.

The Chapter in Review

- Exchange is a tool that helps companies re-engineer the way they do business. Process re-engineering requires a clear understanding of how the organization would ideally process work, given the tools it may not have had in the past. For example, an organization might consider how the development and routing of forms might affect the method by which purchase requests get processed or vacation time gets approved.

- The first step in determining what information needs to be shared is considering an organization's core business. An organization's core product is usually the information that needs to be shared by all departments. The application used to store the core data needs to be determined, as well as its location. Security requirements of the files need to be outlined as well as plans to secure sensitive data.

- After the Exchange designer has assessed the organizational infrastructure, he or she must assess the information technology infrastructure. In doing so, the designer can determine if the infrastructure is based on the organization's physical layout or the logical workflow. An organization without any existing infrastructure may find it easier to design a network solution than an organization needing to redeploy existing equipment. Organizations with existing NT networks need to do server-load balancing and other simulations to confirm that there are enough equipment resources to support the Exchange environment.

- Exchange can improve an organization's communications. But how is it done? To share information more effectively, users would post their documents to an Exchange folder instead of saving files in their private directory. This allows for the entire organization to access that information. Exchange also allows for discussions to occur without needing all participants to be in the same place at the same time. Users can read the topic of discussion, post responses, and read other's responses at a convenient time. This reduces the number of meetings required and increases the number of people who are able to participate. This virtual conversation can be extended to include clients and vendors. A greater number of people can have access to the information if they need it without having to sit in a meeting, and questions have a greater likelihood of being answered completely and accurately when all participants are polled.

- Now that the Exchange network ... ows some key functionality that Exchange pr... ...p is to determine what degree of business process re... ...zation will want and need. In order to allow ... ... degree of re-engineering is usually ... ...ysical size and structure needs to ... ...logy infrastructure needs ... ...igner needs to understand ... ...one person or department ... ... flow chart and unofficial ... ...ion. In order for a virtual ... ... flow chart needs to be man... ... done by re-engin... ...rocedures, and establi... ...ll users must check mes... ... organization's existing w... ...enlightening to see a ...

... company's business goals before

...plemented, Exchange can help a business ...er than without it. But a clear focus on the ...chieve complete success.

... versus information pull.

...hen the message creator determines who he or she ...mation and sends it to them. Information pull is when the ... ...at he or she needs the information and actively searches and ret...

Q. Give exam... ...s of a demand-pull system.
A. The Internet, a company's intranet, and groupware (such as Exchange) folders.

Q. What key features do you need to know about a company's infrastructure before being able to begin assessing its technological needs?

A. The number of users, physical layout of the organization, the logical layout of the organization, the management and communications hierarchy, and the workflow processes of the workgroups and organization.

Q. What are the three main capabilities of Exchange that make it a desirable groupware application?
A. Centralized storage of information, electronic discussion groups, ability to replicate a repository of information.

Q. What are the advantages to posting files in Exchange folders instead of in users' personal directories?
A. Centralized information store, automated information replication, integrated information portability, multiplatform file interchangeability, quick and simple file look up, and the ability to search across multiple file types and formats.

Q. Who has access to virtual conversations?
A. Any user has the ability to participate in virtual conversations if he or she is given security access rights. This includes users within the organization, in remote parts of the organization, or users in other organizations. Exchange is an excellent tool for geographically dispersed organizations and organizations with flex-time employees.

Q. Why do businesses undergo business process re-engineering?
A. To allow for virtual workgroups, businesses often need to rethink how their organization processes tasks.

Q. What are two essential things that need to be evaluated in order to know enough to do business process re-engineering?
A. An organization's physical layout and the organization's existing technology infrastructure.

Q. When collecting information about how a business processes a task, what are examples of information that should be gathered?
A. The interviewer should be informed of the process name (i.e., capital equipment requests), who initiates this process, when and how the process is initiated, and then ask what happens next. This last step should be repeated until the process is completed. How do you know that the process is completed? What are the end results? It is important to get copies of all forms, ideally blank and processed forms. The designer needs to look for places where complete information wasn't provided and decide how that will be handled electronically.

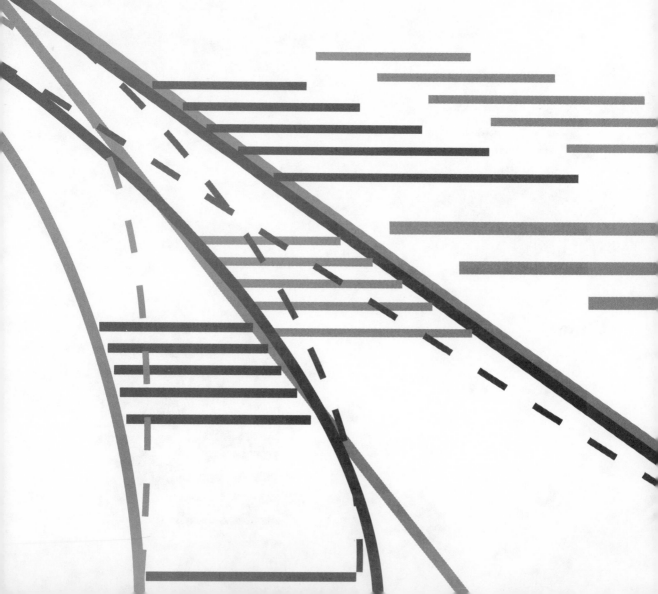

CHAPTER **6**

Migrating to or Integrating into a Microsoft NT Environment

In the last two chapters, we reviewed how an organization would plan and prepare to install Microsoft Exchange in a Windows NT environment. Because Microsoft Exchange is written over Windows NT Server, organizations wishing to standardize and deploy Microsoft Exchange that have a different standard network operating system environment need to consider whether they want to migrate to Windows NT for their organizational operating system or want Microsoft Exchange to coexist with their existing operating environment. This chapter will explore the migration process from Novell NetWare and Banyan Vines to Windows NT Server, as well as the integration and coexistence of Microsoft Exchange in a Novell NetWare, Banyan Vines, and a UNIX-TCP/IP existing infrastructure.

Migrate or Integrate?

The obvious question that an organization needs to ask itself as it prepares to deploy Microsoft Exchange in its environment is whether it will migrate its existing infrastructure to Windows NT, or integrate Microsoft Exchange to work within its existing operating environment.

It is not imperative that an organization replace its entire existing infrastructure with a Microsoft Windows NT infrastructure. When Microsoft Exchange is written on top of Microsoft Windows NT, it acts as an application server to Microsoft Windows NT; thus Microsoft Exchange can easily coexist in a non-Windows NT environment. In fact, because Microsoft Exchange operates as an application server to Windows NT, any environment into which Windows NT integrates is compatible with Microsoft Exchange. This includes Novell NetWare v3.x (bindery mode); Novell NetWare v4.x (NDS mode); Banyan Vines v5.x, v6.x, and v7.x; IBM OS/2 LanServer v3.x and WarpServer; and DEC PathWorks v4.x and v5.x.

Although Microsoft Exchange will coexist in a non-Windows NT environment, there are advantages to implementing Microsoft Windows NT as the core operating environment for Exchange:

- **Single operating system and operating system access** With Microsoft Windows NT as the sole network operating system for all users in an organization running Microsoft Exchange, all users would have the same operating system to access for file and print services as well as Microsoft Exchange messaging and communications access. Users would have a single method that allowed them to access programs, files, data, and electronic messages. If the means to access the network file system is through TCP/IP using Windows NT client access software, that same configuration gives users access to Microsoft Exchange. This eliminates the need to have other network access drivers (like IPX or Vines IP) in order to access file and print services, in addition to the Microsoft NT client drivers to access Exchange.

- **Single security system** Because the network operating system logon provides security, if the network users used the same logon security authentication process for file and print access as well as Microsoft Exchange access, they would only need to log on and type in a password once. Without a single security system, the users may need to log on to the network with a logon name and password, and then re-authenticate themselves to Microsoft Exchange. Additional ways for users on non-NT networks with Exchange to authenticate themselves to Microsoft Exchange will be addressed later in this chapter.

- **Single network administration** With a common logon and security system for users for both file and print network services as well as Microsoft Exchange messaging access, adding a new user is fairly easy. The network administrator simply needs to add the user once to the Microsoft Windows NT user list. Once the user is added to Windows NT, he or she has access to file and print services to Windows NT, and is immediately added to Microsoft Exchange for messaging and groupware access. As an organization leverages both the single inbox and source for user administration provided by Microsoft Windows NT and Exchange Server, it can also choose to link voicemail administration and pager administration directly into the same administration tool as Windows NT and Exchange. This means that when a user is added to Microsoft Windows NT, that user is also immediately added to electronic messaging, electronic scheduling, voicemail access, discussion groups, public shared information, and pager access. If a user, for example, needs his or her name changed, the network administrator can make a single modification, and *all* of the user's access information will be changed. Centralized user administration and management will be discussed in greater detail in Part Four of this book.

A number of network operating systems are currently available in the computer industry. This chapter will focus on three of the most common network operating environments: Novell NetWare, Banyan Vines, and UNIX-TCP/IP. There are a number of ways an organization can integrate and migrate an existing operating environment to Windows NT. If the organization is small enough, a complete migration can occur in a matter of days or weeks. However, if an organization is large or dispersed across a number of sites, a migration from one network operating environment to another could take several months to a year, or more. The key to a successful integration or migration as described in this chapter is to implement the conversion so that its impact on the users of the organization is minimized.

Some organizations will elect to completely migrate from an existing network operating environment to Microsoft Windows NT, while others will choose to run Microsoft Exchange from within an existing network operating system without the intention of migrating to Windows NT. When integrating a non-Windows NT environment into Microsoft Exchange, the organization needs to keep in mind that its users must be able to access their existing file and print servers using some form of client access software to maintain access to their existing network operating environment, while the administrator is adding on the Microsoft Exchange client access software. The coexistence of Microsoft Exchange in other operating environments requires careful attention to the amount of memory the client stations need in order to load both access client software programs, as well as the need to maintain and administer both environments. The following section will cover the integration of three main operating infrastructures, which include the Novell NetWare, Banyan Vines, and UNIX environments.

There are typically four reasons why an organization chooses to maintain the coexistence of an existing operating environment:

- **Investment to convert core operating environments may be prohibitively high** Many organizations have already invested heavily in the implementation of a core network operating environment, from the standpoint of costs ranging from product and software licenses, training of the administration staff, and implementation of the installation. If the core operating environment is considered to be stable and reliable, the desire to migrate to a different operating environment may not be widely accepted or viewed as necessary.

- **Compatibility with an existing application** Some organizations may not be able to convert to a different operating environment because critical business applications will only run on the existing operating system configuration. The need for application compatibility dictates the maintenance of the organization's existing operating environment.

■ **Size of the organization indicates a lengthy migration process**
The sheer size of some organizations require months, if not years to
complete a migration, even if the organization migrated to a different
operating system. The extended period of time from the start of the
migration to the completion requires a reliable and dependable
coexistence between the two environments during the many
transitional months.

■ **Part of the organization is managed or operated by another business
entity in which the ability to dictate a full migration to Microsoft
Windows NT is not feasible** For some organizations with distributed
administrations, portions of the organization may elect to not migrate
from their existing operating environment. This forces the organization
to construct a strategy that would allow for some level of coexistence
between units with different operating systems.

Integrating and Migrating Novell NetWare with Microsoft Windows NT

The first of the three operating environments that will be discussed for
integration and migration will be an existing Novell NetWare operating
environment. Novell has two completely different operating systems: NetWare
v3.x, which runs in a Bindery mode, and NetWare v4.x, which runs under their
NetWare Directory Services (NDS). Novell has traditionally been the market
leader in local area network operating systems, and there are a number of
tools that are available or included with Microsoft Windows NT in order to
provide for the integration and migration of Novell NetWare in a Windows
NT environment.

Organizations with an existing Novell NetWare environment may elect to
maintain Novell NetWare as their core operating system (sometimes referred
to as a "file and print" environment) and access Microsoft Exchange as an
application server function running under Windows NT. Some organizations
would want to standardize their operating environment to include a single
network operating system and a single user administration process.

Background on Novell NetWare Terminology

An understanding of what is involved in integrating Windows NT with
Novell NetWare requires a familiarity with the terminology that is common to

both operating environments. In Chapter 4, we outlined the components that make up Windows NT. Here are the corresponding components in the Novell NetWare environment.

IPX/SPX

The protocol that Novell NetWare uses as its communications standard is IPX/SPX. This corresponds to NetBEUI Windows NT or TCP/IP for a UNIX environment. Novell created and adopted the IPX/SPX standard for its ability to take on the routing capabilities similar to those that have made TCP/IP popular in wide area networks, but Novell simplified IPX/SPX to make it easier to install and manage on an ongoing basis. Unlike TCP/IP, which requires that each workstation be manually assigned an identification number, IPX automatically assigns a node identification number to each workstation. SPX provides the mechanism in which applications can communicate with each other, such as workstation-to-printer communication for printing, workstation-to-server communication for pass-through access to a mainframe, or workstation-to-server for fax communications. To be compatible with a Novell environment, the NT client and NT servers must communicate over IPX/SPX.

Bindery and NetWare Directory Services (NDS)

Networks track user names and resources on the network through a user and resource database and management system. Under Novell NetWare v3.x (NetWare v3.11 and v3.12 are the most common v3.x systems installed), the user name and security information is stored in what Novell calls a *Bindery*. The Bindery consists of a database of the user names, passwords, and security rights that a user is assigned for access to file servers, as well as a database of security access by users for specific files on file servers throughout the network. On Novell NetWare v4.x (NetWare v4.10 and v4.11 are the most common v4.x systems installed), the NetWare Directory Services (NDS) includes information on all network resources including users, printers, file servers, file access, file security, and network resource management. When communicating from a Windows NT environment to a Novell NetWare environment, the two operating environments need to be able to authenticate each other for security access with both Microsoft Windows NT's Access Control List (ACL) and Novell NetWare's Bindery or NDS security lists.

Syscon and Nwadmin Utilities

The utilities used to manage the Bindery or NDS are SYSCON.EXE and NWADMIN.EXE, respectively. The syscon utility is used to add, modify, and delete users to a NetWare v3.*x* environment. This utility also allows the network administrator to specify which files the user should have access to and his or her level of privileges to the files (read, write, create, modify, or delete). The nwadmin utility does the same for a NetWare v4.*x* environment; however, in an NDS environment, the utility also manages printers, file servers, disk volumes, and other resources on the network. The ability to integrate a NetWare environment with Windows NT would allow for the management of NT resources using either the syscon or the nwadmin utility, or the management of the Novell NetWare users using the Windows NT User Manager utility.

Mapping Volumes and Capturing to Printers

To access files and printers in a Novell network, NetWare users are familiar with the MAP.EXE and CAPTURE.EXE commands. The map command allows a user to specify a drive letter to a Novell drive share, for example,

MAP F:=MYSERVER\DISKC:

The capture command allows a user to redirect printing to a network printer, for example,

CAPTURE /Q=LASERPTR

The Windows NT client station maintains full compatibility with a Novell network by supporting the Novell MAP and CAPTURE commands for file and print access to Novell resources.

Core Components Involved in Integrating NetWare to an NT Environment

Novell NetWare has its own set of protocols and methodologies that determine its performance as a network operating system. In order for

Windows NT to support cross-compatibility with a Novell NetWare network, Windows NT needs to provide these core services that characterize Novell NetWare as its unique operating environment.

NWLink

The first issue of importance in retaining compatibility with a Novell environment is communicating using the same network protocol as Novell. As described earlier in the Novell NetWare terminology, Novell developed and standardized IPX/SPX as its communications protocol. In order for Windows NT to be compatible with Novell networks, Microsoft needed to speak the same protocol (IPX/SPX) as Novell. As a result, the NWLink protocol set was developed, which allows a Windows NT server to speak the basic core language of the two environments. NWLink IPX/SPX supports IPX/SPX sockets and NetBIOS APIs. This means that the NWLink protocol has the ability to make a Windows NT server talk like a Novell network server, while retaining the core communication components Windows NT needs to conduct Windows networking.

File and Print Services for NetWare

The File and Print Services program for NetWare is a Microsoft add-in to Windows NT that allows a Windows NT server to appear as a Novell NetWare server. Users who are configured with the Novell client and MAP to disk shares from a Novell client to a Novell server can now MAP to a Windows NT server just as if the NT server is a NetWare server.

The File and Print Services for NetWare provides an organization with the ability to integrate and migrate from a purely Novell environment to a Windows NT environment without having to change all of the existing NetWare client access components. In fact, if an organization replaced its Novell server with an NT server, and had the NT server assume the name of the old Novell server, users who formerly accessed the Novell server will now be granted the same access to the NT server. All this can be performed without ever making a change to the client workstations.

Client Services for NetWare

An organization that has a mix of both NetWare servers and NT servers may want to install the NT client on the Windows 95 and Windows NT Workstation systems while retaining its access to existing Novell servers. To do so, an organization would install the Client Services for NetWare software on the workstations to maintain access to the Novell servers. The network client speaks the same protocol as the Novell network (IPX/SPX) and acts like a Novell client. The Client Services for NetWare software provides the services necessary to MAP to Novell disk shares as well as CAPTURE to network printers.

The Client Services for NetWare software supports NCP, LIP, and Burst, which provide the same client components that make the NT client look like a NetWare client, allowing the NT client to run utilities such as syscon in order to perform Novell network administration from an NT client. The Client Services for NetWare software bridges the migration process where clients and servers can be NT systems; however, the clients can have full access to the NetWare file servers on the network.

Gateway Services for NetWare

For client workstations that need to access both a Novell network and an NT network, and are completing a conversion from NetWare to NT, Gateway Services for NetWare can be installed on an NT server that allows an NT client to access the NetWare server. The Gateway Services provide NT clients with the ability to NET USE disk shares and print shares using the NT client commands while the information is passed through the NT server to a NetWare server.

Directory Service Manager for NetWare

The Directory Service Manager for NetWare (DSMN) is a Microsoft add-in to Windows NT. DSMN consolidates network administration for a dual NetWare and NT environment into a single management function. This will ensure that a user who logs in to NT will be able to also access information on NetWare servers, and vice-versa. When users change their passwords, their security information is automatically updated on both the NT side and the NetWare side.

Migration Tool for NetWare

The Migration Tool for NetWare (NWCONV.EXE) converts Novell network security information, such as a user's login name, file access, and group information, to Microsoft Windows NT-equivalent items. The Migration Tool for NetWare is extremely useful to organizations who want to transfer the login names and basic security information from a previous NetWare network to an NT network, or to organizations that have long-term strategies for the coexistence of NetWare and NT synchronized by Directory Service Manager for NetWare on an ongoing basis.

Initiating an Integration and Migration Process

To integrate or migrate a Novell NetWare network in an NT environment requires that a sequence of events occur in a specific order. The following section outlines that order.

Migrating User Names and Security Information to NT

The first thing that must be accomplished is the security setup for NetWare users on the NT network. Regardless of all other connectivity and migration functions, if NetWare users don't have user names, passwords, and security authentication capabilities in the Windows NT environment, they won't have access to the NT domain.

The utility that allows for the migration of user names from NetWare to NT is the Migration Tool for NetWare.

USING THE MIGRATION TOOL FOR NETWARE   The Migration Tool for NetWare has two separate components that allow the administrator of the network to migrate users as well as files from a Novell network to an NT network. Within the Migration Tool, the NetWare server is selected from which the administrator wants to retrieve user names, as well as the NT server to which the administrator wants the names to be sent. The administrator can select multiple NetWare servers to consolidate user names to a single Windows NT domain, as shown in Figure 6-1.

The administrator has a number of options to choose from regarding key characteristics during the migration process of the user names. They include:

- **Passwords**   The administrator has the choice of migrating with no passwords, having passwords become the users' names, or assigning pre-defined passwords.

- **User names**   Duplicate names will be ignored, overwritten with new information, or have a prefix added to them.

- **Group names**   Duplicate group names will be ignored, or have a prefix added to them.

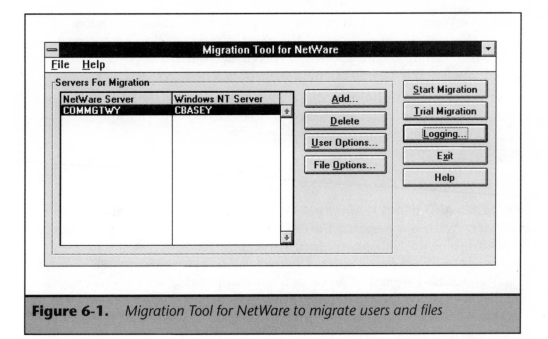

Figure 6-1.   *Migration Tool for NetWare to migrate users and files*

- **Defaults** The migration tool will migrate account restrictions, such as password requirements, minimum password lengths, requirements for users to change their passwords, reuse of existing passwords, or intruder lockouts.

When an administrator migrates user names from NetWare to NT, the users of the network can access the NetWare network, the NT network, or both. The user migration provides basic login security access for the network users and is an option for both coexistence as well as migration processes to NT.

During a migration from NetWare to NT, the Migration Tool also allows an administrator to select the files that should be migrated from a NetWare server to an NT server. The file options enable the administrator to modify file transfer options that include:

- **Migration source and destination** The administrator can choose which NetWare volumes are to be migrated to which NT partitions.

- **Selecting hidden and system files** The administrator can select whether files that are hidden or system files should be transferred from NetWare to NT.

■ **NetWare-specific directories**   Specific NetWare directories such as the \System, \Public, \Login, \Mail, and \Etc directories that are created by NetWare and are specific to Novell NetWare networks can be deselected if they do not need to be transferred.

■ **Selection of individual files and directories**   Specific files and directories can be selected or deselected for transfer from NetWare to NT.

The Migration Tool for NetWare is used to add user names and selected files from NetWare to Windows NT.

CREATING AND USING A MAPPING FILE   To simplify or automate the migration process, a mapping file can be created that will list all of the users and groups on the NetWare file server and allow the administrator to select from a series of text-based options that determine how the mappings between NetWare and NT should be processed. The mapping file is useful when specific users need to have different characteristics for migration than others. This will allow the administrator to select migration characteristics for some users and different migration characteristics for others.

Installation of File and Print Services for NetWare

Once the user names have been migrated from Novell NetWare to Windows NT, the existing Novell users need to have access to the NT file server. The installation of the Microsoft File and Print Services for NetWare enables the Windows NT file server to appear as a Novell NetWare file server. Since the users of the network are Novell NetWare clients that have recently been added to the security list of the NT server in the Migration Tools for NetWare step, the NetWare users will now have access to the NT server without any changes to their client software.

The File and Print Services for NetWare (FPNW) is an add-in to Windows NT and needs to be purchased separately (it costs approximately $100). FPNW is installed with the SETUP command and runs as a service under Windows NT. The administrator has the option of selecting the name of the Novell file server that the Windows NT server will simulate as well as the directories on the NT file server that should be shared and accessed by NetWare users. The configuration option in the Control Panel | FPNW is shown in Figure 6-2.

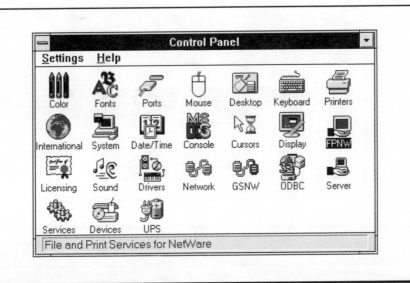

Figure 6-2.   *File and Print Services for NetWare (FPNW) options*

Maintaining Security Synchronization Through Directory Service Manager

If both the Novell network(s) and the Windows NT network(s) are to coexist and may require the synchronization of user names between the two operating systems, the Microsoft Directory Service Manager for NetWare (DSMN) keeps the user names and passwords the same between the two networking environments.

As a Microsoft add-in product, DSMN is sold separately and is installed on a Windows NT server that has access to the Novell NetWare network security information as well as the Microsoft Windows NT security information. Installation is conducted using the SETUP command, as shown in Figure 6-3, and the utility is stored as DSMN, an option in the Control Panel. The administrator chooses which NetWare server and which NT server will be designated to synchronize network names.

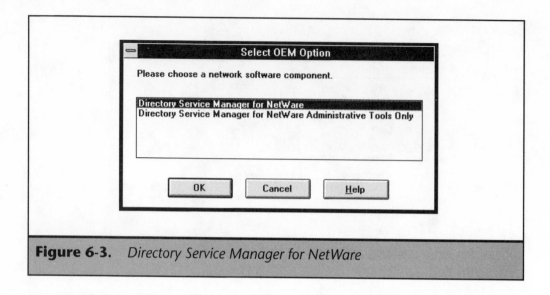

Figure 6-3.   *Directory Service Manager for NetWare*

Installation of Gateway Services for NetWare

After users are migrated from a Novell NetWare client to a Windows NT
client, they still need access to existing Novell NetWare file servers. The
Gateway Services for NetWare that comes standard with Windows NT can
be installed to provide access from NT clients to NetWare disk shares.

The Gateway Services for NetWare is installed from the Control
Panel | Networks | Add Software option and creates a utility in the Control
Panel. The administrator of the NT network has to identify the name of the
NetWare server and volume that will be simulated as a Windows NT directory
share. Once installed and running, the Gateway Services for NetWare provides
a method for NT clients to NET USE Novell volumes and directories without
having to install the Novell client software on individual workstations.

Installing the Client Workstations Software

For Windows for Workgroups, Windows 95, and Windows NT Workstation
systems that require access to a new Windows NT network in addition to an
existing NetWare network, the Windows Networking client software can be
installed on the workstations to provide access to the Windows NT networks.

COEXISTENCE   If a workstation will continue to access an existing NetWare network as well as a Windows NT network, it must have a configuration in one of the following:

- **Access to NetWare:**

  - The Novell client software (DOS ODI or Client for NetWare)

  - The Windows NT client software installed with Gateway Services for NetWare, providing a way to pass through NT clients to a Novell network

- **Access to Windows NT:**

  - The Windows NT client software

  - The Novell client software installed with File and Print Services for NetWare, providing a way to pass through NetWare clients to an NT network

COMPLETE MIGRATION   For a complete migration, the user client software should be replaced—in this case, from the native Novell client software to the native Windows NT client software. For DOS, the Windows NT networking software is the MSCLIENT software for DOS running NetBEUI. The MSCLIENT software is the same software used for a Windows v3.x environment. For a Windows 95 or Windows NT Workstation system, the Windows Networking client needs to be installed.

Completing the Migration Process

To finalize the installation and migration process from NetWare users to Windows NT users, the administrator should clean up unnecessary names, directory shares, files, printer definitions, and other resources that are no longer necessary in the new networking environment. The most common items left over after a migration from NetWare to NT has been completed are users such as supervisor, guest, or FPNW Admin; groups such as ntgateway; and directories such as \Public, \System, \Login, or \Mail. The administrator needs to be careful not to delete any information that may still be used in the Windows NT networking environment, and it is suggested that a backup of all information is conducted prior to the deletion of any information from a network.

Integrating and Migrating Banyan Vines with Microsoft Windows NT

The second of the three operating environments that will be focused on for integration and migration will be Banyan Vines. Banyan Vines has been the industry leader in wide area networks for years. With some of the largest organizations in the world using Banyan Vines as their standard network operating system, some of the largest installations of Microsoft Exchange are expected to be performed for many organizations currently using Banyan Vines.

During the migration process from Banyan Vines to Microsoft Windows NT, the utilities that provide user name population from Vines to NT are the same, as well as the utility that allows an NT network file server to function like a Banyan network file server (File and Print Services for Vines). The difference between a migration and a coexistence process is that the intent of a migration process is to be on the new operating system as quickly and reliably as possible, which is best implemented by short-term conversion steps. A coexistence process, however, is intended to maintain long-term compatibility and interconnectivity, so the utilities used must promote the capabilities of long-term administration and management.

Many organizations running Banyan Vines have elected to either integrate a few Windows NT servers into their environment or to completely migrate to Windows NT. The advantages that Windows NT provides to most Banyan Vines networks include:

- **Larger partition size**   Banyan Vines prior to Vines v6.0 was limited to a network partition size of 2GB. When Vines originally became available in the 1980s, a 2GB disk partition was more than most organizations dreamed they would ever need. However, as databases and archival storage shares increased and the cost of hard drives plummeted, network drive partitions beyond 2GB have become commonplace. By installing a Windows NT file server with a large hard drive subsystem on a Banyan network and providing access to the partition for Banyan users, Windows NT has grown in popularity for providing organizations with the disk access they require.

■ **Compatibility with hardware** Banyan Vines is an operating environment that has historically provided minimal options for support hardware and peripheral options such as tape backup systems, CD-ROM towers, or CD-ROM jukeboxes. Even when add-in peripherals became extremely popular among other network operating environments, if Banyan Vines did not have driver support for the option, the peripheral could not be supported by the Banyan Vines network. Again, if a peripheral is supported by Windows NT and can be installed and made operational on an NT server, once that NT server is integrated into a Banyan environment with the appropriate access utilities for the clients, the peripheral becomes available for the Banyan network.

Even without Microsoft Exchange as a potential catalyst for organizations to integrate or migrate Windows NT into their existing Banyan Vines environment, other factors have created a demand for Banyan Vines administrators to integrate or migrate to a Windows NT network operation.

Background on Banyan Vines Terminology

An understanding of what is involved in integrating Windows NT with Banyan Vines requires a familiarity with the terminology that makes up the core components of both of the operating environments. The following are corresponding components in the Banyan Vines environment.

Vines IP

Banyan Vines, as a core operating system, runs over BSD UNIX and has many of the characteristics of a UNIX operating environment. However, one improvement that Banyan made to the UNIX operating environment was to integrate dynamic TCP/IP addressing into the Banyan Vines operating system. To do so, Banyan created a new version of the transport operating protocol in which Banyan Vines communicates from the clients to the server. The resulting protocol is Vines IP. Vines IP is a routable protocol just like TCP/IP; however,
it has the added benefit of providing condensed server-to-server and client-to-server communications with the ability to dynamically assign user IDs to users on the network.

StreetTalk

The biggest praise that Banyan always receives is for the design of their directory services, StreetTalk. Although many directory services models are limited to networks of less than 256 users, 2,500 users, 10,000 users, or 20,000 users, Banyan Vines, by utilizing the StreetTalk directory services, commonly manages wide area networks with 20,000, 50,000, or even 100,000 or more users.

StreetTalk uses an Organization, Group, and User structure for the naming of users on the network. The components of a user name help to designate in which part of the network or directory the user resides and should have access. The naming scheme separates the three components of the name by an @ sign. Thus a user is *user@group@organization*. This is significant, as the three components of a Banyan name need to be translated to the Windows NT domain structure.

Access Rights Lists (ARLs)

Banyan Vines user and resource administration provides security access through the creation and management of Access Rights Lists, or ARLs. The ARL designates which files, directories, and resources a user should access. The ARLs are important when mapping file level security between an existing Banyan Vines network security model and a Windows NT network security model.

SETDRIVE to Partitions and SETPRINT to Printers

Banyan Vines users access network resources such as disk shares and printers through the use of the SETDRIVE and SETPRINT commands, respectively. Like the Windows NT network NET USE command to access file shares and printers, the SETDRIVE and SETPRINT utilities are used as counterparts in a Banyan Vines environment. The closer Windows NT can provide SETDRIVE and SETPRINT services for Banyan clients, the easier it will be for users to migrate from a Banyan Vines environment to a Windows NT network environment.

Core Components Involved in Integrating Banyan Vines to an NT Environment

Just as for NetWare, there are core components that allow a Banyan Vines network to closely integrate with a Windows NT environment. A few of those tools and utilities include the following.

Banyan Enterprise Client for Windows NT

The Banyan Enterprise client for Windows NT provides Windows NT servers and workstations with the ability to access Banyan Vines file servers running Vines v5.56 or higher. The Banyan Enterprise client for Windows NT provides all of the security controls access, StreetTalk naming system, and other resource access functionality of a normal DOS-based Banyan Vines client.

Banyan File and Print Services

When a Banyan client needs to access a Banyan Vines file server, the user executes the SETDRIVE command. However, during an integration or migration process in which a file server is a Windows NT server, the Banyan client needs to access the NT server. One option is to load the Windows NT client software onto the workstation (in addition to the normal Banyan Vines client software); another is to purchase the Banyan File and Print Services software from Banyan. The Banyan File and Print software, shown in Figure 6-4, enables a Windows NT file server to function like a Banyan file server. The file server can participate as a resource server in the Banyan StreetTalk directory system. Users that normally SETDRIVE to Banyan servers can SETDRIVE to a Windows NT server running the Banyan File and Print Services.

This add-on software to Windows NT provides a Banyan network environment with the ability to access Windows NT servers without having to change any of the client software drivers or access utilities. Additionally, now that the servers are NT servers, the Banyan users can access any of the resources that are normally limited in a native Banyan environment, such as special CD-ROM tower configurations, CD jukeboxes, tape backup systems, or large hard drive partitions.

Banyan Migration Tool

For organizations migrating from Banyan Vines to a Windows NT environment, the Banyan Migration Tool (BMT) provides utilities that enable an organization to migrate user names, groups, and resource security information from a Banyan StreetTalk environment to a Microsoft Windows NT domain environment.

The BMT can be used to simply populate a Windows NT domain with users from the Banyan StreetTalk organization, or to create a long-term coexistence between Banyan resources and Windows NT resources.

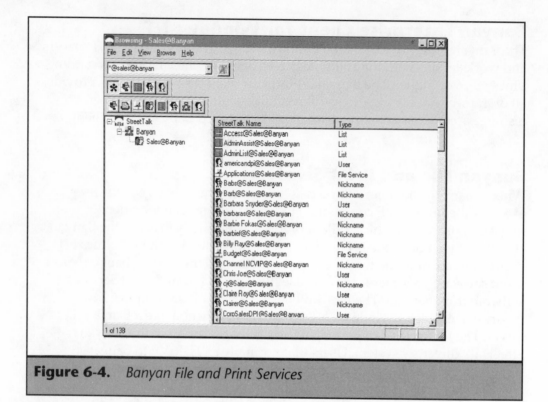

Figure 6-4.   *Banyan File and Print Services*

Initiating an Integration and Migration Process

Integrating or migrating a Banyan Vines network in an NT environment requires that a sequence of events occur in a specific order. The following section outlines that order.

Migrating User Names and Security Information to NT

First, security must be set up for the Banyan Vines users on the NT network. Regardless of all other connectivity and migration functions, if Vines users don't have user names, passwords, and security authentication capabilities in the Windows NT environment, they won't have access to the NT domain.

The utility that migrates user names from Banyan Vines to Microsoft Windows NT is called the Banyan Migration Tool. File security migration from Banyan Vines to Windows NT requires that all users and group accounts have been created on a Windows NT network. Windows NT Access Control Lists (ACLs) only store a security ID (SID) for a file, so when a file is transferred from Banyan Vines with Banyan Access Rights Lists (ARLs) that have user, group, and list names in the security information, if a user or group has not been created, the Banyan Vines ARL will not transfer the security information to the ACL for Windows NT.

As long as the user and group names are imported to Windows NT from Vines, as shown in Figure 6-5, then the BMT can copy Vines file security information to the NT server.

USING THE BANYAN MIGRATION TOOL   The Banyan Migration Tool allows the network administrator to migrate users from a Banyan Vines network to a Windows NT network. The administrator has a number of options to choose from regarding key characteristics during the migration process of the user names. They include:

- **User names**   Migrated names to NT can remain the same as they were in Vines, use the Vines user name, the shortened nickname, the first initial and last name, first name and last initial, or a pre-determined prefix and suffix.

- **Passwords**   The administrator has the choice of maintaining the Vines passwords, utilizing the user ID as the password, selecting a pre-determined password for all users, or randomly generating a password for the user.

- **Account expiration**   During the migration process, the user accounts can be left unchanged, set to never expire, or set to expire on a set date.

- **Group name change**   A Banyan group name can be changed during the migration process to a new or different Windows NT group name. This may be a process whereby an administrator merges multiple Banyan Vines groups into a single Windows NT user group.

Because the Banyan Migration Tool does not migrate files or directory shares, the information migrated from Banyan Vines to Windows NT will need to be migrated separately.

Installation of Banyan File and Print Services

Once the user names have been migrated from Banyan Vines to Windows NT, the existing Banyan users need to have access to the NT file server. The installation of the Banyan File and Print Services enables the Windows NT file server to function like a Banyan StreetTalk file server. Since the users of the network are Banyan clients that have recently been added to the security list

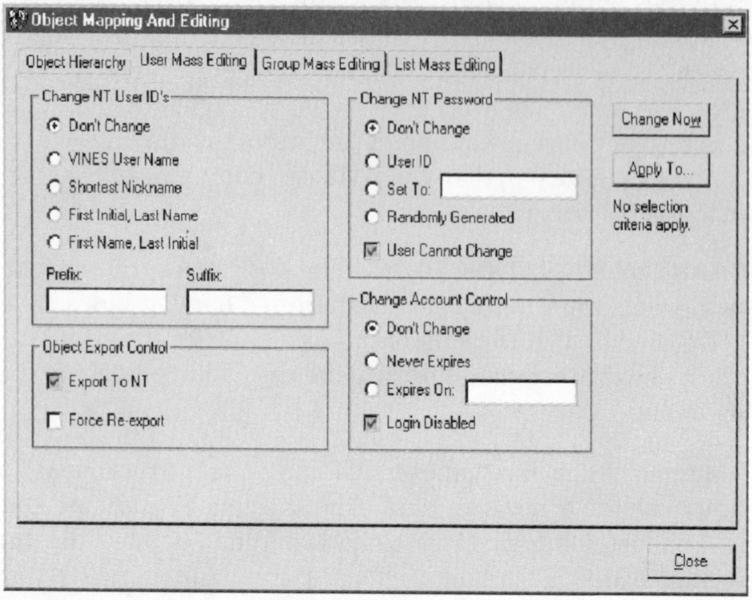

Figure 6-5. *Banyan Migration Tool*

of the NT server in the Banyan Migration Tools step, the Vines users will now have access to the NT server without any changes to their client software.

The Banyan File and Print Services is an add-in to Windows NT and needs to be purchased separately from Banyan. BMT is installed with the SETUP command and runs as a service under Windows NT. The administrator has the option of selecting the name of the Banyan file server that the Windows NT server will simulate as well as the directories on the NT file server that should be shared and accessed by Vines users.

Migrating Programs and Data

Since the Banyan Migration Tool does not migrate programs and data from a Banyan file server to a Windows NT server, the administrator needs to create a process that will complete the migration (such as simply using the XCOPY command to migrate information from one server to another).

Installing the Client Workstations Software

For Windows for Workgroups, Windows 95, and Windows NT Workstation systems that require access to a new Windows NT network in addition to an existing NetWare network, the Windows Networking client software can be installed on the workstations to provide access to the Windows NT networks.

COEXISTENCE If a workstation will continue to access an existing Banyan Vines network as well as a Windows NT network, it must have a configuration in one of the following:

- **Access to Banyan Vines:**
  - The Vines client software (DOS or Windows versions available)

- **Access to Windows NT:**
  - The Windows NT client software
  - The Banyan Enterprise client software installed with the Banyan File and Print Services, providing a way to pass through Vines clients to an NT network

COMPLETE MIGRATION For a complete migration, the user client software should be replaced from the native Banyan Vines client software to the native Windows NT client software. For DOS, the Windows NT networking software is the MSCLIENT software for DOS running NetBEUI. The MSCLIENT software is the same software used for a Windows v3.x environment. For a Windows 95 or Windows NT Workstation system, the Windows Networking client needs to be installed.

Completing the Migration Process

To finalize the installation and migration process from Banyan Vines users to Windows NT users, the administrator should clean up unnecessary names, directory shares, files, printer definitions, and other resources that are no longer necessary in the new networking environment. The administrator needs to be careful not to delete any information that may still be used in the Windows NT networking environment and it is suggested that a backup of all information is conducted prior to the deletion of any information from a network.

Integrating and Migrating UNIX-TCP/IP with Microsoft Windows NT

The third and last of the three operating environments that will be focused on for integration and migration will be a UNIX or TCP/IP environment with Microsoft Windows NT. A TCP/IP environment does not necessarily need to have UNIX systems within the environment; however, since TCP/IP is the standard means of communication for UNIX systems, the implementation and citation of TCP/IP commonly refers to core UNIX system functionality. Microsoft Windows NT probably has one of the best coexistence processes for integrating native UNIX environments into the core network operating environment. Because Microsoft Windows NT supports TCP/IP client and server communications, that same communication process that provides the client access to a UNIX server also allows the user to access the Microsoft Exchange environment. In fact, Microsoft provides utilities that allow for seamless integration of UNIX systems into the NT environment and vice-versa. The integration solutions include some of the core interconnectivity solutions based around TCP/IP networking, including Domain Name Services (DNS) and IP addressing.

Background on UNIX-TCP/IP Terminology

An understanding of what is involved in integrating TCP/IP into a Windows NT environment requires a familiarity with the terminology that makes up the core components of TCP/IP. The following are components in a TCP/IP environment.

TCP/IP

The first term to define is TCP/IP itself. Many people know it stands for Transmission Control Protocol/Internet Protocol; however, beyond the textbook definition of TCP/IP is the functionality it can provide to an organization with a local area or wide area network.

Adding TCP/IP to a Windows NT network provides the following advantages:

■ **The ability to connect traditionally dissimilar systems:** TCP/IP became a de facto standard for organizations primarily because of the popularity of the Internet, which communicates over TCP/IP. Currently, various types of computer systems (UNIX, Novell NetWare, Banyan Vines, Windows NT) that could never speak to each other before can now be configured to communicate with each other over TCP/IP.

- **A standard routable protocol:** TCP/IP is the most complete and widely accepted protocol available. The Internet is based on a TCP/IP backbone, and now organizations can use the same resource to allow their internal networking environments to grow and become as large and dispersed as they wish.

- **The ability to access the Internet:** the exponential growth of the Internet, its status as the largest TCP/IP network, and a plethora of organizations and individuals wishing to be connected to the Internet on a daily basis have all created a demand to configure local area and private networks as TCP/IP networks.

IP Addressing and Domain Name Services (DNS)

Just about every administrator of a TCP/IP network complains about the requirement that every device (workstation, file server, router, or printer) on a TCP/IP network must have a unique address. The IP address is a series of four numbers (from 0 to 255) separated by periods (for example, 204.31.169.1). In a TCP/IP network, the network administrator needs to assign and then keep track of all IP addresses. If the administrator fails to do this and two devices are mistakenly assigned the same IP address, one of the devices will not work on the network.

One way that TCP/IP administrators track IP addresses with common names of the systems is through a Domain Name Service (DNS). The DNS is a cross-reference server that matches a given IP address with a given server name. On the Internet, DNS servers keep track of registered servers like Web servers so that a user can either access the Microsoft WWW server by typing http://www.microsoft.com (and a DNS server will resolve the name to the correct IP address) or the user could type http://xx.xx.xx.xx, which is the direct method of accessing a Web server on a TCP/IP network.

NFS Host and NFS Mounting

In order for UNIX systems to share hard drives, Sun Microsystems, a long-time developer of UNIX and TCP/IP networking systems, developed and made NFS popular. NFS stands for Network File System and an NFS server is one that publishes the contents or a portion of the content of the server disk storage information for access by other users on the network. A system that has NFS mounting capabilities can mount an NFS server shared disk space. The ability to share drive space enables an organization in a UNIX environment to work together as a workgroup.

Pinging an IP Address

In a UNIX environment, clients and servers can ping each other to confirm the existence of the IP addressed user. For example, a user may type PING 204.31.169.1 and either receive a response that the host is not found or the user will receive a response that the host is a determined number of milliseconds away. The ping function in a TCP/IP environment allows users to confirm the existence or nonexistence of a connection to other IP devices.

Managing Client IP Addresses using Dynamic Host Configuration Protocol (DHCP)

To minimize one of the biggest headaches in TCP/IP networking (which is to manually assign and track IP addresses), Microsoft created the Dynamic Host Configuration Protocol (DHCP), which is an NT service installed on a Windows NT server in an NT network. DHCP provides a system in which IP addresses can be assigned and tracked by a server running the DHCP services. This provides an organization with the ability to specify a range of IP addresses (for example, 204.31.169.1 to 204.31.169.31) and allow them to be assigned on a first-come, first-served basis automatically as users log on to the network.

DHCP provides the following benefits to an organization:

- DHCP allows for the dynamic allocation of IP addresses: as users log on to the network, the DHCP server dynamically allocates an IP address to the workstation. This minimizes the need for network administrators to assign an IP address to each workstation.

- DHCP addresses are leased on a limited time basis: if a user's workstation that was dynamically assigned an IP address by the DHCP server no longer uses the workstation (i.e.: system crashes and is replaced by a new system, system is removed from a network and installed on a different network), there is no need to remember which IP address was assigned to that system. The next time a new system logs on to the network, a new IP address is assigned to the new system, and eventually the old IP address assigned to the old workstation automatically expires from nonuse and is reallocated to the DHCP address pool.

■ DHCP provides a trackable method of assignment: since DHCP logs the leases of IP addresses, an organization can keep track of IP addresses that have been assigned to workstations and which IP addresses are still available in the address pool.

Configuring the DHCP Services

DHCP comes free with Microsoft Windows NT v4.0 Server and is downloadable from Microsoft for free for Windows NT v3.51. DHCP is part of the Windows Internet Utilities and is installed as a service using Control Panel | Networking | Add Software.

When configuring DHCP, the administrator will have the option of setting specific parameters. The key to a successful DHCP configuration is the creation of a DHCP Scope. The DHCP Scope is where the administrator enters the range of IP addresses that are available in the pool for dynamic assignment as well as the subnet mask assigned to the clients, as shown in Figure 6-6.

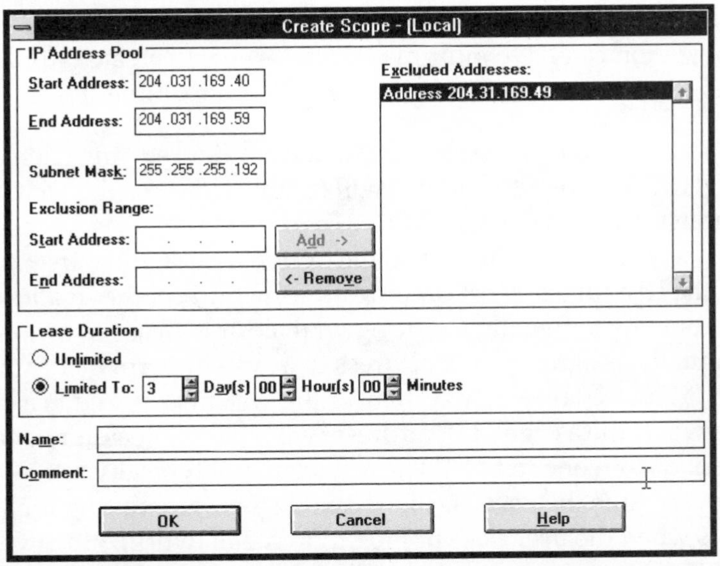

Figure 6-6. *DHCP Scope assignment*

Additionally, the administrator will have the option of configuring the following:

- **Default gateway address** This is the address of the router port on the user's TCP/IP segment that leads to a desired external network (such as the Internet, a WAN connection, a host server farm, or other external segment addresses).

- **Domain Name Service address(es)** The DNS addresses are the IP addresses of DNS servers that the user has access to. The ability to locate a DNS server allows the user to resolve common names (like http://www.microsoft.com) with IP addresses. An organization can utilize multiple DNS servers to resolve names, such as an internal DNS server to resolve intranet server names and IP addresses, or external DNS servers to resolve Internet World Wide Web server addresses.

- **WINS server address** A WINS server address (WINS servers will be described in-depth later in this chapter) will be used to resolve an IP address with a Microsoft Networking common name (such as the name of a file server—like EXCHSRVR—with an assigned IP address). An organization can have multiple WINS servers to create fault tolerance in the event that the primary WINS server is inoperable.

Once the scope of a DHCP server has been configured, any client that requests a DHCP assigned IP address will be able to access the DHCP server pool and receive an IP address.

In the scope, the administrator has the option of assigning an expiration for the lease of the IP address. Most organizations would set the IP address lease timeframe from one to five days. Setting an IP address lease to unlimited is just like manually assigning an IP address to a system permanently. Even if the workstation is replaced by a new system, or the system is moved to a completely different network, the assigned IP address will never be reassigned. By setting the lease period from one to five days, a system will typically retain the same IP address every time the user logs in to the system (accounting for weekends and holidays when the user does not log in to the network). However, if the workstation is moved or removed, the IP address is made available to the IP address pool to be reassigned to another workstation or individual after a relatively short period of time.

DHCP servers are typically configured on the basis of one DHCP server for each segment of the network. If the network is split into four separate segments to minimize the traffic on each segment (to improve network performance), a DHCP server would be installed on each segment. An organization may elect to have just one DHCP server managing a number of network segments. However, in order for a workstation client to find the DHCP server over a router to be assigned a dynamically configured IP address, either the router needs to be configured to support RFC 1542, which allows DHCP requests to be forwarded, or a DHCP Relay Host needs to be configured on the local segment of the user. A DHCP Relay Host can be installed and running on an NT server of an NT workstation. The DHCP Relay Host acknowledges the DHCP query from a workstation and forwards the request over the router directly to the DHCP server. This allows the DHCP client broadcast request to pass over the router and to be assigned a dynamic IP address.

Configuring the Client for DHCP Access

To enable a client workstation to be dynamically assigned an IP address from a DHCP server, the client software needs to be configured to dynamically obtain an IP address, as shown in Figure 6-7. This option is available in the Windows Networking configuration screen on any Windows for Workgroups TCP/IP Option system, Windows 95, or Windows NT system accessed by Control Panel | Networks | TCP/IP Option.

The user has the ability to manually configure gateway addresses, DNS addresses, WINS server addresses, and other information in the client workstation TCP/IP configuration section. If the user leaves the section blank, the client will assume the defaults defined by the DHCP server for these options.

Resolving Windows Networking User Names with IP Addresses (WINS)

The Windows Internet Name Service (WINS) is a way for Windows network workstations to resolve IP addresses with the common Windows networking name (sometimes called the user's NetBIOS name). The NetBIOS name is the name that a user calls the workstation the first time the system is configured (such as NT-BOB, or WIN95-JoesPC, or MarysWS). When a Windows client or server browses the network to find out what other workstations or servers reside on the network, the utilities look for NetBIOS names to list the servers, printers, workstations, and other resources available. This is the information a user sees when he or she clicks on the Network Neighborhood option in Windows 95.

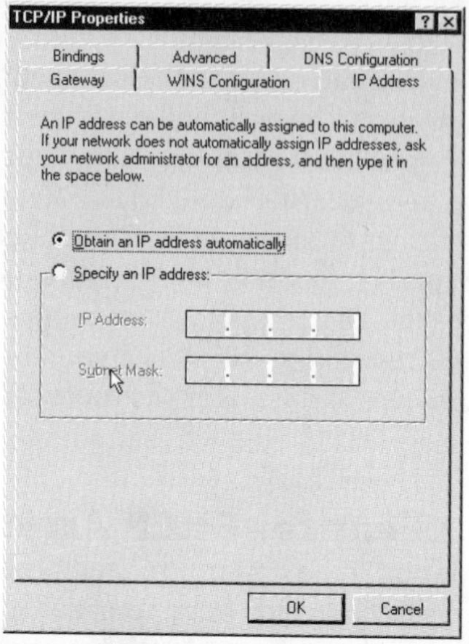

Figure 6-7. *Configuring a workstation client for DHCP access*

However, when a network is running TCP/IP as its sole protocol, or NetBIOS is blocked by routers (since it is nonroutable), workstations, servers, printers, and other resources are not available in the user's Network Neighborhood. The only way a user can see these resources is to run a WINS server that resolves the NetBIOS names with TCP/IP addresses. The WINS server displays the system's NetBIOS name even though the system is communicating over TCP/IP.

Configuring WINS Services

WINS comes free with Microsoft Windows NT v4.0 or is downloadable from Microsoft for Windows NT v3.51. Like DHCP, WINS is part of the Windows Internet Utilities and is installed as a service using Control Panel I Networking I Add Software.

Once installed with the WINS NT service running, the WINS server will maintain a database of IP addresses and NetBIOS names. The names are registered on a temporary basis so that they may be reused if the client stops using the name. WINS clients are responsible for maintaining the leases on their registered names and informing the WINS server when the name is no longer in use.

At any time, the administrator can review the WINS database and compare an IP address with a NetBIOS name, as shown in Figure 6-8. Or, if a user pings an IP address, the WINS server will resolve the IP address and respond with not only the "alive" response but also the NetBIOS name.

Configuring the Client for WINS Access

To enable a client workstation to be tracked by the WINS server for name resolution, the client software needs to be configured to register its information with the WINS server. This option is available in the Windows Networking configuration screen on any Windows for Workgroups TCP/IP Option system, Windows 95, or Windows NT system accessed by Control Panel | Networks | TCP/IP Option. An example of a Windows 95 system naming a WINS server is shown in Figure 6-9. If the user is using DHCP for

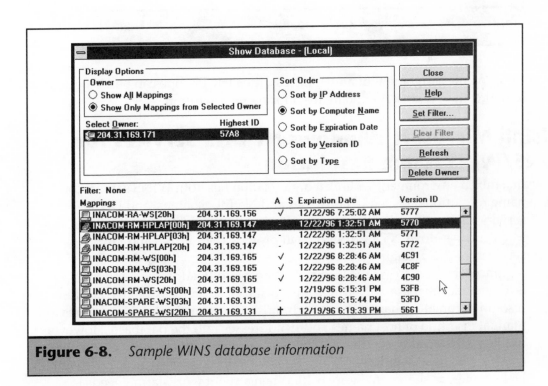

Figure 6-8.   *Sample WINS database information*

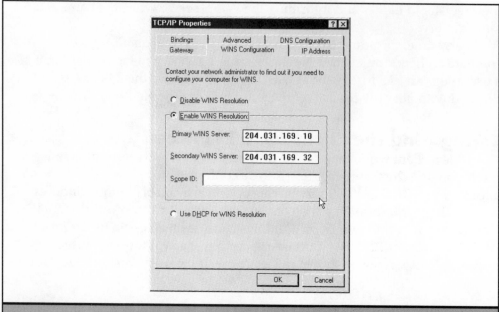

Figure 6-9. *Client workstation naming the WINS server for address resolution*

the dynamic assignment of an IP address, the DHCP scope can be configured to define the WINS server being used for name resolution.

Using Microsoft Windows NT DNS Services for DNS/WINS Name Resolution

In a mixed environment where an organization has both WINS servers for name resolution between IP addresses and NetBIOS names, and DNS servers for name resolution between IP addresses and UNIX host names, Microsoft Windows NT v4.0 Server can provide both WINS and DNS services for the domain.

Since DNS requires static insertion of host and IP addresses, and WINS is a dynamic database of NetBIOS names and IP addresses, the two address resolution functions have different administrative functions. DNS requires a manual insertion of host names and IP addresses into the database. However, unlike a UNIX utility counterpart that requires text editing using crude line editors, Microsoft Windows NT provides a graphical user interface to maintain DNS names, as shown in Figure 6-10. When a client workstation needs to

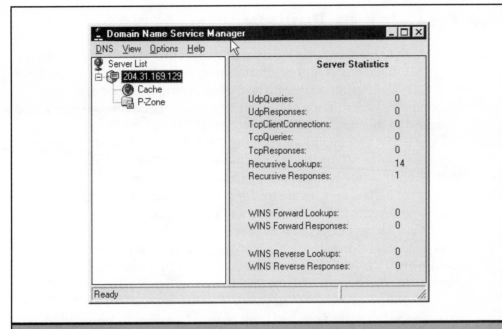

Figure 6-10. *Graphical interface of the Windows NT DNS service*

resolve a name, the NT server running both WINS and DNS can provide the client workstation with the address resolution it requires.

Configuring DNS Services

DNS server services come free with Microsoft Windows NT v4.0. Like DHCP and WINS, DNS server is part of the Windows Internet Utilities and is installed as a service using Control Panel | Networking | Add Software.

Once installed with the DNS NT service running, the DNS server will allow the administrator to add IP addresses and host names to the database. The names are registered on a static basis and must be removed if the host stops using the name.

At any time, the administrator can review the DNS database and compare an IP address with a host name; or, if a user pings an IP address, the DNS server will resolve the IP address and respond with not only the "alive" response but also with the DNS name.

The Chapter in Review

■ Most organizations have an existing infrastructure that needs to coexist with NT and Exchange, either short term as a migration strategy or long term as an integration strategy. The three existing network operating environments other than a Microsoft Windows NT environment that are addressed in this book are Novell NetWare, Banyan Vines, and UNIX-TCP/IP. Organizations running NetWare may choose to migrate from NetWare to NT, or they may choose to have NetWare run File and Print Services while NT functions as an application server. The Client Services for NetWare software bridges the migration process. It allows clients and servers to be NT clients while still allowing them full access to NetWare file servers. Gateway service for NetWare allows an NT client to access information on a NetWare server by passing commands through an NT server to access a NetWare server. Directory Service Manager for NetWare (DSMN) consolidates network administration functions for a NetWare/NT network. The Migration Tool for NetWare assists in the migration process from Novell NetWare to Windows NT.

■ The integration or migration process from NetWare to NT must occur in a specific order to be successful. The migration tool for NetWare is an important tool in the migration process. It allows the administrator to migrate users and files for NetWare to NT. A mapping file is used to give specific users different characteristics for migration than others. Installing File and Print Services for NetWare enables the NT server to appear as a NetWare server on the network. The Directory Service Manager for NetWare is used to synchronize the user names between the two operating systems. To provide NT clients access to NetWare disk shares, administrators can install Gateway Services for NetWare. The administrator needs to identify the NetWare server name and volume that will be shared with NT users. When doing a complete migration, the NetWare client software should be replaced with native NT client software. The final step is cleaning up the files. This includes removing any unnecessary files and old NetWare users including the NetWare supervisor and guest logins.

■ Another well-established network operating system is Banyan Vines. Many Vines accounts are the pioneers of true wide area networking. Vines runs over a variation of UNIX, yet Vines has features not found in UNIX. Vines has dynamic TCP/IP addressing, its own protocol called Vines IP, and a highly respected directory service called StreetTalk. Vines administration is performed through the Access Rights List. Drives and printers are shared via the commands SETDRIVE and SETPRINT. Tools used to integrate and migrate the two networks include File and Print Services for Vines, which is used to populate the NT user name repository. The Banyan Enterprise client allows Vines clients to access NT servers. Use this feature with Vines v5.56 or higher. The Banyan Migration Tool is for use when migrating from Vines to NT.

■ When migrating from Vines to NT, the sequence of events should be:

1. Migrate user names and security access rights to NT.

2. Install Banyan File and Print Services.

3. Migrate applications and data.

4. Install client workstation software.

5. Clean up the network files.

■ Users and group accounts will not be automatically updated on the NT server if they were created on a Vines server. The administrator will have choices to make during the migration regarding user names, passwords, account expiration, and group names.

■ Microsoft Windows NT supports TCP/IP communications. Thus coexistence with NT is relatively easy with UNIX and TCP/IP. The key to this smooth integration is Domain Name Services (DNS) and IP addressing. NFS (Network File System) is used by a server to publish its content for access by other users on the network. Pinging is used to confirm the existence of and connection to other IP-addressed users. DHCP (Dynamic Host Configuration Protocol) allows for a server to assign and track IP addresses within a given range of address options, providing that range of address options is done by the administrator when configuring DHCP services. There is usually one DHCP server on each segment of the network. In order for a client workstation to be able to use DHCP services, it must be properly configured. The WINS server is used to provide other services with the NetBIOS name, or network name, of each device. In order for the WINS server to be able to track client NetBIOS names, the WINS client software needs to be installed and properly configured.

Review Questions

Q. What are the benefits of migrating entirely to Exchange?
A. A single network operating system simplifies network management, security, and administration.

Q. What are some reasons that an organization might have for choosing to maintain a multiple network operating system?
A. 1) Operating-system conversions incur the cost of new operating software licensing; 2) some core applications operate only on certain platforms; 3) if an organization is very large, it may take years to migrate to a new network operating system; 4) parts of an organization may be managed by various departments that may choose differing platforms.

Q. What are Novell's two different versions of NetWare that are most frequently found within organizations?
A. NetWare v3.*x* with its Bindery mode and NetWare v4.*x* with its NetWare Directory Services.

Q. What are the common default protocols for NetWare, NT, and UNIX?
A. IPX/SPX, NetBEUI, and TCP/IP, respectively.

Q. What protocol is common in a NT/NetWare environment?
A. IPX/SPX.

Q. Where do NetWare v3.*x*, NetWare v4.*x* and NT store their databases of user names, passwords, and access rights?
A. The Bindery, NetWare Directory Services, and the Access Control List, respectively.

Q. How would you allow Windows 95 and Windows NT workstations access to both NT and NetWare servers?
A. Install the Client Services for NetWare software on the workstation. This will allow the workstation to access the NetWare server.

Q. What do Gateway Services do?
A. Gateway Services provide NT clients the ability to NET USE disk shares and print shares via NT client commands.

Q. What, specifically, does Directory Service Manager for NetWare (DSMN) provide?

A. It allows users logged in to an NT server to access information on a NetWare server, and vice versa. Security information is updated automatically in both NT and NetWare.

Q. What security information does the Migration Tool for NetWare convert?

A. It converts a user's login name, file access rights, and group information.

Q. Name the order that the integration or migration process of NetWare to NT must occur.

A. Migrate user names and security information; install File and Print Services for NetWare; synchronize security information, if needed; install Gateway Services for NetWare; install the client workstation software; clean up unnecessary names, directory shares, etc.

Q. When using the Migration Tool for NetWare to migrate user names, what options are available to the administrator?

A. The administrator has a choice of how the passwords will be migrated, how duplicate names will be handled, how duplicate group names will be handled, etc.

Q. When using the Migration Tool for NetWare to migrate files, what options are available to the administrator?

A. The administrator can choose which NetWare volumes should be migrated to NT partitions, whether hidden or system files should be transferred, which directories should be deselected, and which specific files and directories should be selected or deselected.

Q. How is FPNW installed and configured?

A. FPNW is installed through the NT Control Panel under network software and runs as a service under Windows NT. Configuration options are in the Control Panel.

Q. How is the Directory Service Manager for NetWare (DSMN) installed and managed?

A. DSMN is installed using the SETUP command. Configuration options are in the Control Panel.

Q. What is the benefit of Gateway Services for NetWare?

A. It provides a method for NT clients that don't have the Novell client software loaded to share NetWare volumes and directories.

Q. If a workstation needs to access both NT and NetWare servers, how should it be configured?

A. To access NetWare, the workstation needs to have either the NetWare client software loaded or it needs access to an NT server that's running Gateway Services for NetWare. To access NT, it needs to have either the NT client software loaded or access to a NetWare server that's running FPNW.

Q. What are the benefits of Microsoft NT over Banyan Vines?

A. Larger partition size, wider hardware compatibilities and options, support for new technology as soon as they become available in the marketplace.

Q. What does the Banyan Migration Tool do?

A. It is a set of utilities that helps organizations migrate user names, groups, and resource security information from StreetTalk to NT.

Q. Why is it important to migrate user names and access rights first in a Vines-to-NT migration?

A. Users will not have access to any services on the NT server unless the server has their names, passwords, and access rights.

Q. What does the Banyan Migration Tool *not* migrate?

A. The BMT does not migrate programs, applications, files, or directory shares. These need to be migrated separately.

Q. Define TCP/IP.

A. Transmission Control Protocol/Internet Protocol.

Q. What are the benefits of adding the TCP/IP protocol to an NT network?

A. TCP/IP is becoming the de facto standard for disparate network communications; TCP/IP allows easier access to the Internet.

Q. What is the purpose of the Domain Name Service?

A. It's a way for administrators to track all their IP addresses with common names.

Q. What are the benefits of DHCP (Dynamic Host Configuration Protocol)?
A. Minimizes the need for administrators to manually allocate IP addresses, old IP addresses get recycled automatically, and administrators can more easily track IP addresses when required.

Q. What is configured in the DHCP scope?
A. The given range of IP address options, default gateway addresses, Domain Name Services addresses, WINS server address, and the expiration date of the IP addresses.

Q. Where is the client configured for DHCP access?
A. In the Control Panel, under Networks, TCP/IP option.

Q. What does the WINS server do?
A. It resolves the IP address with the NetBIOS name.

Q. Why would a TCP/IP network want to use a WINS server?
A. NetBIOS names are not routable. So the WINS server would be set up for users to be able to see all resources on the network.

Q. If a network has a WINS server and a user pings an IP address on the network, what information will they get in response?
A. If the IP address is resolved, they will get the IP address and the NetBIOS name of the resource with that address.

Q. Compare and contrast WINS and DNS services for the domain.
A. Both are repositories of IP addresses. But WINS is dynamic and allocates the address. DNS is static and requires an administrator to assign the address.

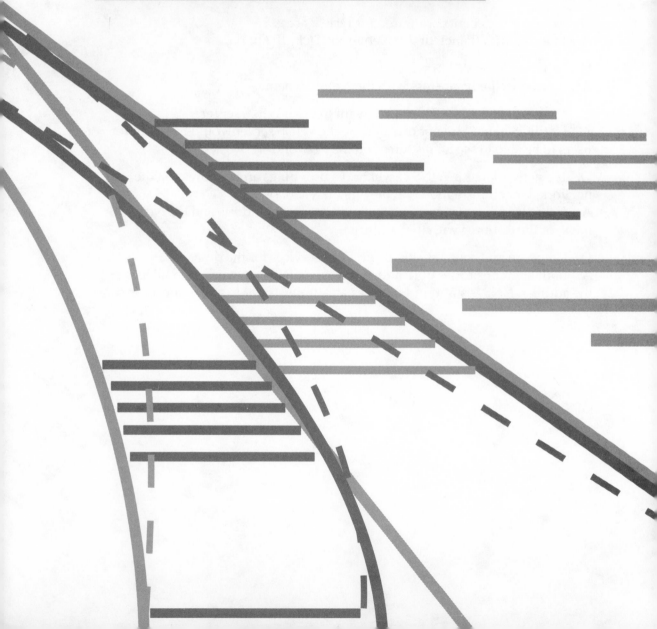

CHAPTER 7

Sizing and Licensing the Microsoft Exchange Server and Workstations

When an organization decides that it wants to implement Microsoft Exchange, the first thing that the designer of the Microsoft Exchange environment will do is begin to size the Exchange file server. After taking examples from the existing electronic mail system, figuring out the currently available latest and greatest system, and throwing in an extra few gigabytes of disk storage, the designer will generally say it's time to deploy Microsoft Exchange.

As you have seen in the past three chapters, there is a great deal more involved in planning a Microsoft Exchange roll out. If designers of the Exchange environment spent the time to think through the entire domain, security, and migration components of an NT and Exchange model, the number and size of servers an organization would require could become a methodical process, instead of guesswork. The previous chapters have provided information that is vital to an organization when it is determining the number of file servers needed, the appropriate processor performance required to manage the demands of its environment, the appropriate disk space necessary according to its storage needs, and its operating systems and general design infrastructure.

This chapter will help to define the appropriate server processor type, memory, and disk storage necessary for an Exchange environment, as well as the software licensing for the organization.

Microsoft Exchange Server Planning

As you have identified in previous chapters, Microsoft Exchange is built on client/server technology, in which the server plays a very important role in the performance and operation of the Microsoft Exchange environment. Additionally, server reliability, as provided by file server redundancy and server fault tolerance, are also important in a mission-critical messaging, groupware, and intranet environment.

E-Mail Only or a Full Groupware Environment?

Key to determining the size and performance of the Microsoft Exchange server(s) is an organization's decision to implement Microsoft Exchange either as an electronic mail-only system or a full groupware system. Many administrators have heard that Microsoft Exchange is very processor-intensive and requires the fastest file server available with a lot of RAM memory and disk storage. However, what is missing from that comment are the services the

Microsoft Exchange Server environment is providing to the user community. In most cases, if an organization currently has an e-mail system and migrates to Microsoft Exchange for basic electronic messaging, the file server needs, performance, and capabilities are generally the same as the old server system. At minimum, however, organizations would begin to take advantage of the basic groupware capabilities of Microsoft Exchange such as personal, group, and resource scheduling of users within the organization, server-based rules for message management, and the out-of-office assistant for schedule notification. Using these features *plus* the basic e-mail functions doubles the core functionality the users have received in the past—thus the need for a faster-performing file server with more disk storage may be necessary for these added functions.

As organizations start to consolidate messages and files into public folders, begin using electronic forms, and add in functionality such as faxing, document routing, and intranet search engines, their need for a more sophisticated environment with better server processor performance, memory and disk storage increases dramatically. For an organization that has been considering a dedicated Web or separate document management server, the ability to consolidate information into a single server will require more capabilities from that server. However, the cost to deploy this single-source solution is considerably lower than a dual operating environment strategy, and the organization's ability to leverage the capabilities of a single messaging and intranet strategy will ultimately provide it with better deployment functionality.

Exchange on NT v4.0

The decision that many organizations must make as they prepare to deploy Microsoft Exchange is whether they should deploy Microsoft Exchange v5.0 on a Microsoft Windows NT v3.51 server, or Microsoft Exchange v5.0 on a Microsoft Windows NT v4.0 server. Basic functionality (such as e-mail and calendar features) are the same for either environment, but if an organization has the ability to deploy Microsoft Exchange v5.0 on Windows NT v4.0, it will benefit from the following:

- **Infrastructure based on NT v4.0**   It's no secret that Microsoft is committed to the Windows NT v4.*x* product for core LAN and WAN infrastructures as well as application server development. The core Windows NT v4.0 integrated functions like Internet, intranet, and Web linked capabilities means that having a robust network operating system like Windows NT minimizes the need to integrate with non-supported operating systems.

Windows NT v4.0 is a stable operating system backed by Microsoft and the integrators that support Microsoft's core BackOffice product line, so Exchange can facilitate better services offerings for users.

Exchange Server Processor/Performance Options

Although every operating environment is unique and configurations from organization to organization differ, there are some relatively simple rules of thumb to use when determining the size of the server to purchase that will function as the Microsoft Exchange Server. As I discussed earlier, many organizations think that Microsoft Exchange requires a "big" server compared to their existing e-mail server. However, if an organization adds functionality or consolidates users into a single Exchange server, the need for a larger file server will become apparent. For example, a standard 100-user e-mail server running Microsoft Mail can run on a 486 or Pentium server under Novell NetWare v4.1 with about 48MB of memory and 2GB of disk space. A similar Microsoft Exchange Server supporting 100 users and running only electronic mail will work just as well with the same server configuration. However, by adding in documenting routing, intranet document management, network faxing, group and personal scheduling, and ten remote dial-up users, the Exchange server will need 64-128MB of memory in a Pentium or multiprocessor Pentium configuration to support all of the new features and functions. One of Microsoft Exchange's big advantages is that it supports the server scalability of Microsoft NT. This means that an organization can start with a 486 or single processor Pentium server,
and upgrade to a Pentium Pro server, multiprocessor Pentium, or a RISC-based Digital Alpha server to either support a larger or attain a more robust messaging environment. Microsoft Exchange supports a number of different processor options as shown in Figure 7-1.

Intel 80486 Server

The typical minimum configuration for a Microsoft Exchange file server calls for an Intel 80486 processor class system. A 486 processor is adequate for a small e-mail environment, mostly due to its limited ability to manage multiple tasks simultaneously in order to accommodate the bandwidth demands of a fully integrated groupware environment. A faster and more scalar server is more appropriate for a groupware-enabled Exchange environment.

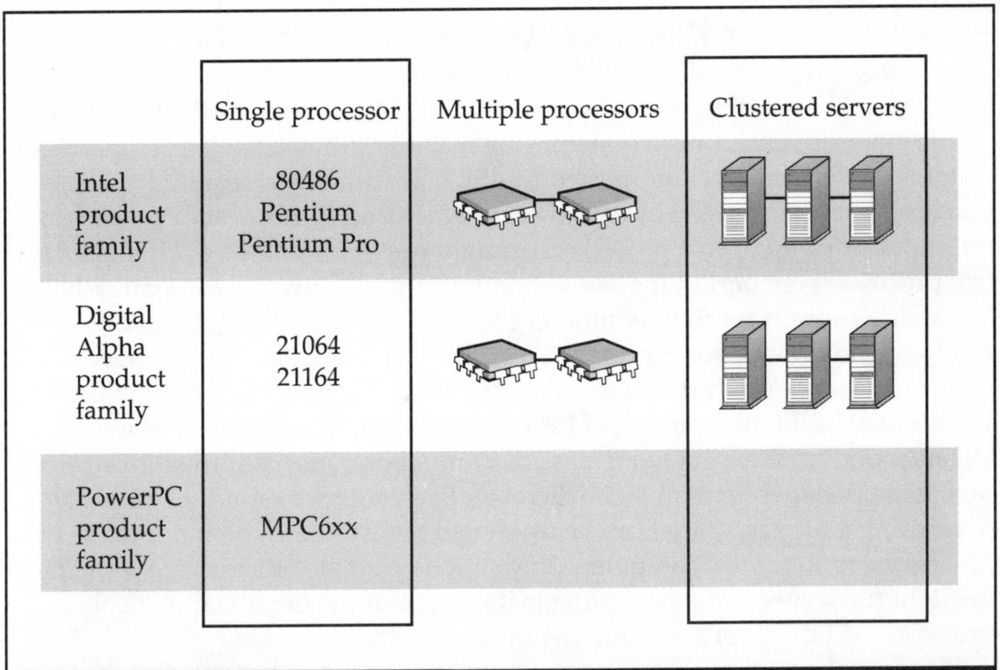

	Single processor	Multiple processors	Clustered servers
Intel product family	80486 Pentium Pentium Pro		
Digital Alpha product family	21064 21164		
PowerPC product family	MPC6xx		

Figure 7-1. *Various processor options supported by Windows NT*

Intel Pentium Server

When Intel released the Pentium processor in 1994, the ability for a file server to conduct multiple tasks simultaneously grew substantially. As the Pentium processor has evolved from a 60MHz version to 166MHz or faster processors, multitasking groupware functionality like Microsoft Exchange became possible for workgroups as large as 50-100 users.

Intel Pentium Pro Server

The Reduced Instruction Set Chip (RISC) Intel Pentium Pro processor has provided organizations with the ability to process even more information on a single processor while still maintaining full compatibility with existing Intel-based software applications. A single processor Pentium Pro server can easily manage the groupware needs of workgroups with up to 150-200 users.

Multiprocessor Pentium/Pentium Pro Server

When an organization outgrows the capabilities of a single processor Pentium or Pentium Pro configuration, it can consider a multiprocessor Pentium or multiprocessor Pentium Pro system. Unlike many previous network operating systems that either never supported multiple processors or required users to purchase a special version of the software, Microsoft Windows NT provides full support for up to two processors straight out of the same box. If more than two processors are part of the server configuration, hardware companies have to provide support for their equipment for Windows NT. Furthermore, most vendors who provide multiprocessor servers do provide the appropriate multiprocessor support drivers to allow their hardware to be compatible with Windows NT with the number of processors the customer owns in the server. Organizations that expect to increase their number of users or their groupware functionality dependent on their Microsoft Exchange Server might consider purchasing a file server that can be upgraded to a system with more than one processor support. Most computers only support a single processor, so selecting the right file server at the beginning is important if the organization expects to add an additional processor in the future.

For organizations with most servers configured for multiprocessor support, the decision to purchase an upgradable system or a multiple processor system from the start may be influenced by what seems like a drastic cost differential. In many cases, however, a dual-processor Pentium or Pentium Pro system will only be a fraction higher in cost than a single processor system, but to upgrade from a single processor system to dual processors can be expensive.

Digital Alpha Server

As organizations increase their performance demands for their servers, they have been turning to Digital Alpha server technology for the next generation of server needs. Because of the Microsoft-Digital Alliance, all core Microsoft products are simultaneously released on both Intel code as well as Digital Alpha code on the same CD, so if an organization installs an Intel server from an NT CD on one day and decides to install NT on a Digital Alpha server the next day, it can use the same CD for the installation of the high-speed RISC-based Alpha system (typically \ALPHA versus \I386 for the source codes).

A single Alpha processor typically runs 20-30 percent faster than a single processor Intel Pentium system. As an organization exceeds the performance capabilities of a multiprocessor Intel-based system, the single or dual Alpha processors are the next step in performance capabilities.

Most organizations equate higher processor performance with faster operating performance of the application software, thus translating to faster response times for users. However, in a Microsoft Exchange messaging server system, the faster processor typically corresponds with the ability to put more users on a single server than previously possible.

Multiprocessor Alpha Server

When a multiprocessor Pentium system reaches its limit of 500-750 users on Microsoft Exchange, a multiprocessor Alpha system can break and exceed 1,000 users on a single Microsoft Exchange Server. In most cases, the cost per user for an Alpha server compared to the cost per user for a multiprocessor Pentium system is fairly similar, and the ability to manage more users on fewer servers can assist in minimizing administration costs. Digital makes generation four and generation five processors with speeds of 200-300MHz in single or multiprocessor configurations, providing an organization with the ability to scale their Exchange resource requirements to meet the needs of the organization.

Server Clusterings

Finally, for an organization in which a single file server or a series of file servers that balance the load of the network is still inadequate, it can consider clustering Windows NT file servers to take advantage of server-to-server scalability. Server-to-server scalability translates to multiple servers providing resource distribution in excess of the capability of a single server in the environment. During a server clustering process, the demands of the workgroup are distributed simultaneously across multiple servers within the organization. The cluster can access and manage resources within the organization at performance levels higher than ever before achieved on a single server environment.

Table 7-1 is an example of the number of users and a common baseline configuration appropriate for an Exchange file server.

Users per File Server	Electronic Mail Only	E-mail/Scheduling/ Document Management/Faxing
20 users	486 processor, 1GB disk space, 32MB RAM memory	Pentium processor, 2GB disk space, 32MB RAM memory
50 users	Pentium processor, 2GB disk space, 48MB RAM memory	Pentium processor, 3GB disk space, 64MB RAM memory
100 users	Pentium processor, 3GB disk space, 64MB RAM memory	Pentium processor, 4GB disk space, 96MB RAM memory
200 users	Dual-processor Pentium, 6GB disk space, 96MB RAM memory	Dual-processor Pentium, 6GB disk space, 128MB RAM memory
500 users	Dual-processor Pentium, 8GB disk space, 160MB RAM memory	Dual-processor Pentium, 8GB disk space, 196MB RAM memory
750 users	3-processor Pentium, 12GB disk space, 196MB RAM memory	3-processor Pentium, 12GB disk space, 256MB RAM memory
1,000 users	Dual-processor RISC, 16GB disk space, 256MB RAM memory	Dual-processor RISC, 16GB disk space, 256MB RAM memory
1,500 users	4-processor RISC, 20GB disk space, 384MB RAM memory	4-processor RISC, 24GB disk space, 512MB RAM memory

Table 7-1. *Sample "per Server" Configurations for Microsoft Exchange*

Although the table suggests server configurations, it is advised that you run the load simulation utility that comes free with Microsoft Exchange, which will provide a more optimal evaluation of the server performance capabilities for your organization's needs.

Exchange Server RAM Memory

In a Windows NT environment, server RAM memory plays as important a role as processor speed in determining the capabilities of the server to manage network resources. The more memory in a Windows NT Server, the more caching on the server disk storage is available, which in turn improves the performance of the network file server. In a network environment in which there are hundreds of users accessing the same file server, if the server has more memory in the system, it can potentially service disk read and write requests from RAM memory rather than having to constantly access the hard disks in the server. When memory is rated in nanoseconds and hard drives are rated in milliseconds, the difference in access performance is significantly improved for the cached information access.

Additionally, as more add-in applications like search engines or document indexing and management utilities are added to Microsoft Exchange Servers, the demand on file server RAM by the applications and add-ins is also increased.

Typically, the rule of thumb for memory in a file server in a highly optimized server configuration is 16MB of base memory plus 4MB of memory for each add-in application (like faxing, search engines, etc.) plus 8MB of RAM for each 1GB of disk storage in the system. Thus, a server with 12GB of disk storage and Microsoft Exchange installed on top of Windows NT should have approximately 116 to 128MB of memory installed. For file servers that have less of a demand on server resources (such as archived data stores or small office servers with large disk space needs), the actual amount of memory for the server can be significantly lower.

Exchange Server Disk Storage

In Microsoft Exchange, the disk storage demands of the file server have a direct relationship to the necessary message storage requirements of the organization. As outlined in Chapter 1 of this book, Microsoft Exchange stores user name and folder information in the directory store, user mailbox information in the information store, and messages in the message database. The administrator of the network does not have to worry about how to manage these storage units. All the administrator needs to do is provide adequate disk storage to handle the storage needs of the organization.

Sizing the Required Disk Storage

When measuring their disk storage needs, if an organization is currently using electronic mail messaging, tracking the growth of disk storage demands on the current messaging system can help in determining the general message demands of the organization. For example, if the organization's existing e-mail storage demands grow over a 30-day period by 10MB and it would like to keep up to three years of messages available to the users, it should consider 3.6GB of storage space to handle the projected messaging needs.

There are many factors that either increase or decrease this storage demand estimate. Some of the variations are caused by the following:

Reasons Storage Demands May Increase:

- Implementation of groupware needs within the organization (such as forms, scheduling, document routing, or faxing).

- Implementation of voicemail integration to Microsoft Exchange.

- Increased capabilities of electronic messaging create an increase in usage of the electronic messaging environment within the organization.

- Increase in the number of users utilizing electronic messaging in the organization.

- User-shift from non-electronic methods of communications (such as voicemail, memo sheets, conference calls, overnight mail packages) to electronic mail and electronic storage within Exchange to fulfill communication needs.

Reasons Storage Demands May Decrease:

- Microsoft Exchange stores only one copy of a message on the server, thus if a big component of an organization's messaging needs involves sending the same message to multiple users, there may be a decrease in the overall demands on disk storage since the Exchange server will more efficiently store only one copy of a message for a group of recipients.

- Microsoft Exchange stores messages as objects within the Exchange message store database, which stores information more efficiently than saving it on a file-by-file basis within the storage environment. For an organization with a number of small messages or attachments, this could gain back significant storage space for the organization.

Disk Fault Tolerance

In addition to evaluating the storage space needs for an Exchange server implementation, an organization needs to evaluate the level of fault tolerance data integrity and security that it needs for its message storage system. The various storage options range from no disk redundancy, which means that a hard disk failure will cause all messaging communications to cease until the storage system is replaced and information is restored from tape, to a sophisticated disk redundancy system that involves two to three different levels of disk failure protection.

The most common disk redundancy options include the following:

- **RAID-1 (Disk Mirroring)**   In a RAID-1 implementation, hard drives in the system are duplicated and information is written to both sets of hard disks simultaneously. In the event that one hard drive or hard drive set fails, the other drive or drive set continues to operate. Disk storage purchase requirements should be double the amount of available disk space desired. Thus if an organization requires 4GB of disk space and would normally purchase one 4GB hard drive, it would purchase two 4GB hard drives and mirror the drives to create a replication of information stored.

- **RAID-2 (Disk Duplexing)**   In a RAID-2 implementation, both the hard drives and the hard drive controllers are duplicated in a system. The same double disk purchase requirements apply as in the previous disk redundancy; however, the organization would also purchase a redundant hard drive controller for the system. In the event of a failure of either one of the hard drives or hard drive sets or the hard drive controller, the redundant set would continue system operation without interruption or loss of information.

- **RAID-5 (Disk Striping with Parity)**   In a RAID-5 implementation, an organization would require a file server and hard drive controller that supports RAID-5 disk redundancy. A RAID-5 disk redundancy system requires at least three hard drives. In an N + 1 model, the equivalent of one drive in the RAID-5 configuration retains a mathematical representation of the fault tolerance parity information. This fault tolerant component is distributed across all of the hard drives in the RAID-5 drive set. In the event that any of the drives in the set fail, the RAID-5 environment continues to run without interruption or data loss. A RAID-5 configuration is more economical than a disk mirror or duplexing system that requires an exact one-to-one relationship between drives. If the subsystem involves three 4GB drives for 12GB of usable disk space, a RAID-5 configuration would require just one extra 4GB drive to make up the RAID-5 N + 1 configuration. However, in a mirror or duplexing scenario, the three 4GB drives would need to be matched with three additional 4GB drives to provide the one-to-one relationship of the mirrored or duplexed configuration.

■ **RAID-6 (Disk Striping with Parity and Online Spare)** A RAID-6 configuration is similar to a RAID-5 configuration in which there is an N + 1 relationship of drives (one extra drive for a series of data drives). However, RAID-6 includes one additional drive, which is an online spare in the environment. In the event that one drive in a RAID-5 subsystem fails, the system continues to operate, but if a second drive fails, all data will be lost and recovery would need to be performed from the last tape backup. With an online spare drive, when the first drive in the subsystem fails, the extra online spare drive will automatically substitute for the failed drive and begin recovery of the RAID-5 configuration. Once recovered to a RAID-5 configuration, an additional drive can fail and the system will still be operational, thus allowing for the potential of an additional failure. In effect, a RAID-6 configuration can have two drives in the drive set fail before the environment is in a fault situation in which data can be lost.

Figure 7-2 shows a graphical representation of the various disk fault tolerance options.

Hardware Versus Software Disk Fault Tolerance

An organization can implement disk fault tolerance either through hardware management or through software management. Microsoft Windows NT provides software disk fault tolerance for disk mirroring and disk striping, whereas hardware disk fault tolerance would require the purchase of a file server and disk controller that supports hardware fault tolerance.

When possible, an organization should consider hardware fault tolerance over software fault tolerance management. The advantages of hardware fault tolerance over software fault tolerance include:

■ **Faster performance** Because hardware fault tolerance is managed by a controller card or other hardware device, processing performance is not compromised in order to provide the fault tolerance functionality for the system. Software fault tolerance requires that a certain level of the operating system and system processor is able to manage the disk fault tolerance of the operating software.

- **Error trapping** If there is a hard drive subsystem failure, a system that uses software fault tolerance may be affected by the subsystem fault, which potentially can cause the server to halt network operating system functions. A hardware fault tolerance system can potentially isolate the disk failure from the operating system functions and protect the operating system from halting processing operations.

If the file server hardware vendor provides utilities to create fault tolerant disk configurations for the server, it is preferable to use the hardware fault tolerance options for disk mirroring, duplexing, or data striping rather than the software options included in the Windows NT Disk Administrator utility.

Separate Boot and Log File Drive

Because Microsoft Exchange is a sophisticated client/server database, the storage and management of information should also take on the characteristics

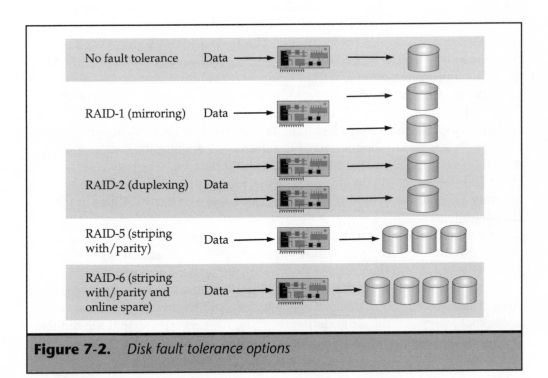

Figure 7-2. *Disk fault tolerance options*

of an optimized client/server environment. An optimized client/server environment typically suggests that data should be stored on a separate drive than the log files and pagefile memory overflow file. This suggests that the Exchange server should have a separate boot drive where it writes error logs, transaction logs, and uses for the server swapfile in the event that the server runs out of memory and needs to use virtual disk storage to manage server operations. On a completely separate disk store, the Exchange server can write message data and other user information. The boot drive may only need to be 1-2GB in size with the bulk of the server's disk storage allocated to the separate data drive component of the server.

Exchange Server Network Adapter

The network adapter in an Exchange server is the portal of communications between the clients and the Exchange server. The network adapter in a Microsoft Exchange file server should be a PCI or EISA adapter to take advantage of the high-speed transmission speeds and capabilities of these adapters compared to standard 16-bit ISA network adapters. If the file server has the option of selecting either a PCI or an EISA network adapter, the PCI adapter will typically provide faster overall performance in communications. An EISA network adapter provides "burst" speeds and throughput for 32-bit communications, but a PCI adapter can typically sustain transmission speeds to the maximum capabilities of the file server bus architecture. In many cases, this can mean two to three times faster performance in communications on sustained server-to-server or client-to-server communications.

Many organizations may elect to install 100MB Ethernet, 100MB token ring, or an FDDI adapter in the file server to achieve faster communication speeds with the rest of the network. As long as the total performance between the client and the server can be improved, the addition of a faster infrastructure can only assist in the overall communications bandwidth capabilities of the Exchange server.

Dependent on the organization's strategy for file server communications bandwidth and performance, it may split its network into segments. On a small network of less than 25 users, all users, file servers, and printers on the network are connected to a single segment. However, as an organization or a workgroup exceeds 50-70 users, it may elect to split the network's physical connections between the workstations and the file server(s) so that the number of users accessing the network is limited. Rather than having 100 users all vying for the single port connection and communication speed with a file server, if an organization splits the network into two separate segments of 50 users each, there will be fewer users on each segment vying for access to the file server, and the performance from the client to the server will improve. Most organizations segment a network so that no more than 75-100 users are on the same physical segment.

As I will discuss in the next chapter on installing and configuring gateways (like a connection to the Internet), there may be a need to install a second network adapter in the file server so that one adapter will service the local area network e-mail users, and the other adapter will communicate to a firewall to the Internet. Unlike network segmentation intended to split the users of the network to decrease file server load on a single adapter, the second adapter in this example is intended to segment security privileges so that users on the internal local area network have access to the Exchange server whereas users on the external Internet connection may only send and receive Internet mail messages.

Modems on the Exchange Server

There are typically two reasons an organization would install a telephone modem on a Microsoft Exchange file server. One reason would be to provide inbound and outbound communications with another electronic mail system such as a gateway to Microsoft Mail, a gateway to cc:Mail, or a gateway to the Internet. Another reason for having a modem on an Exchange server would be for remote access or remote administration to the Exchange server. An administrator may dial in to the network to manage the network or view NT or Exchange operational parameters, or a user may dial in to the Exchange server to check his or her e-mail messages remotely from the network. The remote access functionality of Microsoft Windows NT is included in Microsoft's Remote Access Server (RAS), which will be covered in-depth in Chapter 20.

LOADSIM

To assist organizations in determining whether they have properly sized the Microsoft Exchange file server for their environment, Microsoft includes a load simulation utility, LOADSIM.EXE, with Microsoft Exchange. The LOADSIM program will simulate the following:

■ User action such as sending, receiving, replying to, saving, deleting, and forwarding electronic messages

- User interaction with public folders

- User interaction with Microsoft Scheduler for personal and group scheduling

- Electronic form use, views, and access

Some of these actions are user-initiated and directly impact the interaction between the client and the server. Some of these actions are background processes that impact the performance of the server as the transaction utilizes some of the server's performance capabilities.

Using the LOADSIM Program

The LOADSIM.EXE program resides on the Exchange CD in the support\loadsim directory and is accompanied by a LOADSIM.DOC installation and usage document. LOADSIM is not a standalone modeling simulator, but rather an actual load generating utility. LOADSIM will create actual messages and traffic on a network based on the load parameters specified in the configuration of the LOADSIM utility, so that actual network and server performance can be measured.

Typically, when installing and simulating a network implementation for the simulation of a network of 250 users, it is suggested that the client simulation component be kept to 75-100 client simulations per test workstation, because the load generation will be created by a simulated client system. Thus, for a load simulation test of 250 users, there should be three to four client workstations set up to split the simulation of the 250 users. It is important to note that by only simulating one client workstation for a large test, the actual capabilities of the simulation client workstation may prevent the system from actually simulating that many concurrent transactions. As a result, the simulated Exchange server and the network bandwidth between the client station and the server may be able to handle the demand, but the workstation attempting to simulate 250 clients may not be able to simulate that many systems at the same time.

The end result of a LOADSIM simulation is a graph, similar to the one shown in Figure 7-3, that notes the number of users per server and the weighted average response time of the transactions.

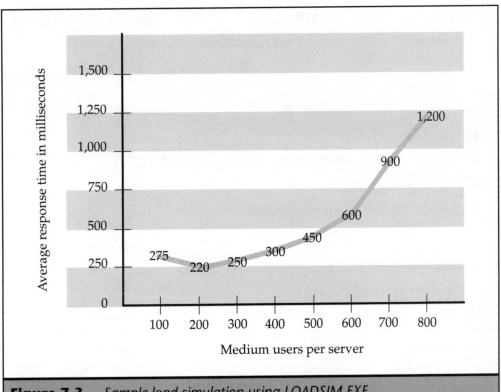

Figure 7-3.   *Sample load simulation using LOADSIM.EXE*

Client Workstation Planning

Now that we have completed the sizing and load capabilities of the server
component of the Microsoft Exchange Server configuration, we will look at the
client component in this client/server environment. In Microsoft Exchange,
the client component of the Exchange environment is just as important as the
server component of the system. While the server manages the messages, the
transfer of the messages from server to server, or from the server to something
like the Internet, the client component manages electronic forms, filtering
of message views, and general rich text viewing and displaying of the
Exchange messages.

Supported Client Workstation Operating Systems

As I covered in Part One of the book, the Microsoft Exchange software supports client workstations including:

- MS-DOS
- Microsoft Windows v3.*x*
- Microsoft Windows 95
- Microsoft Windows NT Workstation (v3.51 and v4.0)
- Apple Macintosh
- UNIX (through POP3 and Web client access)

Workstation Processor Speed and Memory Requirements

The processor speed and memory requirements of the workstation depend in part on the version of the operating system that the client workstation is running. An organization would typically not expect to install Windows on an Intel 80286 workstation, and thus successfully running and installing the Windows version of the Exchange client on an 80286 computer is not anticipated. However, it would be expected that the DOS version of the Exchange client will run acceptably well on an 80286 system. For an organization using Microsoft Exchange only for electronic messaging (no scheduling, forms, or add-in groupware functionality), the RAM requirements for the workstation are far less than for an organization leveraging all of the capabilities of Microsoft Exchange.

Additionally, how fast the Exchange client will perform on a system is just as important (if not more important) than whether the application will simply run on the system. For many product specifications, manufacturers note the minimum configuration, although most administrators would never expect to run the application in a minimum configured system.

The following summary is a generally acceptable performance rule of thumb for each of the processor speeds:

- **Exchange DOS client**   Intel 80386 or faster (with 2MB or more memory)
- **Exchange Windows v3.*x* client**   Intel 80486 or faster (with 8MB or more memory)

- **Exchange Windows 95 client**   Intel 80486 (with 12MB or more memory) or Intel Pentium (with 8MB or more memory)

- **Exchange Windows NT client**   Intel 80486 (with 24MB or more memory) or Intel Pentium (with 16MB or more memory)

- **Outlook client**   Intel 80486 (with 16MB or more memory in Windows 95), or Intel Pentium (with 12MB or more memory in Windows 95), or an Intel 80486 or faster (with 24MB or more memory in Windows NT v4.0)

- **Macintosh client**   Motorola 68040 (with 16MB or more memory with System 7.x) or a PowerPC processor (with 12MB or more memory with System 7.x)

- **POP3 client**   Any operating environment and processor speed that can adequately handle the messaging functions of the third-party POP3 or Web browsing client software

Hard Drive Space Requirements

The hard drive disk space requirements of a Microsoft Exchange client workstation are generally determined by how much of the client software will be installed on the workstation hard drive as well as how much of the messaging data will be stored on the workstation.

Both the full Microsoft Exchange client and the Outlook client each require approximately 40MB of disk space. The client software includes the core messaging forms (.cfg, .ico), applications (.EXE), and operational components (.dll, .ocx). Some of the program components can be centrally stored on a network file server, leaving only a few of the necessary configuration and operational components (like .DLL files) to be saved to the workstation's hard drive. At minimum, there will be at least 8.5MB of files that will need to be stored on the system in which the Microsoft Windows (or Windows 95/Windows NT) application resides. If the organization adds faxing, voicemail integration, document routing, or other add-in groupware functionality to Exchange, the demands on workstation disk storage space may increase.

In addition to the client software program, components stored on the workstation's hard drive would be data files and messages that users want to store on their local hard drives. Typically, there is no need for an office/desktop user to store any of his or her messages or attachments to a local hard drive. The Microsoft Exchange server maintains a copy of all messages, folders, and directory information, so that information never needs to impact the local workstation. However, if the Exchange client is a mobile user who travels with a laptop computer, that user would want a copy of his or her most recent messages stored in the inbox, a copy of his or her appointment schedule, and potentially copies of other personal or public folders on the network. For every message that users want to have available whether they are connected or disconnected from the network, more disk storage space will be required on the portable computer system. This storage information for portable users is called the offline store and is saved in a .OST file on the system's hard drive.

Software Licensing

The selection phase of network file server size, memory requirements, and storage requires that an organization determine the legal licensing for the Microsoft Exchange Server and client software. Organizations are often unsure about whether they need to purchase a Microsoft Exchange client license in addition to a Microsoft Windows NT client license, or whether they need to purchase a license at all (since Windows 95 includes the Exchange client software). All of these common issues require very careful examination of the licensing facts and information noted in the following paragraphs.

Exchange Server Standard Edition

Microsoft Exchange Server is sold in a Standard edition as well as an Enterprise edition. The Standard edition of Microsoft Exchange includes all of the components an organization needs to install and set up a local area network-based Microsoft Exchange Server. The Standard edition software comes in a 10-user or a 25-user license package that provides the organization with the ability to have 10 or 25 mail users (respectively) using the Microsoft Exchange system. Because Microsoft Exchange provides server-based rules and out-of-office notification management on behalf of a user whether that user is connected or logged into the network or not, the licensing for users is based on the number of mailboxes created for users (online or offline), and not merely simultaneous connections like many software application licensing specifications. If the organization requires more user licenses, the client licenses are sold in 1-user, 5-user, 10-user, and 20-user client packs.

Standard Edition Connectors Sold Separately

When an organization purchases the Microsoft Exchange Standard edition of the software, the connectors to other Exchange file servers (the Exchange Connector), to the Internet (the Internet Connector), and to other X.400 networks (the X.400 Connector) are sold separately. It is assumed that a small organization that has neither site-to-site connectivity needs nor wide area connection needs may also have no need for a connection to the Internet or to X.400, so these are sold separately. The options for selecting Microsoft Exchange licenses are shown in Figure 7-4.

If an organization plans to purchase two of the connectors, it should purchase the Exchange Server Enterprise edition.

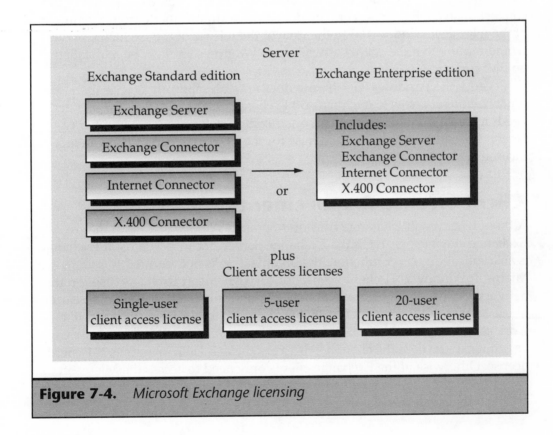

Figure 7-4. *Microsoft Exchange licensing*

Exchange Server Enterprise Edition

The Exchange Server Enterprise edition includes the core Microsoft Exchange Server software, the Internet Connector, the Exchange Server Connector, and the X.400 Connector. Just like the standard edition, the Enterprise edition includes 10-user or 25-user client licenses. Additional licenses are sold separately.

Exchange Client for Windows 95

Although Microsoft Windows 95 includes the Exchange client messaging software and inbox, this does not provide the Windows 95 user with a legal license to access the Microsoft Exchange Server. In fact, the version of the Exchange client that comes with Windows 95 will not even work properly to connect to an Exchange Server. The dozens of additions made from the time of the release of Windows 95 to the time of the release of the Exchange Server would require that the client software for a Windows 95 client be reinstalled on the workstation.

Because the Windows 95 software does not automatically license the organization for access to the Microsoft Exchange Server, each client workstation needs to be accounted for when an organization determines the number of legal licenses it is required to purchase for the Exchange Server and Client License Packs.

NT Client License Requirement

Although Microsoft Exchange runs on Microsoft Windows NT and the Exchange client users access the Exchange Server, because Microsoft Exchange is an application server function, the organization is not required to purchase a Microsoft Windows NT client license for each Microsoft Exchange user on the network. An NT client license will be necessary only if the organization elects to use Microsoft Windows NT as its file and print application software. If a workstation needs to NET USE to access files or print to a Windows NT disk or printer share, then the client needs to also have a valid Windows NT client license. Otherwise, if the Exchange clients only need to access the Microsoft Exchange Server for electronic messages, then the client licenses for Exchange are the only licenses necessary.

The Chapter in Review

- Determining how many servers an organization will need to deploy Microsoft Exchange can and should be accurately measured in a process called *sizing*. If an organization uses Exchange strictly as an e-mail solution, Exchange requires about the same amount of server resources as other mail packages. However, the benefits of using Exchange stem from the groupware features that offer additional functionality, described earlier in the book. Additional functionality requires additional resources. Exchange is scaleable, meaning that it can operate on server hardware ranging from a modest Intel processor system to up to a high-speed multiprocessor RISC-based system. When determining the processing power that a workgroup will require in the future, one strategy is to purchase a server with a single processor but with the ability to add one or more processors in the future. RISC-based processors run faster than standard Pentium-based processors by 20 to 30 percent. By adding processing power to an Exchange Server, an organization increases the number of users the server can support. A multiprocessor Pentium server can support up to 500-750 users. A multiprocessor Alpha server can support 1,000-1,500 users on a single server. Exchange is also well-suited to server clustering. Clusters offer scalability, better resource management, and the option of providing redundancy.

- To improve Exchange performance, one option is to increase the processor speed. Another option is to increase the amount of memory in the server. More memory in a server means the server can respond to processor requests more quickly. If the server is short of memory, it will write additional memory needs to the hard drive of the server, thus causing the system to have to wait for hard drives to respond to its request. The order of magnitude in response-time difference between memory and hard drives is significant, where a task that takes one second for the memory to complete can take tens or hundreds of times longer to complete from read and write tasks to the server's hard drives.

- The relationship between processors and memory/hard drives is that a processor takes data out of storage, manipulates it, and then returns it to storage. Storage for computer systems is the hard drive. Because there is a tremendous disparity between how fast a processor operates versus how fast a hard drive operates, an intermediary is required. That intermediary is the memory, which is a place to store data from the hard drive until it is ready for use by the processor (or until the processor is finished manipulating data and now the new data needs to be returned to its long-term storage location, the hard drive). But memory is a very fast medium storage place, relative to drives. If cost and fault tolerance were not a constraint, the ideal server would have only memory and no drive space. But because memory storage is many times more expensive than hard drive storage and is volatile when the server power is turned off, hard disk storage is necessary. Thus, the relationship between the three components is that data is taken from the hard drive, temporarily stored in memory, processed by the processor, returned to memory, and finally returned to the hard drive for long-term storage.

■ Applications such as search engines, document indexing and forms increase the server memory requirements dramatically. The reason lies within the functions themselves. A search engine must look through files that fit the parameters of the search, and looks for a match between its search word and all the other words. This means that every document within the search parameters must be opened, moved from the hard drive to memory, then to the processor and back again to find all incidents of the word being searched. By having more memory, you increase the efficiency of the processor because the processor itself doesn't have to wait to be given data from the drives.

■ Estimating the size of hard drives in the server is done by measuring the amount of drive space that the organization's current e-mail system uses, and then adding enough drive space to support projected growth of the new system over a desired period of time. What needs to be estimated is the additional functionality that will be demanded of the Exchange server that didn't exist before the migration. Now you can add enough disk space to account for that increased storage demand.

■ In addition to usable drive space, an organization needs to determine what, if any, fault tolerance strategies it would like to implement. By establishing fault tolerant servers, an organization increases its likelihood of successfully recovering from a system failure. Common hardware disk redundancy strategies utilize the following technologies: RAID-1,

RAID-2, RAID-5, and RAID-6. Fault tolerance can also be implemented using software. There are some advantages to using hardware fault tolerance strategies over software fault tolerance strategies. Hardware fault tolerance strategies are faster and generally offer more server uptime in the event of a drive failure.

- The network adapter is an important server component because it is the path that data travels from server to workstation and back. A fast server processor with a slow network adapter can create a bottleneck for the entire network. That is because the server must communicate with several workstations in quick succession. The speed of the server's network adapter is usually measured in relative terms to the speed and quantities of the workstations on that network segment. Workstation network adapters are commonly 16-bit ISA, whereas server network adapters are commonly 32-bit EISA or PCI.

- As the number of network users increases, some organizations look to network segmentation to improve network performance. Network segmentation is when groups of users are connected to the server via multiple network adapters to split the demand for server access by splitting the number of users accessing the server from a single adapter. The benefits of network traffic segmentation is that the fewer number of users that have to vie for the server's single port connection, the faster the access is to the server. Most servers can support multiple network adapters.

- LOADSIM is a load simulation utility that simulates the amount of server resources required based on the number of user requests and based on the server's need to run background tasks. The word "simulation" might be a bit of a misnomer in this situation. The software doesn't do modeling simulation, it actually generates the load of messages and traffic that the network can expect to have based on the number of users configured for the test. This allows an organization to measure its actual network and server performance after the server(s) and cabling are installed but before users are migrated.

- The client configurations are just as important as the server configuration(s) in an Exchange environment. The Exchange client manages electronic forms, filters the message views, and provides the rich text display of messages. The processor speed that the workstation requires and the amount of memory needed are based on which desktop operating system is being used, how many applications are run simultaneously, and how memory intensive each application is. The amount of drive space the client requires depends on whether applications and data files will be primarily stored on the local drive or on the server. Mobile users may require larger hard drives than network users because of their need to access files off-line.

■ Equally important to understand is how Exchange is licensed. This helps an organization determine which software packages and licenses are needed. Exchange users are counted by the number of user mailboxes on the server, not by the number of concurrent users logged on. Exchange comes with either a 10-user license or a 25-user license. Additional user access licenses are purchased in increments of 1, 5, 10, and 20 users. Exchange is sold as either a Standard edition or an Enterprise edition. The Standard edition does not include any connectors, but the Enterprise edition includes the Internet (SMTP) Connector, the Exchange Server Connector, and the X.400 Connector. If an organization needs two connectors, it is more cost-effective to purchase the Enterprise edition.

■ Crucial to the successful operation and use of Microsoft Exchange is the ability to prepare the right server and client configurations to make sure that the client/server environment is sized appropriately for the demands of the organization. This chapter evaluated the performance needs of the organization in order to determine the server and client systems as well as the licensing for the systems.

■ In continuing the design, planning, and migration process to a full Microsoft Exchange environment, the next chapter will evaluate the requirements necessary to integrate Microsoft Exchange into an existing electronic messaging environment. For many organizations, electronic messaging has been available in various forms for many years whether it was a component of mainframe access or a PC local area network electronic messaging system. To replace an existing electronic messaging process and system requires the evaluation of the existing environment to see how Microsoft Exchange can replace the old system with the least amount of interruption of the organization.

Review Questions

Q. What does sizing the server mean?
A. Sizing the server is the process by which the network designer determines how many and what kind of servers the Exchange roll out will require.

Q. What are the benefits of deploying Exchange on an NT v4.0 server versus on an NT v3.51 server?
A. NT v4.0 has Internet-, intranet-, and Web-linked capabilities integrated into it whereas NT v3.51 does not.

Q. What is the minimum recommended server configuration for an Exchange server?
A. 486 Intel processor, 32MB of memory, and 1GB of drive space. This would be appropriate for a small (20-user) workgroup, e-mail only solution.

Q. Name the processor platforms supported by Microsoft Exchange.
A. Intel, Digital Alpha, and PowerPC.

Q. Why might an organization choose to have a single Alpha server over multiple Intel servers?
A. Cost per user is about the same for each option, but the organization may find that by having a single server, network administration is less complicated and less time-consuming.

Q. After reviewing the chart to determine approximately what size server a workgroup requires, what is the next step?
A. Run the Exchange load simulation utility to fine-tune the configuration requirements.

Q. Why is memory so important?
A. The processor receives data from memory and returns data to memory. In order to not keep the processor waiting, the memory should always be available to the processor.

Q. What is a rule of thumb for the ideal amount of memory an Exchange server would have and be able to utilize, assuming that Exchange will be used for complex tasks as well as for e-mail?

A. The rule of thumb for memory in a highly optimized server configuration is 16MB of base memory plus 4MB of memory for each add-in application, plus 8MB of memory for each 1GB of disk storage in the system.

Q. How does an organization estimate the amount of storage it will require for its Exchange server?

A. Estimating the size of hard drives in the server is done by measuring the amount of drive space that the organization's current e-mail system uses and adding enough drive space to support projected growth of the new system over a desired period of time. Also, enough drive space to support the additional functionality that the Exchange server will provide must be estimated.

Q. Why are hardware fault tolerant solutions more desirable than software fault tolerant solutions?

A. Hardware fault tolerant solutions offer faster performance over software solutions and can provide error trapping and recovery where software fault tolerant solutions typically cannot.

Q. Why should Exchange have its data files stored on a separate drive from the pagefile?

A. This separate boot drive is used to write error and transaction logs, and is used for a swapfile if the server runs out of memory. If the server runs out of memory, it can use a hard drive to function as virtual memory; thus, having the pagefile on a separate drive from the data can increase virtual memory performance.

Q. Why might an organization need to install an additional network adapter in the server?

A. To segment user groups for faster performance or to create a secondary communications path with the Internet while providing for greater network security.

Q. Why is the word "simulation" a misnomer in the title LOADSIM utility?

A. It is a misnomer because LOADSIM is a utility that actually generates the load of messages and traffic that the network can expect to have based on the number of users you plan to have.

Q. What clients does Exchange support?

A. DOS, Windows v3.*x*, Windows for Workgroups, Windows 95, Windows NT v3.51 and v4.0, Apple Macintosh, and Web.

Q. What three connectors does Exchange Enterprise edition include that the Standard edition doesn't?

A. Exchange Connector, Internet (SMTP) Connector, and X.400 Connector.

Q. Does every user in an organization need to have an Exchange client access license (CAL)?

A. If the user plans to use Microsoft Exchange, the user will need to have an Exchange CAL for legal access to the Exchange Server.

Q. How does an organization determine whether or not to buy users CALs for NT Server?

A. If the organization is only using Exchange as an application server function, only Exchange client licenses are required. However, if the organization also uses the file and print services of Windows NT to store programs and data files on the Exchange Server or another NT Server in the organization, then CALs for NT are also required.

CHAPTER **8**

Communicating with Other Electronic Messaging Systems

In the previous chapters, we evaluated the design goals of different types of organizations, taking into account the impact that an installation of a new Microsoft Exchange environment would have in an isolated environment. The reality, however, for most organizations is that they already have an electronic messaging system in place. For some organizations, the existing electronic messaging system may not be widely used, so the implementation of Microsoft Exchange may not have a major impact. For others, however, electronic messaging ranks in importance with voicemail and faxes as a primary method of communications within the organization and with clients, vendors, and associates.

When organizations elect to install Microsoft Exchange as their future messaging and groupware environment, their need to maintain the flow of communications with an existing messaging system becomes crucial. The coexistence of two messaging systems may last only a short time while the organization switches from one system to another, or it may be sustained as portions of the organization may choose not to switch to Microsoft Exchange. In organizations with the need to communicate with clients or vendors running different electronic messaging systems, the ability to communicate externally with the Microsoft Exchange system will be just as crucial as the organization's ability to communicate internally.

The more able Microsoft Exchange is to provide smooth integration with other messaging systems, the better it will be able to minimize downtime or interruptions in messaging services for users. Integration is also crucial to the organization's ability to communicate effectively with other departments within the company or with external business partners. This chapter will review and evaluate the general integration needs and requirements of organizations to assist in their integration of Microsoft Exchange with other electronic messaging systems.

Integrating with Other Messaging and Groupware Environments

Similar to our previous environment evaluation processes, we will assess the electronic messaging systems with which the Microsoft Exchange environment needs to communicate in order to consider if and how to integrate the existing messaging system with Exchange. The assessment of the other messaging environments is not necessarily limited to the current message environment of the organization, but could potentially include an evaluation of both the existing messaging system and the other organization(s) that will need communication links and access to information in the new Exchange messaging environment.

The extent of the integration, conversion, and migration process is dependent upon whether the other systems provide only e-mail services or whether the organization is currently using groupware functionality (personal and group scheduling, or forms and document routing). Additionally, if the existing messaging system provides a great deal of messaging and groupware functionality, but the organization needs only to integrate the electronic mail component communication between two divisions, then the demand on the organization to develop a complicated link is minimized. Clearly, a more sophisticated existing messaging system will have a greater need to integrate all its aspects with Microsoft Exchange, resulting in a more complicated integration or migration.

Open Environment or Proprietary Environment

Of great importance in determining the complexity of the integration with Microsoft Exchange is whether the other electronic messaging system supports open industry messaging standards or whether it is of a proprietary format. Because Microsoft Exchange supports the most common industry standard formats of SMTP through the Internet connector as well as X.400 messaging, if the other environment supports one of these standards, it will be able to communicate with Microsoft Exchange. However, even proprietary formats are available for Microsoft Exchange, including gateways to Microsoft Mail, IBM/Lotus cc:Mail, IBM/Lotus Notes, IBM Profs, or DEC All-in-One mail. Microsoft's ability to provide support to a number of messaging gateway formats into Microsoft Exchange as well as third-party support for gateways that Microsoft does not directly support has given many organizations the capability to integrate Microsoft Exchange with their existing environments.

A Gateway Versus a Connector

In many of the readings available on Microsoft Exchange, there are references to gateways to other messaging systems as well as to connectors to other messaging systems. The term that is most commonly used in the industry is gateway. The terms gateway and connector have similar meanings, but their communication capabilities can be drastically different in terms of support or functionality. A gateway is typically a standalone device that allows one messaging system to communicate with another. It acts as a translation system that accepts messages in one format and dispatches them in another format. The more sophisticated the gateway, the better the integration between Microsoft Exchange and the other messaging environment.

Within Microsoft Exchange, the term connector is used to describe a gateway that is tightly integrated into the core Microsoft Exchange communication system. Connectors within Microsoft Exchange tend to support a broader range of message and communications links that include not only electronic mail message interchange, but also capabilities such as appointment schedule interchange and user list name directory synchronization. Rather than acting as an external gateway component that accepts information to and from a Microsoft Exchange organization, the connector resides within the Microsoft Exchange Server, which provides the Exchange system the ability to manage and interpret the information directly with the information and directory stores within Exchange for better services management.

Also, because a connector is integrated into the core directory store, message information management store, and system attendant components of Exchange, it logs all message transmissions and processes directly within the same message and transaction logs used within Microsoft Exchange. With tighter tracking and controls, an administrator is better able to track the status of messages with integrated Exchange connectors than through an external gateway, where limited information, management, and message control exists.

Directory Synchronization

Key to any electronic messaging environment that includes two or more different messaging systems is the ability to update user lists of each organization and make the updated information available to all users. Although the task of maintaining an updated list of users and making it available to all e-mail clients may sound simple, directory synchronization is actually one of the more complicated tasks within cross-platform message administration. Functionally, any time users are added, deleted, or modified as individuals, or added and deleted from messaging groups, the changed information needs to be forwarded to all attached networks. For two small organizations synchronizing user lists, it would be a simple process to simply send an updated user list to the other organization any time information is changed. However, as shared user list distribution grows for larger organizations, the ability to send a modified user list every time there is a change can cause a significant amount of electronic messaging traffic. For example, if an organization with 1,000 employees that communicates with 100 different networks makes a change to their user list, and the electronic messaging system sends the entire user list every time there is a change, the user list could be as large as 250K upon completion of a change, and once sent to 100 different locations could generate a broadcast storm of 2.5MB of traffic. If the organization is connected to the Internet over a 56KB lease line and needs to transmit 2.5MB of user list information, that transmission could saturate the organization's Internet connection for a few minutes.

So, instead of sending the entire user list, including user names, group information, and user communications information with each change, a directory replication system typically only sends and modifies the changed information. If the information for only five users is changed, the content of those five users will be the only information sent and synchronized.

Exchange Source Extractor

For many organizations planning to integrate Microsoft Exchange into an existing network or messaging environment, instead of creating user names from scratch, Microsoft provides a source extractor utility that retrieves user information from the external system and populates Microsoft Exchange with the new user information. The source extractor can be used to populate user lists with the new users, create new user mailboxes, and update address books.

Unlike a directory synchronization process, the source extractor is typically a one-time export and import process. As user names are changed in the other electronic messaging system, a subsequent export from the messaging system and import into Microsoft Exchange will be needed to repopulate the user list that is available to Microsoft Exchange users.

Microsoft Exchange Messaging Integration Support

In order for an organization with an existing e-mail system to integrate with one running Microsoft Exchange, the tools to simplify the integration or to provide seamless coexistence need to be available to assist the organization in conducting cross-platform communications. The following section outlines the utilities that are available to help a Microsoft Exchange organization to communicate with other messaging systems.

Microsoft Mail

Microsoft Mail has been the standard e-mail with optional group scheduling software available from Microsoft since 1991. There are over seven million users of Microsoft Mail, all of whom have the capability to send electronic mail internally as well as communicate externally with users on the Internet, on an X.400 network, through MCI mail, or over fax.

Designed to integrate Microsoft Mail with Microsoft Exchange, the Microsoft Exchange software includes a free connector that allows the Microsoft Mail and Microsoft Exchange messaging systems to seamlessly interchange e-mail messages as well as share personal and group scheduling information between the organizations. The Microsoft Mail Connector installs directly on a Microsoft Exchange server, and through the use of a telephone modem attached to the Exchange server or inband over a network connection, the Microsoft Exchange Server appears to a Microsoft Mail system as another Microsoft Mail external post office. Functioning as an external post office, the Microsoft Exchange Server can send and receive e-mail messages, participate in DirSync directory synchronization processes, and aid in SchDist Microsoft Scheduler free and busy time schedule distribution.

Installing and Configuring the MS Mail Connector

The Microsoft Mail Connector is installed concurrently with Microsoft Exchange. To verify whether the Microsoft Mail Connector has been installed on an Exchange server, within the Exchange Administrator software, go into the Connections section of the Exchange site and verify that there is an MS Mail Connector displayed, as shown in Figure 8-1.

If the MS Mail Connector does not show up in the Connections section of Exchange, it can be installed by performing the following:

1. Run SETUP from the Exchange Server CD.

2. Select Add/Remove.

3. Select the Microsoft Exchange Server and click on Change Option.

4. Select the MS Mail Connector and click on OK.

5. Select Continue.

When the MS Mail Connector is installed, the options need to be configured. To configure the MS Mail Connector, select the MS Mail Connector from the Exchange Administrator program, then select File | Properties to view a screen similar to the one shown in Figure 8-2.

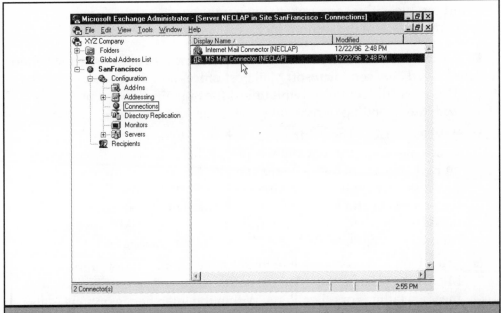

Figure 8-1. *The MS Mail Connector option installed*

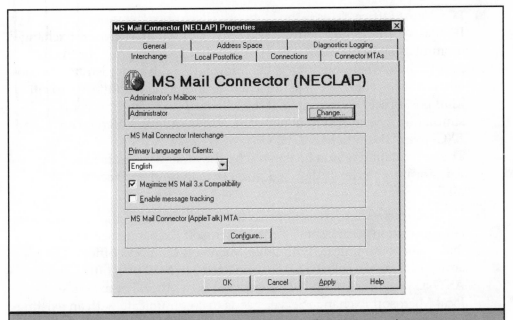

Figure 8-2. *The Microsoft Mail Connector configuration options*

The configurable options are broken down into seven sections. The key components of each of the sections include:

- **General** This section can be used to limit the size of messages sent and received between Microsoft Mail post offices and the Exchange server. This is usually set to No Limit unless the organization has problems with users sending or receiving very large mail messages.

- **Address Space** The Address Space is used to designate the path by which messages are sent and received. When a message is received by an Exchange client designated as an MS (Microsoft Mail) message, the Address Space will route the message to the Microsoft Mail Connector for processing and management. This differentiates an Exchange client message type that may be FAX (for a fax message), SMTP (for an Internet message), or MS (for a Microsoft Mail message).

- **Interchange** This allows you to select the administrator of the Microsoft Exchange MS Mail post office who will receive notices of message failures or other alerts. Within the Interchange options is also the ability to enable message tracking. If logging is desired in tracking messages to and from other Microsoft Mail post offices, the enable message tracking option should be selected.

- **Local Post Office** This is the Network/Postoffice/Sign-on ID/Password for the Microsoft Mail post office that Microsoft Exchange is simulating. In the Microsoft Mail ADMIN.EXE program for the non-Exchange network, this is the information the administrator would enter as the authorized post office to communicate with the Microsoft Mail post office. For example, if the Microsoft Exchange Server is simulating a Microsoft Mail network, it may call itself Network= EXCHNET, Postoffice=EXCHPOST, with Password=PASSWORD. This information would be entered by the other Microsoft Mail Administrator as an authorized post office to send and receive mail messages.

- **Connections** The Connections section correlates with the external administration components for the Microsoft Exchange Server so that it can communicate with other Microsoft Mail post offices. The administrator can select a LAN-connected MS Mail post office, an ASYNC post office or an X.25-connected post office. For example, if the local Microsoft Exchange Server needs to communicate with an existing Microsoft Mail network called Network=MSM-NET, Postoffice= MSM-POST, Password=PASSWORD, this information would be entered in the authorized post office that Exchange will use to send and receive messages.

- **Connector MTAs** This is where the administrator would enter the Message Transfer Agent (MTA) that will be monitoring and performing the sending and receiving of Microsoft Mail messages. The MTA manages specific post offices for Microsoft Mail message management.

- **Diagnostics Logging** The Diagnostics Logging provides the administrator with the option of selecting the level of logging on messages in and out of the Microsoft Mail Connector. Logging can be tracked at three levels: minimum, medium, or maximum. Logging will be covered in greater detail in Chapter 13.

IBM/Lotus cc:Mail

Microsoft Mail's strongest competitor , cc:Mail is the premier electronic mail message system from IBM/Lotus Software. cc:Mail provides users with the ability to send and receive electronic mail messages internally, as well as communicate externally with users on the Internet, to X.400 networks, through MCI mail networks, or over fax.

To integrate cc:Mail with Microsoft Exchange, the Microsoft Exchange software includes a free connector that allows the cc:Mail and Microsoft Exchange messaging systems to seamlessly interchange e-mail messages between organizations. The cc:Mail Connector installs directly on a Microsoft Exchange server and provides organizations with the functions of a cc:Mail router over a network connection to facilitate cc:Mail to Exchange communications. As a cc:Mail router, the Microsoft Exchange Server can send and receive electronic mail messages and participate in the directory synchronization process.

Tips on Implementing the cc:Mail Connector for Exchange

The cc:Mail Connector for Exchange was only made available beginning with Exchange v5.0. Users who have Exchange v4.x should upgrade at least one server to Exchange v5.0 to acquire the functionality of the cc:Mail Connector messaging integration components.

An organization needs at least one Microsoft Exchange Server with the cc:Mail address generator installed so that cc:Mail proxies are generated for the system's recipients. Depending on how the existing cc:Mail environment is configured, the organization may need multiple connections between Microsoft Exchange and cc:Mail in order to perform directory synchronization. If the cc:Mail environment has a centralized Directory Exchange (cc:Mail ADE) configuration, the Exchange server only needs to be configured to communicate directly with the centralized Directory Exchange in order to populate the recipients' information across both platforms.

Installing and Configuring the cc:Mail Connector

The cc:Mail Connector can be installed concurrently with Microsoft Exchange. To verify whether the cc:Mail Connector has been installed on an Exchange server, in the Exchange Administrator software, go into the Connections section of the Exchange site and verify that there is a cc:Mail Connector displayed.

If the cc:Mail Connector does not show up in the Connections section of Exchange, it can be installed by performing the following:

1. Run SETUP from the Exchange Server CD.

2. Select Add/Remove.

3. Select the Microsoft Exchange Server and click on Change Option.

4. Select the cc:Mail Connector and click on OK.

5. Select Continue.

When the cc:Mail Connector is installed, the options need to be configured. To configure the cc:Mail Connector, select the cc:Mail Connector from the Exchange Administrator program and select File | Properties to view a screen similar to the one shown in Figure 8-3. The configurable options are broken down into six sections. The key components of each of the sections include:

- **General** This section notes the cc:Mail post office and path for the data share for the cc:Mail message transfer information. You can also set limits on the size of messages sent and received between cc:Mail post offices and the Exchange server in this section. This is usually set to No Limit unless the organization has problems with users sending or receiving very large mail messages.

- **Address Space** The Address Space is used to designate the path by which messages are sent and received. When a message is received by an Exchange client that has been designated as a cc:Mail message, the

Address Space will route the message to the cc:Mail Connector for processing and management.

- **Import Container** The Import Container notes the location of the inbound cc:Mail messages for the Exchange share.

- **Export Containers** The Export Containers are the locations where Exchange messages are to be sent for distribution to other cc:Mail post offices. Multiple containers can be created to export messages to different post offices or modes of communication (such as cc:Mail post offices over a LAN or cc:Mail post offices on dial-up).

- **Schedule** The Schedule option allows for the timing of imports and exports of cc:Mail messages to and from other cc:Mail post offices.

- **Diagnostics Logging** The Diagnostics Logging provides the administrator with the option of selecting the level of logging on messages in and out of the cc:Mail Connector. Logging can be tracked at minimum, medium, or maximum levels. Logging will be covered in greater detail in Chapter 13.

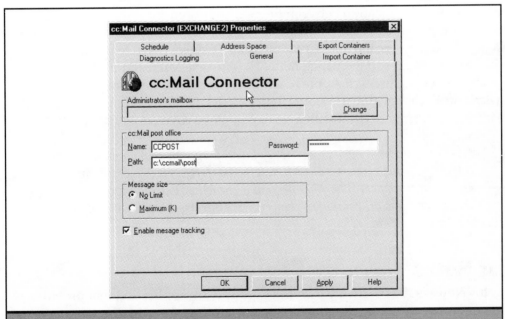

Figure 8-3. *The cc:Mail Connector configuration options*

IBM Profs

IBM Profs is an electronic mail system used by millions of IBM mainframe users around the globe. Through the IBM OfficeVision software, users are provided with personal and group scheduling and electronic calendaring, in addition to electronic messaging.

Integration between Microsoft Exchange and a Profs/OfficeVision environment is provided by third-party add-in gateways to Exchange. Attachmate Zip! for Exchange is one such gateway that allows for the interchange of electronic messages and free and busy calendar information to Profs v2.2.2+ or OV/VM 1.0+. Vendor information on Attachmate and other messaging connector and gateway vendors is provided in Appendix D at the back of this book.

Microsoft Mail for AppleTalk Networks

Microsoft Mail for AppleTalk Networks was Microsoft's electronic mail system for Macintosh computers. Purchased in 1995 by Quarterdeck, Microsoft Mail for AppleTalk Networks has become Quarterdeck's Mail for Macs.

Microsoft Exchange includes a connector for the Mail for Macs that provides inbound and outbound electronic mail messaging as well as directory synchronization between the two environments. Additionally, this connector
is not needed by organizations that intend to connect Macintosh computers directly to a Microsoft Exchange network. With the Microsoft Exchange Macintosh client, users of Apple Macintosh computers can connect to Microsoft Exchange directly from a network. More information on Apple Macintosh interconnection with Exchange will be covered in Chapter 19.

NOTE: Microsoft has two versions of mail programs that support Macintosh computers. One version is the Microsoft Mail for AppleTalk that is an exclusively all Mac mail system. The other version is the Microsoft Mail for PC Networks that is made for PC computers; however, it supports Macintosh computers as a client to the application.

Lotus Notes

Lotus Notes is IBM Software's premier groupware application that provides integrated electronic messaging, document routing, discussion groups, site-to-site data replication, and integrated Web and Internet communications.

A third-party connector, like the one from Linkage Software Inc., provides the interconnection for electronic messaging between a Lotus Notes v3 or v4 environment and Microsoft Exchange. The Exchange-Notes Connector enables full messaging functions, including sending and receiving rich text formatted messages, message status information, and message attachments. Linkage Software Inc. also has a Directory Exchange product that provides directory synchronization between Microsoft Exchange and Lotus Notes.

Vendor information on Linkage and other messaging connector and gateway vendors is provided in Appendix D.

Support for Other Electronic Messaging Systems Through Standard Gateways

An organization running an e-mail system without native connectors to Microsoft Exchange such as Novell Groupwise, Banyan BeyondMail, WordPerfect Office, or DaVinci Mail can use any of the common messaging gateway systems available in order to communicate with Microsoft Exchange. Possible solutions may include using the Microsoft Exchange Internet Connector to communicate with an external SMTP gateway, or using the Microsoft Exchange X.400 Connector to communicate with an external X.400 gateway environment.

Using X.400 as the Common Denominator

Although SMTP Internet gateways and connectors have become the common method of communications for most organizations, X.400 has been and continues to be the common method of host-to-host messaging interchange. As described back in Chapter 1, X.400 is an international standard of messaging communications that was designed specifically to support organizations that span multiple sites, organizational units, and countries. X.400 can efficiently locate and transfer messages through an organizational structure that simplifies message routing management. Additionally, X.400 was designed not only to handle electronic messages, but also attachments and message instruction sets.

Even today, many mail systems like DecMail, WangOffice, or MCI Mail can provide better support and more flexibility in messaging options for X.400

communications than for SMTP Internet connections, because of the exceptional feature sets offered by X.400.

The Microsoft Exchange X.400 Connector provides full X.400 communications support and can be used to communicate directly with other X.400 hosts or X.400 service providers. The Exchange X.400 Connector comes with the Exchange Enterprise edition of the software or can be purchased as an add-on to the Exchange Standard edition of the Exchange Server software.

Using SMTP as the Common Denominator

With so many organizations demanding Internet connections for global mail messaging, most electronic mail programs (new and old) have some form of an SMTP gateway available. The SMTP gateway software allows the electronic mail program to send and receive messages from other users on the Internet.

However, if the organization needs to have a private connection between two or more different electronic mail systems, it can set up an SMTP-to-SMTP connection between the electronic messaging systems. In this scenario, both organizations can set up an SMTP gateway from their electronic mail systems to SMTP. With SMTP as the common link between these locations, they can carry on communications as if they were connected directly.

How SMTP Mail Works

Many organizations do not understand how a mail message from their network utilizes SMTP in order to get the message to another organization. When an electronic mail user in a mail system sends a message to an Internet recipient, the message is first transferred to the local mail system post office. The post office acknowledges the message's destination to a user outside of the local mail system and forwards it to the appropriate gateway. If the message is addressed to an Internet user, it goes to the SMTP gateway. The Microsoft Mail SMTP gateway then needs to log into a smart host (typically a local UNIX-
based "mailhost") to queue up the message on the mailhost. The mailhost is configured to check a message queue to see if there are messages that need to be sent to the Internet. When the mailhost identifies a message in its queue, it opens the message, determines the message's destination, and then logs in to the destination mailhost to establish a connection between the local mailhost and the remote mailhost. Once the connection has been

established, the message is transferred from the local mailhost message queue to the destination mailhost message queue. With the message sitting in the queue destination smart host, the destination's SMTP gateway recognizes a message in its queue, retrieves the message, determines its user destination, and forwards the message to the mailbox of the recipient. This process is diagrammed in Figure 8-4.

The big component in this SMTP link is the mailhost or smart host system. In most environments, this is an $8,000-15,000 UNIX-based system that handles electronic mail communications in a manner consistent with how messaging is conducted over the Internet.

Installing and Configuring the Internet Connector

The Microsoft Exchange Internet Connector can be installed concurrently with Microsoft Exchange. To verify whether the Exchange Internet Connector has

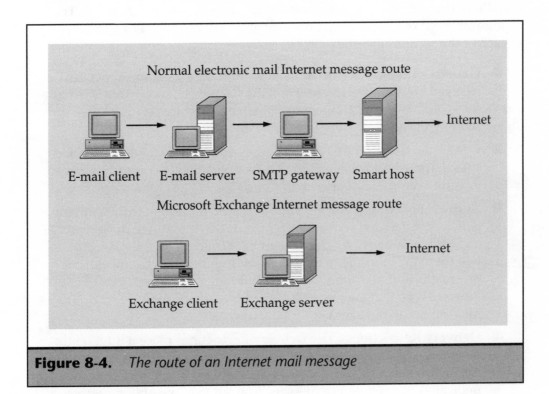

Figure 8-4. *The route of an Internet mail message*

been installed on an Exchange server, within the Exchange Administrator software, go into the Connections section of the Exchange site and verify that there is an Internet Mail Connector displayed.

If the Internet Mail Connector does not show up in the Connections section of Exchange, it can be installed by performing the following:

1. Run SETUP from the Exchange Server CD.
2. Select Add/Remove.
3. Select the Microsoft Exchange Server and click on Change Option.
4. Select the Internet Mail Connector and click on OK.
5. Select Continue.

When the Internet Mail Connector is installed, the options need to be configured. To configure the Internet Mail Connector, select the Internet Mail Connector from the Exchange Administrator program and select File | Properties to view a screen similar to the one shown in Figure 8-5. The configurable options are broken down into ten sections. The key components of each of the sections include:

- **General** This section can be used to limit the size of messages sent and received between the Internet and the Exchange server. This is usually set to No Limit unless the organization has problems with users sending or receiving very large mail messages.

- **Connected Sites** The Connected Sites option allows interconnected sites that support Exchange directory replication to conduct managed directory replication between the sites.

- **Address Space** The Address Space is used to designate the path by which messages are sent and received. When a message designated as an SMTP message is received by an Exchange client, the Address Space will route the message to the Microsoft Internet Mail Connector for processing and management. This differentiates an Exchange client message type that may be FAX (for a fax message) or MS (for a Microsoft Mail message).

- **Delivery Restrictions** The Delivery Restrictions place a limit on the acceptance or the rejection of messages from particular recipients. This can be used either to block messages to the Exchange server from undesired sources, or as a message firewall to allow only messages from authorized recipients to be received by the Microsoft Exchange Server.

■ **Advanced**   The Advanced section provides options relative to the storage, transfer time, and transfer limits for Internet messages. These are typically tuning and logging management functions.

■ **Internet Mail**   The Internet Mail options allow the administrator to set the default for attachment conversions as MIME or UUENCODE types as well as enabling message tracking within the messaging environment.

■ **Queues**   The Queues section shows messages in the queue and the status of the messages in their transmission and communication with other sites. Messages may be stuck in the queue when a destination site is unavailable, thus preventing the Exchange server from connecting to the site to send the message destined to the location.

■ **Connections**   The Connections section allows the Exchange server to be set to allow inbound messages, outbound messages, both, or none. This can be used to designate the role of the Exchange server in splitting the responsibilities of how it manages Internet messages. Within the Connections section, the administrator can designate how long messages are allowed to remain in the queues before notifying the sender of an error. In organizations in which Internet mail is critical to general business operations, the threshold for Connector Message Queue Retry Interval should be set to 2-18 hours so that the sender is notified of a message transmission failure. This should not be set too low, because often destination servers are temporarily down either for maintenance or Internet downtime, and a deluge of returned messages after a single night of destination server downtime may cause undue traffic and user confusion.

■ **MIME Types**   The MIME Types is a translation table between MIME content designations and PC-based file extensions. Thus, a MIME video-formatted attachment would end up with a PC .AVI extension, or a MIME audio-formatted attachment would end up with a PC .WAV extension.

■ **Diagnostics Logging**   The Diagnostics Logging provides the administrator with the option of selecting the level of logging on messages in and out of the Internet Mail Connector. Logging can be tracked at minimum, medium, or maximum levels. Logging will be covered in greater detail in Chapter 13.

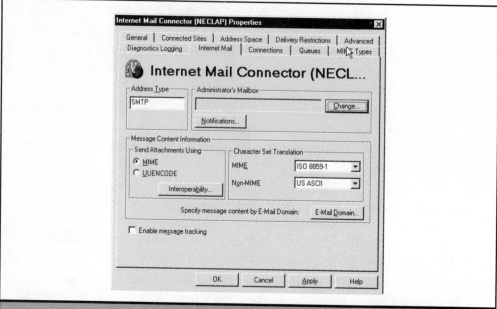

Figure 8-5. *The Exchange Internet Mail Connector configuration options*

The Various Functions of the Microsoft Exchange Internet Connector

The Microsoft Exchange Internet Connector can be used in a variety of roles for SMTP communications. The Exchange server can act as the smart host and communicate directly with another smart host to transfer mail messages. It can also act as an SMTP Gateway Server over a lease line or network connection to forward mail messages to a smart host that is acting as the main mailhost for the organization. Lastly, the Exchange server can function as an SMTP Dial-up Gateway and dial into a smart host acting as the main mailhost in order to send and receive mail messages for an organization.

As the Smart Mail Host

Many organizations are unaware of the significance that the Microsoft Exchange Server can act as the smart host within an SMTP Internet connection link. As the mailhost, the Microsoft Exchange Server eliminates the need for an additional server on the network, as well as minimizes the potential for that extra system to be a place where mail messages need to be stored (and potentially get stuck in transmission). In a sample scenario with Microsoft Exchange as the mail messaging system, a client creates a mail message for an Internet user and presses the send button. The message is received by the Exchange server, which acknowledges that the message is destined to an external address. The Exchange server locates the destination mailhost server, logs in to the mailhost, and transmits the message directly from the Microsoft Exchange Server to the smart host of the destination address. The message is then forwarded by the destination mailhost to the electronic mail system and recipient of the message.

As an SMTP Gateway Server

When an organization already has a smart host that functions as the main mailhost for the organization, the Microsoft Exchange Server can be subordinate to the main mailhost. When a Microsoft Exchange client sends a message addressed to a user on the Internet, the Exchange server forwards the message to the smart host.

This scenario may be common for an organization that has a single centralized mailhost and Microsoft Exchange Servers that manage smaller workgroups within the organization. The smaller Exchange workgroups send information to the main mailhost as the central depository for external e-mail communications. Another scenario is an organization with a variety of e-mail systems in which the other mail systems only support SMTP gateway communications and cannot act as a smart host themselves. Since the organization needs a smart host to provide the services for the other electronic messaging systems, the workgroup using Microsoft Exchange continues to function in the same scenario as the other workgroups and simply forwards messages to the organization's designated smart host.

As an SMTP Dial-Up Gateway

Organizations that lack the volume to justify a full-time lease line connection to the Internet or for whom the cost of a dedicated Internet connection may be prohibitive (for example, an international location or remote site location) may elect to implement a dial-up connection to the Internet. The Microsoft Exchange Server can act as an SMTP Dial-up Gateway in which it dials into a smart host on a predetermined time frame (every 15 minutes, every hour, every few hours), sends mail messages queued up at the Microsoft Exchange Server, and retrieves messages waiting for it at the smart host.

The Chapter in Review

- Coexistence with other e-mail packages is an important requirement for many organizations seeking to incorporate Exchange in their environment. For some, coexistence means the ability to exchange electronic messages between the two e-mail systems. For others, it means integrating schedules, forms, and document routing. The more complex the integration requirements, the more complex the installation will be.

- If the other e-mail package supports industry standards such as SMTP and X.400, Exchange readily supports those standards and can simplify integration. Gateways are available for Exchange to some popular proprietary formats such as MS Mail, cc:Mail, Lotus Notes, IBM Profs, and DEC All-in-One. These connectors and gateways offer support for a wide variety of existing mail systems. Gateways to other messaging systems (called *connectors* in Microsoft Exchange) are tools used to allow Microsoft Exchange to interchange messages with other e-mail systems.

- Directory synchronization is the ability for all attached networks to be able to see current user lists and group lists. Any time a change is made to any of these lists, the gateways must forward those changes to all attached networks. For small organizations, this is a less daunting task. But for organizations with a large number of users or a large number of separate post offices, the concern is how to update all user directories as efficiently as possible. Microsoft Exchange has addressed this issue with a number of its directory management functions.

- A source extractor in Microsoft Exchange is a utility that retrieves user information from the external system and uses it to populate Exchange with new user information. The extractor is a one-time export and import process. The extractor does not continually update the Exchange directory. The extractor has to be run for subsequent repopulations.

- There are a variety of tools to help Exchange integrate or migrate to other messaging environments. Exchange includes a free connector that allows MS Mail and Exchange to interchange e-mail, scheduling, and to participate in Directory Synchronization. IBM/Lotus cc:Mail is a popular, widely installed e-mail application as well. Exchange includes a free connector that allows for cc:Mail and Exchange to seamlessly interchange e-mail. This feature is only available in Exchange v5.0 and higher. IBM Profs is an IBM mainframe-based e-mail application. Integration between Profs and Exchange is provided by third-party add-in gateways. For example, Attachmate offers a gateway that provides the interchange of e-mail and free/busy calendar information.

- MS Mail for AppleTalk has become Quarterdeck Mail for Macs. Exchange includes a connector for Mail for Macs. It provides e-mail interchange and directory synchronization. Lotus Notes is a groupware application that provides e-mail, document routing, discussion groups, data replication between sites, and integrated Web and Internet communications. Organizations with e-mail packages without native Exchange Connectors can communicate via an SMTP gateway or an X.400 gateway. SMTP can be used as a gateway for e-mail applications that use the Internet as their method of transporting messages.

- Many organizations do not realize the value of having the Exchange server being able to function as a smart host. A typical UNIX-based smart host costs $8,000-$15,000. That savings can be recognized directly with an Exchange server. It also eliminates a step in the mail transport of Internet messages, which reduces the complexity of communications via the Internet. The Exchange server can also function as a dial-up gateway to the Internet. This allows Exchange to dial in to a smart host periodically to interchange new messages.

- As organizations consider implementing Microsoft Exchange as their electronic messaging and groupware environment, it is important to have a strategy of how the Exchange environment will communicate with the rest of the organization or with other organizations that may have different electronic messaging systems.

- Microsoft Exchange has some of the best support for interconnecting with other mail messaging and groupware systems, and with the popularity of Microsoft Exchange, support for Microsoft Exchange gateways and connectors will continue to grow.

■ The key to any interconnection between messaging systems is the ability to not only send and receive electronic mail messages, but also to synchronize user names and group information, as well as exchange appointment schedules and conduct intranet groupware functions across multiple operating platforms.

■ For some organizations, the need to have coexistence between an existing electronic messaging system and Microsoft Exchange may be only a short-term one, even if the organization is making a long-term transition to Microsoft Exchange. In the next chapter, we will detail the migration process from other messaging systems to Microsoft Exchange including the tools available to extract user names and migrate user mailboxes and appointment schedules from one environment to another.

Review Questions

Q. What is the difference between a gateway and a connector?

A. Gateways and connectors are both tools used to allow Microsoft Exchange to interchange messages with other e-mail systems. The difference is the degree of sophistication that each offers. Gateways translate e-mails from one format to another. Exchange connectors support schedule interchanges, directory synchronization, or advanced processes for tracking and logging messages.

Q. What is one way to avoid excessive network traffic caused by directory synchronization?

A. One way to avoid excessive network traffic caused by directory synchronization is to configure the network to only send and update information that has been changed rather than sending the entire directory for each new entry.

Q. What is an extractor?

A. An extractor is a utility that does a one-time export of user name information from a messaging system to populate the Microsoft Exchange directory. The extractor does not continually update the Exchange directory.

Q. Using the MS Mail Connector, how does an Exchange server appear to the MS Mail system?

A. The Exchange server appears as another Microsoft Mail post office.

Q. How do you confirm that the MS Mail Connector is installed?
A. From Exchange administration software, go to the Connections section and verify that an MS Mail Connector is displayed.

Q. Which MS Mail Connector configuration option allows you to select which administrator is to receive notices of message failures?
A. Interchange.

Q. What function does the cc:Mail Connector provide?
A. It provides the functions of a cc:Mail router over a network connection. This allows Exchange and cc:Mail to send and receive e-mail, as well as do directory synchronizations.

Q. When does the cc:Mail to Exchange Connector need to be installed only on one server?
A. When the cc:Mail network has a centralized Directory Exchange (ADE) configuration.

Q. What does the Schedule option in the cc:Mail Connector configuration do?
A. It allows for the timing of imports and exports of cc:Mail messages to and from other cc:Mail post offices.

Q. What are Notes features of the X.400 message transport standard?
A. X.400 simplifies message routing management and can handle attachments and message instruction sets as a standard method of message interchange.

Q. What is the key component of SMTP mail link?
A. The smart host system. This is usually a UNIX-based system that handles e-mail in the same fashion that the Internet does.

Q. What are the various functions that Exchange Internet Connector can perform?
A. It can perform smart host-to-smart host communications for message transfers. It can act as an SMTP gateway server to forward messages to a smart host, or it can function as an SMTP dial-up gateway to dial in to a smart host functioning as the main mailhost for the organization.

CHAPTER 9

Migrating to Microsoft Exchange

For many organizations, implementing Microsoft Exchange will require a migration from an existing electronic mail system. During its migration process, an organization would typically want to minimize the task of retyping user names into the new Microsoft Exchange system, and users would want to retain messages and appointment schedules from the old system, and be able to access them in the new system. The more seamless the organization wants the conversion to be, the more steps that will be necessary to ensure a complete migration. This chapter will outline the steps necessary to ensure a successful migration to Microsoft Exchange, including an overview of the utilities available to assist organizations with this transition.

The Migration Process

For a small organization, the migration process might consist of a single weekend's worth of work to convert from one messaging system to another. For a larger organization, the migration process could end up a relatively lengthy procedure, spanning several weeks or months and involving the prolonged coexistence of both the existing messaging system and the new Microsoft Exchange environment. The steps required for both of these types of migrations have been categorized as either single step migration or coexistence long-term migration.

Single Step Migration

Single step migration implies a complete migration from an existing messaging system to Microsoft Exchange, without a transitional period of coexistence. The single step also means that there is no need for gateways from the old system to the new—all users can be migrated simultaneously. As shown in Figure 9-1, an organization can switch from one messaging system to another without the need for backwards cross-compatibility. A single step migration can usually be completed successfully for an organization that meets the following criteria:

- Consists of fewer than 200 users
- Has existing migration tools to assist in the conversion of user mailboxes and existing messages (if desired or required)
- Planned adequately so that the migration can occur in an organized fashion

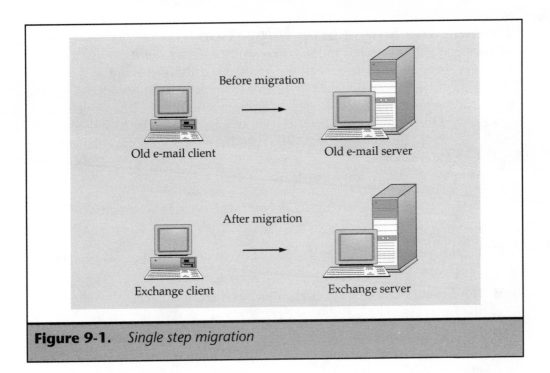

Figure 9-1. *Single step migration*

If the organization generally meets these conditions, it can benefit from the significant advantages to completing a single step migration. The most obvious benefit is the elimination of interim gateways to maintain coexistence of both the old and the new systems. Single step migration allows organizations to avoid the extensive effort necessary to set up and maintain the gateways between the two environments, as well as the difficulty of educating users during the migration process regarding which e-mail address to use.

During a lengthy migration process, some users will reside on the new messaging system, and some users will reside on the old messaging system. This requires that the administrator ensure the appropriate users are residing in the appropriate address book, whether it be the new address book or the old. As users are slowly migrated from one system to the other, they need to be constantly updated about which users are on the new and old systems, so that e-mail messages can be directed to the correct mail system. If the migration process is conducted in a single step, all users will be migrated to the new system simultaneously, eliminating the in-progress confusion.

Planning the Single Step Migration

Completing a single step migration successfully entails careful planning of the entire process and completion of all the necessary components at the appropriate time, which is critical to the final changeover. Although the procedure is referred to as single step migration, a number of phases need to be completed to ensure its success. All components that can be completed and tested prior to the final changeover should be in order to minimize the amount of work on the final day.

The single step migration consists of:

- Installation of the Exchange client software on each workstation
- Installation of the Microsoft Exchange Server
- Prototype testing of the migration of user names, mail messages, and calendars
- Confirmation that all external gateways migrate successfully (such as to the Internet)
- Testing the prototype Exchange client's access to the Exchange server (including successful conversion of users' mailbox messages and appointment calendars)
- Final migration of all users in a "live" migration in a single day

Once all of the components have been tested, the final date of migration can be selected, and the final procedure—the migration of the client workstations to support the new Microsoft Exchange environment—can be implemented.

External Gateways

Because the single step migration has neither internal gateway nor coexistence requirements, the only gateways that need to be installed or tested are external gateways, such as to the Internet (or possibly gateways to other external electronic mail systems the organization needs to communicate with). The ways in which the Microsoft Exchange Internet Mail Connector will change how an organization communicates with the Internet were discussed in Chapter 8, but careful planning and consideration of how the implementation of Microsoft Exchange will impact the new Internet messaging configuration plus the testing of the external gateways from Exchange are necessary to ensure proper inbound and outbound communications after the migration.

Coexistence Long-Term Migration

Any long-term migration will require the coexistence of both the old messaging system and the new Microsoft Exchange environment. Coexistence long-term migration means that gateways from the old system to the new will provide access from the old electronic mail users to the new electronic mail users (and vice-versa) during the period in which two messaging systems are present in the organization. This is shown in Figure 9-2. Organizations that need to migrate their messaging systems over a period of time generally share these characteristics:

- A large number of workstations that cannot feasibly be converted and tested in a single weekend or timeframe.

- An organizational unit spanning multiple locations in which it would be difficult to migrate all locations at the same time to a homogeneous Exchange environment.

- A major division, workgroup, or business unit that is owned or managed by a different organization, making it difficult to plan or coordinate global resources in a single migration process.

- A portion of the workstations that do not meet Exchange's installation requirement. Until they are upgraded, they will only be able to run the older electronic mail system.

Planning the Migration by Workgroups

When an organization decides to conduct a coexistence multiple step migration process, it needs to select the sequence in which groups or workgroups of users are to be converted from the old messaging system to the new. If it can be assumed that the majority of mail messages occur within a workgroup, maintaining the workgroup in the same messaging environment will minimize the potential for messaging interruption within the workgroup.

In a coexistence migration, the planning of the process and completion of all necessary components in a phased process are critical to a successful

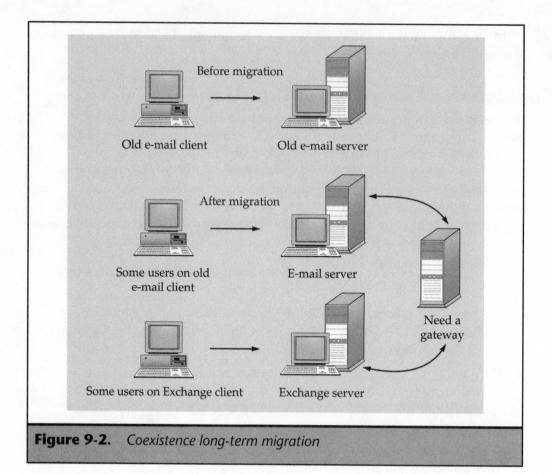

Figure 9-2. *Coexistence long-term migration*

changeover. All aspects of the procedure that can be tested and readied prior to the final changeover should be in order to minimize the amount of work that must be done on the final day.

The procedure includes:

- Installation of the Exchange client software on the workstations
- Installation of the Microsoft Exchange Server
- Prototype testing of the migration of user names, mail messages, and calendars
- Confirmation that all internal gateways meet the functionality necessary to provide a seamless connection between the two messaging environments

- Confirmation that all external gateways migrate successfully (such as to the Internet)

- Testing the prototype Exchange client's access to the Exchange server (including successful conversion of the user's mailbox messages and appointment calendars)

- Workgroup-by-workgroup migration of users over time

Once all of the components have been tested, the group-by-group migration can take place.

Need for Internal and External Gateways

Unlike the single step migration, a coexistence multistep migration from an old messaging environment to a new Microsoft Exchange environment requires internal gateways between the old and new environment so that users can communicate in an organization in which two messaging systems exist. As users within the organization attempt to send internal e-mail messages, they need to know in which messaging system the recipient resides. As users are migrated from the old to the new messaging system, all users within an organization need to be notified of the change in user residence.

Also, during the migration process, the external gateways such as those to the Internet (or possibly gateways to other external electronic mail systems) need to reinstalled and tested.

Migration Tools

The existence of tools to assist the administrator in migrating user names, mailboxes, appointment calendars, and other information from the old to the new messaging system is also extremely important during the migration process. For organizations that are dependent on their electronic mail system for business communications, the need to migrate messages and other electronic mail information is critical. Microsoft provides tools to assist in the migration of this critical information.

Exchange Source Extractor

As described in Chapter 8, the Exchange Source Extractor is an important tool that allows an organization to begin populating its user list for the Microsoft Exchange environment by exporting user names from other electronic messaging systems into Microsoft Exchange. The Exchange Source Extractor retrieves user names (and in many cases group and user access information) from an existing electronic mail system or network operating system and prepares a file that can be imported into Microsoft Windows NT or into Microsoft Exchange to automatically create users in the new messaging environment. The Exchange Source Extractor minimizes the potential for typographical errors as user names are entered into the new messaging system, and, for organizations with a large number of users, it can save dozens if not hundreds of hours of retyping basic user information.

Exchange Migration Wizard

The Microsoft Exchange Migration Wizard, shown in Figure 9-3, is an entirely automated process that provides the Microsoft Exchange administrator with an easy way to extract user names, as well as convert users' mail messages, folders, and appointment schedules, from an existing messaging system, and

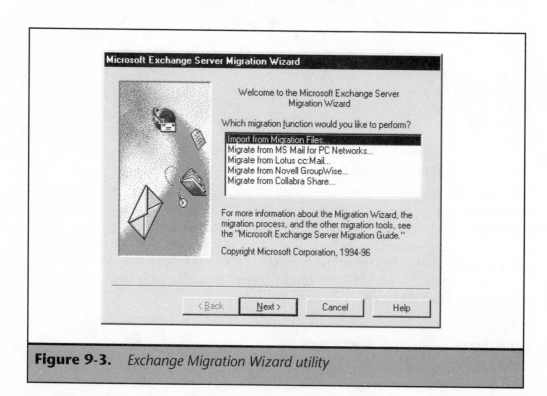

Figure 9-3. *Exchange Migration Wizard utility*

then migrating them into Microsoft Exchange. The Migration Wizard is an invaluable tool for an organization interested in converting to Microsoft Exchange. Users or groups of users can be selected from the organization's user list to be migrated to Microsoft Exchange. By selectively choosing users to migrate, an organization can migrate to Microsoft Exchange as quickly or as slowly as it desires. Through the use of import templates, individual users or groups of users can take on specific Microsoft Exchange characteristics without having to manually reenter information for each individual user.

Connectors or Gateways

During a long-term coexistence migration process, the availability of a gateway or connector from the new to the old electronic messaging system will help provide continuous communication across the two messaging environments until the transition period ends and the entire organization is on Microsoft Exchange. Some organizations may choose to continue to have gateways or connectors installed to support communications and access by users external to their organization.

Directory Synchronization

Also important during a long-term migration process is the ability to keep user address books and user names updated on both the Exchange and the old electronic messaging system. The directory synchronization helps to inform users within an organization where a user resides during the migration period, which can change very quickly: on one day, the user may reside on the old messaging system, and on the next day, the user may reside on the new Microsoft Exchange system. Directory synchronization maintains the user list that keeps track of the mail addresses for users within the organization.

Migrating an Existing Messaging System

Microsoft Exchange provides support for migration from a number of existing electronic mail and network operating environments. The following are the main environments supported for migration and a description of the extent of the migration functionality between the existing messaging system and Microsoft Exchange.

Microsoft Mail

The migration from Microsoft Mail to Microsoft Exchange is a common procedure, because the product line path for Microsoft Mail is the Microsoft Exchange Server product. Microsoft realized that this was going to be the migration path for existing Microsoft Mail users, so the tools available for migration and coexistence are very well developed for Microsoft Mail.

The tools available to migrate from Microsoft Mail to Microsoft Exchange include:

- **Source Extractor** The Source Extractor for Microsoft Mail extracts the user names in Microsoft Mail and populates both Microsoft Windows NT Server as well as the Microsoft Exchange software with core user information.

- **Migration Wizard** The Migration Wizard for Microsoft Mail converts a user's personal mailbox (his or her MMF file) to Microsoft Exchange. This includes all messages and attachments that the user stored in his or her message box, including the inbox and private folders. The Migration Wizard also converts Microsoft Scheduler v1.0 calendars into the Microsoft Exchange Scheduler format.

- **Microsoft Mail Connector** The Microsoft Mail Connector provides seamless communication between a Microsoft Mail post office and a Microsoft Exchange site and organization. The Microsoft Mail Connector may be used in a coexistence slow migration process as an internal gateway, or to communicate from Microsoft Exchange to external clients, vendors, or other business units using Microsoft Mail.

- **Directory Synchronization** Microsoft Exchange provides a DirSync Directory Synchronization program that maintains user name synchronization between Microsoft Mail and Microsoft Exchange. The directory synchronization minimizes the administration that needs to be conducted when updating user lists between multiple messaging environments.

Because of the large numbers of migrations from Microsoft Mail to Microsoft Exchange, a later section of this chapter will be dedicated to defining the migration steps from Microsoft Mail to Microsoft Exchange.

Novell GroupWise

GroupWise is in its second generation of Novell Inc.'s fuliy integrated groupware application environment. Evolved from WordPerfect Office, GroupWise provides electronic mail messaging, personal and group scheduling, discussion groups, and intranet-like information sharing.

Microsoft Exchange Server provides an extractor to collect names from within an existing Novell GroupWise environment to populate a Microsoft Exchange user list. The extractor can be used to create both Microsoft Windows NT user accounts as well as Microsoft Exchange users.

To interconnect a GroupWise messaging system with Microsoft Exchange for internal coexistence communication, the organization would need to select something similar to the X.400 gateway or the SMTP gateway as the common link between the two environments.

Netscape Collabra Share

Netscape Collabra Share is the messaging system and collaborative intranet communication system available from Netscape Communications. Microsoft Exchange Server provides an extractor to collect names from within an existing Netscape Collabra Share environment to populate a Microsoft Exchange user list. The extractor can be used to create both Microsoft Windows NT user accounts as well as Microsoft Exchange users.

To interconnect a Netscape messaging system with Microsoft Exchange for internal coexistence communication, an organization would likely use the SMTP gateway as the common link between the two environments.

UNIX Mail

New to Exchange v5.0, Microsoft provides the migration tools for UNIX mail. The migration tools for UNIX mail takes sendmail account information from a UNIX host and populates a file that can be imported into Microsoft Exchange to create both Microsoft Windows NT user accounts as well as Microsoft Exchange users.

To interconnect a UNIX mail messaging system with Microsoft Exchange for internal coexistence communication, the organization would likely use the SMTP gateway as the common link between the two environments.

IBM Profs

IBM Profs is the electronic messaging system used by millions of IBM mainframe users and is a focus source for Microsoft, who has targeted Profs users for migration to Microsoft Exchange during distributed server migration processes as well as distributed desktop implementation processes.

Microsoft Exchange provides an extractor that retrieves notes, notelogs, calendars, reminders, and address books from Profs/OfficeVision and imports them into Microsoft Exchange.

Additionally, through a third-party vendor, Attachmate Inc., a gateway between a Profs environment and a Microsoft Exchange environment provides inbound and outbound mail message interchange and communications.

DEC All-in-One

DEC All-in-One (DECMail) is the electronic messaging system used by hundreds of thousands of DEC minicomputer users. Microsoft Exchange provides an extractor that retrieves notes and calendar information from All-in-One and imports them into Microsoft Exchange.

As a process to interlink a DEC All-in-One messaging system to Microsoft Exchange, an organization can select either the X.400 route or the SMTP Internet route to provide core communications between the legacy messaging system and Microsoft Exchange.

Verimation Memo

Verimation Memo is a minicomputer-based electronic messaging system that provides full office messaging management including basic mail messaging, personal and group scheduling, and notes and memo pad functionality.

Microsoft Exchange provides an extractor that retrieves notes and calendar information from Verimation Memo and imports them into Microsoft Exchange.

Additionally, through a third-party SNADs gateway, users running Memo, IBM OV/MVS or IBM OV/400 can have a gateway connection between the older messaging system and basic groupware environment and provide inbound and outbound mail message interchange and communications.

Microsoft Mail for AppleTalk Networks

The migration from Microsoft Mail for AppleTalk Networks to Microsoft Exchange is a common procedure for many Macintosh Mail networks.

Although Microsoft Mail for AppleTalk has been sold to Quarterdeck Inc., the tools designed to assist in the migration process from Microsoft Mail for AppleTalk to Microsoft Exchange are excellent.

The tools available to migrate from Microsoft Mail for AppleTalk Networks to Microsoft Exchange include:

■ **Source Extractor** The Source Extractor for Microsoft Mail for AppleTalk Networks extracts the user names from the Macintosh environment and populates both Microsoft Windows NT Server as well as the Microsoft Exchange software with core user information.

■ **Migration Wizard** The Migration Wizard for Microsoft Mail for AppleTalk Networks converts a user's personal mailbox to Microsoft Exchange. This includes all messages and attachments that the user has stored in his or her message box including the inbox and private folders.

■ **Microsoft Mail for AppleTalk Network Connector** The Microsoft Mail for AppleTalk Network Connector provides seamless communication between the Macintosh mail system post office and a Microsoft Exchange site and organization. The Microsoft Mail for AppleTalk Network Connector may be used in a coexistence slow migration process as an internal gateway, or the Connector may be used to communicate from Microsoft Exchange to external clients, vendors, or other business units using Microsoft Mail for AppleTalk.

■ **Directory Synchronization** Microsoft Exchange provides a Directory Synchronization program that maintains user name synchronization between the Microsoft Mail for AppleTalk users and the new messaging system. The Directory Synchronization minimizes the administration that needs to be conducted in updating user lists between multiple messaging environments.

Migrating from Microsoft Mail to Microsoft Exchange

Because Microsoft Mail has a large installation base and is the predecessor to Microsoft Exchange, the tools available to migrate from Microsoft Mail to Microsoft Exchange are quite extensive. The following section details the migration process from Microsoft Mail to Microsoft Exchange, and summarizes how the two environments are structurally configured, how they interconnect, and how an organization would migrate from Microsoft Mail to Microsoft Exchange.

Understanding How MS Mail and Microsoft Exchange Work Together

To better understand how to migrate from Microsoft Mail to Microsoft Exchange, a brief understanding of the infrastructure backgrounds of both environments is helpful. The various components, including the client, the server, and internal and external gateways make up the core components of the messaging systems.

An MS Mail Environment

For Microsoft Mail, the electronic messaging system includes the basic components of the client software and a Microsoft Mail file server. Some organizations also elected to purchase the Microsoft Scheduler add-on for personal and group scheduling. An organization with multiple Microsoft Mail post offices of users would typically have an External Gateway—more technically known as a Microsoft Message Transfer Agent (MTA)—to route messages from one post office to another. The external gateway manages the sending and receiving of mail messages, acts as the component that distributes appointment schedules across multiple post offices, and also manages the directory synchronization of user address lists across the post offices. A Microsoft Mail environment is shown in Figure 9-4.

As a Microsoft Mail organization needs to communicate externally from the post office, gateways are purchased to manage inbound and outbound communications with the Internet, for faxes, for MCI Mail, for ATT mail, for MHS mail, for SNADs mail, or to an X.400 messaging network. In most cases, these external gateways are standalone systems with separate connections from the Microsoft Mail Server to the external messaging source.

MICROSOFT MAIL CLIENT   Microsoft Mail has a variety of client software programs available including DOS, Windows, and Macintosh. The Microsoft Mail client software programs access the Microsoft Mail "maildata" information on the file server to gain access to messages and attachments. For the Microsoft Windows version, the user's mailbox information is converted from text-based messages and attachments and stored in a Mail Message File

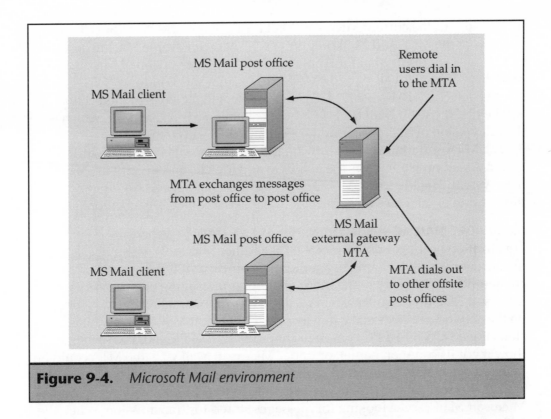

Figure 9-4. *Microsoft Mail environment*

(MMF). The user's MMF has a copy of all of the user's mail messages and attachments for messages in his or her inbox as well as messages stored in private message folders. Some organizations centralize their MMF files on a network file server, and some choose to store their MMF files on the local hard drives of the user's workstation.

An MMF file grows as users open and read messages and store them in their private folders. However, MMF files never shrink in size or automatically reoptimize how the information space in the MMF is managed, so optimizing and managing MMF files will be an issue that will be discussed in the migration steps outlined later in this section.

MICROSOFT MAIL SERVER   The Microsoft Mail Server is similar to a database application that stores information and manages the messages and attachments so that users can access the information from their client software. There are a number of versions of the Microsoft Mail Server, which vary from the versions of the current Microsoft Mail for PC Networks (version 3.5) to versions of the Microsoft Mail program exclusively for Apple Macintosh computers (Microsoft Mail for AppleTalk), as well as a version of Microsoft Mail that comes with all Windows for Workgroups and Windows NT Servers. The versions of the Microsoft Mail program we will focus on in this section will be the Microsoft Mail for PC Networks version 3.0, 3.2, and 3.5, which is the full version of Microsoft Mail for PC Networks software.

The Microsoft Mail Server software is typically installed on a network file server. An administrator has the ability to add, delete, and modify users in the mail system. The Microsoft Mail Server software manages the receipt and distribution of mail messages internal and external to the organization.

MICROSOFT MAIL MESSAGE TRANSFER AGENT (MTA) When an organization needs to communicate with another Microsoft group of electronic mail users typically residing in another post office, or if it needs to communicate externally to the Internet or other messaging environments, a Microsoft Mail Message Transfer Agent (MTA), or external gateway, is set up on the network. An external gateway under Microsoft Mail v3.0 or v3.2 is a standalone DOS-based PC computer that runs an EXTERNAL.EXE program (how it got its common name), or under Microsoft Mail v3.5, the MTA could be integrated as a service under Microsoft Windows NT.

The external gateway looks at the queues in the maildata directories of the Microsoft Mail Server, looking for messages stored for transmission. When the MTA finds a file, it processes the message, either sending it to another post office or another mail system. This process is shown in Figure 9-5.

MS Mail Directory Synchronization

As organizations communicate with other Microsoft Mail post offices, the need to update user lists becomes important, because users need to view the mail users in the address list in order to select the proper recipient of their mail messages. Many organizations that work with multiple post offices are now accustomed to exporting the user list to other post offices anytime a change is made to it. This is commonly done by selecting the export user list from the Microsoft Mail ADMIN.EXE program.

Although this manual method of user name distribution is extremely functional, the way Microsoft Exchange updates user changes from Microsoft Mail to Exchange, and vice-versa, is through the use of the Microsoft Directory Synchronization (DirSync) program. Even if a Microsoft Mail administrator

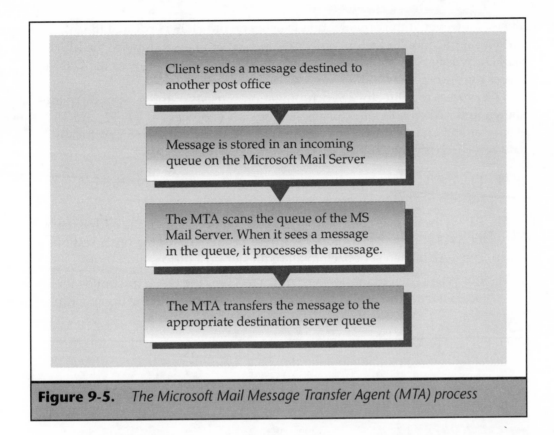

Client sends a message destined to another post office

Message is stored in an incoming queue on the Microsoft Mail Server

The MTA scans the queue of the MS Mail Server. When it sees a message in the queue, it processes the message.

The MTA transfers the message to the appropriate destination server queue

Figure 9-5.   *The Microsoft Mail Message Transfer Agent (MTA) process*

attempts to export the MS Mail user list to a Microsoft Exchange network, the new user list will not be updated in Exchange. The formal DirSync process needs to be in place to automatically update user names and lists between a Microsoft Mail and a Microsoft Exchange system.

DIRECTORY SYNCHRONIZATION SERVER AND REQUESTER   The process of Directory Synchronization between Microsoft Mail and Microsoft Exchange requires one Microsoft Directory Synchronization Server and one or more Microsoft Directory Synchronization Requesters. Most organizations that are already using Microsoft Mail Directory Synchronization already have a DirSync Server and at least one DirSync Requester. If the Directory Synchronization process is working fine, the organization can easily configure the Microsoft Exchange Server as an additional DirSync Requester and begin participating in Directory Synchronization with the other Microsoft Mail post offices. However, if the organization is using an old DOS version of the DirSync application in an MS Mail environment or plans to replace the MS Mail DirSync Server, the Microsoft Exchange Server can operate as the DirSync Server for the organization.

The process for Directory Synchronization consists of three separate phases known in the Microsoft Directory Synchronization process as T1, T2, and T3 events, as shown in Figure 9-6. These timed events exchange mail addresses between Directory Synchronization Servers:

- **T1**   The T1 event has all requester post offices send their post office address list to the DirSync Server.

- **T2**   In the T2 event, the DirSync Server compiles all of the addresses it receives and creates a Global Address List (GAL) for the organization. The GAL is then sent back to all requester post offices.

- **T3**   When each requester post office receives the GAL, it rebuilds its local Global Address List to update the list of users in the organization.

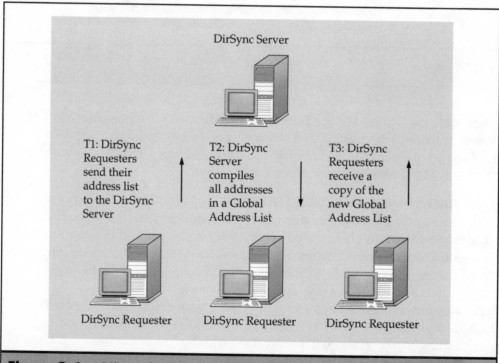

Figure 9-6.   *Microsoft Directory Synchronization process*

Microsoft Mail Remote Client

In Microsoft Mail, remote mail clients use a separate mail program than local mail clients. The remote mail client software comes in two versions, one supporting remote Windows users and the other supporting remote DOS users. Most organizations use the Windows version of the software, which will be detailed in this section.

MICROSOFT MAIL REMOTE FOR WINDOWS CLIENT   The Microsoft Mail Remote for Windows software allows a remote mail user to dial into the Microsoft Mail network to send and retrieve mail messages. The Remote Mail for Windows program stores mail messages in an MMF similar to the way a local MS Mail user stores his or her files in an MMF when they are attached to the network. The Remote Mail program supports a store and forward messaging process in which a user can create messages and queue them up as the messages are created. When the user is done writing messages, he or she can connect to the network and send any stored messages as well as automatically retrieve messages from the MS Mail Server stored for his or her receipt. This store and forward messaging in Microsoft Mail is a proprietary format process that is not supported by Microsoft Exchange Server and will need to be addressed during the migration process.

DIALING IN TO THE EXTERNAL GATEWAY   The remote mail user in Microsoft Mail dials in to the same external gateway that is used to process internal mail messages between post offices as well as sends messages to other post offices over a dial-up asynchronous connection. The external gateway just needs a modem connected to it and remote users can dial in to the external gateway as their point of connection for message transport. An organization can have multiple external gateways servicing a number of remote messaging users.

An Integrated MS Mail/Exchange Environment

In an integrated Microsoft Mail and Microsoft Exchange environment, the various components of the Microsoft Mail system need to be connected to the Microsoft Exchange environment. This includes not only the sending and receiving of electronic mail messages between the two application environments, but also synchronizing address lists between the two systems as well as providing remote access support for remote users.

Within Microsoft Exchange, the Exchange server has a Microsoft Mail Connector that comes free with the Microsoft Exchange Server software. The Microsoft Mail Connector includes multiple components, shown in Figure 9-7,

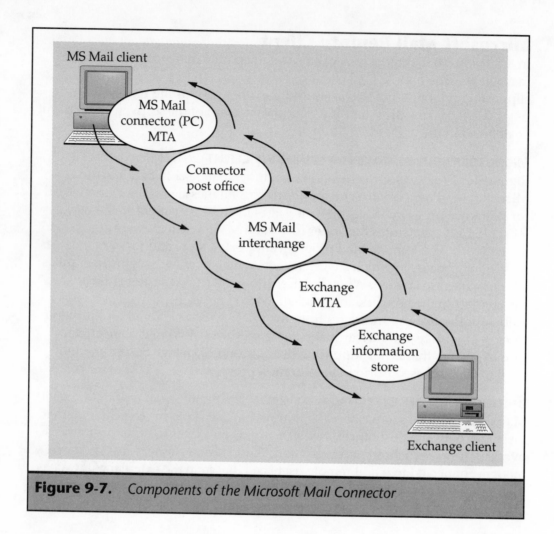

Figure 9-7. *Components of the Microsoft Mail Connector*

that facilitate message transfer between the Microsoft Mail and Microsoft Exchange systems. The components include:

■ **The Microsoft Mail Connector Message Transfer Agent for PC Networks (MTA)** The MTA is similar to the Microsoft Mail external gateway that routes messages between Microsoft Mail post offices. On a Microsoft Exchange Server, the MTA Connector additionally routes messages between the Microsoft Mail post offices, the Connector post office, and the Microsoft Exchange Server.

- **The Connector Post Office**   The Connector post office manages the file structure used to store messages between the Exchange server, Microsoft Mail, and message gateways.

- **The Microsoft Mail Interchange**   The Microsoft Mail Interchange translates and then transfers messages stored in the Connector post office to the Microsoft Exchange Server and vice-versa.

EXCHANGE AS THE MTA   The Microsoft Exchange Server can act as the Message Transfer Agent (external gateway) for the Microsoft Mail environment. If an organization has multiple post offices managed by a Microsoft Mail external gateway to route messages between them, after one of the post offices migrates to Microsoft Exchange, the Exchange server can run the Microsoft Mail Connector Message Transfer Agent for PC networks to provide the functionality of an external gateway for message routing. As a service within the Microsoft Windows NT environment, the Connector MTA can better maintain and manage message interchange within Exchange.

EXCHANGE AS THE DirSync SERVER OR REQUESTER   An additional NT service available in Exchange is the Microsoft Exchange Directory Synchronization Agent (DXA). The DXA can be configured as a DirSync Server or as a DirSync Requester. The Exchange Server can manage all directory synchronization of a Microsoft Mail as well as a Microsoft Exchange Server.

Conducting the MS Mail to Exchange Migration

A number of steps are necessary to complete the migration from Microsoft Mail to Microsoft Exchange. Careful attention to not only the procedural steps but also the completion sequence of the steps is crucial in determining whether the migration will be simply completed, or completed successfully. Delays in the migration process can often be attributed to failure to complete a portion of a sequence in the correct order, which means going back and redoing that step.

Verifying the Domain, Organization, Sites, and Servers

As outlined in Chapter 4, the Microsoft Windows NT domain design, organization and site structure, and server placement are extremely important when determining the infrastructure of the Exchange environment. Since the Windows NT domain design dictates the user access and administrator management of the Exchange environment, creating the appropriate domain structure before the installation of the first Microsoft Exchange Server is very important. And since the Exchange organization and site information cannot be modified once it is installed without complete reinstallation of the Exchange software, it is wise to be absolutely certain that the server, site, and organizational characteristics of the organization are properly designed before implementation.

Verifying DirSync Is Operational

If an organization needs to synchronize user names between the Microsoft Exchange Server and Microsoft Mail post offices, and since the manual Admin | Export option in the Microsoft Mail ADMIN.EXE program for distributing user names does not work within the Microsoft Exchange environment, it should set up the directory synchronization process. Since DirSync acts as the same function for the Microsoft Mail and the Microsoft Exchange connection to Microsoft Mail, setting up and successfully conducting DirSync should be completed before the Microsoft Exchange environment is deployed.

For an organization with no experience of DirSync, setting up the DirSync Servers and the DirSync Requesters and confirming that the user information is properly synchronized between the various post offices within the organization can be a full day's worth of work.

Planning and Preparing for Internal and External Gateway Communications

Since an organization would want to maintain internal and external electronic messaging communications with others, there is a definite need during the migration process to ensure that gateways between the various environments are operational. The gateways are not necessarily difficult to set up and install, but it can be quite hard to understand how the gateways will share the load of traffic between the Microsoft Mail and the Microsoft Exchange systems, decide which external gateway will manage Internet or fax traffic (in a gateway consolidation), and determine whether all of the information that is expected to transfer from one environment to the other is actually transferring across the gateway (such as rich text fonts, graphics, and attachments).

USING THE EXCHANGE MTA FOR INTERNAL MESSAGE ROUTING   The Microsoft Exchange MTA can be used to manage Microsoft Mail external gateway functions such as post office-to-post office message routing as well as directory synchronization tasks. Just as all of the message routing, downstream post office route designations, or Async modem dial-out functions of the Microsoft Mail external gateway are handled by the normal Microsoft Mail external gateway, the same functions can be configured in the administration functions of the Microsoft Mail Connector MTA configuration options as shown in Figure 9-8.

MIGRATING EXTERNAL GATEWAYS   In many cases, gateways can be or may need to be redundant for both the Microsoft Mail and the Microsoft Exchange environments. In some cases, a fax gateway that works for Microsoft Mail users may not work for Microsoft Exchange users. When an organization has both operating environments, the need for two fax gateways may be necessary. How the organization will manage the inbound routing of faxes to one versus

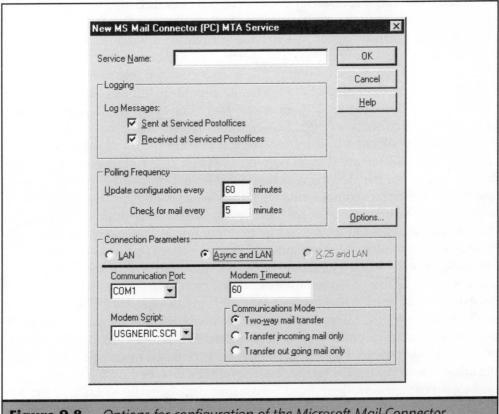

Figure 9-8.   *Options for configuration of the Microsoft Mail Connector*

the other fax gateway and then to the user, needs to be planned and prepared. For other gateways, such as an Internet connection, the organization may elect to consolidate, so that there is only one gateway for both the Microsoft Mail and the Microsoft Exchange environment. During a gateway consolidation, incoming and outgoing routes from within the message administration programs need to be modified to select the destination gateway where messages should be sent or retrieved by the messaging programs. In this scenario, Microsoft Mail uses the concept of a "downstream post office" that manages gateway functions and resides on a different Microsoft Mail post office. In the case of integrating Microsoft Exchange with a Microsoft Mail post office, the Exchange server will be a downstream post office of the Microsoft Mail network with the Microsoft Exchange Internet Connector managing all inbound and outbound SMTP Internet traffic. This process is shown in Figure 9-9.

Installing the Exchange Client Software

Once the infrastructure components of an Exchange migration have been designed, planned, and tested, the Exchange client components can be installed. Although many organizations have already begun to install the Exchange client before any planning has been conducted, the need to prepare and plan for the installation of the Exchange client is extremely important.

As described in Chapter 2, there are two separate client software programs available for Microsoft Exchange Server, the Exchange client and the Outlook client. The Outlook client is a more current version of the client software with some added functionality that an organization may want. However, because it does not allow for the viewing of schedules with the standard Exchange client, and some of its server components are either incompatible or inoperational with the standard Exchange client (such as message voting or 32-bit forms), the limitations of the Outlook client in an integrated environment that may have a need to implement the standard Exchange client (for DOS users, Macintosh users, Windows v3.x users, or other users for which the Outlook client is not available) need to be assessed prior to deployment.

Additionally, the Exchange client that comes with Windows 95 is incompatible with the Microsoft Exchange Server software. Because there were dozens of updates from the time that Windows 95 was released in the summer of 1995 and the time that Exchange was initially released in the spring of 1996, the latest version of the Exchange client should be installed on the users' desktops. Furthermore, there have been a number of interim releases of the Exchange client included with each revision release of Exchange, so the version of the Exchange client that is installed on the users' workstations

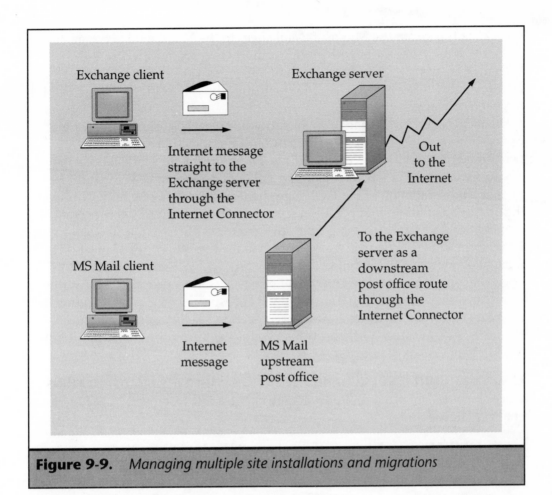

Figure 9-9. *Managing multiple site installations and migrations*

should be the version of the Exchange client that came with the Microsoft Exchange Server software that is being installed.

USING THE EXCHANGE CLIENT WITH MICROSOFT MAIL   During installation of the Exchange client for Microsoft Mail use, because the client software takes 15-20 minutes per workstation on average, installation of the Exchange client for a workgroup of 100 users can take up to an entire week. Depending on the size of the organization's workgroup, it may elect to install the Microsoft Exchange client on all workstations and use the Exchange client while accessing the Microsoft Mail Server.

The Microsoft Exchange client software has support for the installation, access, and use of both a Microsoft Mail post office as well as a Microsoft Exchange Server. In many cases, organizations take this opportunity to convert users over time from the Microsoft Mail client to the Microsoft Exchange client software. It provides users with an opportunity to learn how to use the Exchange client to send and receive mail messages, thus minimizing the learning curve necessary to train the users after the Microsoft Exchange Server has been converted.

Installation of the Exchange client software on each workstation over a period of time can also help to spread out installations that need to be performed on troublesome workstations. These "problem" workstations may have a variety of deficiencies, including not enough disk space or insufficient memory, or installation of the Exchange client software may negatively impact the operation of another application software. Additionally, if the clients' workstations are not only being upgraded from the Microsoft Mail client to the Microsoft Exchange client, but also from Windows to Windows 95, users will most likely need additional time to become familiar with their new desktop operating environment. The fewer new things a user needs to learn all at the same time, the smoother the transition will be, especially for an application as mission-critical for the users and the organization as electronic messaging. Figure 9-10 shows how a Microsoft Exchange client program can support both MS Mail and MS Exchange Server access.

EFFECTS OF USING THE EXCHANGE CLIENT ON OTHER MS MAIL FUNCTIONS

Once a user is converted to the Exchange client, a few Microsoft Mail functions change. They include:

- **MMF Message File is converted to a PST file**   During the conversion from Microsoft Mail to the Microsoft Exchange client, the user's Mail Message File (MMF) is converted to an Exchange Personal Message Store (PST). The conversion process retains all user inbox messages as well as private folders and folder messages so that functionally the user will use the Exchange client just as if it was an MS Mail client (but with a new user interface). A conversion of the message file to the PST means that a user cannot easily switch back to the Microsoft Mail client software. The MMF to PST conversion is essentially a one-way conversion process. If a user switches back to the Microsoft Mail client, he or she will begin using an MMF file again; however, this time the MMF file will be empty (since all messages transferred to the PST file). If the user sends and receives messages while in the Microsoft Mail software program, the new messages will again begin to populate the MMF file. When the user returns to the Exchange client, any messages sent or received by the user while he or she was in the Microsoft Mail client will not automatically be populated into the Exchange client. Migrating a user to the Exchange client should be a one-time process, and the user should not be able to return to the older Microsoft Mail client software.

■ **User defaults to the Scheduler v7.5 schedule function, not the older Scheduler v1.0** Because installation of the Microsoft Exchange client software also installs the latest Microsoft Exchange Scheduler software program, when the user receives an appointment scheduling request, the Microsoft Exchange client software will automatically populate the Scheduler v7.5 scheduler, not the user's Scheduler v1.0 schedule. A user may elect to continue to use Scheduler v1.0 while using the Exchange client to maintain compatibility with full schedule viewing access with older Microsoft Mail/Scheduler v1.0 users. (As noted in Chapter 3, Scheduler v1.0 and Scheduler v7.5 users can see only free and busy times on each others' schedules, but the function of viewing appointments or making appointments across the two different versions of the Scheduler software is no longer possible.)

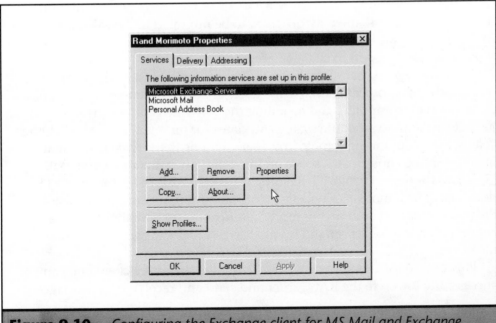

Figure 9-10.   *Configuring the Exchange client for MS Mail and Exchange access*

Configuring a RAS Server for Remote Mail Users

The implementation of Microsoft Remote Access Server (RAS) as the remote access system for mail users is required for users that will be converting from Microsoft Mail to Microsoft Exchange prior to the conversion to Microsoft Exchange Server, as well as for all users accessing Microsoft Mail remotely, since the Exchange server does not support the older Microsoft Mail Remote client software.

During an Exchange migration, because the Microsoft Exchange Server store for user messages and message management is different for the Microsoft Mail environment (as described earlier in this chapter about the effects of using the Exchange client in an MS Mail environment), once a user converts to Microsoft Exchange as his or her client software (even if he or she is using Microsoft Mail Server as a messaging system), the user needs to begin using RAS for remote access to messaging rather than the Microsoft Mail Remote for Windows application to the MS Mail external gateway. The client software version used in the office needs to be the same client software used remotely, and a user who converts to the Microsoft Exchange client software is now using a PST file for message storage. When that user accesses the network remotely, he or she also needs to be using a PST during the remote connection.

Additionally, because the Microsoft Mail Remote for Windows remote mail software does not support access to a Microsoft Exchange Server, all users remotely dialing in to the network need to be migrated to the Microsoft Exchange client and use RAS for their remote mail access prior to the conversion to Microsoft Exchange Server.

The remote mail user migrations are typically the most challenging aspect of the conversion process because the users are by definition remote users, and accessing their computers and installing the software is time-consuming. It can be quite difficult to schedule systems updates for remote users as well. Other challenges in upgrading remote user workstations to the Exchange client include having enough disk space on the remote system (about 40-60MB [35-40MB for the Exchange client software, plus 10-20MB for the user's PST data file]). The remote user will also require training regarding the basics of the new messaging system, but more significantly, on how to establish a connection to a RAS Server and invoke the sending and receiving of mail messages.

However, once all remote users are using the Exchange client and can successfully log on to the RAS Server and send and receive mail messages with Microsoft Mail, when the organization finally switches to Microsoft Exchange, the most difficult stage of configuring the core workstation software and end user training will already be completed.

Exchange Migration Wizard

Once all of the infrastructure functions of the NT Server, Microsoft Exchange Server, desktop clients, remote clients, and internal and external gateways have been configured and tested, the final procedure involves conducting the migration from Microsoft Mail to Exchange.

It is typically suggested that the migration process be tested in a prototype prior to a live migration. The advantages of prototype testing on the migration process include:

- Ability to test all user mailboxes to make sure they converted properly

- Ability to test any gateways or sending and receiving of electronic messages across platforms

- Ability to sample workstation changeovers from MS Mail to Exchange

- Ability to time the migration process to make sure enough time is allocated to convert the server as well as switch designated users from Microsoft Mail to Exchange in the time allotted

EXTRACTING AND MIGRATING USERS   During the Microsoft Mail to Microsoft Exchange migration process, the Migration Wizard will walk the administrator through the conversion. The administrator will be prompted to specify the Microsoft Mail post office that is designated for migration and the destination Exchange server that will be the recipient of the new users. The Migration Wizard will extract user names from the Microsoft Mail post office and migrate the user names to the Exchange server.

During the migration process, the Exchange Migration Wizard will convert users' MMF files to an Exchange client message format on the Exchange server for those users who did not migrate their MMF file to an Exchange client file. During the server conversion of the MMF file, no new file is created. Since the Exchange server software is a client/server database, messages in users' MMF files are imported into the Exchange server message store. During the migration process of the MMF files, if a user has a corrupt message file, the Migration Wizard will recognize it as a corrupted file, skip the migration of the user configuration, log the error, and continue on with the rest of the message files for conversion. In order for the completion of the conversion of that specific user message file, maintenance will need to be done on the MMF file. To fix a corrupted MMF file, the following process can be followed:

1. Identify the corrupt MMF file from the logs of the Migration Wizard.

2. Identify the user to whom the MMF file belongs by running the LISTUSER.EXE utility, which is a shareware utility available on the Microsoft home page (http://www.microsoft.com), on CompuServe, or on the Microsoft TechNet support CD-ROM.

3. Have the user to whom the MMF file belongs launch the Microsoft Mail program; however, when the user presses the ENTER key after typing in his or her user name and password to open the Microsoft Mail program, hold down the right SHIFT key until a screen shows up asking if you want to conduct maintenance on the message file. Select OK to clean up the corrupt message file. This process may take five minutes to over an hour, depending on how large the user's MMF message file is. Another option that can be used by administrators is the DBFIX utility, available on Microsoft's TechNet, which is a DOS command line MMF file maintenance utility.

4. Once the corrupt message file has been cleaned up, the administrator can rerun the Migration Wizard and only select the user who had the corrupt message file. This will complete the migration for that particular user.

What the administrator will come to realize during this test migration process is how long it will take to migrate users. In addition, it will allow the administrator to identify corrupt message files prior to a live migration so that users can have a chance to clean up their message files. If during a live migration a number of message files are corrupt and need to be fixed before they get converted, the live migration may be stalled and need to be canceled until a more successful, problem-free migration can take place. If the administrator can identify corrupt message files before the live migration process, it can minimize the number of errors during the migration process.

The migration process from an MMF to the Exchange server store requires that the user's MMF file resides on the Microsoft Mail Server for the Exchange Migration Wizard to find the file to complete the migration. Many organizations request that their users save their MMF files to local hard drives. If a user's MMF file resides on his or her local hard drive, the administrator needs to have the MMF files moved to a central location on the Microsoft Mail Server for automatic file conversion.

In addition, during the test migration process, the administrator may be able to identify users with thousands if not tens of thousands of messages saved, and prior to a live migration, he or she may be able to convince users to do some housekeeping of their mail messages to decrease the number of messages stored, and thus decrease the time that it takes for the Migration Wizard to convert the user from Microsoft Mail to Microsoft Exchange.

MIGRATING USERS WHO ALREADY HAVE PSTs   Microsoft Mail users who are already using the Microsoft Exchange client will have already converted their MMF file to a PST file, thus the Migration Wizard process needs only to copy the user name information and basic security information from Microsoft Mail to Microsoft Exchange. This can drastically minimize the amount of time it will take for the administrator of the network to run through a complete Migration Wizard process.

Once the Migration Wizard has completed the migration of users from Microsoft Mail to Microsoft Exchange, the Microsoft Exchange client user workstations need to be changed from the Microsoft Mail service to the Microsoft Exchange service. The services are controlled by the Mail and Fax utility (typically run by running CONTROL MLCFG32.CPL), which shows the services the client software has access to. When the user's service is changed from Microsoft Mail to Microsoft Exchange, the next time the user logs into Microsoft Exchange, he or she will have access to the Exchange server message store.

If users converted their inbox and personal folders to the Exchange client, they will have both an Exchange server personal message store as well as an Exchange PST message store, which are two separate message stores. It is recommended that users move their messages from their PST to the Exchange server message store. Messages that reside in the PST are only stored in the PST. If the PST file gets corrupted or if the user dials in remotely to the network and does not have access to the PST file, the messages are not available to the user. If the user's messages are transferred to the Exchange server store, the messages are securely stored on the Exchange server and are accessible from either a LAN network connection or from a Remote network connection.

CONVERSION OF THE USER'S PERSONAL ADDRESS BOOK   Part of the Migration Wizard process is the conversion of the user's Personal Address Book (PAB). The personal address in Microsoft Mail is converted to the user's

Personal Address Book in Microsoft Exchange. The migration process will send the user an electronic mail message, providing him or her with an attachment that includes the old Personal Address Book with instructions on how to import this address book into the new Microsoft Exchange client software. The process involves saving the attachment that includes the personal address book and running the Exchange client address book import function.

Completing a Live Migration

Once a pilot test migration has been completed and the administrator has been able to identify corrupt MMF files, knows how long it will take to migrate from Microsoft Mail to Exchange, tests the gateways, and tests a handful of client systems, then the organization can complete a full migration from Microsoft Mail to Microsoft Exchange.

Debugging Problems in the Migration

Some of the common problems after a migration include the following:

- **Replying to MS Mail Messages after the conversion to Exchange** When users are converted from Microsoft Mail to Microsoft Exchange, all of the mail messages in their inbox and personal message folders are also converted. If a user replies to a message, he or she will probably receive an error message after they send the message. The message is commonly one that refers to a "transport error." This message occurs because the reply to the message is attempting to route the message back through the old Microsoft Mail system. Because the user is now on Microsoft Exchange, he or she needs to create a new route for that message to travel for a return response. Instead of selecting "reply" to the message and using the existing name on the reply, the user should change the name on the reply and select the new name of the intended recipient from the new address list. This will select the user from the Microsoft Exchange user list and provide a new route back to the original of the message.

- **Old addresses in Personal Address Books** Another problem similar to the reply to function occurs when users select an e-mail address from their old Personal Address Book. By default, the Microsoft Exchange client software sets the user's personal address list before the Microsoft Exchange address list. If the user types in the name of the recipient in the To: or Cc: section, when he or she sends the message, the Exchange client will pull the recipient's address from the user's personal address list. It is likely that the user's Personal Address Book contains the old Microsoft Mail addresses for users on the network, not Microsoft Exchange addresses. Thus, the user will get a "transport error" again when sending the message. This can be minimized if users specifically go into the Global Address List or Exchange server recipients list to pull names for messages they wish to send. Or, the users can go into their Exchange client software, select Tools | Options | Addressing and move the Personal Address Book below the global address book in the order in which the Microsoft Exchange client pulls user names. By selecting from the Global Address List first, the user's name will be pulled from the current Microsoft Exchange user list rather than from an old user name list.

Migrating from Lotus cc:Mail to Microsoft Exchange

Lotus cc:Mail is the next most popular electronic messaging system from which users migrate to Microsoft Exchange. The tools, gateways, connectors, and directory synchronization utilities for a cc:Mail migration are very sophisticated for helping to integrate cc:Mail post offices into a Microsoft Exchange environment.

Because Lotus cc:Mail has a large installation base, the tools available to migrate from Lotus cc:Mail to Microsoft Exchange are quite extensive. The following section details the migration process from Lotus cc:Mail to Microsoft Exchange including a summary of how the two environments are structurally configured, how they interconnect, and how an organization would migrate from Lotus cc:Mail to Microsoft Exchange.

Understanding How cc:Mail and Microsoft Exchange Work Together

To better understand how to migrate from Lotus cc:Mail to Microsoft Exchange, an introduction of the infrastructure backgrounds of both environments is helpful. The various components such as the client, server, routers, and external gateways make up the core components of the messaging systems.

A Lotus cc:Mail Environment

For cc:Mail, the electronic messaging system includes the basic components of a client software, and a cc:Mail file server. Some organizations may have elected to purchase Lotus Organizer, the add-on for personal and group scheduling. For an organization that has multiple Lotus cc:Mail post offices of users, the organization typically has a "Router Gateway," or more technically known as a cc:Mail router, to route messages from one post office to another. The router not only manages the sending and receiving of mail messages, it also is the component that distributes appointment schedules across multiple post offices, as well as managing the directory synchronization of user address lists across the post offices. A sample Lotus cc:Mail environment is shown in Figure 9-11.

Because a cc:Mail organization may require you to communicate externally from the home post office, links and servers are purchased to manage inbound and outbound communications for faxes, MCI Mail, UUCP mail, and MHS mail, and with the Internet and a Lotus Notes messaging network. In most cases, these external links or gateways are standalone systems with separate connections to both the cc:Mail home post office and the external messaging source.

LOTUS cc:MAIL CLIENT Lotus cc:Mail has a variety of client software programs available for DOS, Windows, OS/2, World Wide Web, Mobile, and Macintosh. The Lotus cc:Mail client software programs access the cc:Mail post office information on the file server to gain access to messages and attachments.

LOTUS cc:MAIL SERVER The Lotus cc:Mail Server is similar to a database application that stores information and manages the messages and attachments for users to access the information from their client software. There are a number of versions currently in use of the Lotus cc:Mail Server, varying in difference from the current Lotus cc:Mail (release 6) to Lotus cc:Mail (release 3). The version of Lotus cc:Mail program we will focus on during this section will be Lotus cc:Mail release 6.1, which includes Lotus Organizer.

The cc:Mail Server software typically is installed on a network file server. An administrator has the ability of adding, deleting, and modifying users in the mail system. The Lotus cc:Mail Server software manages the receipt and distribution of mail messages that are internal and external to the organizations.

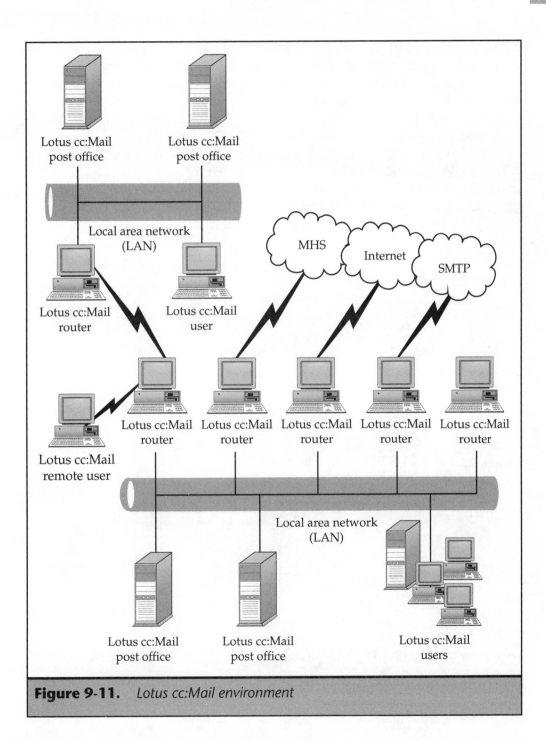

Figure 9-11. *Lotus cc:Mail environment*

LOTUS cc:MAIL ROUTER When an organization requires communications with another group of electronic mail users typically residing in another post office, or if the organization wants to exchange messages with other messaging environments, a Lotus cc:Mail router messaging exchange configuration, or router, is set up on the network. A router under Lotus cc:Mail is a standalone DOS-based or OS/2 PC computer that runs the ROUTER program.

There are two main Lotus cc:Mail router connections, Type 1 and Type 2. A Type 1 connection, shown in Figure 9-12, consists of a single router that transmits messages between cc:Mail post offices, where the respective data directories are mapped directly by the router. A Type 2 connection, shown in Figure 9-13, consists of a router on each of the cc:Mail post offices that sends messages to the router on the opposite side of the connection, which can be

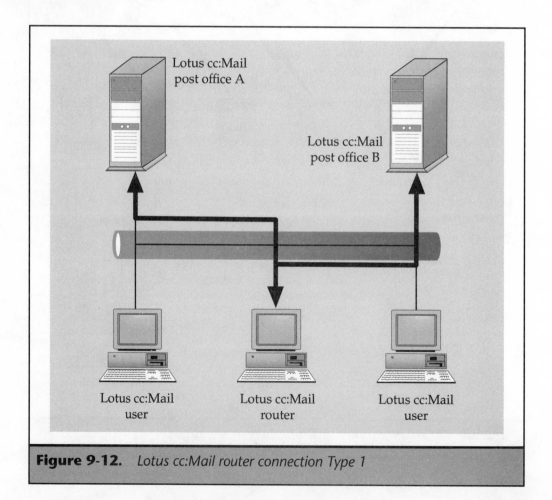

Figure 9-12. *Lotus cc:Mail router connection Type 1*

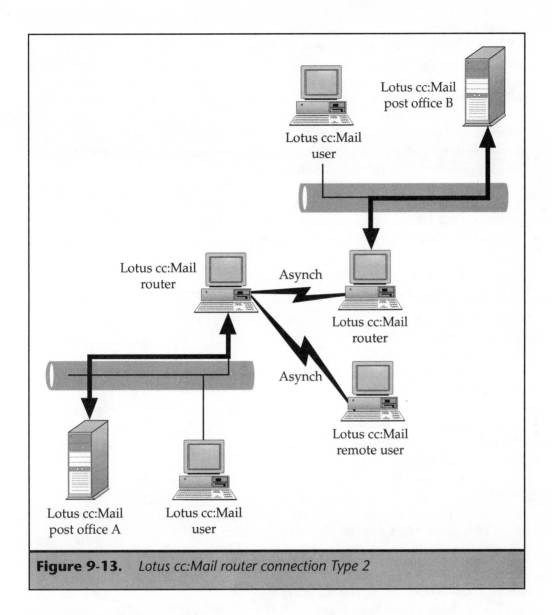

Figure 9-13. *Lotus cc:Mail router connection Type 2*

dial-up or WAN. Type 2 router connections support a variety of transport protocols but would require a separate router session for each of the protocols needed.

The external gateway looks at the queues in the CCDATA directories of the cc:Mail Server, searching for messages stored for transmission. When the router finds a file, it processes the message, sending it to either another post office or another mail system.

Lotus cc:Mail Directory Synchronization

As organizations communicate with other Lotus cc:Mail post offices, a need to update user lists becomes important so that users can see mail users in the address list and select the recipient to send a message to. Many organizations that work with few post offices have gotten used to simply synchronizing the directories manually by exporting the user list to other post offices anytime a change is made to the user list. This can be time-consuming, as the entire directory is sent to the other post office.

While this manual method of user name distribution is functional, the way Microsoft Exchange updates user changes from Lotus cc:Mail to Microsoft Exchange, and vice versa, is through the use of the Automatic Directory Exchange (ADE). The ADE allows the incremental directory updates to be propagated to the participating post offices automatically, rather than requiring the administrator to manually send them. This also reduces the volume of traffic generated by the full synchronization.

ADE RELATIONSHIPS   The ADE relationship refers to the type of directory information two post offices will exchange with each other. Which relationship is chosen depends on whether centralized or distributed control of directory information is needed. With centralized control, one post office has the master directory and sends updates out to all other post offices. With distributed control, the sending and receiving post offices compile their own directories. Centralized directory control is a good choice for cc:Mail systems that are managed from a single post office, whereas distributed directory control is a better choice for locally managed cc:Mail systems.

The predefined ADE relationships are Superior-Subordinate, Broadcaster-Broadcaster, Division-Division, Enterprise-Enterprise, and Peer-Peer. The Superior-Subordinate is the only centralized relationship. It is important to note that a single cc:Mail post office can have different types of relationships with different post offices.

Lotus cc:Mail Mobile Client

In Lotus cc:Mail, remote and local mail clients use separate mail programs. Lotus cc:Mail Mobile supports DOS, Windows, and Mac clients. Most organizations use the Windows version of the software, so that version will be detailed in this section.

LOTUS cc:MAIL MOBILE   The Lotus cc:Mail Mobile software allows a remote mail user to dial in to the Lotus cc:Mail messaging system to send and retrieve mail messages. The Mobile Mail program stores mail messages locally and supports the store and forward messaging process—where a user can create messages and queue them up as the messages are created. When the user has completed writing messages, he or she can connect to the network and send any stored messages, as well as automatically retrieve messages from the Lotus cc:Mail Server that are stored for receipt. This store and forward messaging to a dedicated rouer in cc:Mail is a proprietary format process that is not directly supported by Microsoft Exchange Server, and will need to be addressed during the migration process.

DIALING IN TO THE cc:MAIL ROUTER   The mobile user in Lotus cc:Mail dials in to the same router that is used to process internal mail messages between post offices, as well as to send messages to other post offices over a dial-up asynchronous connection. Once a modem is connected to the router, the mobile users can dial in and use the router as their point of connection for message transport. An organization can have multiple routers servicing a number of remote messaging users, to distribute the load and provide more dial-up connections.

An Integrated Lotus cc:Mail/Microsoft Exchange Environment

In an integrated Lotus cc:Mail and Microsoft Exchange environment, the various components of the cc:Mail system need to be connected to the Microsoft Exchange environment. This is necessary not only for sending and receiving electronic mail messages between the two application environments, but also for synchronizing address lists between the two systems and for providing access support for remote users.

Within Exchange, the Microsoft Exchange Server has a cc:Mail Connector that comes free with the Microsoft Exchange Server software. The cc:Mail Connector includes multiple components that facilitate message transfer between the Lotus cc:Mail and Microsoft Exchange systems. The components, shown in Figure 9-14, include the message transfer store, the cc:Mail MTA, and a directory synchronization service. The cc:Mail Connector directory synchronization service allows the Microsoft Exchange Server to participate in the ADE process.

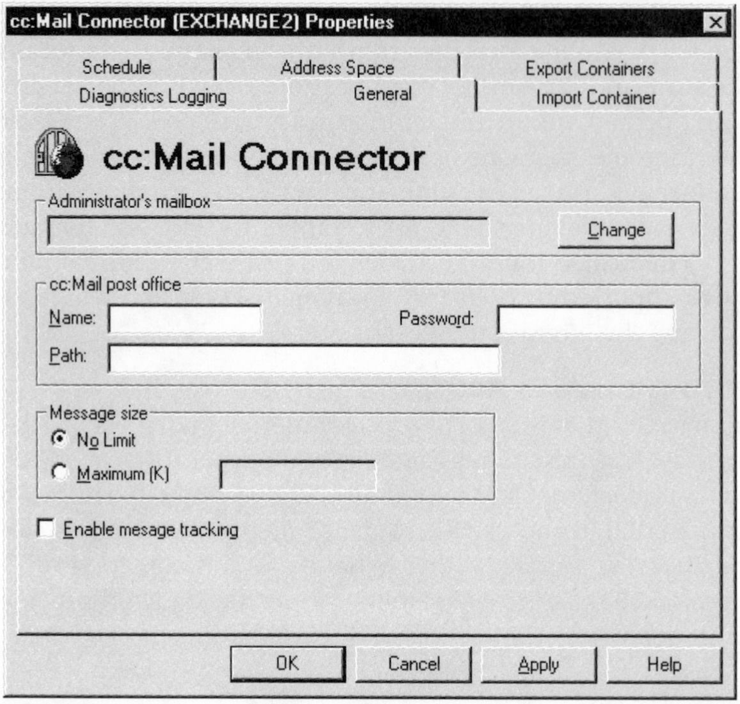

Figure 9-14. *cc:Mail Connector options in Microsoft Exchange*

Conducting the Lotus cc:Mail to Exchange Migration

During a Lotus cc:Mail to Microsoft Exchange migration, there are a number of steps necessary to complete the migration. In addition, the sequence of steps is crucial in determining whether the migration will be completed and how successful the migration is. In a migration process, delays are usually caused by a failure to complete a portion of the process in the right order, forcing the administrator to go back and redo a step.

The tools available to migrate from cc:Mail to Microsoft Exchange include:

- **Source Extractor** The Source Extractor for cc:Mail extracts the user names in cc:Mail and populates both Microsoft Windows NT Server as well as the Microsoft Exchange software with core user information.

■ **Migration Wizard**   The Migration Wizard for cc:Mail converts a user's personal mailbox to Microsoft Exchange. This includes all messages and attachments a user has stored in the message box, including the inbox and private folders.

■ **Exchange cc:Mail Connector**   The cc:Mail Connector provides seamless communication between cc:Mail post offices and a Microsoft Exchange site and organization. The cc:Mail Connector may be used in a coexistence slow migration process as an internal gateway, or may be used to communicate from Microsoft Exchange to external clients, vendors, or other business units using cc:Mail.

■ **Directory Synchronization**   Microsoft Exchange provides Lotus cc:Mail Automatic Directory Exchange (ADE) services for Directory Synchronization between cc:Mail and Microsoft Exchange. The Directory Synchronization minimizes the administration that needs to be done in updating user lists between multiple messaging environments.

Verifying the Domain, Organization, Sites, and Servers

As outlined in Chapter 4, the Microsoft Windows NT domain design, organization and site structure, and server placement are extremely important in setting in place the infrastructure of the Exchange environment. Since the Windows NT domain design dictates the user access and administrator management of the Exchange environment, it is important to understand and review the appropriate domain structure even before installing the first Exchange server. And since the Exchange organization and site information cannot be modified once installed, without complete reinstallation of the Exchange software, making sure the server, site, and organizational characteristics of the organization are properly designed before implementation should be your top priority.

Verifying ADE Is Operational

If the organization has a need to synchronize user names between the Microsoft Exchange Server and Lotus cc:Mail post offices, then the ADE should be fully operational in the cc:Mail messaging systems prior to migration. This will ensure that time is not spent trying to diagnose directory propagation problems on the Lotus cc:Mail messaging system during the migration process.

Planning and Preparing for Internal and External Gateway Communications

During the migration process, because the organization would want to maintain internal and external electronic messaging communications with others, there is a need to ensure that the gateways between the various environments are operational. The gateways are not necessarily difficult to set up and install, but the difficulties lie in understanding how the gateways will share the load of traffic between the Lotus cc:Mail and the Microsoft Exchange systems, which external gateway will manage Internet or fax traffic (in a gateway consolidation), and whether all of the information that is expected to transfer from one environment to the other is actually transferring across the gateway (such as rich text fonts, graphics, and attachments).

MIGRATING EXTERNAL GATEWAYS   In many cases, gateways can be or may need to be redundant for both the Lotus cc:Mail and the Microsoft Exchange environments. In some cases, a fax gateway that works for Lotus cc:Mail users will not work for Microsoft Exchange users. An organization would then need to plan for two fax gateways, and more specifically, how to manage the inbound routing of faxes to one versus the other fax gateway. For other gateways, such as an Internet connection, the organization may elect to consolidate, leaving only one gateway for both the Lotus cc:Mail and the Microsoft Exchange environment. During a gateway consolidation, incoming and outgoing routes from within the message administration programs need to be modified in order to select the destination gateway where messages should be sent or retrieved by the messaging programs.

Installing the Exchange Client Software

Once the infrastructure components of an Exchange migration have been designed, planned, and tested, the Exchange client components can be installed. As described in Chapter 2, there are two separate client software programs available for Microsoft Exchange Server, the Exchange client and the Outlook client. Even though the Outlook client is a more current version of the client software with some added functionality that an organization may want, its limitations need to be taken into account prior to deployment. For instance, it does not allow for the viewing of schedules with the standard Exchange client, nor are some of the server components compatible or operational with the standard Exchange client (such as message voting or 32-bit forms). These limitations, especially in an integrated environment that may have a need to implement the standard Exchange client (for DOS, Macintosh, Windows v3.*x*, or other application users where the Outlook client is not available), need to be assessed before installation.

Additionally, the Exchange client that comes with Windows 95 is not compatible with the Microsoft Exchange Server software. Because there were dozens of updates from the time that Windows 95 was released in the summer of 1995 and the time that Exchange was initially released in the spring of 1996, the latest version of the Exchange client should be installed on the users' desktops. Furthermore, there have been a number of interim releases of the Exchange client included with each revision release of Exchange, so the version of the Exchange client that is installed on the user's workstations should be the version of the Exchange client that came with the Exchange server software being installed.

USING THE EXCHANGE CLIENT WITH LOTUS cc:MAIL   While the Microsoft Exchange client does not provide for access to a Lotus cc:Mail post office, there are third-party add-ins which will allow the Exchange client to use a cc:Mail post office. When installing the Exchange client for Lotus cc:Mail use, because the client software takes 15-20 minutes per workstation on average, the installation of the Exchange client for a workgroup of 100 users can take an entire week to just install the client software. Dependent on the size of the organization's workgroup, the organization may elect to install the Microsoft Exchange client on all workstations and use the Exchange client while accessing the Lotus cc:Mail Server.

The Microsoft Exchange client software has the support for the installation, access, and use of both a Lotus cc:Mail post office as well as a Microsoft Exchange Server, through the use of third-party add-ins. In many cases, organizations take this opportunity to convert users over time from the Lotus cc:Mail client to the Microsoft Exchange client software. It provides the users an opportunity to learn the Exchange client to send and receive mail messages, minimizing the learning curve necessary to train the users after the Exchange server has been converted.

The installation of the Exchange client software on each workstation over time can also spread out any problem of some workstations where the Exchange client cannot be easily installed. This may be a workstation that does not have enough disk space, have enough memory, or where the Exchange client software may impact the operation of another application software. Additionally, if the clients' workstations are not only upgraded from the Microsoft Mail client to the Microsoft Exchange client, but also from Windows to Windows 95, there may be an additional need for time for the users to get familiar with their new desktop operating environment. The fewer things a user needs to learn all at the same time, the smoother the transition would be, especially for something that may be as mission-critical for the users and the organization as electronic messaging.

Configuring an RAS Server for Remote Mail Users

The need to implement Microsoft Remote Access Server (RAS) as the remote access system for mail users is required for users that will be converting from the Lotus cc:Mail Mobile to the Microsoft Exchange prior to the conversion to Exchange server, as well as a requirement for all remote users accessing cc:Mail remotely since the Exchange server does not support the older proprietary cc:Mail Mobile client software.

During an Exchange migration, because the Exchange server store for user messages and message management is different for the cc:Mail environment, once users convert to Microsoft Exchange as their client software (even if they are using the Lotus cc:Mail post office server for their messaging system), the users need to begin using RAS for remote access for messaging rather than the Lotus cc:Mail Mobile client application to the Lotus cc:Mail router.

Additionally, because the Lotus cc:Mail Mobile software does not support access to a Microsoft Exchange Server, all users remotely dialing in to the network need to be migrated to the Microsoft Exchange client and use RAS for their remote mail access prior to the conversion to Microsoft Exchange Server.

The remote mail user migrations are typically the most challenging in the conversion process because the users are by definition remote users and sometimes getting access to their computers and installing the software takes time or is difficult to schedule when they can have their systems updated. Other challenges in upgrading remote user workstations to the Exchange client involve having enough disk space on the remote system—about 40-60MB (35-40MB for the Exchange client software, plus 10-20MB for the user's data file.) The remote user will also require training. Training, not as much on how to send or reply to a message, but also for how to establish a connection to a RAS Server and invoke the sending and receiving of mail messages.

However, once all remote users are using the Exchange client and can successfully log on to the RAS Server and send and receive mail messages with the Lotus cc:Mail post office, then when the organization switches to Microsoft Exchange, the hardest part of configuring the core workstation software and end user training will have been completed.

Exchange Migration Wizard

Once all of the infrastructure functions of the NT Server, Microsoft Exchange Server, desktop clients, remote clients, and internal and external gateways have been configured and tested, the final process is conducting the migration from Lotus cc:Mail to Microsoft Exchange.

It is typically recommended that the migration process be tested in a prototype prior to doing a live migration. The advantages of doing prototype testing on the migration process include:

- Ability to test all user mailboxes to make sure they converted properly

- Ability to test any gateways or sending and receiving of electronic messages across platforms

- Ability to sample workstation changeovers from cc:Mail to Exchange

- Ability to time the migration process to make sure enough time is allocated to convert the server as well as switch designated users from Lotus cc:Mail to Microsoft Exchange in the time allotted

EXTRACTING AND MIGRATING USERS   During the Lotus cc:Mail to Microsoft Exchange migration process, the Migration Wizard, shown in Figure 9-15, will walk the administrator through the conversion. The administrator will be prompted to specify the cc:Mail post office that is desired to be migrated and the destination Exchange server that will be the recipient of the new users. The Migration Wizard will extract user names from the cc:Mail post office and migrate the user names to the Microsoft Exchange Server.

Also during the test migration process, the administrator may be able to identify the users that have thousands if not tens of thousands of messages saved, and prior to a live migration, the administrator may be able to convince the users to do some housecleaning on their mail messages to decrease the number of messages stored, and thus decrease the time that it takes for the Migration Wizard to convert the user from Lotus cc:Mail to Microsoft Exchange.

Completing a Live Migration

Once a prototype migration has been completed and the administrator knows how long it will take to migrate from Lotus cc:Mail to Microsoft Exchange, tests the gateways, and tests a handful of client systems, then the organization can complete a full migration from Lotus cc:Mail to Microsoft Exchange.

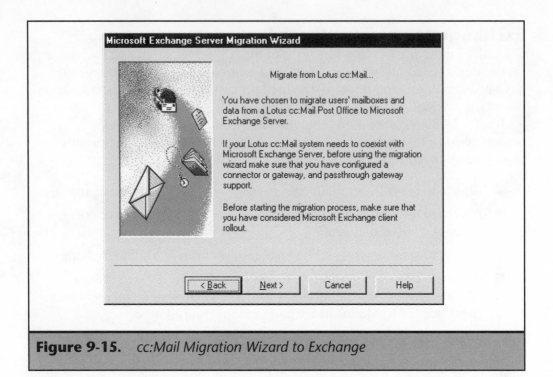

Figure 9-15. *cc:Mail Migration Wizard to Exchange*

Debugging Problems in the Migration

Some of the common problems after a migration include the following:

■ **Replying to cc:Mail messages after the conversion to Exchange**
When users are converted from Lotus cc:Mail to Microsoft Exchange, all
of their mail messages in their inbox and personal message folders are
also converted. If a user replies to a message, he or she will probably
receive an error message after they send the message. The message is
commonly one that refers to a "transport error." This message occurs
because the reply on the message is attempting to return the message
back through the route of the old cc:Mail system. Because the user is
now on Microsoft Exchange, the user needs to create a new route for
that message to go for a return response. Instead of selecting "reply" to
the message and using the existing name on the reply, the user should
change the name on the reply and select the new name of the person
they want to respond to from the new address list. This will select the
user from the Microsoft Exchange user list and provide a new route
back to the original of the message.

■ **Old addresses in Personal Address Books** Another problem similar to the reply to function is if a user selects an e-mail address from the user's old Personal Address Book. By default, the Microsoft Exchange client software sets the user's personal address list before the Microsoft Exchange address list. If the user types in the name of the recipient in the To: or Cc: section, when he or she sends the message, the Exchange client will pull the recipient's address from the user's personal address list. More than likely, the user's personal address has all of the old cc:Mail addresses for users on the network, not Microsoft Exchange addresses. Thus, the user will get a "transport error" again when sending the message. This can be minimized by having users specifically go into the Global Address List or Exchange server recipients list to pull names for messages they wish to send. Or, the users can go into their Exchange client software, select Tools I Options I Addressing and move the Personal Address Book below the global address book in the order in which the Microsoft Exchange client pulls user names. By selecting from the Global Address List first, the user's name will be pulled from the current Microsoft Exchange user list rather than from an old user name list.

The Chapter in Review

■ Many organizations will choose to migrate their mail system to Exchange. The duration of the migration process will largely be influenced by the size of the organization. The greater number of users, the greater the number of sites, and the more complex the mail system, the longer the migration is likely to take. The single step migration happens all at once and without a need for transitional gateways. A single step migration is feasible if an organization has fewer than 200 users, if the migration is adequately planned for in advance, and if a migration tool exists for any messages that need to be migrated.

■ A long-term migration will require a coexistence strategy. Pivotal in that strategy is the interim gateway between the old and the new message systems. An organization is more likely to require a coexistence migration strategy if it has more workstations that need to be converted and tested than it can do in that timeframe, if it has more than one location which makes it prohibitive to be able to migrate all the users at once, if it has workgroups with differing management which makes coordinating schedules and resources difficult, and if some workstations are too old to support Exchange.

■ Migration tools provided with the Microsoft Exchange Server software provide the ability to assist the organization to migrate to Microsoft Exchange from other networking or messaging environments.

■ Exchange supports migrations from many different e-mail applications and network operating systems: Microsoft Mail, IBM/Lotus cc:Mail, Novell GroupWise, Netscape Collabra Share, Profs, Verimation Memo, DEC All-in-One, and UNIX mail.

■ There are a number of different versions of MS Mail Server available. There is MS Mail for PC networks, v3.5, MS Mail for AppleTalk, and MS Mail that comes with Windows for Workgroups and Windows NT servers. A Mail Message Transfer Agent (MTA) is used to communicate to other post offices within the organization or outside the organization. The external gateway under MS Mail v3.0 or 3.2 is a standalone DOS-based PC computer than runs an executable program called EXTERNAL.EXE. Under MS Mail v3.5 the MTA can be a service under Windows NT. If an organization's post office communicates with one or more other post offices, those post offices need to share updates to their user lists. By updating user lists, users on both networks can see all mail users on their network and select the appropriate recipient. This data exchange can be made manually via the ADMIN.EXE program. The DirSync program is used to automatically update user lists.

■ A successful MS Mail-to-Exchange migration requires a number of steps to be completed in the correct order. Delays with the migration are usually caused by a step not being completed or not being completed in the correct sequence. The Exchange domain structure, including the server, site, and organizational characteristics, must be finalized before installing even the first Exchange server. If the organization needs a connector between the MS Mail network and the Exchange network, the DirSync server should be configured before the Exchange environment is deployed.

■ Some common migration problems include:

   ■ Problems replying to existing e-mail messages

   ■ Old addresses in users' Personal Address Book

■ Similar processes are noted to assist in the migration from cc:Mail to Exchange including the migration of cc:Mail clients, cc:Mail routers, and the cc:Mail Server. All of these components are migrated in an outlined sequence to get from cc:Mail to Microsoft Exchange.

Review Questions

Q. What are the benefits of doing a single step migration?
A. The configuration and maintenance of an interim gateway are not necessary and the end users do not need to be instructed on how to utilize an interim gateway.

Q. What is the process for a single step migration?
A. Install the Exchange client software on each workstation; install Exchange on the server; prototype the migration of users, mail messages, and calendars; confirm that all external gateways migrate successfully; prototype the client access to the Exchange server to confirm that users' mailboxes and calendars migrate successfully; do the final migration of all users in a "live" migration in a single day.

Q. What does a Source Extractor retrieve?
A. A Source Extractor retrieves from the old mail system users' names, and often retrieves user group and security information.

Q. What tool can take existing user data and reform it to have Exchange characteristics?
A. The Exchange Migration Wizard can do this through the use of import templates.

Q. If an organization migrates to Exchange but wants to continue communicating with external clients, vendors, and business units via MS Mail, what product would it use?
A. The MS Mail Connector.

Q. What does the Migration Wizard for cc:Mail convert?
A. It converts users' personal mailboxes to Exchange, including all messages and attachments stored in their inboxes and private folders.

Q. The IBM Profs-to-Exchange gateway is included in Exchange, true or false?
A. False; it is an add-on third-party product offered by Attachmate.

Q. Why is the DirSync application required between MS Mail and MS Exchange post offices?
A. DirSync is a tool that automatically updates user lists between the two post offices. It is needed because the manual method of exporting user lists will not be accepted by Exchange.

Q. What are the benefits of using the Microsoft Exchange Server as the MS Mail MTA?
A. Under NT, the Connector MTA can better manage and maintain message interchange within Exchange.

Q. If I install Windows 95 on my client workstations, I don't need to install the Exchange client software, true or false?
A. False; the Exchange client that comes with Windows 95 does not work with Microsoft Exchange Server. It needs to be upgraded to the client software that comes with the server.

Q. Is end user training recommended to be scheduled before or after the switch is made to Exchange Server?
A. It is suggested that users be trained on Exchange when the client software is installed and before the Exchange server is brought online.

Q. Which utility shows which server users have access to?
A. The Mail and fax utility, launched by running CONTROL MLCFG32.CPL.

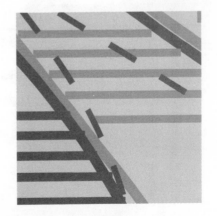

CHAPTER 10

Finalizing the Microsoft Exchange Installation Plan

O ver the last six chapters, we have reviewed everything from Microsoft Windows NT domain security and the Microsoft Exchange Server site and organization schemes to the integration and migration of Microsoft Exchange in existing messaging or networking environments. The planning process is now complete. At this point, we need to consolidate the information we have gathered and begin allocating the resources necessary to begin the deployment of Microsoft Exchange.

This chapter will link the previous planning and design chapters, and begin to identify the physical resources necessary to implement the Exchange environment. We will review the creation of a GANTT chart, which we will use as a road map to implement the Microsoft Exchange organizational environment.

Consolidating the Exchange Design and Planning Information

The first section of this chapter will recap the information from the previous six chapters, with the intent of combining the information already gathered in an effort to determine how it will relate to the installation of the Exchange Server environment. The consolidation process will be helpful in creating the GANTT chart for the implementation process to follow.

The Structural Business Chart

One of the critical design plan steps we took was to evaluate the physical business structure of the organization in order to identify the organizational units and sites which will dictate the need for connectors and site-to-site connectivity.

The following information will be needed in the next section to complete the implementation GANTT chart:

- Name of the organization
- Sites within the organization
- Type of connection between sites
- Protocols selected to communicate between sites
- How each site will be administered and managed
- How many users and who they are at each site

The Operations Structure Chart

The next component of importance in creating the organization's infrastructure is the preparation of the Windows NT domain model. The NT domain model dictates the security and access administration on an information systems level for the networking infrastructure. The domain design will also dictate the placement of domain controllers and Exchange servers within the organization.

The following information will be needed in the next section to complete the implementation GANTT chart:

- Which NT domain model desired (single domain, fully trusted, master domain, multiple master domain)
- Which system and where the primary domain controller will be placed
- Which system(s) and where the backup domain controller(s) will be placed
- Who will administer the domain(s) and the overall network
- What security is needed between domains and throughout the organization
- Who is responsible for managing the network and the messaging system

The Workflow Chart

Commonly overlooked but extremely valuable in determining whether the domain design or site infrastructure design is appropriate for the organization is the ability to look at the general workflow and workgroup processes involved in the Exchange environment. The decisions made regarding the organization's workflow will affect how replication should be set between domain servers and used to analyze the traffic between clients and between servers within the organization.

The following information will be needed in the next section to complete the implementation GANTT chart:

- Virtual workgroup configuration of the organization
- General workflow of information currently and projected within the organization
- Consensus on how server-to-server replication should be designed

Networking: New Network, Migration, or Integration with an Existing Network

If the organization has no existing local area or wide area network, the decision to implement a Windows NT network is a simple one. However, assuming that the organization already has an existing network, the need to determine if the organization will retain its existing network or migrate to a Windows NT networking model will impact the implementation schedule. If a network needs to be installed or an existing network needs to be replaced, the completion of either of these processes must be taken into account when planning the implementation of the Exchange environment.

The following information will be needed in the next section to complete the implementation GANTT chart:

- What is the existing network
- Is it designed to maintain the existing network infrastructure
- Is it designed to replace the existing network infrastructure with Windows NT

Microsoft Exchange: New Installation, Migration, or Integration

In addition to the existing network operating system infrastructure, an organization must decide whether Microsoft Exchange will be the first and only electronic messaging system, whether existing users and messages from an older messaging system will be migrated to Microsoft Exchange, or whether the existing operating environment will dictate immediate or future solutions.

The following information will be needed in the next section to complete the implementation GANTT chart:

- What is the existing electronic messaging system
- Is there a desire to retain the existing electronic messaging system
- Is it possible to block any communications required by the cable operator

Product and Licensing Selection and Procurement

Based on the number of Exchange servers, type of users, and the flow of information and necessary replication, an organization can determine the number of Exchange server and client licenses that it requires, as well as the number of servers, processor speeds, disk configuration and other information about its core server configurations. The following information will be needed in the next section to complete the implementation GANTT chart:

- How many Exchange servers will be installed on the network
- How many client licenses will be needed for the users of the Exchange environment
- How will each of the Exchange servers be configured

Creating the Implementation GANTT Chart

Before we begin creating the GANTT chart that will be used as the road map for our implementation of the Microsoft Exchange environment, it is important to thoroughly explain exactly what a GANTT chart is so that it will be easier to gain an understanding of the terminology that will be used to describe components of the GANTT chart, as well as knowledge of how to track information, resources, and progress on the GANTT chart.

What is a GANTT Chart?

A GANTT chart is a tool used by project managers that tracks information about the tasks of a project in both a text and graphical format. The GANTT chart lists information about each task, and displays the duration of those tasks with start and finish dates. The relative positions of the GANTT tasks (and graphical bars) show you the order in which the tasks should be completed, and which tasks should overlap within the framework of the larger project.

GANTT charts are created by using a project management program like Microsoft Project. Like any application program, the information that comprises the project plan needs to be entered by the user of the application software. If information is left out of the project plan, the project management software does not have the ability to tell the project manager that a step has been missed.

GANTT charts are used to:

- Arrange the tasks of a project in order so that the project manager can ensure that the project tasks are completed in sequence

- Keep track of project tasks, including the duration and costs of each component, ensuring that the project is kept on schedule and within budget

- Establish sequential relationships between tasks so that the project manager can see how changing a task may affect the start and finish dates of other tasks in the project, which can ultimately affect the project completion date

- Provide the project manager with the information necessary to assign personnel and other resources to project tasks and to make sure that resources are used as efficiently as possible

- Track the progress of the project by comparing its original baseline expectation with its actual progress by checking the percentage of each task that is completed

Terms and Terminology

The following are some of the terms and terminology of project management and project planning that are used to describe the components or processes of a project plan:

- **Scope of Work** The scope of work of a project is a compilation of its goals, expectations, available resources, required resources, expected effort for completion, and available budget that is written down, specifically outlining what the project is expected to entail. In many cases, the scope of work consists mainly of the originator's brainstormed ideas in outline form. Essentially, it delineates the conceptual view of the project and provides as much information about the project as possible.

- **Workplan** The workplan of a project takes a scope of work and forms the guideline in which the GANTT chart is developed. The GANTT chart is the sequential text and graphical representation of the project process, or of the project's entire workplan. The workplan identifies the requirements of the project and the resources that will be necessary to complete it.

- **Phases** Most projects, especially those that span a relatively lengthy period, are broken down into smaller subprojects, or phases. The phases of a project are typically defined by the different kinds of work performed in each of the phases. The phases shown in Figure 10-1 are major phases, such as planning, installation, and optimization. Breaking a project into smaller subsets allows an organization to track and manage a project in more manageable pieces.

■ **Resources** Resources can be anything that needs to be allocated for a project, such as people, equipment, time, or money. A project's resources are typically allocated at its start, and the success of the project is often dependent on whether the resources are used as efficiently as possible without last-minute, unplanned demands for additional resources. Some resources are scarce, such as a high-level engineer's consultation time, which needs to be managed carefully so that the utilization of the resource can be maximized. In Figure 10-1, the resources are displayed as the user names for internal personnel, and are denoted as Vendor XYZ for a subcontracted resource.

■ **Milestones** The milestones of a project are the significant steps that demonstrate the successful completion of a major task or phase. A milestone may provide the organization with the knowledge that the project is being completed on time and as planned, or it may be an indicator that the next step in the project is ready to be initiated. Milestones are often keyed to the major goals of the project. In Figure 10-2, the milestone at the end of the installation phase is called out by a diamond at the end of the section.

■ **Tasks** Tasks are the steps of a project that need to be completed. There are typically two levels of tasks that can be identified. Some tasks are major components of a phase of a project, and some are minor details within a phase of a project. Major tasks are categories that typically have a number of detailed steps are associated with the specific task. In Figure 10-3, the major tasks shown are items such as "Install the Primary Domain Controller," or "Install the first Microsoft Windows NT Server." Minor tasks shown in Figure 10-3 are the detailed steps of the major tasks and include details such as "Configure the PDC Server (Memory, HDS, NIC)." Tasks of a project will have a start date, ending date, duration of time, allocation of resources, and allocation of costs associated with them.

■ **Parallel Processes** Some processes within a project can be completed concurrently without placing overwhelming demands on project resources. Parallel processes may occur when work is being completed in multiple locations or in multiple workgroups simultaneously. For example, in Figure 10-2 work is being completed in multiple cities at

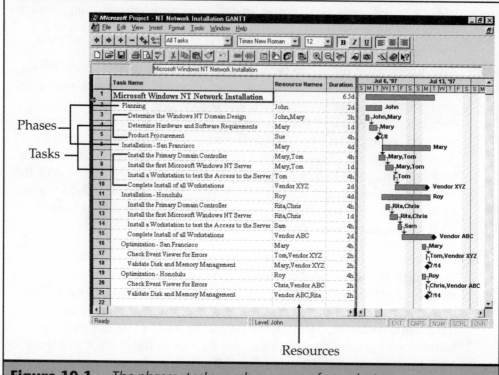

Phases —

Tasks —

Resources

Figure 10-1. *The phases, tasks, and resources of a project*

the same time, and the two processes can take place in parallel, which results in an overlap of installation dates for these tasks. If use of the resources needed to complete the work does not overlap, completing tasks simultaneously can minimize the time necessary to finish the task, phase, or project.

■ **Linked Processes** Some processes are sequential and can only be started once a specific event has taken place. In other words, the delay of a preceding event can affect whether the next sequential task can be completed. For example, the configuration of a server cannot be completed until the equipment arrives. Subsequently, the equipment cannot arrive until a purchase order is placed. And, the equipment cannot be ordered unless its configuration is determined. Each of these tasks is linked, and a delay or change in any of them will affect the initiation of the final task. In Figure 10-2, configuration of the server cannot be started without the receipt of the equipment. Thus, the

Milestones

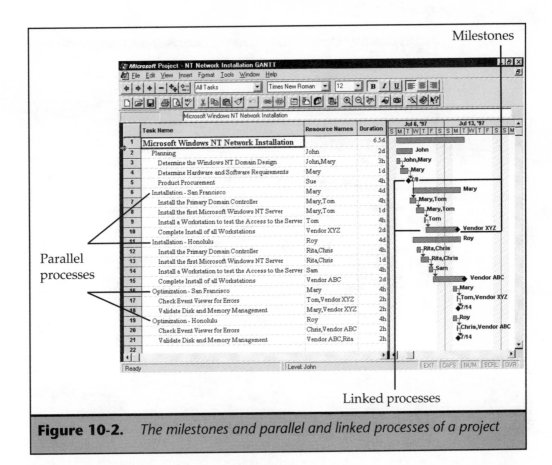

Parallel
processes

Linked processes

Figure 10-2.   *The milestones and parallel and linked processes of a project*

required task must be completed, or the preceding task is said to be
"linked" to the current task. The project management software has the
ability to link tasks in this way so that a delay or change in preceding
tasks can be made, and the subsequent effect upon the balance of the
project can be visually displayed for analysis.

Where Do You Start?

The task of creating the project plan and the GANTT chart for the
implementation process is usually a real challenge for most project managers.
The creation of the GANTT chart is typically viewed as an entire project in
itself, but the fear engendered by the need to create the GANTT chart is often
caused by the project manager's approach. All too often, project managers end

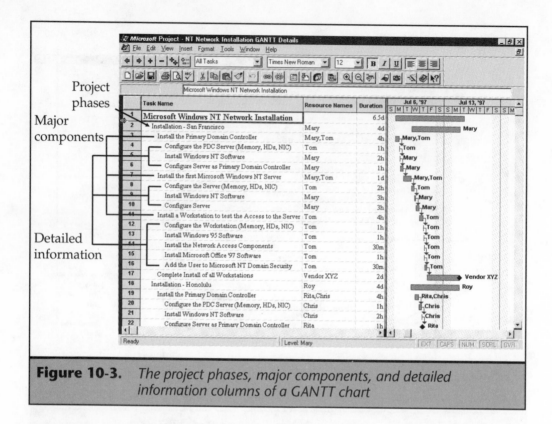

Figure 10-3. *The project phases, major components, and detailed information columns of a GANTT chart*

up sitting in front of project management software and attempt to "work the GANTT chart" rather than think through the scope of work and the workplan.

Instead, a GANTT chart should be thought of as a glorified spreadsheet. Most people do not become overwhelmed when working with a spreadsheet. Generally, information in a spreadsheet is filled in from the top to the bottom of the far-left column. When a new line needs to be added to the spreadsheet, a simple insert command adds a new line. The description of the new line is then entered.

If the project manager thinks of the GANTT chart in the same manner, its creation can be completed in a logical and manageable sequence.

Gathering the Components of the GANTT Chart

A GANTT chart cannot be created without knowledge and information about the project that will be undertaken. Typically, research will need to be done in order to consolidate the goals, expectations, functions, resource availability, and technical implementation needs of the project. Depending on the complexity of the project, project planning can be as quick and simple as an interview with the person or team that originated the project, or as in-depth as a series of interviews with a number of key individuals and searches for information about the available resources or technical components of the project.

The tasks of a GANTT chart can be broken down into three separate columns: the major phases of the project, its major components and milestones, and its detailed components.

Project Phases: The First Column of Information

The first step that needs to be determined when outlining the tasks of the project are the project phases. This information makes up the "First Column" of information on the GANTT chart. The project phases can typically be described in one or two words, and may include planning, designing, resource acquisition, prototyping, training, implementation, and ongoing support. They are essentially descriptions of the type of work that will be completed in the particular phase of the project.

Major Components and Milestones: The Second Column of Information

The second step is outlining the major components and milestones of the project. This procedure typically takes the title of each phase of the project and breaks down the information into a sequence that can be identified as a subcategory of the phase. Under the installation phase of the project some of the major components, like the ones detailed in Figure 10-3, may include the installation of the Primary Domain Controller, the NT server, or the NT workstations.

Detailed Information: The Third Column of Information

The third step is to break down the major components into detailed and sequential procedural information. This would involve taking the component that identifies the installation of the workstation and separating it into smaller and more specific components, such as the installation of memory and network adapter into the workstation, installation of Windows 95 on the workstation, and the installation of Microsoft Office and the Exchange client on the workstation. This is similar to the detailed task information shown in Figure 10-3.

Determining the Phases and the Tasks

At this point, it should be clear that the phases and tasks of any project need to be determined. In many cases, a project can be outlined from finish to start, beginning with the final goals and expectations of the project and then returning to the workplan. By working backwards, each of the preceding events of the project can be identified as well as the major phases and tasks necessary for successful completion of the project. As the project manager reviews the workplan, new tasks can be identified and added to the project GANTT chart by using the INSERT key. By filling out the phases and tasks of the project without having to worry about the resource demands or the timetable of each component at this time, the project manager can concentrate on making sure that each step in the project has been identified and flows in a logical, sequential format.

Determining the Resource Needs

Once the phases and tasks of the project are identified, the resources needed to complete the tasks must be identified. For example, an outline of the skills necessary to complete each task should be performed to assess human resource needs, and the required tools, equipment, or other components should be identified and linked to specific tasks to fulfill equipment resource needs. When both the personnel and equipment requirements have been identified, the cost of the equipment can be determined, thus providing the budget allocation resource for the project. Essentially, in order to determine resource needs, the project manager needs to match up the general skill set or equipment demands of the project outline with the corresponding lines on the project GANTT chart.

Determining the Timetable

Once the resources for the project are determined, the length of time they will be needed can be identified. When tasks are linked in sequence, resources can be utilized on a flowing rate process. When tasks are parallel, the demand for limited resources must be planned and managed so that the requirements of the resource do not result in overlapped processes. It is in this final step that the starting dates, ending dates, and length of time the resource is needed are determined, and thus the corresponding bar on the GANTT chart can be drawn.

Sequence of Events for the Installation Process

During the creation of the GANTT chart, the sequence of events for the installation process will be outlined. By combining the information gathered earlier in this chapter about the domain structure, site names, and other component information along with the information on how to create a GANTT chart, we will utilize the following steps to finally create the outline of the implementation GANTT chart. We will only be focusing on the first two task columns on the GANTT chart, leaving the minor details open for the project manager to identify and expand.

Planning and Design Components

The first phase of the GANTT chart creation needs to start with the Planning and Design components of the Exchange implementation process. Many of these components are the pieces that we have gathered in previous chapters, but some are new processes that also need to be included.

Identifying the Installation/Implementation Project Manager

One of the first steps in the project plan development is the selection of the project manager. Although it may seem obvious that the project manager should be the person who creates the GANTT chart, that is actually not necessary. In many implementations, there may be multiple project managers involved who are each in charge of a specific area, such as project planning, implementation of the servers and infrastructure, or desktop workstation configurations, upgrades, and user training.

Of course, the key to a successful implementation with multiple project managers is that they all have the experience and expertise to plan, manage, and implement their aspect of the project. In many cases, contracting an external project manager experienced in this specific line of work can produce more effective results, while an internal project manager can be the central point of contact for overall communication during the final implementation of the project.

In either case, a single project manager will be in charge of the project's ultimate success, and needs to be the central point of all project communications.

Administrator Training for Exchange Administration Personnel

Proper personnel training may be necessary to help the people that will be planning, designing, deploying, and supporting the implementation of the project. Gaining background expertise in the technology prior to its implementation can help the administrator or manager of the project to be better able to make good decisions and choices during the design and implementation process.

TAKING MICROSOFT TRAINING COURSES ON EXCHANGE   Expertise can be acquired through the training courses that Microsoft offers through their Authorized Technical Education Centers (ATECs). Microsoft offers a training course on Microsoft Exchange Administration that covers the design, installation, and support of the Microsoft Exchange product. While the Microsoft Exchange training is good textbook product training, actual experience with planning, installing, and supporting Microsoft Exchange is always preferable, and will help ensure a successful installation.

ATTAINING MICROSOFT CERTIFICATION FOR EXCHANGE   Microsoft offers certification designations for individuals wishing to take a series of training courses and exams in order to prove their expertise with the Microsoft products. Microsoft has three types of certifications:

- **Microsoft Certified Professional (MCP)** The Microsoft Certified Professional is a specialist who passes a core Microsoft Windows NT certification test as well as a specialization exam. In the case of a Microsoft Exchange certification, an individual would take the Windows NT Enterprise Networking exam as well as the Microsoft Exchange Server exam. The content knowledge required to pass these exams is taught in the ATEC training courses on the products and technologies.

■ **Microsoft Certified System Engineer (MCSE)** The Microsoft Certified System Engineer is required to pass a series of exams including core Microsoft Windows NT certification tests as well as a number of electives. The certification is more comprehensive across a handful of specializations, demonstrating the individual's technical expertise in a variety of fields and practices.

■ **Microsoft Certified Solution Developer (MCSD)** The Microsoft Certified Solution Developer is required to pass a series of exams including core Microsoft Windows NT certification tests plus a focus on application development tools such as C++, or Visual Basic. The certification is focused on developers, whose expertise will be in the creation of application-based solutions.

Acquiring External Expertise

When choosing whether to build versus buy experience and expertise in the design, implementation, and support of a sophisticated product like Microsoft Exchange, organizations may elect to acquire external expertise from a variety of sources. The expertise may be obtained from a consultant with extensive experience with a similar design and implementation process, or from a consulting firm that specializes in the type of deployment project being undertaken. More information on acquiring external expertise will be covered later in this chapter.

Developing the Scope of Work and the Workplan

The intent of the creation of the GANTT chart is to develop a scope of work and workplan that can be followed during the deployment of the Microsoft Exchange environment. The development of the scope of work and workplan should be reflected with the creation of a document that outlines the expectations and goals of the Exchange implementation project, defines the resources available from the organization to complete the project, and defines the external resources that need to be contracted or acquired to complete the project on time and within budget.

Creating the Infrastructure Design and Plan

The information collected throughout this and previous chapters should be enough to enable you to complete the first phase of the Microsoft Exchange implementation project. Some of the tasks that would be designated by the analysis of the plan and design information would include developing the equipment list for server and software purchases. The planning and design portion of the GANTT chart should look similar to Figure 10-4.

Resource Acquisition Components

After the design and planning processes have been completed, the organization needs to begin acquiring the resources necessary to implement the project and process. As defined earlier in this chapter, the resources needed for a project may include personnel time, equipment (hardware and software), expertise, time, and money.

Product Procurement

The equipment and software licensing acquisition list created during the planning and design phase of the project will designate the hardware and software necessary to complete the installation and implementation. In many cases, the product procurement would be split into multiple rounds. The first round of product acquisition would typically consist of the products necessary to prototype the installation; for example, this could be a server to install Microsoft Exchange and a handful of workstations to simulate a fully operational Microsoft Exchange environment. After the prototype is completed and everything is tested and found to be operational, the balance of the equipment and software licensing acquisition can be completed.

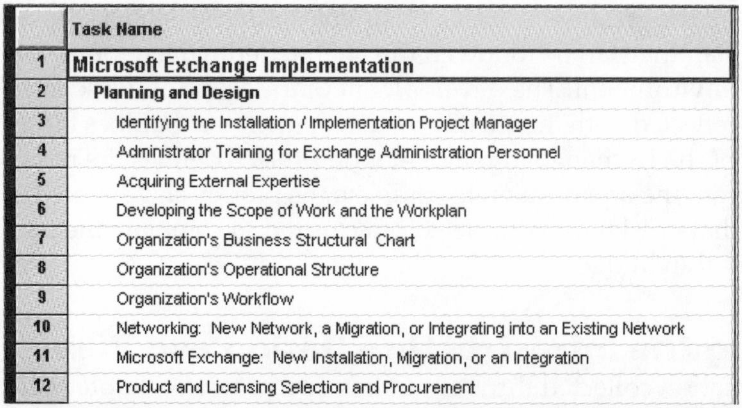

	Task Name
1	**Microsoft Exchange Implementation**
2	**Planning and Design**
3	Identifying the Installation / Implementation Project Manager
4	Administrator Training for Exchange Administration Personnel
5	Acquiring External Expertise
6	Developing the Scope of Work and the Workplan
7	Organization's Business Structural Chart
8	Organization's Operational Structure
9	Organization's Workflow
10	Networking: New Network, a Migration, or Integrating into an Existing Network
11	Microsoft Exchange: New Installation, Migration, or an Integration
12	Product and Licensing Selection and Procurement

Figure 10-4.   *The planning and design portion of the GANTT chart*

Acquiring Personnel Resources

In general, most organizations do not have the spare personnel resources readily available to assist with the prototype project and installation of Microsoft Exchange. In order for the implementation of Microsoft Exchange to be completed, an organization would need to evaluate the current workload of its personnel and decide how many hours during a day or a week could be allocated to the Exchange deployment project. When personnel resources are unavailable or the skill set required to complete tasks in the workplan is lacking, an organization may consider the option of contracting the work to be completed.

Acquisition Phase GANTT Chart Summary

The acquisition phase components to the project plan GANTT chart should look similar to this:

III 10

13	Resource Acquisition
14	Product Procurement
15	Acquiring Personnel Resources

Prototyping and Testing Components

When the hardware and software needed to begin the prototyping phase becomes available, the first round of installation and testing can begin. This is an opportunity for the organization to install and test theories on domain designs, migration processes, gateway processes, and client access functions. This is also an opportunity to rerun LOADSIM to confirm server performance functionality and network load capabilities, so that the assumptions made about Exchange Server performance modeling can be verified.

Client Configuration

The project manager and Exchange administrator will discover that they must be prepared to devote large chunks of time not only to the planning process of a Microsoft Exchange deployment, but also to the installation of Exchange's client software. During the prototype testing phase, assumptions are made about the time needed to install the client, configure it, and if applicable, convert user mailboxes to the Exchange client so that they can be tested.

PLANNING FOR USER DOWNTIME   The prototype phase for client configuration can be used to determine how long it will take on average to install, configure, and test a client workstation configuration of the Exchange client. This information can then be utilized to estimate the user downtime during the implementation process. A downtime estimate is needed because implementation time should be taken into account for deployment, and also because users should be informed of downtime that will take place on their workstations (if the installation takes place during business hours).

COEXISTENCE OF THE USER CLIENT SOFTWARE   To minimize the effects of client downtime and the need to do initial end user training, an organization can elect to install the Microsoft Exchange client software, test all software configuration functions, and prepare the workstation for Exchange access to the prototype system. However, the user's existing electronic mail software can remain on the system and be used until Microsoft Exchange is brought live on the network.

UPGRADING THE USER CLIENT SOFTWARE   If the organization elects to upgrade user client software programs overnight, the resulting scenario can mean that on the day after the users had access to their old electronic mail software, their workstations have been modified to run only the Exchange client. This procedure will force users to convert to the new Exchange configuration. If the implementation of the Exchange server is set up to minimize training or downtime functions, a number of users could be converted to the Exchange client in a relatively short period of time. To ensure the success of the implementation, group training sessions are advised to ensure that users clearly understand how the new client software operates.

Server Configuration

One of the major tasks during the installation process is the configuration of the Microsoft Windows NT and Exchange servers in the environment. Unless the organization plans to implement Microsoft Windows NT as the network operating system within the organization, the NT servers will typically be the organization's domain controller installation.

IMPLEMENTING THE DOMAIN DESIGN   A component of the server installation will include the installation of the domain. This would include the installation of the primary domain controller as well as any backup domain controllers identified for the organization. During the implementation of the domain design prototype installation, the organization will have an opportunity to test trusts between domains, domain security, and group and user security models that have been planned and deemed appropriate.

INSTALL EXCHANGE SERVERS   Once the domain controllers are installed and the domain structure is set for the organization, the Exchange servers can be installed and integrated into the prototype domain. The Exchange server installation will involve testing the Exchange Administrator functions of the servers, testing public folder structures, testing replication between multiple servers and sites, and testing load balancing.

Prototype Phase GANTT Chart Summary

The prototype phase components to the project plan GANTT chart should look similar to this:

16	Prototyping and Testing Phase
17	Client Configuration
18	Planning for User Downtime
19	Co-existence of the User Client Software
20	Upgrading the User Client Software
21	Server Configuration
22	Implementing the Domain Design
23	Install Exchange Servers

End User Services Components

As the administrators for the Exchange and network environment test the design plans for the Exchange configuration, users within the organization should begin training on how to use Microsoft Exchange. Training for end users within the organization can be conducted in a few separate rounds. The first round of training will be an introduction to the Exchange product. The second round of training can be conducted after the users have had a chance to use the Exchange software and want to know how to use some of its more advanced features.

Introductory Training for the Exchange or Outlook Client

The introductory training for the end users within the organization should show the basics of the Microsoft Exchange or Outlook client software applications. If users are already familiar with electronic mail programs, teaching them about Microsoft Exchange can be a relatively simple process. If users are unfamiliar with electronic mail programs, the training will need to include information about the concepts of replying to mail messages, forwarding mail messages, using address books, or other simple messaging functions that may not be obvious to the new users of electronic messaging. The entire training process prior to the installation of Microsoft Exchange does not necessarily need to be extensive unless the users are relatively sophisticated. In that case, it would be beneficial to provide them with training on some of the groupware capabilities of Microsoft Exchange.

Intermediate and Advanced Training

If users are experienced with electronic mail messaging or have the ability to understand the more sophisticated groupware capabilities of Microsoft Exchange, the initial training can include the more advanced functions. Intermediate and advanced training on Microsoft Exchange may be more appropriate for users after they have had an opportunity to become familiar with the basic features of Microsoft Exchange and are ready to learn about its groupware functions, such as forms or public folder usage, or to work with third-party add-on applications like document routing, faxing, or voicemail integration with Exchange.

End User Services Phase GANTT Chart Summary

The End User Services phase components to the project plan GANTT chart should look similar this:

24	End-User Services Phase
25	Introductory Training to the Exchange or Outlook Client
26	Intermediate and Advanced Training

Implementation Components

When the project manager believes that the prototype process has provided the administrators of the network with adequate experience in testing and understanding the installation or migration process with Exchange, the actual implementation for Exchange can commence. This process includes implementing the domain design, Exchange servers, gateways, client workstations, and all components of the Microsoft Exchange installation in a live production installation.

The implementation phase has a number of components that have been identified and will be outlined in the next chapter of this book. The completion of the implementation phase of the GANTT chart development will be continued in the next chapter as well.

Future Phases Components

Once the installation of Microsoft Exchange has been completed and all user functions are working, the design, planning, prototyping, and implementation phases of Microsoft Exchange have been completed. The additional phases that could be a part of the project GANTT chart include tuning and maintenance of the Exchange server as well as future implementations of groupware functionality of Exchange.

Tuning and Maintenance

Although a Microsoft Exchange Server implementation may go smoothly, the project is not necessarily finished. Part of a follow-up to the installation process is testing the performance of the Microsoft Exchange Server and analyzing whether the server is operating at its highest capability. This may include tuning and maintenance of the Exchange server(s), tuning the Microsoft Windows NT domain design, or optimizing the overall operation of all communication functions for the new messaging infrastructure. The components for tuning and optimizing an Exchange environment will be covered in Chapter 14 of this book.

Attaining External Expertise

As with any project process, the successful planning and implementation of the project may require the assistance of external expertise. The assistance may be in the form of validation of an implementation plan or design specification, and may involve the management of the project, or out-tasking desktop workstation client component installation. There are a number of resources available for an organization that needs assistance in the planning, designing, prototyping, installation, training, or tuning of a Microsoft Exchange environment deployment.

Microsoft Consulting Services (MCS)

Microsoft Consulting Services (MCS), a division of Microsoft, works with large organizations or with organizations that have very unique or extremely strategic Microsoft integration implementation needs. MCS works on a consultative arrangement with clients in conjunction with specialized Microsoft Solution Providers to assist clients with their Microsoft Exchange plans or implementation needs.

Microsoft Solution Providers (MSP)

Microsoft has a number of independent organizations around the globe called Microsoft Solution Providers that specialize in working with Microsoft products and technologies. Each Microsoft Solution Provider has specialties that range from design planning, installation, training, application development, or support services on Microsoft products from the desktop application products like Windows 95 or Office 97, to the Microsoft BackOffice products like Microsoft Exchange, System Management Server, and SQL Server to organizations specializing in application tools such as C++, ActiveX, or Microsoft Access.

Microsoft Solution Provider Member

Microsoft has two levels of solution providers. The first level is referred to as Microsoft Solution Provider Members. There are over 11,000 Solution Provider Members worldwide who specialize in Microsoft products and technologies.

Microsoft Solution Provider Partner

Microsoft's second level of solution providers are called Microsoft Solution Provider Partners. A partner-level solution provider is in the top ten percent of solution providers who have committed to a higher level of technical certification and additional training on Microsoft products. Solution Provider Partners receive priority technical assistance from Microsoft as well as additional training and resource allocation. If they are experienced in a product line or technology, Microsoft Solution Provider Partners can be among the best resources available on Microsoft technologies.

Microsoft Certified System Engineer/Microsoft Certified Professional—Exchange

As described earlier in this chapter, Microsoft has a technical certification program that challenges the technical knowledge of individuals who wish to prove their knowledge and expertise in Microsoft technologies. The Microsoft Certified Professional has passed a core Windows NT exam, and a Microsoft Certified System Engineer has passed a series of Windows NT exams, networking technologies, and specialization exams that can include Microsoft Exchange, Microsoft Internet technologies, SQL Server, SNA Server, or System Management Server.

Microsoft Certified Solution Developer (MCSD)

An organization in need of technical assistance with developing forms, add-in applications, or specialized application functions utilizing Microsoft application development tools can turn to Microsoft's Certified Solution Developer certification, which recognizes the qualifications of individuals with application development expertise. The MCSD can be extremely helpful for an organization in creating a solution to a component within an application environment that may help it achieve a specific desired product functionality.

Experience with Microsoft Exchange

In addition to people with technical certifications, there are a number of individuals and organizations that have expertise that goes beyond simply knowing the Microsoft Exchange product. These other resources may have experience or expertise with third-party add-ins to Exchange, such as document routing, voicemail integration with Microsoft Exchange, Internet connectivity to Microsoft Exchange, inbound and outbound faxing with Exchange, or the interconnection of Exchange with SQL client/server databases.

Because Microsoft Exchange has a number of capabilities that go beyond just the core functions of the product, seeking out the experience of individuals with specializations in products and technologies relative to the organization's needs could prove to be valuable in providing the organization with a complete system solution. The vendors that provide add-in products to Exchange have a list of integrators who best represent their organization's product or technology.

Professional Business Consulting and Project Management

Beyond simply product expertise is the need to consider individuals or organizations who understand the practical business functionality of a product like Microsoft Exchange and can provide professional business consulting expertise to assist an organization in identifying how a product like Microsoft Exchange can improve how it conducts its business. Furthermore, an organization can seek out an individual or organization that specializes in the management of a project implementation to get an idea of how a project moves through the stages of design, planning, and implementation to completion.

For most organizations, the success they can achieve in implementing a project can be determined by their past successes in implementing similar projects. Evaluating previous business projects can be indicative of their ability to successfully implement future projects or processes.

The Chapter in Review

■ This chapter ties together the previous planning and design chapters and begins to identify the physical resources required to deploy Exchange. In addition, it takes us through the creation of an implementation GANTT chart which is used as a road map to implementing Exchange.

■ Earlier in the book we evaluated the physical business structure of the organization. The purpose was to identify the organizational units and sites which dictated the need for connectors and site-to-site connectivity. We then created a Windows NT domain model. The NT domain model dictates the security and access administration for the network administration. The domain design also gave us suggestions on the placement of the domain controllers and Exchange servers.

■ In order to help confirm that the domain design and site infrastructure design is appropriate for the organization, the administrators can look at the organization's general workflow and workgroup processes that are affected by the Exchange environment. The organization's workflow will affect how replication between servers is set and what kind of traffic patterns to expect between clients and servers. Additional information required to create a GANTT chart includes the virtual workgroup configuration of the organization, the current and future (estimated) workflow of information, and a consensus on how server-to-server replication should be designed. Additional information required to create a GANTT chart includes knowledge of what the existing network operating system infrastructure is, how much of the infrastructure will be retained in the new Exchange network, and whether an existing network infrastructure is going to be replaced with Windows NT.

■ With that information acquired, we could create a GANTT chart. Using text and graphs, a GANTT chart helps project managers track information about the individual tasks that comprise the project plan by outlining each task in a text chart with its start and end dates. The relative position of each task to the other shows the sequence of tasks required to complete the project. The purpose of a GANTT chart is to arrange the project tasks in order to make implementation easier for the project manager to manage, to track the cost and time required to complete each task, to help keep the project on time and on budget, to develop a sequential relationship between tasks so the project manager can see how changing one task affects the entire project, to help the project manager gather appropriate resources and ensure they are being used efficiently, and to track the progress by comparing the planned installation schedule with the actual installation schedule.

■ The first task in developing a GANTT chart is to think through the process to determine what needs to be done. After an outline is developed, the plan can be further refined and developed. Research needs to be done to determine the project goals, expectations, functions, availability of resources, and technical needs to successfully complete the project. The tasks outlined in a GANTT chart can be classified as major phases of the project, major components of each phase, minor components of each phase, or project milestones. Once the phases and tasks are outlined, the necessary resources can be identified. The first step is to outline the personnel skills necessary to complete the task. Equipment resource needs include hardware, software, tools, equipment, and configuration space needed to perform each task. Once the resources are identified, the project manager needs to determine the length of time each resource will be needed for each task. Ideally, a project manager will have the experience necessary for this kind of project, and the expertise to properly plan, manage, and implement all tasks they are responsible for.

■ To help ensure the success of a project, many organizations contract an external project manager with the appropriate expertise. The internal project manager is someone from the organization who functions as a single point of contact who will ensure that the organization's needs and goals will be met. Internal staff may need to be technically trained on the new application being implemented.

Review Questions

Q. Why is it important to begin planning for an Exchange implementation by evaluating the physical business structure of the organization?
A. The purpose is to identify the organizational units and sites, which dictate the need for connectors and site-to-site connectivity.

Q. Name some components of the project plan.
A. Scope of work, work plan, phases, tasks, resources, milestones, parallel processes, and linked processes.

Q. What is a milestone?
A. Milestones are the significant steps that denote the successful completion of a major task or phase of the project.

Q. What is the difference between parallel processes and linked processes?
A. Parallel processes are tasks that can be performed at the same time. Linked processes require that the first process be completely finished before the next process can begin.

Q. What is required before beginning any GANTT chart?
A. Research is required to determine the project goals, expectations, functions, availability of resources, and technical needs to successfully complete the project.

Q. What happens once the phases and tasks are identified?
A. Once the phases and tasks are identified, the necessary resources can be identified.

Q. Give examples of resources required in an Exchange project.

A. Required resources are usually broken down by personnel and equipment. Examples of personnel resource needs include a project manager, project planner(s) and designer(s), implementation engineers, etc. Equipment resource needs include hardware, software, tools, equipment, and configuration space. Time and money are also required resources.

Q. How are the baseline timelines and implementation dates established?

A. Once the resources are identified, the project manager determines the length of time each resource will be needed for each task. This is the final step in determining baseline dates including starting dates, ending dates, and amount of work required from each resource. With this information, the project manager can draw the implementation dates on the GANTT chart for each phase.

Q. Name some components of the planning and design phase.

A. Identifying the project manager, train internal personnel, acquire external expertise, develop a scope of work and a work plan, and create the infrastructure design and plan.

Q. After investing in all that training, why might an organization need to acquire expertise from outside the organization?

A. While the training classes address design, installation, and support of Exchange, having assistance from a person or organization that has done many Exchange projects increases the organization's likelihood of success. Both training and experience are desirable to ensure a high level of project success.

Q. What is the first round of installation and testing called?

A. The first round of installation and testing is called the prototyping phase.

Q. What are some professional services that Microsoft recognizes to assist organizations with their Exchange rollouts?

A. Microsoft Consulting Services, Microsoft Solution Providers, and Microsoft Exchange Specialists.

CHAPTER **11**

Installing the Microsoft Exchange Environment

In the previous chapters, we designed and planned the Microsoft Exchange environment, as well as began the creation of a GANTT chart to map the Microsoft Exchange implementation. This chapter will complete the implementation phase of the Microsoft Exchange environment, including the installation of the Microsoft Windows NT domain controllers as well as the Microsoft Exchange servers and clients.

Installing the Core Local Area Network

The installation procedure for Microsoft Exchange begins with the installation of the core Microsoft Windows NT components, such as the primary domain controller, backup domain controller(s), and Microsoft Windows NT servers (shown in Figure 11-1). These components create the main infrastructure for Microsoft Exchange and the security access to the Exchange server and public and private information stores, as well as define the group security functions of the network.

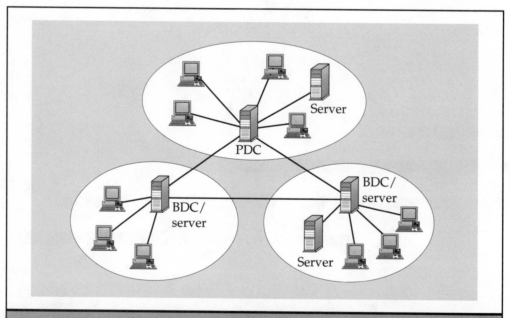

Figure 11-1. *Sample network with one PDC and a handful of BDCs and servers*

As discussed in Chapter 4, the placement of the primary and backup domain controllers, as well as the servers in the network, is done for specific, strategic reasons based on the network security configuration and the distribution of its administration.

Installing Microsoft Windows NT Server

The Microsoft Windows NT Server software, which is at the heart of the Microsoft Exchange environment, is available either as a standalone product or bundled with Microsoft BackOffice. As I discussed in the previous chapters on designing and sizing the Exchange server, the "hardware" of the Microsoft Exchange Server should be thoroughly prepared and tested, taking into account:

- An appropriate amount of RAM memory to cache the hard disk capacity of the server, and to optimally run the add-on applications on the server.

- An appropriate amount of disk storage plus the proper hard disk fault tolerance that has already been configured and tested and found to be in a clean format.

- A network adapter that is appropriate for the communications infrastructure of the organization.

Once the hardware is configured and tested, the installation of Microsoft Windows NT Server can begin.

The installation of Microsoft Windows NT Server software should follow this procedure:

1. Format the boot partition of the server with DOS (skip this step if the installation is on a Digital Alpha or PowerPC system).

2. Run the Windows NT setup program by going into the I386, ALPHA, or PPC directory on the Microsoft Windows NT CD-ROM. The installation setup program can be started by running the WINNT.EXE program for the Intel systems or the automated installation for the Alpha and PowerPC systems. The initial installation will copy the default configuration files for the server into temporary directories. The Windows NT system will complete the file copy and will reboot the server.

3. Upon automatic reboot of the server, the initial installation screen, as shown in Figure 11-2, will be displayed. Throughout the installation process, the administrator will have the opportunity to move to the next screen or back a screen.

4. The next screen will be the Setup Options for the Windows NT installation. Since the server will be an application server and not a user's workstation, many of the standard components of Microsoft Exchange Server do not need to be installed. The "typical installation" of the Windows NT Server software is all that is necessary as a framework for the Exchange server installation.

5. One of the next screens to appear will be the option for the Computer Name, as shown in Figure 11-3. As previously noted, the naming conventions of the Exchange environment dictate that the computer name is the name that the client workstations need to identify as their default server for their client software installation. The server name should be easy to remember and potentially indicative of the location or site of the server, so when users need to connect to the server, they will be able to easily figure out or remember its name.

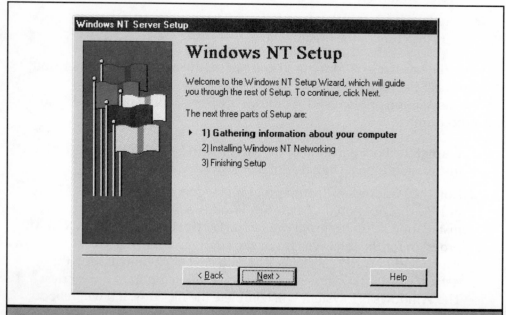

Figure 11-2. *Initial Windows NT setup screen*

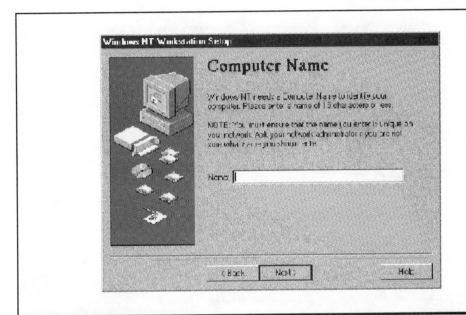

Figure 11-3.   *Selecting the name of the Microsoft Windows NT Server*

6. The installation will proceed with the administrator being asked to provide the server user name and company name. The administrator will also be asked to enter a Product Identification number for software licensing authentication.

7. Next, the administrator will select a password for the server's administrator name. If this is the first server to be installed for the domain, this will be the logon password for the administrator that will be used to manage the Microsoft NT domain.

8. The next step of the Windows NT Server installation is the configuration of the Windows NT setup options. You will see a Windows NT setup screen similar to the one shown in Figure 11-4. From among the networking components options later in the installation, you will be able to select the appropriate network adapter(s) as well as the protocols. You will have the option to select one, two, or all three of the protocols. They include TCP/IP, IPX, and NetBEUI and should be selected based on your network environment's integration compatibility and WAN connectivity needs.

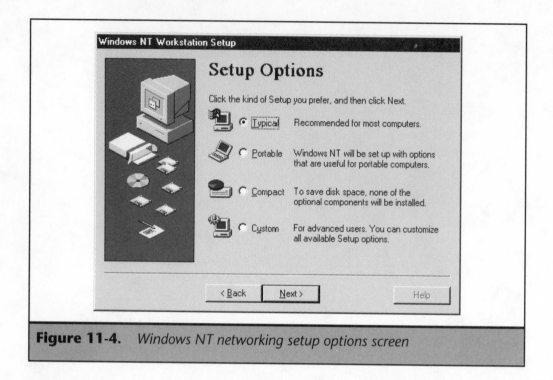

Figure 11-4. *Windows NT networking setup options screen*

Primary Domain Controllers/Backup Domain Controllers

During the installation process, you will have the option to select whether this server will be the network's primary domain controller, a backup domain controller, or just a server on the network. It is crucial that the appropriate option is selected at this time.

If the system will be the primary domain controller, the name of the domain will need to be entered. Since it is assumed that the primary domain controller is the first system in the new domain, the domain name selected must be unique on the network. If after the installation process the new primary domain controller finds another primary domain controller with the same domain name, errors will occur.

If the system will be a backup domain controller, after the network adapter and networking protocols have been selected, the installation process will look for the primary domain controller to connect the new server and begin the domain controller replication process for the new backup domain controller. If the backup domain controller cannot find the primary domain controller during the installation process, the installation of the system will fail. The installation would need to be restarted from the beginning when the primary domain controller is available and accessible to the server being installed.

Servers

If the new server is designated simply to be a server in the domain, it will be added into the domain as a resource server. It is important to note, however, that it will not be possible to promote this server to domain controller status in the future. Once installed as a server, the system will always remain a server. If at some point in the future there is a need to promote the server to primary or backup domain controller status, the option must have been selected during the installation process or the server software will need to be reinstalled from scratch. At any time, a domain controller can become a server, but a server cannot become a domain controller.

After the installation process has been completed, the server will reboot to the logon screen for the network, as shown here:

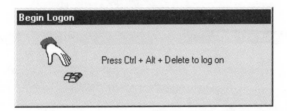

Installing the Exchange Servers

Once the core Windows NT networking components have been installed, the next step is the installation of the Microsoft Exchange Server software. This is where the main Microsoft Exchange components will be installed for the organization, sites, connectors, and public folders. To begin the installation of the Microsoft Exchange Server software, run the SETUP.EXE program on the Microsoft Exchange Server installation CD-ROM.

Installation of the First Server

During installation of the first Exchange server in the organization, you will be asked to enter the organization name and site name from a screen similar to the one shown in Figure 11-5. As I discussed in Chapter 4, selection of an appropriate organization and site name is important because these names cannot be changed later without performing a complete reinstallation of the Microsoft Exchange software.

Adding a Server to the Same Site

If this will be a new server added to an existing site, rather than adding a new organization and site name during the installation process, you will need to select the option to add a new server to an existing organization, as shown in Figure 11-6. All servers within a site need to share administrative security privileges with the domain of the existing organization and site. Thus, prior to the installation of the new server, the server either needs to be a part of the existing Windows NT domain, or trust relationships between the new server and the existing organization need to be configured. Otherwise, the installation of the new server will fail.

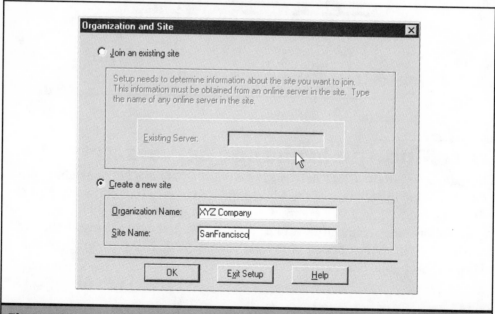

Figure 11-5. *Entering the organization and site name for the first Exchange server*

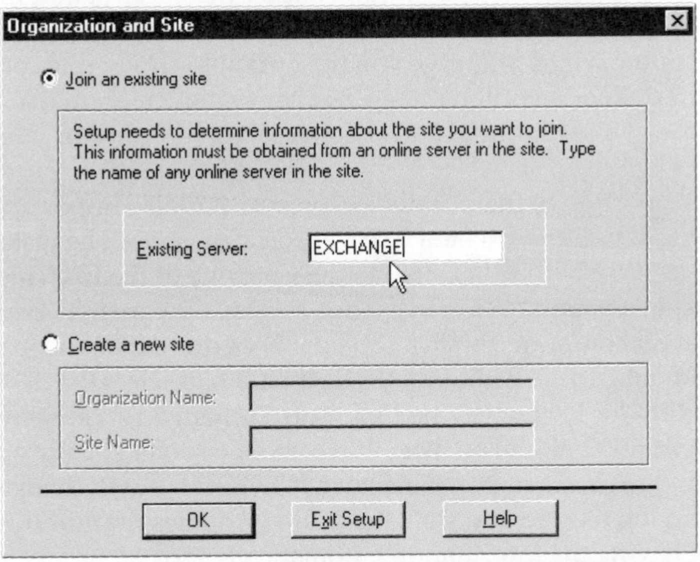

Figure 11-6. *Adding a server to an existing organization or site*

Creating a New Site in an Exchange Organization

If the new server is part of an existing organization but is a new site, enter a server name of an existing server in the organization as the configuration option in Figure 11-6. Because sites are connected through site connectors, the interconnection between the new Exchange server and the existing Exchange network does not necessarily need to be configured during the initial installation process.

Installing Exchange Connectors

During the installation of the Exchange software, you will have the option to select a typical installation or a custom installation, as well as the location to which you want to install the Exchange server files. If this will be the first server in an isolated network environment, the typical installation is fine; however, if this server will be connected to other Exchange servers or other networks such as the Internet, the custom installation should be selected. By default, the installation of Microsoft Exchange Server does not install any of the connectors. They can be easily installed after the initial standard Exchange server installation. Or, during the installation process, select the custom installation option, which will give you the option to choose the connectors. The connector options selection screen, similar to the one shown in Figure 11-7, will allow you to highlight and checkmark each connector you wish to install.

During this portion of the installation process it is also important to select the directory to which the Exchange server software should be installed. By default, the software will be installed to the C> drive of the Exchange server. However, the destination for the Exchange server software may be a D> or E> drive for a server configured with a separate boot drive than the main programs and data drive. Although this is the time to select the destination of the program files for Exchange, the Microsoft Exchange Server software has an optimization utility that will analyze the Exchange server software after its installation and suggests more efficient ways to install the Exchange software, data store, and log files. In addition, the utility provides the administrator with the option of having the information automatically moved and reoptimized. The optimization tool for Exchange will be discussed in Chapter 14.

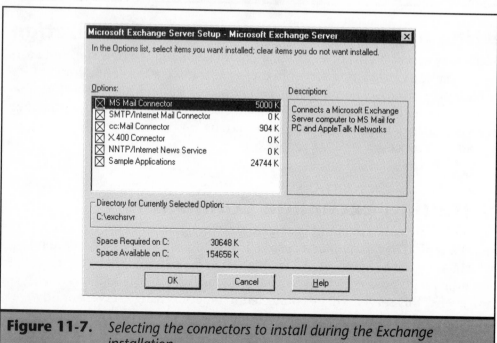

Figure 11-7. *Selecting the connectors to install during the Exchange installation*

Exchange Connector

If this server will be connected to other Microsoft Exchange servers, when the new server joins another site, the Exchange connector will be installed for the system. The Exchange connector provides options for replicating public folders, the time of day to replicate folders, primary and secondary connector routes, and the method of connection. Use of the Exchange connector does not require the servers to be a part of the same site or members of the same organization. Many organizations may want to connect their servers together to have a private network-to-network connection for secured electronic mail transfers. Other organizations may want to replicate public folders between organizations to facilitate the sharing of information.

Internet, X.400, MS Mail, cc:Mail Connector

Microsoft Exchange Server has a number of other connectors, including connectors to the Internet, X.400, Microsoft Mail, and cc:Mail. All of these connectors and their installation and configuration were covered in Chapter 8.

Installing Clients

Once the Microsoft Exchange Server infrastructure is configured and operating, the installation of the client software is the next step. For many application programs, the installation of the client software is fairly simple and quick. For Microsoft Exchange, however, installation of the client software is in many cases the hardest part of an Exchange environment deployment.

The Exchange client software installation can easily take over 85 percent of the time and effort necessary to successfully complete the Exchange installation. Among the many challenges faced when migrating the Microsoft Exchange client software include ensuring that there is enough disk space and RAM memory on the workstation to support the software, and that the transport drivers for the Exchange client on the workstation are compatible.

There are two methods generally used to install the client software on a workstation. They vary depending on whether the client software is being installed on a system with no existing electronic mail, or whether the software is being installed on a system with an existing electronic messaging system that requires the coexistence of the old and the new messaging systems.

The user client software installation process includes:

- Verifying that the user's workstation has the minimum hardware requirements to support the Microsoft Exchange client software. The minimum requirements are

  - **RAM** 4MB minimum for the DOS client, 8MB minimum for the Windows/Windows 95 client, 24MB minimum for the Windows NT client, 12MB minimum for the Macintosh client

  - **Disk Space** 8MB minimum disk space per user on the hard drive that has the user's Windows and windows\system directories, or 36MB minimum if the full client software is installed for each user

  - **Processor Speed** Any processor speed that adequately supports Microsoft Windows or Windows 95 software (typically a 486 or faster, but the DOS client for Exchange will perform adequately on a 286 or 386 computer)

  - **Local Area Network Connection** All users on a Microsoft Exchange network must have the components necessary to establish a local area network connection such as a network adapter, network access drivers, cabling, and wiring hubs. The currently supported network operating systems include Novell NetWare (v3.x and v4.x), Microsoft Windows NT (v4.x, v3.5x, and v3.1), Microsoft LanManager, IBM OS/2 WarpServer and LanServer, and Banyan Vines (v6.x and v5.x).

- Determining which transport method you wish to use in order to access the Exchange server. Although this is not mentioned in any common Microsoft Exchange client installation guide, you can actually choose either the Exchange client or the Exchange server to function as your transport protocol. Thus, if you are currently using Novell NetWare and Novell's IPX/SPX protocol in order to access your LAN, you can use TCP/IP or NetBEUI as your primary transport for Exchange. This is important for many organizations that are considering standardizing their company transport standard to a protocol such as TCP/IP or those who prefer to have client/server communications over their wide area networks to run over TCP/IP rather than NetBEUI or IPX/SPX. The Microsoft Exchange client transport options include RPC, IPX, TCP/IP, Vines IP, and Named Pipes.

- Installing the Exchange client software on the workstation. Once you determine the core configuration of your Exchange client software, you can begin installing it on the workstation. You can either install the entire Exchange client software on the local hard drive of the workstation (a total of around 40m of disk space will be needed), or you can install it in a shared location on a network file server and only install the local configuration files and require support files (DLLs in a Windows-type environment) on the local workstation. The support files that are installed on each workstation's Windows directory still take up around 10m of disk space. The obvious advantage to installing the Exchange client software on a shared network directory is saving around 30m of disk space on each workstation's hard drive. However, sharing the workstation client software will result in more network traffic, as all access to the Exchange client software will need to be done from the network shared location. Of more importance than disk space requirement issues and speed is the fact that a shared installation of the workstation client software does not allow new users to be added when someone is using the shared version of the Exchange client software. Because the Exchange client is running from a shared directory, if someone is using the shared Exchange client software, a few of the shared files will be open and in use, thus preventing the installation of new users until all users close out the Exchange client software. If you have the luxury of disk space on each user's workstation, it is advisable to perform a full installation of the 36MB of Exchange client software on each workstation.

- As you install the Exchange client software, you have the option of which services you want to access during the installation (access to Exchange Server, an old Microsoft Mail e-mail system, cc:Mail, a Lotus Notes server, access to CompuServe e-mail, etc.). If you are migrating to Exchange and plan on using the new Exchange client to access your old e-mail system in the interim, you need to install the services to include your old e-mail system (MS Mail or cc:Mail) as well as Exchange server.

- At about the time that the Exchange client software is installed on the users' workstations, you may want to provide them with training materials or a training class so that users can become familiar with the Exchange client software. Most users who have e-mail proficiency may need only a few minutes to figure out how to send messages, read messages, reply to messages, and use the new Exchange client software on their own. However, users who are part of organizations that have never had electronic mail may need assistance in gaining familiarity with the use of the Exchange client software.

Installing the Windows v3.x, Windows 95, and Windows NT Exchange Clients

The installation of the Exchange client software is initiated by running the SETUP.EXE program from the Exchange Server CD. The Windows v3.x client software resides in the WIN16 subdirectory, and the Windows 95 and Windows NT client software resides in the WIN32 subdirectory. The initial installation screen, as shown in Figure 11-8, will ask whether you want to install a typical or a custom version of the installation. If you want to install the Microsoft Exchange Server service option so that the client can access Microsoft Exchange, the standard option is all that needs to be selected. If you want to install the service or the services to connect to Microsoft Mail, to a POP3 Internet server, or any other messaging service, select the custom option and choose the services you need during this installation phase, or you can elect to add the other mail services later.

In the initial installation screen, you will also be given the opportunity to select the directory to which you want to install the client software. If you want to install the client software in a centralized location on a shared server, select the directory of the server at this time.

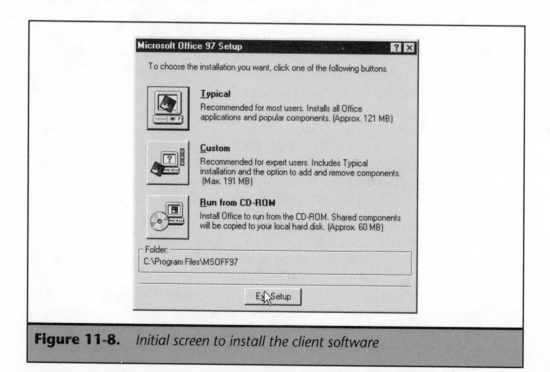

Figure 11-8. *Initial screen to install the client software*

Using the Exchange Automatic Profile Generator

For an organization that will be installing the Microsoft Exchange client on a number of workstations, use of the Exchange Automatic Profile Generator can minimize the number of times the installer of the Exchange client software needs to press the ENTER key or select *yes* or *OK* during the installation process. In fact, all the installer needs to do is make a few minor changes to the default profile and then run SETUP to install the client software.

During the installation of the Microsoft Exchange client software, the setup program looks for a file called DEFAULT.PRF. If it finds the file, it will spawn the NEWPROF.EXE program that creates a user's profile based on the settings within the DEFAULT.PRF program. The use of default profiles assumes that the installation of the Exchange client software is invoked from a subdirectory on a server hard drive and not from the Exchange CD-ROM, so the DEFAULT.PRF can be edited and copied into the subdirectory for use. The default profile configuration file can be configured to automatically install the following options for a user:

- **Profile Name** This is the default name given to a user's profile.

- **Services** These are service options, such as the Microsoft Exchange client or Microsoft Mail client support, personal address book option, or personal folders.

- **Mailbox Name/Home Server** The profile can be configured to automatically select a user name or a default server during the installation process.

- **Path to Personal Address Book/Path to Personal Folders** The profile can be configured to automatically select the directories where the user's personal address book or personal folders will be stored.

A sample DEFAULT.PRF is shown below:

```
; Section 1 - Profile defaults.
[General]
ProfileName=Default Exchange Profile
DefaultProfile=Yes
OverwriteProfile=No
DefaultStore=Service2
; Section 2 - Services in profile.
[Service List]
Service1=Microsoft Exchange Client
```

```
Service2=Microsoft Exchange Server
Service3=Personal Address Book

; Section 3 - Default values for each service.
[Service1]
NotifyPlaySound=TRUE
NotifyChangeCursor=TRUE
NotifyShowPopup=FALSE
WarnOnDelete=TRUE
EmptyWastebasket=FALSE
ShowTooltips=TRUE
SelectEntireWord=TRUE
AfterMoveMessage=0
IncludeMessageText=TRUE
IndentMessageText=TRUE
CloseOriginalMessage=TRUE
GenReadReceipt=FALSE
GenDeliveryReceipt=FALSE
DefaultSensitivity=0
DefaultPriority=1
SaveSentMail=TRUE

[Service2]
ConversionProhibited=TRUE

[Service3]
PathToPersonalAddressBook=c:\exchange\mailbox.pab
ViewOrder=1

; Section 4 - Mapping for profile properties.
[Microsoft Exchange Client]
SectionGUID=0a0d020000000000c000000000000046

[Microsoft Exchange Server]
ServiceName=MSEMS
MDBGUID=5494A1C0297F101BA58708002B2A2517
MailboxName=PT_STRING8,0x6607
HomeServer=PT_STRING8,0x6608
OfflineFolderPath=PT_STRING8,0x6610
OfflineAddressBookPath=PT_STRING8,0x660E
ExchangeConfigFlags=PT_LONG,0x6601
;        The following values are possible:
```

```
;        VALUE          RESULT
;        4              Normal
;        6              Ask whether to connect or work offline at
                        startup.
;        12             Allow clients to be authenticated via the
                        Internet
;        14             Combination of 6 and 12.

[Personal Address Book]
ServiceName=MSPST AB
PathToPersonalAddressBook=PT_STRING8,0x6600
ViewOrder=PT_LONG,0x6601
```

Installing the Microsoft Outlook Client

The installation of the Microsoft Outlook client is initiated by running the SETUP.EXE program of the Microsoft Office 97 CD. During installation, the user will have the option of installing all of the Office 97 components, including Word, Excel, or PowerPoint, or the user can simply elect to perform a custom installation and select the Outlook client component, as shown in Figure 11-9. During the installation of the Outlook Client, the installer will have the option of selecting the Exchange server information, user information, and directory to which the Outlook client should be installed.

Installing the Macintosh Client

Chapter 19 of this book will cover the installation and integration of Macintosh computers into a Microsoft Windows NT and Microsoft Exchange network. Please refer to that chapter for detailed installation information.

The Chapter in Review

- This chapter completes the implementation phase of Microsoft Exchange. The main infrastructure of the Exchange network includes the primary domain controller, backup domain controller, and NT servers. The hardware that runs Microsoft Exchange needs to have the appropriate configuration for its intended use. That includes enough memory, appropriate drive space and fault tolerance, and a sufficient

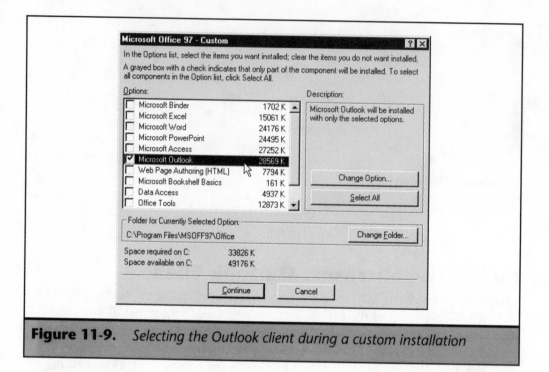

Figure 11-9. *Selecting the Outlook client during a custom installation*

network adapter. The installation of an NT server begins by running the Windows NT setup program and answering the installation questions the server will prompt the installer for.

■ The installation continues with the next screen for setting up options. The Typical installation option is usually adequate when configuring NT for an application server, such as with Exchange. The primary domain controller needs to be installed on the network first, then backup domain controllers and servers can be installed. Regular servers cannot be promoted to become either a primary domain controller or a backup domain controller without reinstalling the Windows NT operating system on the server.

■ The next step is to install Exchange on the server. For the first Exchange server, it will prompt for the organization name and site name. If this server is being added to an existing site, instead of typing in the organization name and site name, the configuring engineer would select the option to add a server. All servers within a site need to share administration security privileges. Thus, the server needs to be part of the existing Windows NT domain, or a trust relationship must be established between the new server and the existing organization.

- By default, Exchange does not install any connectors. So if there is to be more than one server or an Internet connection, the custom installation option of Exchange should be chosen.

- The next step is to configure the clients. Installing the client portion of Exchange can be the most time-consuming part for some organizations. Each client must have adequate resources available, including free drive space, adequate memory, and a compatibility of transport drives for the Exchange client workstation. First, confirm that the workstation(s) has (have) an adequate amount of resources available. Then, the organization must choose which transport protocol will be used between the Exchange Server and clients. The organization does not necessarily have to run the same transport between Exchange servers and clients as it runs on the rest of the network.

- To speed the client installations, the configuring engineer can use the Exchange Automatic Profile Generator. This allows for the client options to be selected once and installed for many, significantly reducing the amount of information required for each workstation.

Review Questions

Q. What happens during an NT installation after NT has completed the file copy?
A. It will automatically reboot, at which point the installation continues.

Q. Which stage of the NT installation process are network protocols chosen?
A. When NT installs the networking components.

Q. If a new server is part of an existing organization but located at a new site, what server name would be entered?
A. The name of an existing server on the network.

Q. What transport providers can the Exchange client support?
A. RPC, IPX, TCP/IP, Vines IP, and Named Pipes.

Q. What options can the Automatic Profile Generator automatically install?
A. The profile name, services, mailbox name/home server, and the path to the personal address book and folders.

PART THREE

Administering, Optimizing, Tuning, and Managing a Microsoft Exchange Environment

In the first half of this book, we reviewed the entire Microsoft Exchange Server product and its capabilities, and designed a plan to configure, install, and migrate to Microsoft Exchange and Microsoft Windows NT. In Part Three, we will examine the installed Microsoft Exchange Server environment and suggest ways to optimize the installation as well as review its administration, security, and management in order to make Microsoft Exchange a more efficient and effective messaging tool.

CHAPTER 12

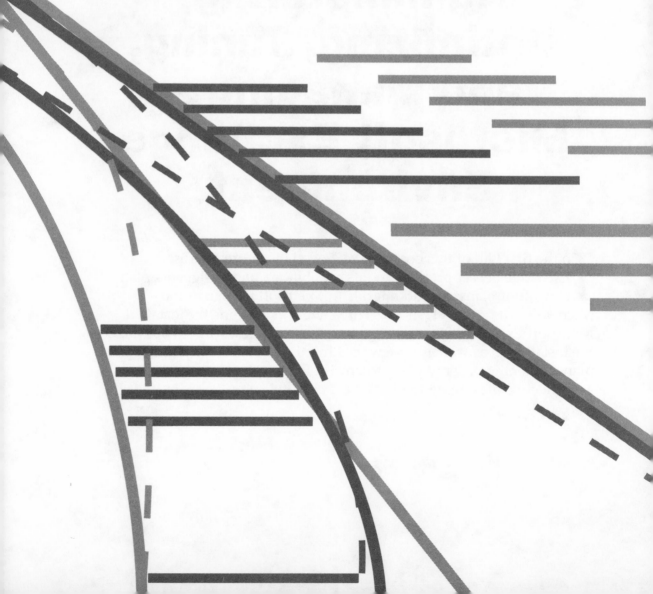

Administering a Microsoft Exchange Environment

Administering a Microsoft Exchange environment involves not only daily user management tasks such as adding, modifying, and deleting but also securing the network both internally and externally. In this chapter, we will summarize the daily administration functions of Microsoft Exchange as well as explore various client-to-client, and server-to-server security administration functions available within Microsoft Exchange.

Adding, Deleting, and Modifying Users

The first thing that comes to mind when someone refers to administering a messaging system is the daily task of adding, deleting, and modifying users. We will review these basics and also examine the administration of groups and resources in Exchange, as well as how Exchange's various user and resource administration components affect daily and operational usage.

Adding and Managing Users in Microsoft Exchange

The administration of users within Microsoft Exchange begins when users are added to the system. Users are added and user functions are modified in Exchange through the use of the Exchange Administrator utility. By default, the Exchange Administrator utility is added to the Exchange folder on the Exchange server during installation. When administrators of the Exchange environment run the utility, they have the ability to select the site they wish to administer, and the server to which they wish to add a new mailbox. The procedure to add a new user to Microsoft Exchange, as shown here, is to enter File | New Mailbox within the Exchange Administrator program.

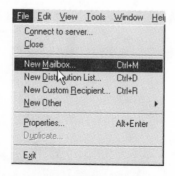

When the new user screen appears, the administrator has ten tabs of options in which to enter information. This information includes the user's first name, last name, and mail groups he or she belongs to, as well as dozens of other options.

General Information Tab

On the General information tab (shown in Figure 12-1), the administrator has the option of making the following selections. The options and their importance are as follows:

- **First Name/Middle Initial/Last Name** These options identify the user. The Exchange user information can essentially become a company directory because of the Exchange administration utility's ability to track information in addition to the user's name and mailbox. If the organization's strategy is to use the Exchange administration information as its database, populating the information with as much detailed information as possible can be very beneficial.

- **Displayed Name** This is what appears in the Global Address List (or address book) of the network. If the organization wishes to store users according to their last names, first names, Internet addresses, or some other method, this is where the user information is generated.

- **Alias** When a user's information is searched from the network address book, the Exchange client software will find the user based on either the user's displayed name or alias. If a user's formal name is James, his displayed name may appear as *James*, but he may also have an alias, *Jim,* in the user configuration information. This allows other users to find him as James or Jim.

- **City, State, Zip, Country, Title, Company, Department, Office, Assistant, Phone** Detailed information about users can be entered into the Exchange user properties and used within the organization to search or find information about specific individuals.

NOTE: Administrators can create a default to determine the way that the Display Name and the Alias Name are concatenated, such as first name then last name (John Smith), first initial then last name (Jsmith), or first name and last initial (JohnS), etc. This can be selected as an Exchange Administrator default by selecting Tools/ Options. The administrator will have the option of selecting something similar to %First %Last (which will place a space between the first name and the last name) or %1First%Last (which will take the first letter of the first name and the entire last name).

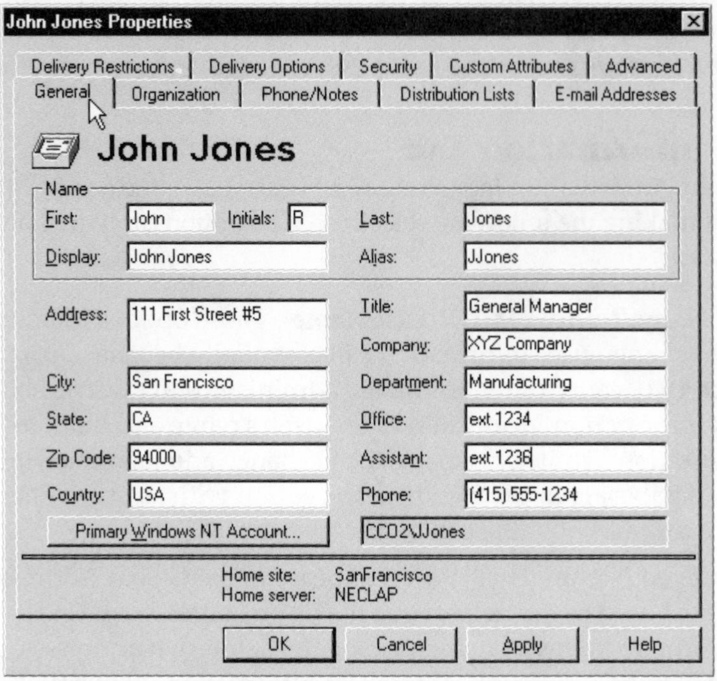

Figure 12-1. *Exchange administration user General information tab*

Organization Tab

The organization section of the user properties can be used to set up an organization's chart tree. An individual user's manager can be selected from the list of Exchange recipients as well as the persons who report to the user. Anyone searching the organization's address book using the Exchange user properties can move up and down the organization chart simply by selecting names in the address book.

Phone/Notes Tab

The phone and notes section provides the administrator with the ability to add in a variety of phone numbers for each individual. The various phone options include: business (which will be the same as the phone entry from the general tab), business two, fax number, assistant's phone number, home phone, second home phone number, mobile number, and pager number. There is also a section to which you can enter general notes for the individual which could be additional information not included in a default field of the administrator program.

Distribution Lists Tab

The Distribution Lists tab is used to track the Microsoft Exchange groups to which the user belongs. This may be a distribution list of "all e-mail users," a list of "all San Francisco Managers," a list of "all Worldwide Marketing Executives," or the like. Selecting an existing distribution list adds the individual to the distribution list.

E-mail Addresses Tab

E-mail addresses serve as the definitions for users' Internet addresses, Microsoft Mail addresses, or X.400 addresses. By default, an addressing scheme is created for the user. If an individual user address needs to be changed, the e-mail address section can be used to modify it. Users can have multiple addresses as well, which is of use to organizations when users change their names. For example, a user would probably want to begin using his or her new name as an Internet address, but Microsoft Exchange would need to be able to route messages correctly for the user's old Internet address name as well. The e-mail address section allows users to modify their address names or have multiple address names.

Although users can have multiple addresses for incoming messages, they can only have one return or reply address that recognizes the user for return replies. The Set as Reply Address option allows the administrator to select the default return reply address. A sample of e-mail address options for users is shown in Figure 12-2.

Delivery Restrictions Tab

Within the Exchange Administrator, restrictions can be placed on incoming messages for each Exchange user in the organization. The administrator can select the name of an individual or individuals from whom messages will be either accepted or rejected. This function can be used to prevent messages from being sent directly to helpdesk personnel instead of to a helpdesk request message queue.

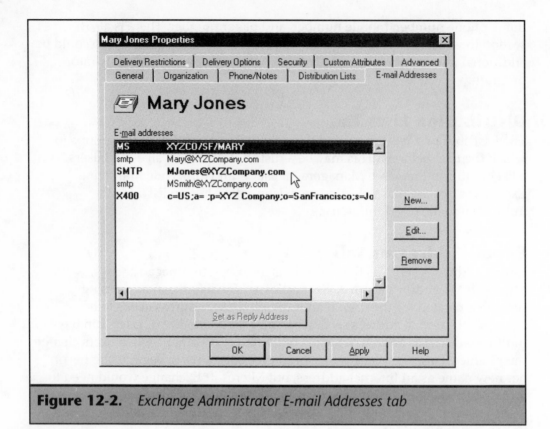

Figure 12-2. *Exchange Administrator E-mail Addresses tab*

Delivery Options Tab

The Delivery Options tab of the user properties allows the administrator to grant certain users the privilege to give their assistants Send on Behalf of messages permission, as well as alternate recipients for messages. These options can be set up by each individual user; however, the administrator may want to set up a messaging relationship between a manager and a secretary, or an individual and his or her personal assistant so that the assistant is able to send or receive messages on behalf of the manager.

Security Tab

The security section provides the administrator with the ability to enable, recover, and revoke advanced messaging security. This includes enabling digital signatures and encryption. Security information will be covered in-depth later in this chapter.

Custom Attributes Tab

An administrator can configure up to ten custom attributes for an organization. These attributes may include information such as an employee badge number, an individual mailstop number, or other unique information that an organization wants to enter specifically for individuals. The custom attributes are initially customized and created for the organization by going to the Configuration section of the Exchange site hierarchy as shown in Figure 12-3, selecting the DS Site Configuration container, File | Properties, and the Custom Attributes tab.

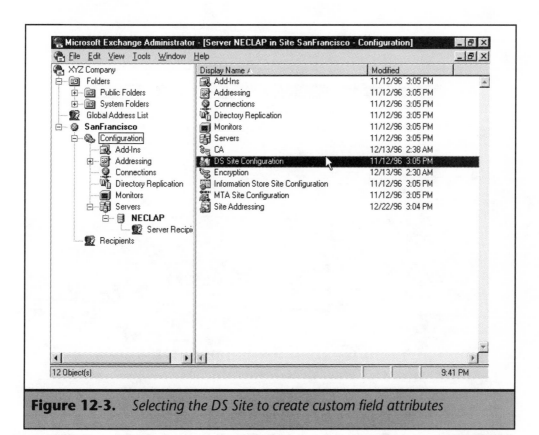

Figure 12-3. *Selecting the DS Site to create custom field attributes*

Advanced Tab

The Advanced tab in the user properties options contains detailed user information and choices for messaging handling functions for each user in Exchange, as shown in Figure 12-4.

- **Simple display name** This is the name that can be used by an individual to communicate with a system that cannot interpret the user's normal display name. This may be required for a naming structure that has special characters or name lengths that are supported by Microsoft Exchange, but not supported by other messaging systems.

- **Directory name** The directory name is the given name defined on the General page of the user properties.

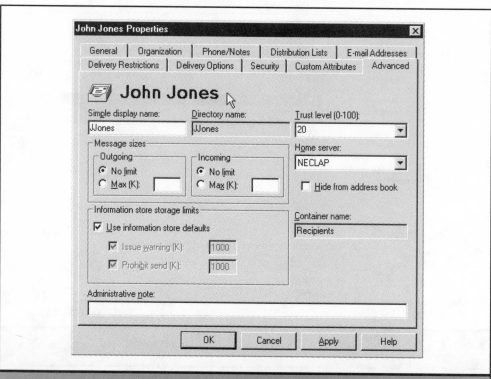

Figure 12-4. *The Advanced tab in the user properties information*

- **Trust level** The trust level of a user is used to determine if the information about the user will be replicated to other mail systems during directory synchronization. If the user's trust level is higher than the trust level set for the container being replicated, the information about the user will not be replicated. This is useful for organizations that want some, but not all users to be seen in the address book in remote sites of the organization. At these remote sites, the presence of irrelevant user information about users who are unconnected to the specific site will simply clutter up the organization's directory.

- **Outgoing message size limit** The size of outgoing messages in Exchange can be limited. This function can prevent users from sending extremely large files that take up a large percentage of the organization's WAN or Internet bandwidth capability, or it may be used to prevent a user from e-mailing large company databases outside of the organization. By default, the message size limit is set to unlimited.

- **Incoming message size limit** An administrator can also limit the size of files being retrieved by any individual. This can prevent a huge file from being sent to users within an organization that may potentially take up all of the available disk space of the Exchange message store. By default, this option is set to unlimited incoming message size.

- **User's home server** The user's home server can be selected to define where the user will, by default, login and authenticate to the Exchange organization.

- **Hide the user from the organization's address book** Some users may not need to be seen in the address book. These users may be special alias message boxes for individuals within the organization, or particular support individuals who may not want their addresses publicly available. Within the Exchange Administrator program, the administrator has the option of either viewing visible recipients or all recipients including hidden users.

- **Information store storage limits** When the information store of the individual exceeds the maximum limit defined for the user, warnings are generated and sent to the individual. This can be used to prevent users from saving any and all messages and storing hundreds or thousands of megabytes of messages without performing periodic housecleaning.

- **Administrative note** There is a field in which the administrator can enter additional notes on the individual user.

Groups and Resources in Exchange

Many electronic messaging systems do not differentiate between a user or a resource within the organization. Users send and receive messages as well as have appointment calendars and participate in group discussions. A resource, however, like a conference room, needs an appointment calendar that is available to users in a messaging system, but it has no need to send or receive messages or to participate in discussion groups.

Microsoft Exchange does not drastically alter the process of creating a resource compared to creating a user, but there are specific functions for the creation, maintenance, and management of resources that should be properly handled.

Creating and Managing Resources

Creating a resource is exactly the same as creating a user, which was outlined earlier in this chapter. The key functions in creating a resource should follow these steps:

1. Click on File | New Mailbox.

2. **General tab**   There is no need to have a First, Middle, or Last name for a resource, so just fill in the display name with the way you want the resource to appear on the address book, and fill in the alias with a word or phrase that help users to be able to search for this resource. Select the Windows NT security for the individual who will be the administrator of the resource to allocate security privileges and do periodic maintenance on the schedule. The balance of the information is not applicable for a resource.

3. **Delivery Restrictions tab**   Select to reject messages from all users since no one should be sending messages to the resource.

4. **Advanced tab**   Set the incoming and outgoing message sizes to 0K since this resource should not be sending or receiving messages. The Trust level should be set high since most resources are only applicable for use by local users and users in other sites or connections have no need to see or schedule a resource in another site.

5. Organization/Phone/Distribution Lists/E-mail Addresses/Custom Attributes/Security/Delivery Options have no application information for a resource.

6. On a workstation, create a new Exchange profile for the new resource.

7. Launch the Schedule+ client for the new resource.

8. Create a new scheduler file for the new resource.

9. In the Scheduler software, select Tools | Set Access Permissions and set up access privileges for users within the organization to access and schedule appointments for the resource.

Creating and Managing Groups

Groups of users are created as Distribution List members in the Exchange Administrator program. To create a new distribution list, select File | New Distribution List and fill in the options for the distribution list properties, as shown in Figure 12-5.

The options include selecting a display name for the group. Just like the display name for users, the display name for a group appears in the address

Figure 12-5. *A user distribution list or group of users in the organization*

book. Many organizations start group names all with the same starting letter or set of letters such as *XYZ Managers, XYZ Administrators,* and *XYZ Sales* so that all a user has to do is go to the XYZ section of the address list to see all of the available groups of users.

The administrator can either add users to the distribution list in the distribution list properties section, or add users individually within the user's property section.

Granting Security Rights

When a new mailbox is created within the Microsoft Exchange Administrator program, a Windows NT user account can be created or an existing NT user account can be used at the same time. The mailbox and its contents, such as messages, private folder information, and appointment calendars, can be accessed through the proper entry of the user's logon name and password.

If a user tries to access another user's mailbox and does not have Windows NT security, he or she will receive an error notification stating that he or she does not have security rights to that user's mailbox. An error dialog box, similar to the one shown here, will appear.

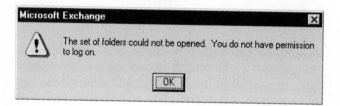

Deleting Users

A user can be deleted within the Microsoft Exchange client by selecting the user name from the Exchange Administrator address list and selecting File | Delete. The deletion of a user from within Microsoft Exchange does not automatically delete that user from the network domain for file and print access services. If an Exchange administrator wants the user to be deleted from Windows NT at the same time that the user is deleted from Microsoft Exchange, then from the Exchange Administrator program, select Tools | Options, Permissions, and then select the option "Delete primary Windows NT account when deleting mailbox."

Microsoft Exchange Security

One aspect of the administration of a Microsoft Exchange environment is ensuring the security of the network both for client-to-client as well as server-to-server communications. The client-level security guarantees that only the users who are allowed to access the server and send messages gain access to the network. The server-level security ensures that information that passes between the Exchange server and another server environment is secure. This server-level security also encompasses remote-access security to the Exchange server environment, such as access to the server over the Internet.

Digital Signatures and Encryption

Critical to advanced security in the Microsoft Exchange environment is the use of digital signatures and encryption. Although Windows NT-level security or even mailbox-level security can minimize the potential of unauthorized access to a user's mailbox and messages, a common network security breach is all it takes to compromise the security of information authentication. One of the most common security breaches can occur when a user is logged into the network e-mail program and steps away from his or her desk for just a moment to go to lunch, the restroom, or even down the hallway to get a fresh cup of coffee. Within seconds, anyone can access the user's unattended workstation and e-mail messages.

Security can become more of an issue when an organization implements document routing that requires the authentication of an individual in order to approve a process. For example, an electronic route can be utilized to approve an office supply order, or approve a pay increase. Once these procedures are implemented, the potential for users to send an approval request and self-approving the request by accessing a manager's workstation at a strategic time can become a security problem on the network.

Through the use of digital signatures, a message is authenticated by a security process that requires a user to enter a password for each message that requires validation. If the user's security key matches the server-registered security key, the message is sent. If there is a mismatch in security key authentication or if the user's password does not match the password registered with the Exchange server, the message is not sent. Digital signatures can be used to confirm transmissions on a message-by-message basis based on whether the authorized password was entered at the time the message was sent.

Encryption Algorithms in Exchange

Microsoft Exchange uses a hybrid encryption system that contains both a public key and a secret key cryptography system. Microsoft Exchange takes advantage of the benefits of public key cryptography to easily and securely distribute keys between users, and it relies on secret key cryptography to encrypt the content of messages because the secret key system is better suited to manage bulk encryption of message data.

Public key cryptography was developed by Ron Rivest, Adi Shamir, and Leonard Adleman in the late 1970s, and is called *RSA public key cipher*. Public key cryptography works on the principle of two halves called a key pair. The key pair consists of a public key and a private key. Matching the appropriate public key with the appropriate private key creates the authentication of a digital signature or an encrypted message.

Microsoft Exchange supports both the CAST (originally developed by Carlisle Adams and Stafford Tavares) and the DES (Data Encryption Standard) security algorithms. CAST supports a flexible encryption standard that can vary between 40 and 128 bits. The longer the key, the more secure the message will be. Microsoft Exchange supports CAST 40, which uses a 40-bit encryption key as well as CAST 64 in a 64-bit key. DES is a fixed length 56-bit key. To comply with U.S export laws, only the CAST 40 can be exported outside the United States and Canada. An organization that wants more secure encryption than the standard 40-bit system can request a more sophisticated encryption version of the software from Microsoft as long as it is a registered owner of Microsoft Exchange residing in the United States or Canada. Certain countries, like France, prohibit any form of encryption; thus the French version of Microsoft Exchange includes no support for a Key Management Server or tabs for Advanced Security.

The use of the same password system that is used in digital signature authentication allows messages to be encrypted and sent to a Microsoft Exchange user with encryption support to be read. If both the sender and the receiver of a message complete the authentication process for a message, the message can be encrypted and unencrypted.

The Key Management Server

The processes of both digital signatures and digital encryption are the result of the implementation of a Key Management Server (KM Server) in the Exchange environment. The Key Management function is a service on an NT server that can run on an existing Microsoft Exchange server or on any NT server in the Exchange domain. The Key Management function manages the allocation and authentication of the digital signatures and encryption on the network.

Installing the KM Server

The Key Management Server software comes free with Microsoft Exchange and is stored in the EXCHKM directory of the Exchange Server CD. The process to install the Key Management Server is as follows:

1. Run the SETUP.EXE program for the KM Server software.

2. Select a directory in which to install the KM Server software.

3. When prompted, put a floppy diskette into the floppy drive which will have a KM Server file copied to the diskette. This file will need to be accessed (on floppy) every time the Key Management Server is initiated. This is typically done at the time of server boot-up. If a Key Management Server cannot find the floppy diskette when prompted the next time during boot-up, the Key Management Server service will not start.

4. After the initial installation of the Key Management software, the Key Management Server service needs to be configured so that it will automatically start on boot-up. To configure the automatic starting of the Key Management Server, on the server that the Key Management software was installed, select Start | Settings | Control Panel | Services. Scroll down to the Microsoft Exchange Key Manager option. Select Startup and change the Startup Type to Automatic. Select Start to start the Key Management Server software.

Granting a User Advanced Security Privileges

Once the Key Management Server software is installed and started, the administrator can select which users within the organization should have access to advanced security. This includes configuring a component in the Exchange Administrator program for each user, as well as configuring a client component on each Exchange client for use of the advanced security functions.

To update the user's configuration on the server, go into the Exchange Administrator, select the user's name and select File | Properties. Select the Security tab and choose "Enable Advanced Security." The administrator program will display a security token message similar to the one shown here:

Write this information down. Users will need to enter the token during the configuration of the client component of the security installation process in order to have security management operational.

Invoking Advanced Security on the Client Workstation

When the administrator provides users with their security tokens, they can now configure their client components with advanced security. To do this, users would select Tools | Options and select the Security tab. From the Security tab, users should choose "Setup Advanced Security." A user screen, similar to the one shown in Figure 12-6, requests information about the token provided by the administrator, designates where the user's security profile file should be stored, and requests the password that will be used to digitally sign and encrypt messages.

User Level Security

The user level of security for the network may include use of encryption as well as digital signatures to authenticate communications.

Client-to-Server Encryption

In a client-to-server communication process that may include communication to a server over a local area network, a wide area network over a lease line, dial-up access to a server by telephone modem, or access over the Internet, the need to secure the transmission between the client and the server becomes an important process.

The Microsoft Exchange encryption process requires a user to encrypt a message by selecting the File | Properties option while composing a message,

Figure 12-6. *Configuring the client workstation to authenticate the user*

and selecting the Security tab and enabling the encryption option, as shown in Figure 12-7. When the user attempts to send the message, the Exchange client will prompt the user to enter his or her password. When the proper encryption password is entered, the message is sent. When the recipient receives and opens the message, he or she is prompted to enter the password. Through a series of encryption authentication processes, the private key and public key are compared and confirmed, and the document is subsequently made available to the recipient. If the proper password is not entered, the message remains encrypted.

Client-to-Client

When users communicate with each other, two security functions can be useful. One is the use of digital signatures to authenticate a user's message to the recipient of the message, and the other function is the use of digital encryption. Digital signatures can confirm whether the individual sent the message or not, since a properly signed document can be confirmed as an unaltered message state.

A message can also be digitally signed for user authentication. A digitally signed and authenticated message can confirm that the person who sent the

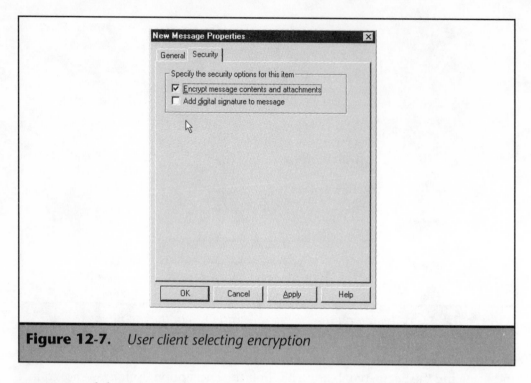

Figure 12-7. *User client selecting encryption*

message and the user whose name appears as the sender are the same person. Client-to-client authentication is used for verifying document routing, document approval processes, and confirmation of individual messaging.

Server-to-Server Security

As an organization grows beyond the interconnections of the local area network, the need to authenticate servers between locations on a wide area network becomes important. Unlike client-to-client security authentication, which is most often used to verify the sender of a message, server-to-server security allows two servers to communicate securely with each other and minimizes the potential for message tampering or unauthorized viewing of message content.

The Chapter in Review

- Chapter 12 is the first of three chapters in Part Three that focus on administering, managing, and tuning an Exchange environment. Specifically, Chapter 12 covers how to administer an Exchange server by utilizing the tools for administration, security, and management of the Microsoft Exchange Server product. Exchange administration includes adding, modifying, and deleting users; setting up appropriate security; and managing the network to perform efficiently.

- Network administration begins by managing the user accounts. These functions are performed by the administrator of the messaging system through the Microsoft Exchange Administrator utility. The first of all administration functions is to add new users. Users can be added manually one at a time through the Exchange Administrator program in which user options are selected individually, or a user template can be created to automatically populate specific fields for the new user, thus minimizing the keystrokes needed to add a user to the Exchange environment. A new user needs to have a displayed name that is seen in the Global Address List, be a member of workgroups within the organization, have a translation of his or her name into an Internet and X.400 name, as well as have a correlation between the logon name in the Windows NT security environment and a user name in the Exchange messaging system. All of these options can be defined in a user template for simplified user creation.

- Once a user is added to the Exchange environment, his or her security or access rights can be modified by the administrator at any time. This can include adding or deleting the user from a designated workgroup or changing the user's name after a marriage. By changing the user information within Microsoft Exchange, any add-in applications (such as faxing, document routing, integrated voicemail applications) that are integrated with the Microsoft Exchange user administration, will also have the information changed for that add-in application function.

- Once an Exchange environment is operational, the implementation of a security system becomes a logical next step. Exchange security is set at both the client level and the server level. The client-level security ensures that a particular client is supposed to access that server and the group of users associated with the security configuration. The server-level security ensures that server-to-server communications between specific servers is permitted, thus minimizing the chance of unauthorized messaging communications external to the Exchange environment. Server-level security also protects remote access, such as server access over the Internet.

■ Microsoft Exchange includes two advanced security functions, digital encryption and digital signatures. Digital encryption is a message security process that functions on a message-by-message basis and requires the sender to encode the message with a passcode. When the recipient receives the message, he or she enters a personal passcode which completes the authentication process and validates the message, and then unencrypts the message contents for viewing. Additionally, Exchange supports digital signatures. This security function checks message authenticity by requiring the sender to enter a message authentication password. When the recipient receives the message, he or she can verify if the sender of the message entered the authorized passcode to authenticate the message. Digital signatures is used in document- routing processes that require management approval or other process approvals for automated document authentication.

Review Questions

Q. When adding a user to Exchange, how do the displayed name and the alias name differ?
A. The displayed name is the name shown on the formal directory or Global Address List of the users, whereas the alias name enables an individual to use the "check names" options in the Exchange client software to look up users by either their formal or their alias name.

Q. What configuration option allows the administrator to add the user to a workgroup user list?
A. The distribution list in the User Properties tab.

Q. When configuring an Exchange user's appointment schedule configuration, where does the user allow access privileges to his or her schedule?
A. In the Scheduler software, select Tools I Set Access Permissions.

Q. How does the network administrator modify the messaging characteristics of an existing Exchange user?
A. Enter the Exchange administrator program, go to the recipients branch of the hierarchy, and select File I Properties to edit the user's messaging characteristics.

Q. Where does the network administrator go to add users to the distribution list?

A. The administrator can add users to the distribution list in the distribution list properties section, or individually within a user's properties section.

Q. How does a network administrator set the default to automatically and simultaneously delete a user from both Windows NT and Exchange?

A. From the Exchange Administrator program, select Tools | Options, choose Permissions, and then select the option "Delete primary Windows NT account when deleting mailbox."

Q. What does the Key Management Server do?

A. The Key Management Server manages the allocation and authentication of the digital encryption and digital signatures on the network.

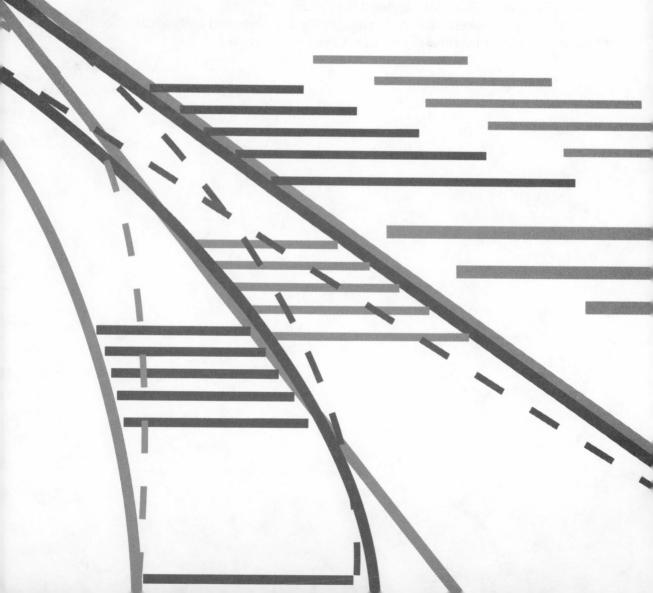

CHAPTER 13

Managing a Microsoft Exchange Environment

Managing any information infrastructure requires the ability to react to system failures or problems and to create solutions that can resolve those problems, as well as the ability to prepare proactively for system downtime with a defined plan and strategy that will address problems as they arise. In this chapter, we will identify the steps that administrators can take to develop disaster recovery planning processes as well as define the procedures necessary to determine the source of a system problem by evaluating the error and operation logs of the Microsoft Exchange Server environment.

Proactive Environment Management

The intent of every information system organization should be to plan proactively and manage system downtime in order to minimize the potential for system crashes that decimate user productivity. The challenge, however, is to allocate the time necessary to create disaster recovery plans, test recovery procedures, and prepare the documentation to implement a planned system recovery in an environment that demands the time and effort of all personnel to maintain its existence—essentially, firefighting—as well as typically working within a limited operational budget.

When an organization is able to allocate properly the time and resources to develop proactive environment management procedures before crises occur, it tends to spend less time and effort trying to recover from a system or environment failure. The need to prepare and plan for downtime of a product like Microsoft Exchange, the communications infrastructure core of many organizations, is as crucial as ensuring that the lights and air conditioning are functioning every single day.

Creating a Baseline

Key to any process evaluation procedure is the ability to create a baseline, so that administrators will know what the environment should look like during normal operations. Baselines for a Microsoft Exchange Server need to be recorded for processor performance and utilization, disk space usage, time needed to send and receive messages, and the response time to message transfers. It is very difficult to determine if there is a system problem when it is not possible to determine whether the system performance, disk space usage, or other pertinent system operational functions are working the way they should be.

Understanding the Microsoft NT Performance Monitor

One of the tools that Microsoft ships with the Windows NT Server software is the PERFMON.EXE performance monitoring utility. PerfMon provides the Windows NT network and Microsoft Exchange administrator with a tool to monitor dozens of statistics and operations on the network, similar to the performance trace shown in Figure 13-1. PerfMon tracking options typically fall into three categories that include:

■ **Percentages** A performance monitor tracking process may track the percentage of an available resource, like the percentage of available system buffer memory. The percentages are based on resource availability. When the availability threshold is excessive, the server resources may need to be upgraded to improve performance or minimize the chance for system failure.

■ **High Counts** The high count is determined by the attainment of a particular level during the performance monitoring period. For example, this may be the high count of the number of users connected to the system. High counts can show the maximum sessions or events occurring on the Microsoft Exchange Server, which are used to determine the extent of the demand for the resources in the Exchange environment.

■ **Events per Time** Another statistic generated by the performance monitoring tool is the tracking of an event over a period of time. This time period may extend over the duration of the monitoring period, such as the number of messages sent since the performance monitoring was started, or the time period may be per minute or per second, such as the number of messages read or written per minute.

Most of these performance monitoring traces are meaningless without a baseline to help administrators determine what is normal over time for the environment, compare the events per time to the percentage of resources used or allocated, and know what should be appropriate for the statistic. The combination of monitoring events can indicate whether there are bottlenecks on the network, the resources of the network or the server are inadequate and should be upgraded, or the new stress put on a server during an upgrade, scaled over time, will exceed its capabilities, based on historical data.

It takes time to figure out what information the performance monitoring tool contributes, but once you have, it can prove to be extremely helpful in

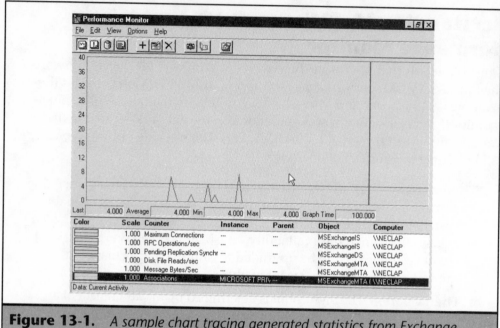

Figure 13-1. *A sample chart tracing generated statistics from Exchange*

providing snapshots of the capabilities of the Exchange server(s) in its environment. As users are added, new add-in tools are implemented, or the Exchange environment undergoes changes, the effects of these changes can be quantifiably traced and projected to determine the maximum threshold of the server within the environment.

Some of the performance monitoring options commonly traced to determine the effectiveness of the server include:

■ **Exchange Database Monitoring** Verification of the database cache hits, the percentage of the cache buffer in use, and the number of buffer bytes read and written per second can be used to determine how efficient the Exchange database is running within the environment and how much stress is being placed on it. Typically, when the percentage of cache buffer in use is excessively high, the amount of RAM within the server to buffer the database cache may need to be upgraded. That determination is based on the amount of information read and written to the database over time, which is based on the number of transactions enacted, which is determined by the number of users added to the environment over time.

- **Directory Store Monitoring** Address book browsing, reads and writes, access violations, and replication updates per second in the directory store monitoring components reflect the usage of the directory information within the Exchange environment. Because the Exchange directory store is accessed any time messages pass through the Exchange server, the percentage statistics from the directory store can indicate an excess of transactions, which may indicate a need to upgrade the processor of the server so that it can handle more transactions.

- **Information Store Monitoring** Active connections, active users, database session percentage hit rate, maximum connections, RPC operations per second, and RPC requests on the information store indicate the volume of information of the transactions on the server. Many of these statistics are maximum numbers of connections or active sessions that set the upper limit of current resource demands. The amount of resources used compared to the percentage ratios of the server's ability to handle peak capabilities indicates whether the server can handle additional traffic or interactions.

- **Private and Public Information Store Monitoring** Average time for delivery, folder opens per second, messages delivered per minute, and messages submitted per minute provides valuable information on transactions over time on the server. The transactions over time tell how much volume is being handled by the server during peak times of the day. Although an average taken over a long period of time will indicate that the server is idle 75 percent of the time, it must be able to handle peak periods during production hours to be efficient. These statistics provide a snapshot that tells whether the server can handle the demands of peak traffic times in its environment.

- **Exchange MTA** Disk file opens, reads, writes, and deletes, LAN transmits and receives, and messages bytes per second of the Exchange MTA show the routing capacity of the server. This may vary for organizations that do a lot of external messaging compared to internal messaging, but it also may indicate that the distribution of external resources may need to be updated. If there is excessive traffic over an Exchange Connector link or over an SMTP link, these MTA sessions may indicate that the addition of users on either side of the link will increase the demands, which may in turn require an increase in bandwidth between the links (faster lease line) or the splitting of the current Exchange server to distribute communications across multiple systems.

When choosing an option to add to the performance monitoring chart, select Edit | Add to Chart and then select the object category and the counter to be tracked, as shown in Figure 13-2. The performance monitor will begin tracking the resource.

In addition to monitoring Microsoft Exchange-specific events, the performance monitor can also track Windows NT-specific events such as processor utilization, available disk space, bytes read or written to disk over time, network adapter transmit and receive statistics over time, or general server resource allocation and availability. These additional statistics expand the view of the performance characteristics and demands of the network server in determining the ability of the server to handle scalability of traffic and resource demands.

Link Monitor

The link monitor in Exchange can be configured to check for problems with the transportation of message connections or network connections with other servers or other messaging systems (internal and external) to ensure valid communication links are active. Link monitors are configured in the Exchange

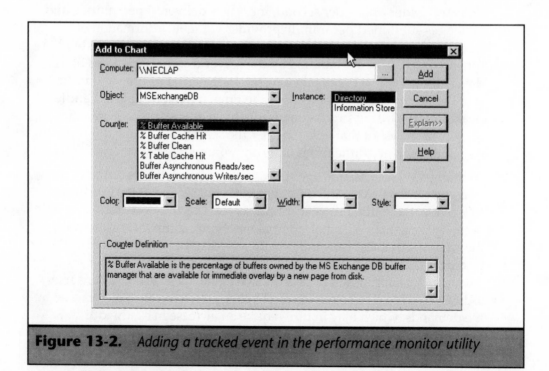

Figure 13-2. *Adding a tracked event in the performance monitor utility*

Administrator program and can perform *pings* to other messaging systems or servers with the anticipation of a response. If a threshold is reached without a response, the remote device can be declared offline. When this occurs, an alert can be generated in the form of an electronic message sent to a designated individual or group of individuals on the network, or the alert can be logged on a server in the network domain. In either case, the alerts may be linked to an external pager system to inform the administrator of a system failure or potential problem.

A link monitor is created by the Configuration | Monitors section of an Exchange site within the Exchange Administrator program by selecting File | New Other | Link Monitor. The link monitor properties, similar to the one shown in Figure 13-3, will allow the administrator to create link tests including where the recipient ping test should be sent, the elapsed time that determines whether an error has occurred, and who should be notified in the event of an error. A number of parallel events can be created and run simultaneously to check the connections to a number of different destinations, checking the links to other Exchange servers, to Internet sites, or to connector and gateway sites like an MSMail Server, cc:Mail Server, or an X.400 provider.

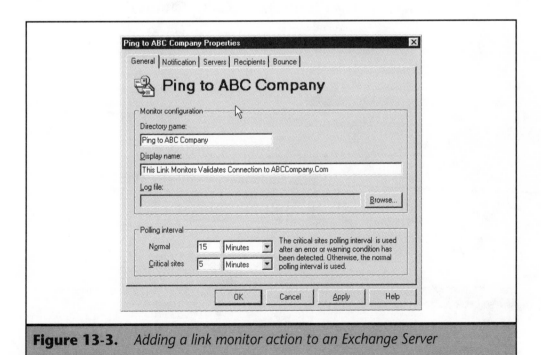

Figure 13-3. *Adding a link monitor action to an Exchange Server*

Server Monitor

The server monitor is similar to the link monitor, except that the server monitor checks for the existence of other Exchange servers in the organization. The server monitor may be used to confirm that a server designated as a public information store for the environment is still operational. While the public information store server provides public information storage capabilities to the organization, it does not have general electronic messaging capabilities that can be traced in something like the link monitor.

A server monitor is created in the Configuration | Monitors section of an Exchange site within the Exchange Administrator program by selecting File | New Other | Server Monitor. The server monitor properties, similar to the one shown in Figure 13-4, will allow the administrator to create a check process to determine if another Exchange server and all of its services are operational. In the event of an error, the monitor can be sent a notification via an electronic mail message or a network alert can be generated. Independent

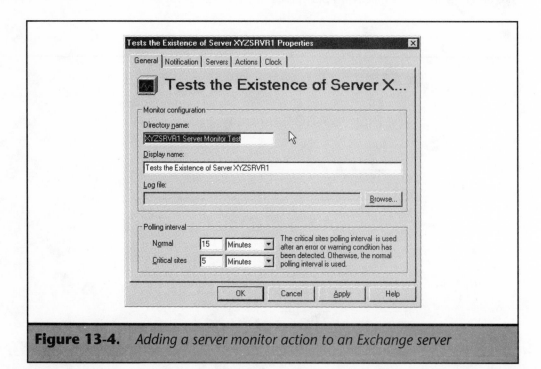

Figure 13-4. *Adding a server monitor action to an Exchange server*

of the notification, the server monitor can also be configured to take no action or can attempt to restart the service or to restart the server.

By setting up strategic server monitors, an administrator can proactively search for system failures and attempt to automatically resolve the problem or at least receive notification of the problem.

Checking User Storage and Last Logon Information

A helpful tool for most network administrators is the ability to determine the size of the message store for each user on the Exchange server and the last time the user has logged on to check his or her messages. This information can help an administrator to determine how much disk space and how many messages a user has stored. By determining the date of the user's last logon, the administrator can verify whether a user is accessing his or her Exchange mailbox frequently to check messages. If users are storing large amounts of message data or not bothering to check their e-mail frequently, administrators with this information can back up their requests for users to be more conscientious with actual data about their habits.

All of this information is in the private information store section of the Exchange Administrator program. By selecting the Sitename | Server Name | Private Information Store and then selecting the Mailbox Resources tab, the administrator can sort the information based on user name, logon name, last logon, NT account information, total disk space used, and the total number of messages stored.

Disaster Recovery Planning

Regardless of how well an organization proactively monitors and manages its environment, system failures do occur. The organization's ability to minimize the downtime caused by a system failure will be the determining factor of its success in conducting disaster recovery planning. Disaster recovery procedures may be as simple as having a tape backup available to restore a failed server and a subsequent rollback to the time of the last backup. An organization that cannot afford downtime on a mission-critical messaging system may have mirrored servers and offsite recovery centers to handle and manage system failures.

Exchange Server Backup

Microsoft Exchange includes a backup program, NTBACKUP.EXE, with the Microsoft Exchange Server software. This replaces the NTBACKUP.EXE program that comes with Windows NT Server. The program is the same, but the version that comes with Microsoft Exchange has been upgraded to support the online backup of Microsoft Exchange databases.

Online backups of the Exchange databases mean that the Exchange server can be backed up even while it remains operational to send and receive messages. During the backup process of an Exchange server, the various components such as the information store, directory store, and message database all need to be backed up. The process involves the creation of a checkpoint, where all of the databases on the Exchange server are in sync. In general, the backup state of the files will be different for each database being backed up because the backup process for all of the databases can take place over a matter of minutes or hours, and because sending, receiving, and message managing transactions can still take place on the server. To ensure that the state of the databases is in sync, the checkpoint is used during a restoration process to make the determination of the state of the system at a common point in time.

Components to Backup

The components that need to be backed up on an Exchange server include:

- The Exchange information store

  - Private Information Store \exchsrvr\mdbdata\PRIV.EDB

  - Public Information Store \exchsrvr\mdbdata\PUB.EDB

- The Exchange directory store

  - \exhsrvr\dsadata\DIR.EDB

- The message database

- The Microsoft Exchange Server programs and data files

- The log files (which include the checkpoint files)

  - Information Store Transaction Logs \exchsrvr\mdbdata*.LOG

  - Directory Store Transaction Logs \exchsrvr\dsadata*.LOG

- The server security registry information

- User public address books (PABs), schedule files (SCDs), personal folders (PSTs), and offline folders (OSTs)

  - PABs, SCDs, PSTs, OSTs commonly stored on the user's local hard drive

Backing Up the Server

The Exchange server can be backed up using the Microsoft-provided tape backup software, or there are a number of third-party backup vendors (like Cheyenne Software or Seagate Software Arcada Backup Exec) whose products allow administrators to conduct attended and unattended backup procedures of Exchange server(s).

Backing up the entire Exchange server and its components involves selecting the server as well as selecting the necessary services and options. A sample selection of the server, directory, and information store from the NTBACKUP.EXE program is shown in Figure 13-5.

The key to the checkpoint files and the transaction logs is Microsoft Exchange's ability to conduct transaction recovery based on log entries within the system. Because log entries are entered immediately into the transaction

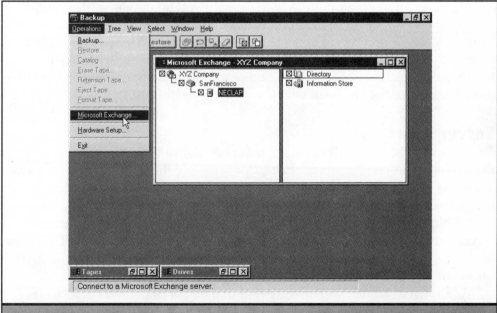

Figure 13-5.   *Selecting the server and services to back up*

logs before the data is written to the information or directory store or to the message database, a current copy of the transaction log with the proper checkpoint pointer to the last full or incremental server backup can recreate the processing of all messages within the organization.

The most important factor in transaction recovery is the implementation of a backup system on the Exchange server that utilizes the Exchange backup APIs, which provide the transaction tracking to do a checkpoint-based recovery. The backup must be a full or incremental backup with circular logging disabled. In this configuration, once a tape backup has been completed, the transaction log will be purged and then maintained until the next backup. By default, the transaction logs are set for circular logging and need to be reconfigured to disable circular logging. In the event of a single drive failure of an optimized server configuration in which the log files are written to a different physical drive than the message database, the data lost will be from the log files. However, the message database will remain intact, or if some part of the message database is lost, it can be restored from tape and then brought up-to-date by replaying the transaction logs.

Server Fault Tolerance

Organizations that have a very low tolerance for downtime need to implement a server fault tolerance system. A fault tolerant system may involve redundant file servers within the organization continuously backing up information from a primary server, or a redundant file server configuration may be a delayed process that can bring the organization back up and running within two to four hours. The choice of server redundancy is dependent on how fast the organization needs to be back online after a system failure.

Server Clusters

One option for server fault tolerance that provides full server redundancy is the implementation of a server cluster. Most people think of server clusters as a method of providing faster server performance because two or more servers integrate their processing performance resources to provide performance capabilities that exceed those of a single server. However, another feature of a server cluster is its ability to maintain server redundancy. In the event that one of the servers fail, the other server(s) in the cluster will continue to operate, thus eliminating downtime caused by failure of a server.

As shown in Figure 13-6, in the event that one of the servers of a cluster fails, the remaining server(s) will continue to operate, alleviating system downtime.

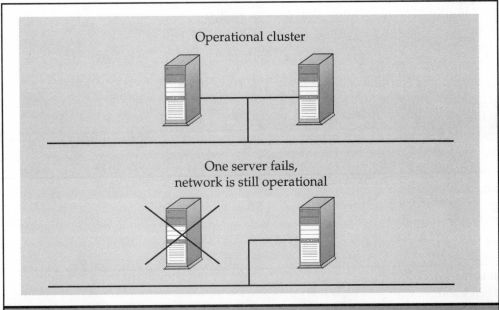

Figure 13-6. *When one server in a cluster fails, the other server maintains operations*

Online Standby Server

An online standby server is a system that operates in tandem with the primary server of the network which typically saves information simultaneously to the standby server. In the event of a primary server failure, with a few minor changes to the standby server configuration, the standby server can be brought online within 30-60 minutes as the new primary server with no loss in stored information.

Unlike the server configurations of a mirrored server environment that need to be equivalent or identical to each other, the configuration of the online standby server needs only to have comparable disk storage with the primary server. This allows an organization to place a lower-powered server or possibly an older server in the standby role, thus minimizing downtime and the cost to do so.

Standby server products like the Vinca Standby Server provide administrators with the ability to replicate both the server configuration as well as the data on the server, thus creating a completely redundant server environment. As shown in Figure 13-7, in the event of a primary server failure, the primary server can be brought offline and the standby server can be brought online as the primary server in about an hour's time.

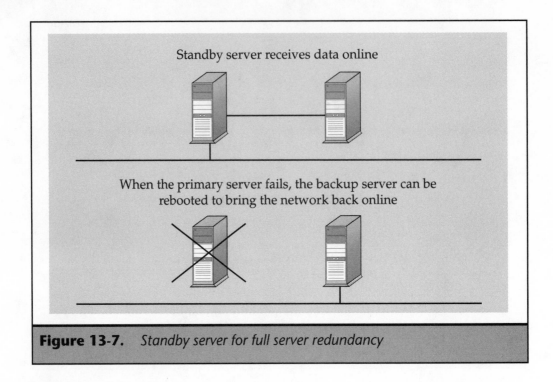

Figure 13-7. *Standby server for full server redundancy*

Hot Spare Server

Some organizations elect to have a less automated method for server recovery, which involves having a server fully configured and prepared to accept a restoration of tape information on the hot spare server. Like the online standby server, the hot spare server does not necessarily need to be the same make or model as the primary server; only the disk storage needs to be comparable.

In the event of a primary server failure, the most recent tape backup can be restored on the spare server, which should already be configured and operational. This process is shown in Figure 13-8.

An alternative to the hot spare server configuration, which requires a tape backup restoration to return the system to operational status, is the creation and configuration of a hot spare server with an identical hard drive, memory, processor boards, and network adapters. This hot spare server must be kept ready and available at all times, because when a component in the primary server fails, the component will be transferred from the hot spare server to the primary server. For example, this procedure could easily and quickly remedy problems such as a failed processor board, a failed network adapter, or an entire failed hard drive subsystem. When a component can be replaced

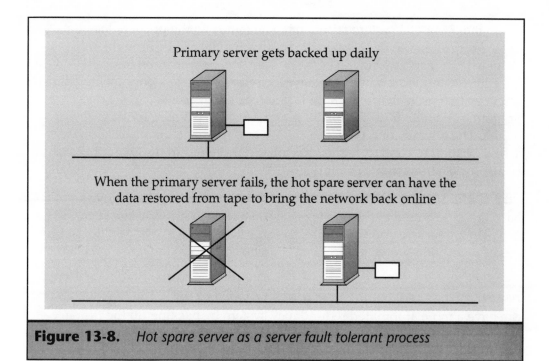

Figure 13-8. *Hot spare server as a server fault tolerant process*

between servers, administrators can eliminate the time necessary to complete the restoration and the loss in data from the time of the last backup to the time of failure.

Server-to-Server Connections

Another disaster recovery procedure involves placing redundant servers (either online or hot spare servers) in an offsite location. Having redundancy in another location may be extremely beneficial when distributing the disk for data loss or downtime caused by a locale-specific disaster such as a fire, flood, earthquake, hurricane, or localized power failure.

Offsite Secondary Data Center

The most common offsite replication process involves an offsite secondary data center. The center may be on the other side of town, in a different part of the state, or on the other side of the country. It doesn't matter as long as the center has the ability to replicate programs and data and the processing capabilities to manage data access from a redundant site.

In the event of a system failure or a site failure in the primary location caused by a site-specific disaster, the redundant site can be brought online to provide the organization with data services. The organization may also have a lease line connected from the primary location to the secondary offsite data center so that users in the primary location can gain access to the same programs and data from the offsite center during a primary location server failure. The organization may also choose to implement an offsite secondary access location to connect to the secondary data center in the event that the client workstations in the primary location are unavailable.

HOT SPARE SERVER WITH A RECENT BACKUP   An organization may have tapes delivered to the offsite center on a regular basis. In the event of a primary location server failure, the tape is restored to a hot online spare server to provide server service to users who can access the remote secondary offsite center.

ONLINE HOT SPARE SERVER REPLICATED OVER T1 LINE   The organization can have a more automated redundancy system by backing up the primary server(s) over a T1 lease line during a replication process either as an online standby server or as an online hot spare server. If the primary server fails in this environment, the spare server on the other side of the T1 lease line can be activated as the primary server.

Replicating Data Link Connections from Site to Site

An organization's ability to maintain some level of fallback between its site connections often translates to an additional need for redundancy. This need is an important aspect of the disaster recovery process involving lease line connections, whether it is for an online hot spare server replicating a primary server in an offsite data center, or part of the wide area network configuration of multiple sites in an Exchange environment communicating over lease lines.

To back up a data link line, an organization may install a backup high-speed dial-up ISDN line between the locations that can provide 128KB data speeds on a dial-up and pay-per-minute basis. If an organization has three or more locations, it can triangulate lines so that if a line between two locations fails, the messages will be rerouted and communications will continue, as depicted in Figure 13-9.

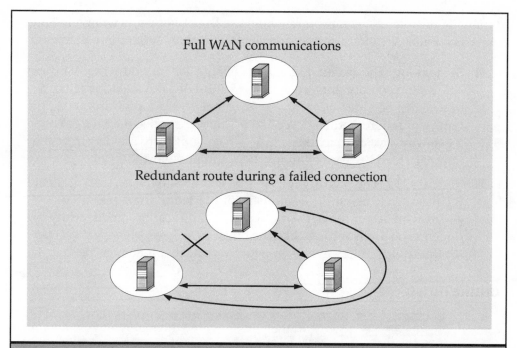

Figure 13-9. *Redundant paths for lease line connections*

Reactive Environment Management

Although proactive planning will not catch all errors and a disaster recovery process will not cover all components of a system failure plan, the last resort when systems crash is the administrator's ability to perform reactive environment management. Of course, all administrators wish that reactive responses to problems could be eliminated, but the reality is that the majority of administrative problems require some form of reactive response to fix, so the ability to analyze the problem and utilize the available tools is extremely important.

Understanding the Windows NT Event Viewer

The key to all Microsoft Windows NT environment and application server functions is the information provided in the Windows NT Event Viewer. The NT Event Viewer acts as a depository for a variety of server and communication errors. A sample list from the Event Viewer is shown in Figure 13-10. The Event Viewer information is logged in three separate sections:

- **System log** The system log records events generated by the Windows NT system components, such as the failure of a device driver (like a mouse driver, video adapter driver, or network adapter driver), or the failure or failure notification of an NT Server service (like the failure of a gateway service to load because of a corrupt software driver, or the failure to load because of an invalid login password).

- **Security log** The security log records changes to the security system of the network to assist the administrator in identifying a potential security breach of the network, server, or application. The security log depends on audit settings like the ones in the User Manager software to set thresholds or key events in which a security breach has been enacted.

Date	Time	Source	Category	Event	User	Computer
1/4/97	3:15:44 AM	EDK GWPerf	None	1034	N/A	NECLAP
1/4/97	3:02:39 AM	MSExchangeSA	General	5004	N/A	NECLAP
1/4/97	3:02:34 AM	MSExchangeSA	General	5003	N/A	NECLAP
1/4/97	2:28:33 AM	EDK GWPerf	None	1034	N/A	NECLAP
1/4/97	2:00:37 AM	MSExchangeSA	General	5000	N/A	NECLAP
1/3/97	11:49:25 PM	MSExchangeKMS	None	1036	N/A	NECLAP
1/3/97	11:49:24 PM	MSExchangeKMS	None	1037	N/A	NECLAP
1/1/97	11:45:14 PM	EDK GWPerf	None	1034	N/A	NECLAP
1/1/97	11:40:13 PM	MSExchangeKMS	None	1010	N/A	NECLAP
1/1/97	11:39:18 PM	MSExchangeKMS	None	1008	N/A	NECLAP
1/1/97	11:39:18 PM	MSExchangeKMS	None	1056	N/A	NECLAP
1/1/97	11:38:22 PM	MSExchangeKMS	None	3034	N/A	NECLAP
1/1/97	11:35:59 PM	MSExchangeIS Priv	General	1016	N/A	NECLAP
1/1/97	11:31:49 PM	MSExchangeKMS	None	1056	N/A	NECLAP
1/1/97	11:06:03 PM	MSExchangeKMS	None	1056	N/A	NECLAP
1/1/97	11:05:31 PM	MSExchangeKMS	None	1056	N/A	NECLAP
1/1/97	11:04:42 PM	MSExchangeKMS	None	1056	N/A	NECLAP
1/1/97	11:04:13 PM	MSExchangeKMS	None	1001	N/A	NECLAP
1/1/97	11:04:13 PM	MSExchangeKMS	None	1036	N/A	NECLAP
1/1/97	11:04:13 PM	MSExchangeKMS	None	1037	N/A	NECLAP
1/1/97	11:04:12 PM	MSExchangeKMS	None	1014	N/A	NECLAP
1/1/97	11:04:11 PM	MSExchangeKMS	None	1000	N/A	NECLAP
1/1/97	11:03:38 PM	MSExchangeKMS	None	1022	N/A	NECLAP
1/1/97	11:03:38 PM	MSExchangeKMS	None	1076	N/A	NECLAP
1/1/97	11:03:38 PM	MSExchangeKMS	None	1075	N/A	NECLAP
1/1/97	11:03:34 PM	MSExchangeKMS	None	1073	N/A	NECLAP

Figure 13-10. *A sample NT Event Viewer summary list*

■ **Application log** The application log tracks events logged by the server applications such as events generated by the Microsoft Exchange Server. Microsoft Exchange records changes to the information store, directory store, key management server, and the MTA of the Exchange server to the application log. This may include the consolidation and generation of the Global Address List, the creation of a security certificate by the key management server, the creation of a new user on the network, the starting and stopping of services, the starting and stopping of the information store and directory store, migration notes as users are migrated from one platform to another, etc.

The events logged in the NT Event Viewer from Microsoft Exchange are configurable within the Microsoft Exchange Administrator program. The administrator has the option of configuring the Microsoft Exchange Server software to log information in four different levels. They include:

■ **No Logging** No events will be logged.

■ **Minimum-Level Logging** Only fatal conditions will be logged. Examples of fatal conditions include a gateway service that fails to load, which means that no messages can be sent or received, or the return of a message due to the lack of a connection to the external source.

■ **Medium-Level Logging** Fatal and near-fatal events will be logged. An example of a near-fatal event is when a user attempts to send an encrypted message to a user who does not have encryption and receives a notification of a security error. Although this event was prevented because of a security problem, its outcome was not fatal, and the user was notified. The medium-level log noted the change.

■ **Maximum-Level Logging** The logging of fatal and near-fatal events as well as informational events. An example of an information event would be tracing an Internet connection link for a message that is sent from one user to another, or the addition of a user to the network. Although these may be significant events, they have no negative impact on the operation of the network, so they are not considered events of noted value. However, an administrator who is used to seeing transaction logs and general communication logs, or who is attempting to evaluate the performance and usage of the network would find it very helpful for these informational events to be logged.

Although the maximum level of logging provides the greatest amount of logging information available, a network with 50 users sending and receiving mail messages with maximum-level logging enabled for all event options in the Exchange Administrator utility will log 20-30 events per second. Obviously, maximum-level logging can log so many events so quickly that it can become very difficult to find a specific piece of information even by utilizing filtering to categorize the messages.

To enable event tracking, within the Exchange Administrator, select the site, and then select the server. A series of display names for the directory service, directory synchronization, message transfer agent, private and public information store, and system attendant will be available. Select one of the services, choose File | Properties and then select the Diagnostic Logging tab. There will be a series of event options and the four different levels to select for the events. As soon as the event logging level is selected and Apply or OK have been selected, the Exchange server will begin logging events within the Event Viewer. For connectors to the Internet, X.400, MS Mail or cc:Mail sites, the options for diagnostic logging are found in the Sitename | Configuration | Connections section of the Exchange Administrator tree.

The events most commonly tracked include user logons and message details to ensure that users can get into the system and messages are sent. As a result, these events generally have maximum logging; however, by updating the address book or performing consistency checks on the information store these events only need to have alerts when a fatal error occurs. The breakdown of common logging events is as follows:

- Minimum Logging Events to Track:

    - Directory Services

    - Message Transfer Agent Services

    - Information Store | System | General

    - Information Store | Public | Replication

    - Information Store | Public | Transport

    - Information Store | Public | General (except Logon, Access Control, and Storage Limits)

    - Information Store | Private | Transport

- Information Store | Private | General (except Logon, Access Control, and Storage Limits)

- Medium Logging Events to Track:

  - Directory Synchronization

  - Information Store | Public | General (Storage Limits and Access Control)

  - Information Store | Private | General (Storage Limits and Access Control)

- Maximum Logging Events to Track:

  - Information Store | Public | General (Logon)

  - Information Store | Private | General (Logon)

  - Sitename | Configuration | Connections (for all connectors)

After setting these suggested log levels, the administrator should let the server run for a few days of normal use and then check the Windows NT Event Viewer to see if the messaging and information logging levels are appropriate for the organization. The level of logging will vary with the administrator's desire to track or find the specific information required.

Exchange Message Tracking

Message tracking is an important tool so that administrators can verify that messages are being sent and received properly between users. By providing the administrator with the ability to track messages, it minimizes user complaints about lost or never received messages. The message tracking system tracks the message from its origin time to its receipt time through the Exchange server and gateways. Throughout the entire process, the administrator can determine whether the message is being functionally transported.

By default, message tracking is disabled. To enable message tracking, the administrator needs to go into the Exchange Administrator program and select Sitename | Configuration | Information Store Site Configuration. On the general

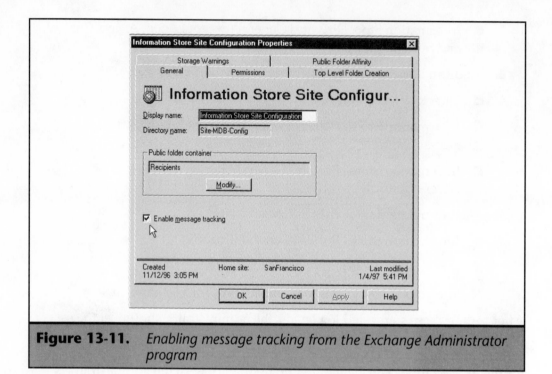

Figure 13-11. *Enabling message tracking from the Exchange Administrator program*

tab of the Information Store Site Configuration option is the option to select "Enable message tracking," as shown in Figure 13-11. Message tracking will be enabled for the server by selecting Sitename | Configuration | MTA Site Configuration and then selecting the "Enable message tracking" in the General tab.

Verifying Message Tracking

To verify whether a message has been transferred through the message tracking system, the administrator needs to run the Message Tracking Center program. This is implemented within the Exchange Administrator program by selecting Tools | Track Message. By selecting the name of the sender, the name of the recipient(s), and the number of days to search, the administrator will receive a time and date list of messages sent and received that match the criteria specified, as shown in Figure 13-12.

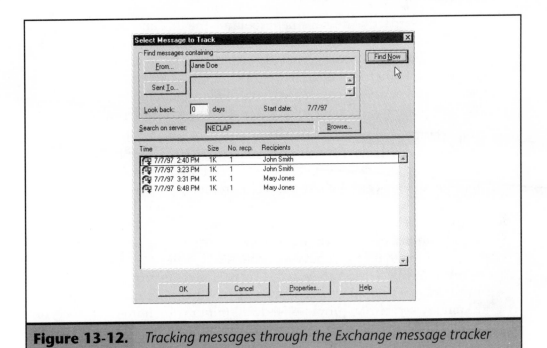

Figure 13-12.   *Tracking messages through the Exchange message tracker*

The Chapter in Review

■ In this chapter, we explored the tools available to the messaging administrator which help manage an existing Microsoft Exchange environment. These include options to develop proactive monitoring and Exchange management functions, disaster recovery planning, and reactive messaging management. Obviously, the goal of organizations should be to proactively plan and prepare for system failure to minimize the impact that downtime can have on the organization; however, in any environment, the reality of disaster planning is challenged by the occasional firefighting in reactive support.

■ Key to proactive management is to create a baseline where the administrator knows what the network operations normally look like in the administration tool (such as the performance monitor). By having a baseline, key statistic changes can lead to diagnosing and resolving system problems when the administrator checks the network performance monitor.

- Two other proactive management tools are the link and server monitors. These two utilities provide the ability for an Exchange server to monitor connections across wide area networks, or across local area networks of other Exchange server operations, as well as to monitor general server operations. If a server or link is inoperable, an administrator can be made aware of a pending system problem.

- Important in any mission-critical environment is the ability to implement a disaster recovery process. It may be as simple as having a tape backup and restoral process, or it could involve having an offsite location in the event of a natural or environmental disaster. Disaster recovery might be as sophisticated as the organization's budget will allow and is based on the tolerance for downtime relative to the organization's budget to minimize and manage downtime. For an organization that cannot have any downtime, a need for fault tolerant servers may be a necessity where a server failure is protected by the presence of a backup or secondary server. Other interim options include a standby server that provides 30- to 60-minute downtime tolerance, or a mirrored hard drive subsystem that provides the replication of drive data in the event of a hard drive subsystem failure.

- When all planning and fault tolerant functions fail, the need to reactively resolve problems typically involves the Windows NT Event Viewer and the Exchange message tracking utilities. The Windows NT Event Viewer requires diagnostic logging to be enabled in the Exchange Administrator program in order to adequately track operational functions of the messaging system. There are four levels of tracking: minimum, medium, maximum, and none. The minimum tracking level notes all fatal system errors. The medium level of tracking notes all near fatal as well as fatal system failures, and finally, the maximum level of tracking notes fatal and near fatal errors but also tracks information messages such as the confirmation of message transfers.

- The Exchange message tracking utility tracks messages from source to destination. In conjunction with the NT Event Viewer, an administrator can track a message from the time the message was sent from a client through the Exchange messaging system, to its final destination. In the event a message fails to transfer, the administrator can track the message to determine at which level or layer of communication the message failed to complete its transaction.

Review Questions

Q. What utility allows the administrator of an Exchange environment to determine the processor utilization of the Exchange server?
A. The Performance Monitor utility.

Q. Where would the administrator go to verify the amount of disk space a user is taking with his or her message store?
A. Total disk space usage by a user can be found in the Exchange Administrator program by going into the Sitename I Server Name I Private Information Store, and then selecting the Mailbox Resources tab. The administrator can sort the information based on user name, logon name, last logon, NT account information, total disk space used, and the total number of messages stored.

Q. What term is used to describe multiple computers linked together to provide faster server performance as well as mirror server redundancy?
A. Server clustering.

Q. How can an organization leverage the integrated server-to-server components of Exchange to minimize the risk of losing server information caused by a system failure?
A. By implementing server-to-server data store replication, an organization can protect its storage of information by having a duplicate copy of information reside on a separate Exchange server.

Q. What's wrong when the administrator goes into the Event Viewer and discovers that only the fatal and near fatal errors are being logged?
A. This means that the administrator has only a medium level of diagnostic logging enabled which is capturing only fatal and near-fatal errors. By changing the diagnostic logging to maximum, the informational messages will also be logged in the NT Viewer utility.

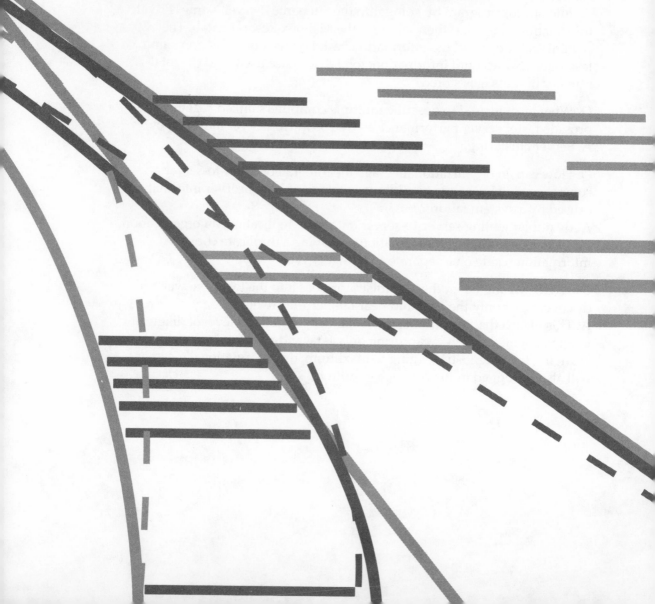

CHAPTER 14

Optimizing and Tuning the Exchange Server

In the past two chapters we have reviewed the administration and management of an Exchange server with a focus on keeping the server operational and developing strategies to make Exchange servers more dependable and easier to troubleshoot. In this chapter, we will look for ways to optimize and tune the existing Exchange server to improve the overall performance of the Exchange environment. We will further discuss some of the tools mentioned in previous chapters that can be used to understand the baseline of the server environment and to improve overall system performance.

Optimizing the Server

The initial task that needs to be performed when you are optimizing your server is deciphering general statistics and baselines to determine which components of the information gathered on the Exchange environment can be optimized. The information generated by the tools and displayed as statistics does not automatically flag areas of inefficiency. It requires the ability of an administrator to determine the baseline and optimal levels for the organization, set a threshold, and tune the server to optimize and improve its performance within its configuration and environment.

Faster Doesn't Necessarily Mean Better

When configuring and optimizing a server configuration, it is important to remember that adding more processing speed and memory to a server will not necessarily pay off. In many cases, the addition of resources to a server may only mask an inherent configuration problem on the system. If the server is properly optimized, a system can function adequately with a lot less hardware and will actually run more efficiently over time. In fact, adding more hardware to mask a performance problem can reach a point of diminishing returns in performance as well as decrease the operational life of the hardware and possibly lead to a premature server component failure.

Comparing the Baseline to a Current Test

As we discussed in the previous chapter on proactive environment management, statistics provide a snapshot of the current configuration and operation of the server. However, a number of factors can cause the statistics being generated from a server to be interpreted differently. The factors include changes made to a server, the ways in which the changes affect the baseline, and the analysis of the baseline compared to optimal performance for the server configuration.

As we will discuss throughout this chapter, the key to our analysis will be the ability to take a good baseline measurement, make changes to the server configuration, and then determine how those changes affect the performance and operation of the server. Additionally, during our server performance comparisons, we will evaluate performance statistics during strategic periods of the day. Obviously, taking a snapshot of server performance when no one is on the server does not provide a realistic picture of in-use server operation. However, averaging server traffic and performance over a two-week period that includes nights, early mornings, and weekends will also provide inaccurate results. If the majority of user access occurs during business hours Monday through Friday, then the performance baselines and comparisons should also be taken during those times.

Poor Performance Does Not Necessarily Equal Slow Performance

Improving server efficiency will not only help the server to perform faster, but it may also minimize premature server failure caused by unnecessary stress to the server's components. When the server runs out of RAM memory and requires spooling to disk to a pagefile, the additional reading and writing to the disk not only causes the server to run sluggishly because of the disk I/O, but more importantly, it can cause additional strain on the hard drive subsystem. The additional reading and writing to disk can weaken the server drive and possibly cause the drive to fail before it would normally have problems.

Adding More Disk Space Without Checking the Pagefile Usage

An example of an organization adding more hardware without checking the server statistics is the addition of more disk space without first checking the server's pagefile usage. When a Windows NT Server is configured, the installation utility automatically assigns a pagefile for memory overflow to disk. The size of the pagefile is typically equivalent to the amount of memory in the file server; thus, if a server has 128MB of memory, the NT Server software will automatically allocate a 128MB pagefile. In many cases, 128MB of memory is enough to allow the server to run optimally within the confines of the RAM memory and the pagefile is seldom used. In this case, the pagefile is taking up disk space that can be freed for application usage. To verify the usage of the pagefile, run the WINMSD.EXE program that comes with Windows NT, select the Memory tab, and view the pagefile space at the bottom of the utility, as shown in Figure 14-1. The total pagefile space will be shown, which will be the allocated amount of disk space, and the peak use will show how much has ever been used of the pagefile. If the peak use is significantly lower than the total pagefile space, the pagefile can be reduced. To change the size of the pagefile, go into Start | Settings | Control Panel | System and select the Performance tab, and then change the virtual memory in the system. For servers with 256MB or even 1GB of RAM memory, the effects of modifying the pagefile size can free up a significant amount of disk space for application usage.

Background Processes in Use

Server performance is not necessarily affected by the number of users logged on to the server or the amount of messages being sent to and from the server,

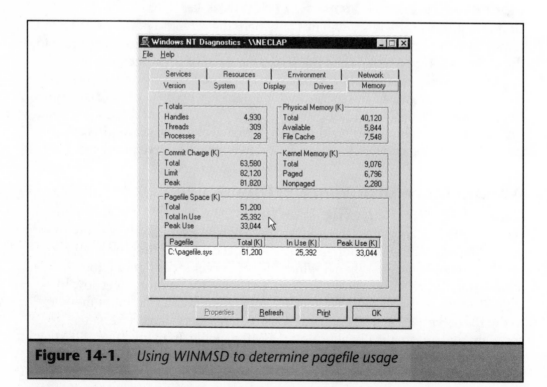

Figure 14-1. *Using WINMSD to determine pagefile usage*

but rather the culprit may be the other background services that the server is managing. Instead of splitting the Exchange site into multiple servers so that the electronic mail load is distributed, try to evaluate the background processes on the server that can result in negative performance effects, such as when the server acts as a primary or secondary domain controller, or as a file and print server.

By reviewing the processor utilization of the server and the amount of CPU time being allocated to various server services, an analysis of the server resources can be performed. To view the server processes, run the NT Task Manager software by running the TASKMGR.EXE program and selecting the Processes tab. A screen of processes similar to the one shown in Figure 14-2 will be displayed. By clicking on the CPU Time column header, the processes will be sorted based on the time the function has taken of the server's CPU capacity. If the server is managing application tasks as opposed to server tasks, the administrator should consider moving the application to another server.

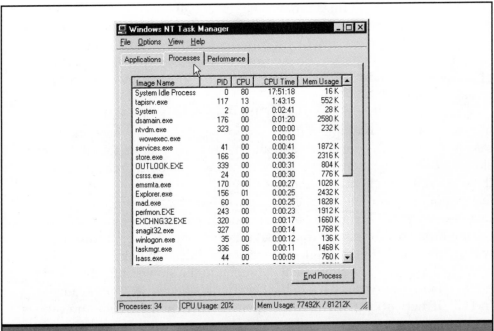

Figure 14-2. *Task Manager showing the CPU time being used on a server*

Understanding How Messages and Information Are Routed

When evaluating the performance between a workstation and a server, immediately jumping to the conclusion that higher bandwidth network adapters are needed, like a 100Mbps adapter configuration instead of a 10Mbps adapter configuration, may be incorrect. The organization should first evaluate and test the message transfer route between the client and the server, especially in the Microsoft Exchange client and server environment.

By default, the Microsoft Exchange client and server software load the transport drivers for NetBEUI, TCP/IP, and IPX/SPX. If the adapter drivers are loaded for all three protocols, the method that the client is communicating to the server is not necessarily assured. Although the organization may have a Novell backbone, communicate between the Novell servers with IPX/SPX, and communicate with the Internet with TCP/IP, the organization may, unbeknownst to the administrators, be communicating from the client to the server over NetBEUI. Although this is not an immediate problem, if an organization thinks it is communicating exclusively over IPX/SPX and TCP/IP on its backbone and its clients are communicating with the Exchange server over NetBEUI, a third protocol has essentially been introduced to the backbone and every protocol communicated over a network takes additional bandwidth from the entire network communications infrastructure. In many cases, the addition of an additional protocol decreases the overall performance of the network bandwidth by one-half for two protocols, by one-third for three protocols, etc.

Organizations that are running TCP/IP as the only protocol on their network may have multiple routes to an Exchange server, where one route may be over a LAN connection and another may be a redundant link over a slower WAN connection. Although administrators would probably assume that the Exchange client is communicating with the Exchange server over the faster communication link, the client may in fact be communicating by default over the slower WAN connection. It is important to remember that most devices communicate over the same route that they have previously used, and if there was an interruption in the higher speed communication link between the client and the server and the client defaulted to the slower link, the client may not automatically switch back to the faster link when it becomes available. In TCP/IP networking, each route is given a "cost," and the communications route is determined by the lowest-cost route for the communication link. However, when many organizations configure TCP/IP networking in a Windows NT environment, they do not properly assign the costs for the various communication links, which can cause the organization to have the same cost on all routes regardless of their actual performance. Thus, the default communications path from the client to the server will be based on the last successful route of communications, regardless of its level of performance.

There are a number of tools you can use to help establish the path between an Exchange client and the Exchange server. First, determine the appropriate protocol that will be used for communication between the client and the server. The only way to ensure a constant link between the client and the server over a given protocol is to set up the Exchange client so that it will only communicate over a predefined protocol configuration. The configuration can be set by modifying the line in either the EXCHNG.INI for Windows v3.x, or by editing the registry for Windows 95 or Windows NT under HKEY_LOCAL_MACHINE, Software | Microsoft | Exchange | Exchange Providers for the Rpc_Binding_Order that by default are ncalrpc (for RPC communication), ncacn_ip_tcp (for TCP/IP communication), ncacn_spx (for IPX/SPX communication), ncacn_np (for Name Pipe communication), netbios (for NetBIOS communication), and ncacn_vns_spp (for Banyan Vines communication). If the organization expects to communicate solely over TCP/IP, all of the binding orders with the exception of the ncacn_ip_tcp should be deleted. The next time the client software is loaded, assuming that the client and the server can normally communicate over TCP/IP, the client will now access the server via TCP/IP for mail messaging. If the client cannot communicate with the server, standard TCP/IP communication link tests such as ping should be run to verify successful TCP/IP communications.

Once the client software is configured to communicate over a specific transport, a trace should be performed to confirm that the route that the client is using to communicate with the server is correct. Under TCP/IP networking, this can be accomplished using the TRACERT.EXE utility that comes with the Windows software and is installed simultaneously with TCP/IP networking. By using the TRACERT utility, an organization can run a trace between the client and the server to check whether the route that the link is actually taking and the one the administrator assumes it is taking are the same. Figure 14-3 shows how the TRACERT can determine the actual route of an assumed link.

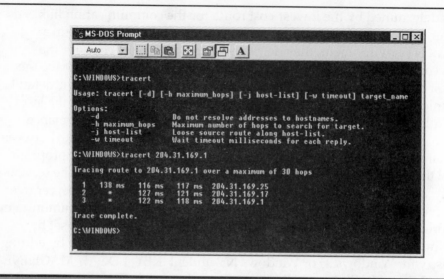

Figure 14-3. *Using TRACERT to confirm an assumed TCP/IP link*

Areas to Improve Performance and Operation Optimization

The three major areas of Exchange server performance that can be optimized include processor performance, disk drive performance, and memory management of the server. As I discussed earlier in this chapter, a common quick-fix approach to sluggish performance is to upgrade the processor, add more disk space, and add more memory to the Exchange server. However, strategic upgrades and server optimization can give far better results while creating an environment based on efficient operations that will also minimize unnecessary server failures caused by undue functional stress.

Processor Performance

As I just discussed, to increase the performance of an Exchange server, the conclusion most organizations leap to is to upgrade the server to a faster processor (200MHz instead of a 133MHz) or to add another processor to the system. Although this will increase the performance of the server, the decision to upgrade or add a processor should be systematic and planned.

The first thing to check when evaluating the server processor performance optimization is whether the server is configured to maximize throughput for network applications rather than for file and print management. This option can be set by running Start | Settings | Control Panel | Network | Services | Server. A screen similar to the one shown here will be displayed.

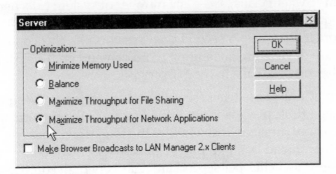

By selecting "Maximize Throughput for Network Applications," network applications like Microsoft Exchange will be given priority over file cache access to memory. Additionally, the amount of memory allocated to the server service for functions that include paged memory, thread counts, free connections, and in-process items will be optimized for a network application server function.

The way to determine if the processor in an Exchange server needs to be upgraded is to use the Performance Monitor (PERFMON.EXE) utility on the Exchange server. The key components to view in the Performance Monitor, as graphed in Figure 14-4, are described as the following:

- **Processor** % Processor Time (or System: % Total Processor Time for multiprocessor systems)—The % Processor Time shows the percentage of time that the system processor (or processors) is being utilized. When the processor time is utilized in excess of 70 percent, the system processor may be a bottleneck.

- **Processor** Interrupts/sec—If the % Processor Time is excessively high, the next thing to check is the interrupts per second on the processor. This will reveal whether the CPU activity is being caused by an application request like Microsoft Exchange functions, or if it is being caused by hardware interrupts. When over 1,000 interrupts per second are being generated, hardware devices in the server that are CPU-intensive should be evaluated. These devices would include 16-bit controllers or PIO devices that require a processor cycle to manage the hardware adapter. Many older network adapters, IDE or 16-bit SCSI hard drive controllers, or even video adapters require these processor cycles. Devices that do not require PIO processor interrupts such as PCI network adapters or bus mastering controllers can minimize the demand on the server processor.

■ **System** System Calls/sec—The number of system calls per second is the frequency of calls made to the Windows NT services. When there are more interrupts per second than system calls, this confirms that the hardware devices are generating more demand on the system processor than the software calls to the NT services.

■ **System** Context Switches/sec—If you are trying to determine whether a RISC processor server will increase the performance of your environment, first confirm whether the rate of switches from one thread to another thread is a high processor activity on your existing server. If the context switches per second are relatively high compared to total processor time, a RISC processor can improve system performance.

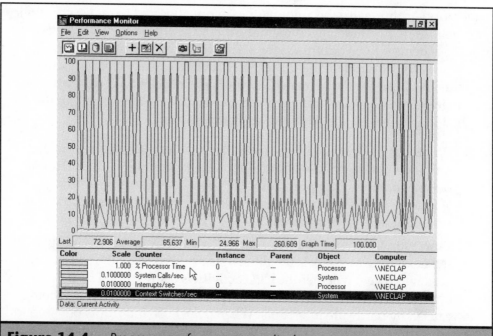

Figure 14-4. *Processor performance monitoring*

In many environments, a faster processor may be indicative of faster performance, but an additional function of faster processing speed for an Exchange server is that it can provide the capacity to add more users to a single server. Unlike file-based messaging systems that typically have limited options for server scalability, Microsoft Exchange can be scaled to add more processors or to upgrade to a RISC-based processing system at a time when processor performance of the existing server exceeds the available current processing performance.

Disk Performance and Optimization

The second thing an organization can do to increase the performance of an Exchange server is to evaluate the method and process of implementing a disk storage strategy. Key to the disk performance strategy is how log files and message databases are distributed across the available hard drives in the server. If a server disk subsystem with a number of 2GB or 4GB drives is configured as one large server drive with the Exchange log files and message database writing to the single logical disk, the system is not properly optimized. A server disk subsystem is better optimized by placing the log files and the message store on separate drives so the information can be written to two separate subsystems simultaneously. Additionally, the pagefile and event logs can be split on two separate drives for improved disk performance.

The way to determine if the disk subsystem in an Exchange server needs to be upgraded or modified is to use the Performance Monitor (PERFMON.EXE) utility on the Exchange server. Before disk performance can be tracked, the counters need to be activated on the server. To activate disk counters, the program DISKPERF-Y must be run on the server. The key components to view in the Performance Monitor, as graphed in Figure 14-5, are described as the following:

- **Paging File** % Usage—The paging file usage percentage tells how much of the paging file is being used at any given time. When the paging file exceeds 90 percent, it is dynamically increased. When the paging file needs to be increased, it not only takes server performance to manage its update, but it is also increased in a noncontiguous disk configuration. The paging file is initially a single contiguous block of disk space that can be efficiently written and read when it is created, but it should be maintained to minimize the need to dynamically change the file.

- **Physical Disk**   % Disk Time—The physical disk percentage time is the amount of time a disk read or disk write is conducted on the server. When the percentage of disk time is in excess of 65 percent, the disk subsystem may be a bottleneck on the server. A number of options can be invoked to improve disk performance caused by excessive disk access, which will be discussed later in this chapter.

- **Logical Disk**   Disk Bytes/sec—The disk bytes per second is the volume of information being read or written to the disk at any given point in time. By tracing the amount of information that is read and written to disk, it can be evaluated whether the demand for disk throughput (whether a Fast SCSI-2, Fast Wide SCSI, or a cached disk subsystem) is necessary for the amount of actual disk throughput demands made on the server.

- **Current Disk Queue Length**   The current disk queue length shows how many disk I/O requests are pending processing. When the disk queue length exceeds two, the pending request transactions for the server may indicate the need for a faster controller card or distributed disk read or write subsystem.

- **Average Disk sec/Transfer**   The average disk transfer shows how many seconds a read or write request takes to complete. When the average disk transfer exceeds .05 seconds, a caching disk controller may improve disk read and write performance on the server.

Disk Caching Controllers

Disk caching controllers can significantly improve the performance of a server with heavy disk reads and writes. A messaging server, by definition, manages information transfers from user to user as well as the transport of messages in and out of directory and messages stores. When the PerfMon thresholds are excessive, a disk cache controller can minimize the bottleneck on the disk subsystem. A caching controller can provide better scalability for users on a server as this typically translates to more transactions and more messages on a server at any given time.

RAM Memory in the File Server

The third aspect that can help an organization increase the performance of an Exchange server is to evaluate whether the amount of memory in the file server is adequate for the demands of the environment. Key to the server memory

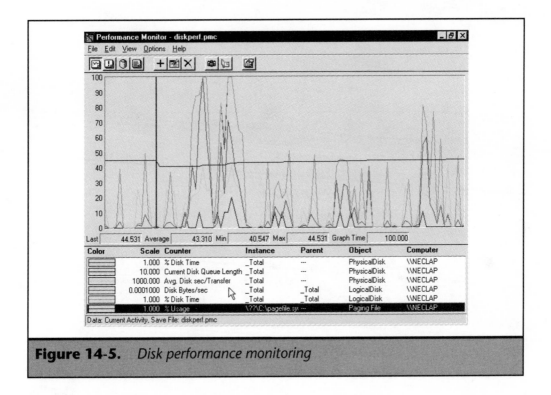

Figure 14-5. *Disk performance monitoring*

management is whether the amount of memory in the server is sufficient to cache disk read and write requests and to store directory store information in order to minimize the number of times the server needs to read information from disk.

One way to determine whether the memory management in an Exchange server is optimized is to use the Performance Monitor (PERFMON.EXE) utility on the Exchange server. The key components to view in the Performance Monitor, as graphed in Figure 14-6, are described as the following:

■ **Memory** Available Bytes—The available bytes is the amount of memory available for use. When the memory bytes available drops below 4MB, paging is occurring on the server and the system may require more memory to minimize the number of times it needs to page to disk.

■ **Memory** Pages/sec—The memory pages per second is the number of memory pages being read and written to disk that were not cached in memory at the time of request. When the pages per second exceeds 15 pages per second, the system is most likely destroying the disk and

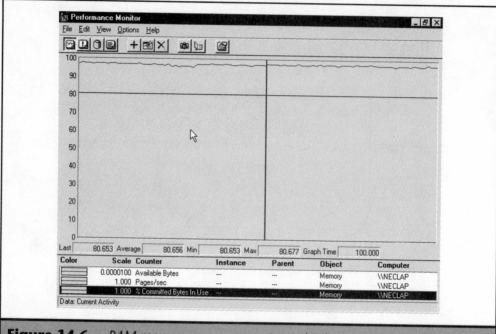

Figure 14-6. *RAM memory management monitoring*

either more RAM memory should be added or a cached disk controller should be added to the server.

- **Memory** % Committed Bytes in Use—The percentage of the committed bytes in use is the ratio of committed bytes to the committed limit, which is the amount of virtual memory that is in use. When the committed percentage exceeds 90 percent, the server may reallocate memory for the paging file, causing a decrease in performance as the paging file is updated.

Ways to Improve Performance and Operation Optimization of the Exchange Client

In addition to optimizing the Exchange server to enhance overall environment performance, there are a number of ways to improve the performance of the client workstation that need to be explored as well. Given that Microsoft Exchange is a client/server environment, a portion of the performance characteristics and capabilities of the system are dependent on the performance of the client workgroups.

Use of a 32-bit Operating System

An organization using a 16-bit operating system for its client workstations can gain significant client performance by going to a 32-bit desktop operating system such as Windows 95 or Windows NT Workstation. The 32-bit desktop operating systems do not have the same barriers to memory management as their 16-bit counterparts. Better memory management capabilities mean that a workstation can have multiple network access protocols operating at the same time, thus allowing a workstation to communicate to a network operating system as well as a messaging operating environment with efficiency. Additionally, a 32-bit version of the Exchange client software can load more of the application into memory at a time than the 16-bit version, minimizing the number of times the application has to separately read and write information to disk.

If an organization elects to implement the use of the Outlook 97 client software, it will find that the features built into the Outlook client for Exchange, including the implementation of the 32-bit electronic forms designer, will not only improve functionality, but also overall access performance quite significantly.

Faster Connection from the Client to the Server

As with any client/server application environment, the performance between the client and the server becomes important in determining how fast information can transfer from the client to the server. As organizations increase the user functionality of a groupware and intranet-capable product like Microsoft Exchange, the client demands to do more with their communications systems also increases.

The ways to increase the connection performance between a client and a server include increasing the bandwidth between the client and the server, such as upgrading to 100Mbit Ethernet, Token Ring, or FDDI speeds, or by increasing the efficiency of the network by segmenting the network into smaller workgroups.

The costs to implement 100Mbit networking have dropped dramatically, enabling organizations to implement cost-effectively a 100Mbit solution for higher performance between the client and the server.

As for the implementation of network segmenting, an organization hoping to increase networking performance without upgrading to 100Mbit can split up large clusters of users currently communicating on a single Token Ring segment or on the same Ethernet segment, and can gain communication infrastructure performance by splitting the networking segment. Decreasing the number of users on a segment to less than 40-60 can minimize the number of collisions caused by a congested network in an Ethernet environment, or minimize the token rotation time for a large Token Ring segment.

These changes can increase the overall throughput between the Exchange client and the Exchange server.

Running the Exchange Optimization Wizard

A utility that is run at the time of the Microsoft Exchange Server software installation is the Optimization Wizard, which can also be run after the server has been running for a while as well. The Optimization Wizard analyzes the server configuration with respect to disk configuration, physical and logical disk allocation, server service component configuration, and other core server component and attempts to optimize the server and allocate the resources of the system.

Optimization Wizard Functions

The Optimization Wizard is implemented by running the Optimization Wizard icon in the Exchange folder on the Microsoft Exchange Server. The Optimization Wizard collects information about the server configuration as well as provides a menu of configuration options for an administrator to select, as shown in Figure 14-7. During the optimization process, the Optimization Wizard analyzes the current hardware available for the system and provides suggestions on reallocating the current server configuration to improve overall system performance.

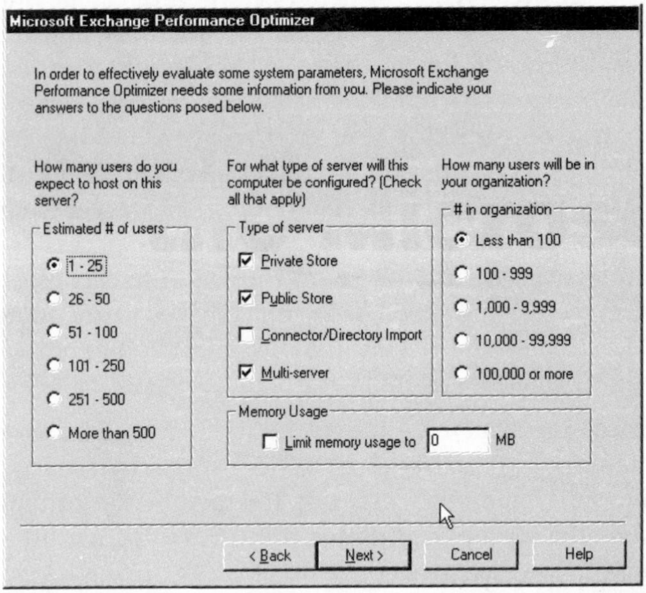

Figure 14-7. *Selecting optimization characteristics for the Exchange optimization wizard*

The Chapter in Review

- The last chapter in Part Three of the book, Chapter 14, addresses the tuning and optimization of an Exchange server. While many organizations have begun the implementation of an Exchange environment, the key to maintaining the environment to work properly is to constantly tune and optimize it to meet the changing demands of the organization. Many organizations mask inherent design flaws by adding more memory or buying a faster file server when in fact it is the environment that needs to be adjusted. Masking design flaws can cause an Exchange environment to prematurely fail. Thus, it is important that an organization does whatever it can to see that the Exchange environment is configured to work to its full potential.

■ There are three areas where system performance can be improved. They include upgrading the processor, the memory, and finally the disk subsystem. Many administrators have been taught through the years that a faster processor will make the system operate faster. This is obviously true on a desktop computer where a 166MHz Pentium processor definitely loads and calculates a spreadsheet faster than an 80486 33MHz processor. However, in the client/server environment, other factors are just as crucial to the performance success of the system. For example, the amount of RAM in the server to cache system requests, as well as the speed of the hard drives to adequately store information to disk as efficiently as possible, need to be considered when judging overall system performance.

■ A fast processing system with inadequate RAM can be slowed by the lack of memory to properly cache disk reads and writes to the server's hard drive subsystem. By increasing the memory, information can be accepted by the server client faster, thus providing a buffer for the information to be queued and written to disk during a slower processing cycle of the system.

■ In addition to improving the performance of the Exchange server, an organization also needs to take into account the performance of the client system. Because Microsoft Exchange is a client/server operating environment, the performance of the client system is just as important as that of the server system. The upgrade from a 16-bit DOS or Windows environment to a 32-bit Windows 95 or Windows NT environment will increase system performance due to the faster capabilities of the operating system.

■ Finally, an Exchange Administrator can use the Exchange Optimization Wizard to automatically optimize an Exchange server. The Optimization Wizard reviews memory in the server, disk storage capacity and capability, and the implementation of requirements of a server environment. By properly implementing solutions relative to the capabilities of the server, an Exchange implementation can operate with minimal end user downtime.

Review Questions

Q. When does faster not necessarily mean better?
A. When an Exchange or any network environment is not running to its utmost efficiency, not only is the system's performance poor, it can also prematurely fail. By adding a faster server to the environment, the organization does not necessarily resolve the core efficiency problems of the system.

Q. True or false, Microsoft Exchange automatically optimizes system performance at the time of the software installation?
A. False. While an Exchange server has an Optimization Wizard to attempt to improve system performance, there are still functions in the server's operation that need to be manually tuned.

Q. How should information stored on a server with multiple hard drives be configured?
A. If a server has multiple hard drives, it is preferred to have the Exchange message store, the NT pagefile, and the log files write to separate hard drives. Since these tasks are frequently written to the disk simultaneously, having multiple hard drives can improve disk write performance.

Q. How can an organization improve system performance at the desktop?
A. An organization can upgrade a desktop's operating environment from a 16-bit DOS or Windows environment to a 32-bit Windows 95 or Windows NT workstation environment. Additionally, the connection between the workstation and the server can be upgraded to a faster transport system such as 100-Mbit Ethernet instead of the standard 10-Mbit Ethernet.

PART FOUR

Advanced Business Uses for Exchange

In the past three sections of this book, we have reviewed the basic features and functions of the Microsoft Exchange product, how to plan for a successful installation and configuration of the Exchange environment, and how to manage, optimize, and tune the Exchange system. Most installation guides, user manuals, and third-party books would end after these topics had been covered. Throughout this book, however, the goal has been to both thoroughly explain Microsoft Exchange basics and also to demonstrate that the value of the Microsoft Exchange product lies not only in what the product can do off the shelf, but also in the ways in which it can improve how users and organizations work, communicate, and provide services with and for each other. It is this value that will be covered in the last part of this book, which includes implementing Microsoft Exchange as a full communications environment, and the expansion of Exchange functionality through the use of third-party add-in products that demonstrate its full capabilities.

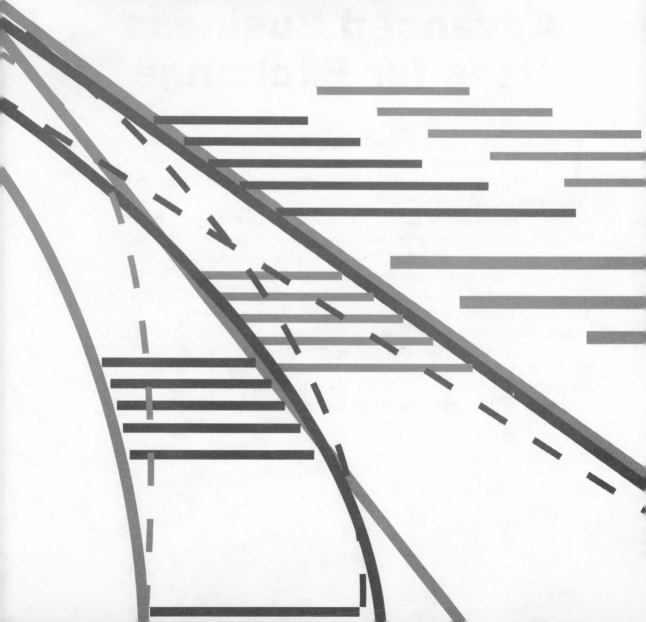

CHAPTER 15

Using
Microsoft
Exchange as
an Intranet

One of the hottest topics in today's corporate environment is the deployment of an intranet to manage corporate communications. The appealing functionality of an intranet is its ability to centralize corporate information, such as forms, policies, procedures, group discussions, etc. This concept is not new to organizations, who have been distributing corporate information in many ways, including placing word processing documents on local area network file servers and data on mini-computers and mainframes, storing the information residing in files in filing cabinets, and placing information in various formats in corporate databases. A new concept, however, is the ability to use a single method to search and access this information, which is basically an intranet's strongest appeal to business executives and information managers.

Many organizations are taking a dual approach by upgrading their electronic mail system to include groupware capabilities and at the same time developing a strategy to create a corporate intranet. In this chapter, we will highlight the ability of Microsoft Exchange to be both the corporate groupware communication system as well as the company intranet document and information management system.

Microsoft Exchange includes all of the infrastructure components of a good intranet system, such as a public and private storage system with integrated file and folder security, and with the addition of third-party search engines and document viewers, Microsoft Exchange rivals traditional Internet and intranet solutions.

What Is an Intranet?

An intranet is essentially the consolidation of information so that users in an organization can quickly and easily find that information in the centralized storehouse and access it on an as-needed basis. Additionally, an intranet is a way for users to share ideas, participate in discussion groups, and carry on communications and business electronically through virtual processes, eliminating the need for physical meetings, conferences, or a traditional paper trail system.

Strategies for Deploying a Separate Intranet

Organizations developing an intranet strategy are consolidating data files, graphic files, paper-based contracts, forms, procedures, and other company information to centralize all forms of organizational communications. A traditional intranet that uses a Web server such as the Netscape Server or Microsoft's Internet Information Server converts text files to Hypertext Markup Language (HTML), or converts forms and contracts to Portable Document Format (PDF) file formats for universal access by any Web browser software. The standard Web-based formats allow for universal sharing of common information.

Although this is one of the more common methods for Web-based intranet server file and information management strategies, other options for managing files are also available. In an effort to minimize the tedious need to convert existing word processing documents to HTML formats or to scan forms using a desktop scanner into PDF formatted files, tools are now available to store document files on a Web server in their native format. These plug-ins to Web browser software allow users accessing a file to view it in a native file format, as long as the user has an application that will be able to view the file (such as Microsoft Word or Microsoft Excel). By eliminating the need to convert standard documents into HTML and thus leaving them in their native formats while making the information available to other users in the organization, the time and effort required to administer the documents is drastically reduced.

The challenge for many organizations is the consolidation of information and the maintenance of this information. Some information is archived on desktop PCs, some is actively used on network file servers, some is stored on Macintosh workstations, and some is stored on UNIX servers. Clearly, the lack of a central file storage system becomes a problem. Although many organizations have cross-platform methods that save information to common file servers using a shared NetWare, NT, or NFS server, a strategy for file sharing across multiple platforms is rarely defined on an organization-wide basis.

An additional problem with keeping files in their native format is the need to have either the native application to retrieve the file (for example, Word or Excel), or a "viewer" that will allow the user to accept the file and perform a file conversion to view the document onscreen. If all the organization's users are running the same applications, native file access is not an issue. However, for an organization running multiple desktop operating systems (such as DOS, Windows, Macintosh, and UNIX workstation systems), all with different support requirements, the need for a browser that can support all of these formats becomes more of a challenge.

The Intranet Capabilities of Microsoft Exchange

Just as organizations are deciding how to implement a cross-platform intranet system to share information and improve communications, Microsoft released the Microsoft Exchange messaging and groupware product. At first, many organizations saw Microsoft Exchange as just another electronic mail system. However, as early users of Microsoft Exchange Server began to deploy the Exchange server environment and utilize the capabilities of the core product as well as added-in third-party applications, Microsoft Exchange soon became an obvious solution that addressed many of the challenges of a traditional intranet.

Benefits of Microsoft Exchange as an Intranet

As was noted in the last section, an intranet needs the following capabilities:

- Ability to centrally store information for access by a system of any operating platform
- Ability to quickly and easily search for information
- Ability to logically store information in a hierarchical format for structured information management

The benefit of a Microsoft Exchange environment is that it performs the basic functions of an intranet as well as goes beyond the functions of information storage and retrieval. Microsoft Exchange and third-party Exchange add-ins give organizations these capabilities:

- Ability to manage documents and maintain document controls on stored information

- Ability to route documents using digital signature authentication
- Ability to not only passively store and retrieve information, but to actively manage all forms of information such as voicemail messages, fax messages, and task and project management information

Universal Inbox and Multiplatform Client Support

As outlined earlier in this book, the Universal Inbox can hold electronic messages as well as fax documents, voicemail messages, form documents, or even application documents like Microsoft Word document files or Lotus 1-2-3 spreadsheet files. Similarly, the private and public folders in a Microsoft Exchange environment can act as receptacles for a variety of information documents. An organization no longer needs to have a shared hard drive directory for word processing documents, a contact management database to store e-mail or text-based communications, and a filing cabinet to store fax messages. By using the inbox to drag and drop information into common client folders, different types of information can be stored and shared across a domain.

In addition to different information formats, an organization can also have different client operating systems, all supported by Microsoft Exchange. Because Exchange has client software that will support users of DOS, Windows, Windows 95, Windows NT, and Macintosh, as shown in Figure 15-1, and virtually any other client through the universal Web client for Exchange, the various information formats for text, graphics, forms, or schedule information become available to virtually all users in an organization. Through the use of the same technology that a Web server infrastructure uses to support the storage of files in their native file format which are then shared through viewers to other platforms, Microsoft Exchange provides the "front end" support to centrally store, transport, and provide viewing capabilities for information across multiple client platforms.

Robust Electronic Mail

Key to any good communications system serving as an intranet is its ability to distribute information, ask questions, seek approvals, invoke queries, or request confirmations. Although many intranet solutions depend on an add-on electronic messaging system or process to fulfill these needs, Microsoft Exchange is built on one of the most sophisticated electronic messaging systems available.

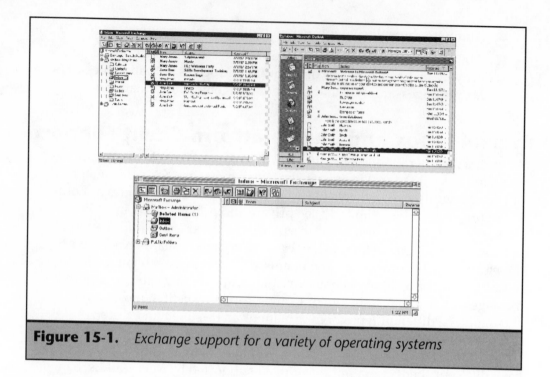

Figure 15-1. *Exchange support for a variety of operating systems*

The components that I will cover later in this chapter regarding intranet users' need for a highly sophisticated messaging system is an intranet's ability to conduct the functions of a sophisticated document routing system.

Saving Information in its Native Format in a Hierarchical Folder Structure

Microsoft Exchange is built on a system that sees all information as objects, which allows it to accept files for storage in folders in their native format as well as in certain formats that do not require special conversion for support by other client operating software. Using a hierarchical directory storage system, information can be stored on Exchange servers as the central depository for all operating system environments. And because Microsoft Exchange is a client/server environment, it can operate as a file management system for virtually any client operating system through nothing more than the standard Microsoft Exchange messaging client software front end.

Out-of-the-Box Solutions

The key to Microsoft's success with Microsoft Exchange as an intranet is the add-ins created by third-party software developers that enhance its ability to act as an extremely sophisticated intranet server solution. Although many intranet document management, information management, and communications systems require special CGI scripting, HTML document creation, and specialized security and authentication systems created by a programming specialist over a period of weeks or months, Microsoft Exchange has dozens of utilities and applications available to facilitate intranet communications without lengthy or complicated programming or application development.

As a result of the industry-wide popularity of Microsoft Exchange, many software development companies are strategically creating add-in software applications and utilities for Exchange. The competition between the multiple companies developing Exchange applications is a real benefit to the user, because the multitude of products encourages competition in both cost and quality. Unlike Microsoft Exchange, other groupware or intranet application environments do not have as much industry third-party development support, and the availability of off-the-shelf options is limited.

Using Microsoft Exchange to Store and Retrieve Information

Utilizing Microsoft Exchange as an intranet involves the integration of core Microsoft Exchange functions with third-party add-in products to provide an advanced complete solution. The various components that make up an Exchange intranet environment are noted in the next section.

Microsoft Exchange File and Folder Management

Microsoft Exchange stores electronic messages in folders. A folder can have subfolders, just as a directory in a hard drive hierarchy can have subdirectories. For example, a folder can be labeled CLIENTS with subfolders for ABC Company, XYZ Company, and the like, as shown in Figure 15-2. Electronic mail messages can easily be dragged and dropped from the user's inbox to a folder.

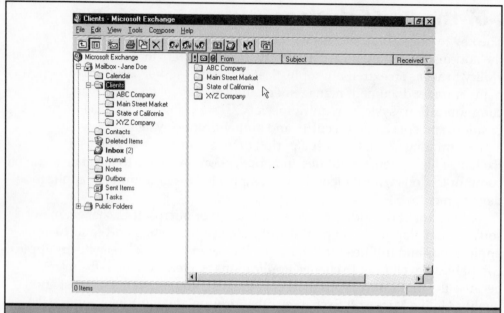

Figure 15-2. *Folder structure to support the organization of information*

In Microsoft Exchange, there are also private folders and public folders. A private folder is a group of messages that only a user can access, whereas a public folder is a group of messages that is made available for viewing, editing, or deletion (depending on public folder security) by other users in the messaging domain. With Microsoft Exchange v5.0, public folders can be selected to be hidden from specific users or groups of users on the network.

Since Microsoft Exchange treats documents as objects, an entire subdirectory from a hard drive can be dragged and dropped (using File Manager or Windows Explorer) directly into an Exchange folder, eliminating the need to create message files or headers documents for each file. Many organizations have taken common directories from their file servers and dragged and dropped entire directories of hundreds and thousands of files directly into Microsoft Exchange to consolidate storage locations and utilize the capabilities of Exchange search engines and viewers to retrieve information.

This ability to drag and drop files into Exchange and make the files available to any Exchange client (including clients of mixed operating system platforms), as well as the need to implement a file and storage system based on NFS, NT, or NetWare with dedicated support for file sharing can be eliminated in favor of Microsoft Exchange.

Additionally, as messages are dragged and dropped into public folders, they can be screened for appropriateness of content automatically. This process can ensure that the right information is stored in the right folders, or that a folder administrator has the ability to preview information before authorizing the posting of information into a public folder.

The entire folder process system in Exchange is an included function that is built into the Microsoft Exchange product.

Information Reference (Search Engines)

One of the most important third-party add-ins to Exchange are search engines, which index information on the server for future reference capabilities in just seconds. Not only do these search engine utilities search the file name or subject of the information, they can also open document files and read and index the information within objects stored on the Exchange server, providing a two-to-three second look-up time for any information stored in Exchange folders.

Once vital information is stored in common Microsoft Exchange folders, the ability to find it when you need it becomes crucial. Microsoft Exchange has a basic FIND utility built into the Tools menu of the Exchange client that will search for information based on the sender, the recipient, the subject of the message, or the text content of the message. Although this is adequate for simple reference in small groups of messages, it could take in excess of 30-40 seconds to look through 1,000 text e-mail messages to find a match. Furthermore, the FIND function within Exchange will look only at the text portion of a message, not within the contents of an integrated attachment.

There are a few third-party search engines available for Microsoft Exchange that index folder messages including attachment documents within a folder. The advantage of these third-party add-ins is their ability to index documents during idle time on a server, thus making the search function significantly faster once the information has been indexed. On an administrator-level configuration option, new messages or documents dragged and dropped into an Exchange folder can be immediately indexed by the Exchange server or indexed during an off-hour process. Because this indexing is performed as a central server process, instead of as an on-request basis, a search of 1,000 messages will take only a few seconds to find the corresponding documents. Furthermore, since attached application documents (like raw word processing documents, spreadsheet files, or encapsulated text files) are also indexed, the contents of documents themselves are searchable and retrievable by the search engine.

Search engines for Exchange have the ability to gather, index, and provide search capabilities for all types of document content and information. Although there are a handful of third-party add-in search engines for Exchange, I will be highlighting Fulcrum FIND! from Fulcrum Technologies throughout the balance of this section on search engines.

Search Engine Indexes

Indexes are an extremely important component of functions designed to provide high-speed reference to information stored in Exchange folders. By maintaining an index service on the Exchange server that monitors mailboxes and public folders in order to find items that have been added, updated, or deleted from the folders, the search engine can automatically update its index. In addition, an administrator can choose the level of indexing by indicating whether information should be indexed manually or automatically on a set routine basis.

Common search engine indexing functions include:

- Automatic maintenance of synchronized indexes for folders stored on multiple Exchange servers using the native Exchange synchronization process
- Specification of which folder(s) will be indexed
- Automatic association of newly created subfolders into the index
- Determination of how often the index will be updated
- Determination of where the index system files will be stored

Before a user can perform a search on a newly created folder, that folder needs to be defined as a default index folder, as shown in Figure 15-3. Otherwise, by default, folders are not automatically indexed. This minimizes both the amount of information that may not need to be indexed and the overhead necessary to manage folders that have little value in a searchable index system.

Searching for Information

Once information has been stored and indexed, the next step is the ability to search for information in the indexed folders. Search engine look-up criteria, as shown in Figure 15-4, should allow users to reference information including

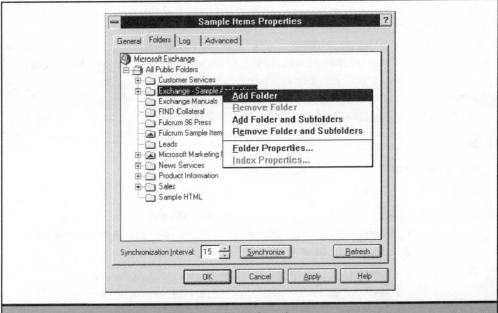

Figure 15-3.   *Adding a folder to be indexed*

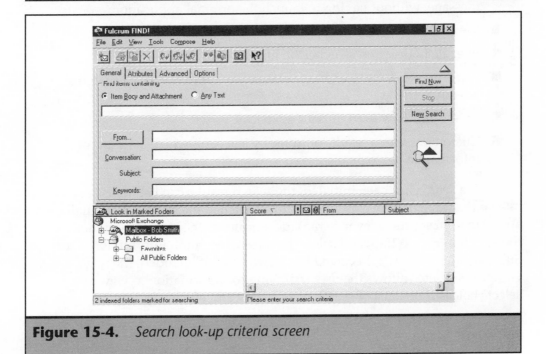

Figure 15-4.   *Search look-up criteria screen*

from whom a message was sent (From), the subject of the message (Subject), the key word or words in the body text or attachment of the message (Keywords), as well as providing users with the ability to select date ranges for messages to search. The more flexible the searching methodology, the greater likelihood that users will be able to narrow down the criteria and find the information they are looking for.

Search engines for Exchange typically have the following capability to:

- Search multiple mailboxes
- Search multiple private folders and personal stores
- Search public folders
- Search files or message attachments in a wide variety of formats, including word processing, spreadsheets, presentation packages, and Adobe Acrobat PDF files
- Search for items using multiple terms, Boolean logic, wildcards, proximity searching, and word variations (for example, *word, words, word's*)
- Display any retrieved item, even an attachment to a Microsoft Exchange message, without having to launch the original application
- View retrieved items, enhanced with search-term highlighting
- Execute high-speed searches on gigabytes of data
- Perform follow-up searches for items similar to one or more items already retrieved
- Save commonly used queries as special Views
- Customize search result columns, by selecting which columns of information are to be displayed

After a search has been initiated, the search results can list items based on a relevant ranking of how closely each item matched the criteria. Essentially, the ability to both see the relevance ranking (similar to the information found in the search in Figure 15-5) and select the message column information (From, Subject, Title, Sent Date, Received Date, Attachment Included, Message Urgency Key, etc.) allows the user searching for information to view and select choices from a list of search hits quickly and efficiently.

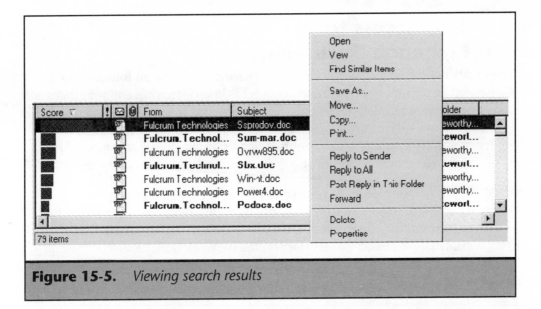

Figure 15-5. *Viewing search results*

Viewing Information

Once the search criteria finds the matching information, the Exchange client needs to view the information with or without the original application in which it was formatted. The addition of an integrated viewer to the system means that users can select a message and view it whether it is a word processing-formatted document, spreadsheet information, or in any of several graphical formats. Additionally, the user should have the ability to edit or print the information if that is what the property rights of the information will allow.

The Management of Documents and Document Control

When information is stored for common access or use, it needs to be managed in order to minimize the ability of unauthorized users to access the information, add more information to the file system, and modify or delete the information. In addition, there should be some method of metering or controlling the process by which information is stored in an Exchange intranet environment.

Controlling Access to Stored Exchange Documents

The implementation and enforcement of a security system on folders is vital to the proper management of common documents in order to prevent unauthorized access or unauthorized changes or deletion of stored information. Microsoft Exchange provides certain security functions on folders, which include the ability to specify variable access rights based on individual Exchange users or by an Exchange group definition. Security rights fall into two categories:

- **Own, All, or None** To receive folder security privileges, users can be configured so that they can only manipulate information submitted to the folder by themselves (*own*), so that they can manipulate any information stored by any user on the network (*all*), or so that they have no rights to manipulate any information in the folder (*none*).

- **Attributes** The attributes of a modification include the ability to create, delete, or read messages, or create other subfolders within the folder.

Access control determination is selected by either the Exchange administrator or by the owner of the folder. The folder owner(s) are also defined in the permissions security properties for the folder, as shown in Figure 15-6.

Through the use of security implementation, an organization can create a messaging hierarchy that can adequately manage its access to information. By providing a common filing system with a variety of management capabilities, the organization can give itself a number of information storage options.

Metering or Controlling Stored Information

Once information can be stored, easily searched, and secured, the next step for the organization is to meter and control the information while retaining the ability to note changes or modifications made to it. When information is set for read-only privileges, the only thing that needs to be limited is the security privileges to access the information. However, when users are given the authority to modify and delete information, a system needs to be implemented so that revision changes or controls can be tracked for other users to see. The implementation of this system is the next step in document sharing and management.

Within the Exchange environment, each folder can be assigned predefined rules for manipulating stored information. By defining the modification rules

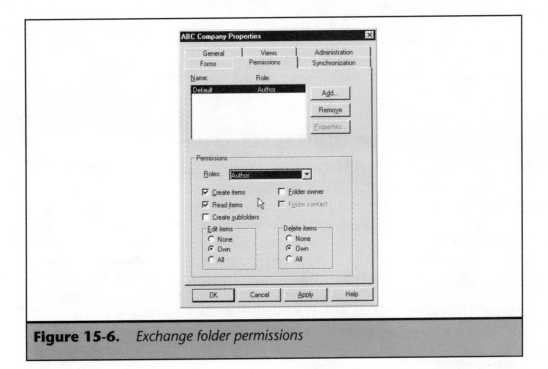

Figure 15-6. *Exchange folder permissions*

for the information stored within an Exchange environment, an archive of revisions can be developed by moving the existing document automatically to a common storage area, which means that the new version of the document in the primary folder or information store becomes the primary document, retaining its modifications or edits. Notifications can be configured so that Exchange administrators, information administrators, folder owners and the contact individuals defined for the folder access receive notice of edits made to certain documents. Additionally, rules can interface with data contained within a document, including the form in which a document has been placed.

Forms and Templates

One way to control how information is stored and managed is to designate the format in which information in an Exchange environment is stored. This can be done through the use of Exchange forms and template documents. As outlined in Chapter 3 of this book, Microsoft Exchange includes the Electronic Forms Designer (EFD) software, which gives an organization the ability to create standard forms that can be used as default guidelines for information entry. Forms can be configured to require specific information so that a form entry cannot be submitted to an information folder if all of the key fields on the form have not been completed. Please refer to Chapter 3 for information on the creation and management of forms and templates in an Exchange groupware environment.

Implementation of Digital Signature and Digital Encryption

The final component in the management and control of information within a message or common document storage system is the ability to encrypt the information for general access and use as well as the ability to authenticate the information to ensure its validity. Chapter 12 of this book covered the use of digital signatures and digital encryption within documents. These functions are crucial when sensitive data may be categorized within a common folder section of information but should be individually restricted for access and review. Through the use of digital encryption, a single message within a common folder can be identified as restricted and can be encrypted to require that access and viewing are conducted only by an individual who has the authority to access the information.

As we move into the next section of this chapter on document routing, once messages are sent, received, routed, and moved for the purpose of approval or comment criteria, the need for an approval process requires that users have the ability to confirm the information before it is forwarded to the next individual in the process. Authorization or authentication are critical when electronic decisions on information need to be made, similar to a confirmation or consensus process for information discussed in a conference or an in-person group setting.

Using Microsoft Exchange to Route Documents

As an organization's intranet evolves, it will be expected to go beyond simply storing and retrieving information in central folders to routing documents and information among users both internal and external to the organization in order to invoke queries and responses to that information. Document routing within Microsoft Exchange requires the purchase of document routing software and can leverage the components within Exchange, such as digital signatures, to electronically approve and authenticate a document route, utilize digital encryption to maintain security of the information being routed, and implement document revision control procedures to ensure that the information being routed can be validated for changes.

Document Routing

Although Microsoft Exchange has the ability to provide very basic document routing capabilities directly from the Exchange software, some of the third-party document routing add-in programs add very sophisticated document routing functions to the existing Exchange environment, enhancing the capabilities of its routing functionality. While there are a handful of document routing programs available for Exchange, we will focus on a product made by KeyFile Corporation called KeyFlow for Exchange.

Workflow management products for Microsoft Exchange Server enable professionals to easily visualize business processes, like the one shown in Figure 15-7, to allow professionals to automate processes, monitor their progress, and modify them in real time to improve efficiency and respond immediately to changing business needs.

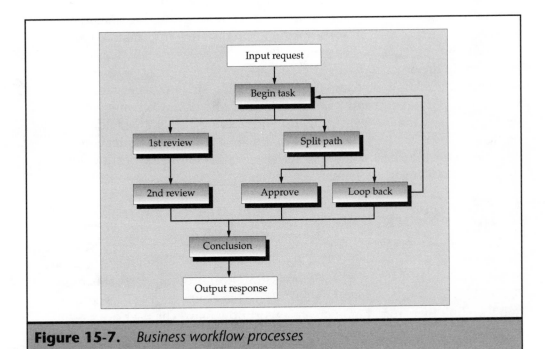

Figure 15-7. *Business workflow processes*

With a document routing or workflow product, documents can be automatically circulated through a review cycle according to predetermined criteria. Customer and client issues can be addressed promptly by the appropriate personnel. And functional groups can collaborate more effectively, eliminating wasteful steps and improving the organization's efficiency, sometimes even paring down lengthy processes such as a product's time-to-market. Workflow systems empower corporate professionals to apply their expertise to design efficient business processes that can be used by anyone within a department or across the entire corporate enterprise.

The key elements most critical for automating business processes are:

- The ability for any user to graphically map out a process and create a workflow that automates that process.

- The ability for authorized users throughout an organization to monitor a workflow process and dynamically modify the workflow while it is in progress.

- The ability to interconnect departmental workflow processes across an entire enterprise.

A workflow can be as simple as routing a document to several workers for their information and input. Or, it can be as complex as routing documents and decision processes to specific recipients, requesting information based on document contents, and automatically routing the workflow to anyone anywhere in the organization.

The best workflow programs integrate seamlessly into the Microsoft Exchange environment, and take advantage of Microsoft Exchange's client user interface, standard messaging, user addressing, and public folder and replication facilities. Any user is able to initiate a workflow and respond to workflow task messages by simply selecting and running a workflow form from within Microsoft Exchange.

Creating a Workflow

To create a new workflow, a user can select a workflow template by choosing from an integrated Compose | New Form menu option within the Exchange client software. By using the workflow's graphical user interface, shown in Figure 15-8, a user can select the steps desired to emulate a business process and then link them together to create a workflow map. The user can assign one or more recipients to a step by selecting their names from the Microsoft

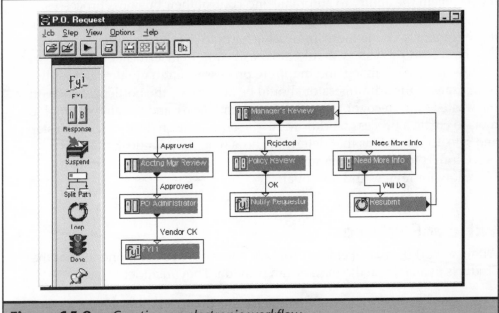

Figure 15-8. *Creating an electronic workflow*

Exchange Address Book. If the user is not sure who the manager is for each department in the enterprise, he or she can select the "Manager" role. When a user starts the workflow, Microsoft Exchange automatically selects that user's manager through the use of the Exchange administrator manage and report to functions.

By integrating into the Exchange client software, other controls such as "simple," "voting," and "conditional" prerequisites enable the creator of the workflow to tightly map even the most complex business processes. Once a workflow has been completed, it can be stored in a private folder, or the workflow process can be shared as a corporate-wide workflow template through the use of Microsoft Exchange public folders and folder replication.

Effects of Workflow in Organizational and Business Processes

Workflow functions should allow an organization to empower its users. By putting the power of the workflow in the hands of management professionals, it gives them the ability to automate and control their business processes. Managers will have the ability to modify electronic business processes and to continuously create more innovative ways to get the job done.

The workflow system should also easily automate critical business processes. By visualizing and mapping processes manually throughout the organization, the administrator should be able to see the bottlenecks, identify the wasted steps, recognize the endless redundancies, and use simple graphical tools to create a process workflow. As the organization designates each step and sets up conditions that determine how work should flow, the next procedure is to preassemble supporting information and attach it to the workflow for review and approval.

Workflow Features

Within a workflow application program, there are key components that the products available on the market can provide. They include:

- **Complete Microsoft Exchange Server Integration** The workflow application should integrate seamlessly into the Microsoft Exchange environment, taking advantage of Microsoft Exchange's comprehensive information management and communications infrastructure. Users work directly through Microsoft Exchange's graphical user interface to compose, address, monitor, and control workflows. Participants in active workflows receive task messages and related attachments via their Microsoft Exchange inbox. Microsoft Exchange also provides the storage and replication facilities that enable a user to share workflows throughout the organization.

- **Graphical Interface** Creating workflows should be easy. A user should be able to simply click the steps needed from the step palette, draw lines between them, and complete the properties page for each step.

- **Attachments** Users should have the ability to attach documents and other relevant files to a workflow. Attachments can include Microsoft Exchange files or messages, as well as OLE objects or OLE object links. The attachment feature is invaluable for processes that require recipients to review or process information.

- **Monitoring Workflows** Workflow users should have the ability to monitor the progress of active workflows by viewing a graphical map of the workflow, like the one shown in Figure 15-9. Color codes indicate which steps are active, complete, or pending. You can also monitor the progress of recipients' task messages by viewing the recipient status.

The recipient status window displays a list of recipients for each step and indicates when a recipient has received, viewed, or completed the step. Recipient status can be exported to any SQL/ODBC database to produce reports that will help users to analyze the efficiency of a workflow and identify bottlenecks in a process.

- **Complex Prerequisites** A workflow administrator should be able to define simple, voting, or combinations of the two with AND and OR operators as prerequisites for any step in a workflow. This capability is useful when an action is dependent on the recipients' responses to one or more of the previous steps. You can also nest prerequisites to create complex Boolean expressions.

- **Voting** A step's prerequisite can include voting. Voting lets you specify how many recipients must select ("vote") a particular response in order for the prerequisite conditions to be met. An example of a prerequisite condition statement is "If one of five recipients rejects this Engineering Change Order (ECO), then initiate the design review process." Voting also allows you to specify a percentage of recipients. For example, "If 60 percent of the recipients approve this Engineering Change Order (ECO), then initiate the purchase order process." You can also combine the voting conditions to review whether more recipients selected one response over another, and if a certain percentage of recipients selected the response you specified.

- **Looping** Looping allows users to automatically reroute workflows, eliminating manual intervention. The loop step supports prerequisites, defining the conditions that cause the loop to occur. The loop step continues indefinitely until the step's prerequisites are no longer met.

- **Time-of-day Alerts** Time-of-day alerts allow you to build date and time deadlines into your workflows. Alert messages are sent to recipients to remind them of when they must respond to an FYI or response task message.

- **Launching Flows** Use the launch step to create workflows that automatically start other workflows. Launching workflows is useful for automating workflows that span multiple departments. For example, the Manufacturing Department's Engineering Change Order (ECO) workflow may include launch steps that start the Engineering Department's Product Design Review workflow and, if approved, Purchasing's Purchase Order Request workflow. Launching workflows empowers professionals to make use of the streamlined procedures created by the appropriate expertise centers within an organization.

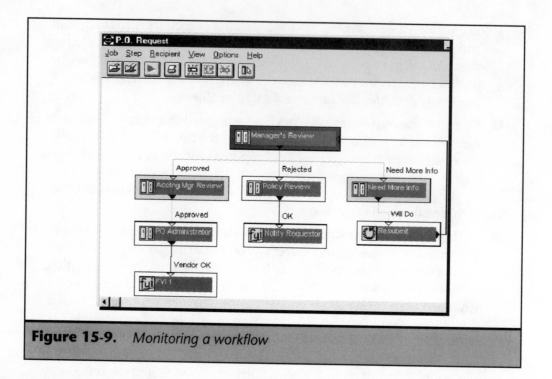

Figure 15-9. *Monitoring a workflow*

The Chapter in Review

■ The last section of the book, Part Four, takes the Microsoft Exchange product and provides real-world uses of the Exchange environment in order to assist businesses to improve organizational efficiencies and corporate communications. Chapter 15 starts the section by outlining how Microsoft Exchange can work as an intranet. An intranet is the ultimate paperless office, and in today's technology environment, the term intranet conjures up visions of open communications and easy access to information anywhere within an organization. Many organizations are implementing intranets as well as upgrading their electronic messaging system in parallel. Upgrading to a product like Microsoft Exchange, an organization can improve its messaging system and at the same time take advantage of Exchange's intranet capabilities for corporate communications.

- The biggest benefit of Microsoft Exchange is its ability to provide a Universal Inbox for the storage of virtually any form of electronic information, whether it be an electronic mail message, an appointment schedule confirmation, an incoming fax document, or a voicemail message. Microsoft Exchange sees information as objects, not as file types, thus a piece of information can be stored in the folder hierarchy of Microsoft Exchange in its native file format. Additionally, because Microsoft Exchange supports a variety of different desktop clients, the integration of Exchange into a multiplatform environment can also simplify the need to intercommunicate across such a diverse desktop.

- An important third-party add-in to a Microsoft Exchange environment for helping to improve Exchange's intranet capabilities is the addition of a search engine, one that will assist users of the organization in finding information stored in the Exchange environment's folders. While users can easily and freely store information in an Exchange hierarchy, an important factor is whether they can find the information when they need it. With third-party search engines, information can be stored and indexed on an Exchange server as the search engine creates a sophisticated index table. When a user wants to look up information on the Exchange server, he or she can find any information stored in virtually any file format, and find information when needed.

- In addition to storing and finding information in an Exchange intranet environment, an organization can also manage and control documents stored in the Exchange system. Other benefits of Microsoft Exchange are the ability of the messaging system to retain historical copies of stored information, and the ability to link with desktop office tools like Microsoft Word to provide document editing and revision control consistent throughout the organization. By implementing forms and templates within the organization, stored information can resemble structured information stores, giving a consistent look to all documents.

- Finally, as in any document management or document control system, Microsoft Exchange offers the ability to route documents throughout the organization in a manner that supports an authenticated approval process all along the document information route.

Review Questions

Q. What makes Microsoft Exchange a functional intranet?
A. Exchange supports the storage of virtually any kind of file, whether it is a mail message, word processing document, graphic file, fax message, or voice message. With add-in search engines and document routing software, Microsoft Exchange can be turned into an intranet for centralized storage of information with minimal additional training to the users of the messaging and groupware environment.

Q. How does information from within a Windows-based application get stored in an Exchange folder?
A. In a Microsoft Exchange-aware application, the application supports the ability to File | Post information straight from the application directly into an Exchange folder. Just as an application typically supports the ability to File | Save a file, using File | Post saves information directly to an Exchange folder system. If the application does not support direct posting of files to the Exchange structure, the user can run File Manager or Windows Explorer and drag and drop files directly into an Exchange folder.

Q. How does a third-party search engine differ from the built-in Microsoft Exchange Tools | Find function?
A. The Tools | Find function within Microsoft Exchange allows the user to search text fields of a message and conducts the search at the time of the query. However, third-party search engines like Fulcrum FIND! indexes text-based fields but will also index attachments. All of the indexed information is stored on the Exchange server. Information can be searched within seconds through the use of a search engine product.

Q. What level of security is available on folders within Microsoft Exchange?
A. The creator of a folder (as well as the Exchange administrator) has the ability to set folder level security on the information stored within the folder. By selecting the Properties | Security function, a user can enable another user or a group of users to have access to create messages in the folder, and delete and modify messages created by the individual and others.

Q. How can workflows improve communications?

A. A workflow with a form can provide a manager with the ability to set up processes in which information is routed within the organization. When left to an ad hoc method of communications, users can accidentally or purposely circumvent procedures or processes; however, in a managed document routing process, the flow of the information, the fields of information required, and the deposition of information routed can be controlled through the document routing process.

CHAPTER 16

Maximizing the Microsoft Exchange Groupware Capabilities

As I discussed in Chapter 3, Microsoft Exchange provides organizations with the opportunity to utilize its many groupware capabilities, including personal and group scheduling, public discussion forums, workgroup shared folders, and electronic forms management functions. Together, these features create the infrastructure for an electronic groupware environment.

In this chapter, I will expand on the standard groupware capabilities of the Microsoft Exchange environment and evaluate third-party groupware add-ins that greatly enhance an organization's ability to leverage Microsoft Exchange in a full groupware integrated communications system. The add-ins covered in this chapter include integrated network faxing, voicemail integration into Exchange, and virus protection for message communications.

Faxing from Within Exchange

The first function that does not ship with Microsoft Exchange Server that most organizations elect to implement is the ability to send and receive faxes. Integrated faxing allows users to receive faxes, which are sent directly to their inbox message box—in exactly the same way that users would receive incoming electronic mail messages. Integrated faxing also allows individuals to send faxes to recipients that may not have electronic mail available to them. Although many organizations are now using electronic mail as a standard method of communications, there are still many organizations that continue to use faxes as the primary communication means. A tightly integrated fax solution within Microsoft Exchange bridges the gap between many current organization processes that use faxing as an authorized or accepted form of communications.

Why Is Network Faxing from Exchange a Favorable Solution?

A number of faxing solutions are available for local area network users as well as individuals to send and receive faxes from laptops or desktop systems. In the past, many organizations elected not to implement network faxing because of the time and effort involved in supporting yet another network add-on service. Now that faxing can be tightly integrated into Microsoft Exchange, however, the effort to administer and manage the faxing solution is integrated into the functions of administering and managing Microsoft Exchange.

Using Existing Microsoft Exchange Resources for Sending and Receiving Faxes

One of the many advantages that an integrated Microsoft Exchange fax solution can provide is the Exchange server's ability to receive incoming faxes, which eliminates worries about maintaining a local workstation and ensuring that it is on and has the proper fax receiving software loaded and operational. Additionally, the fact that incoming faxes appear on the Microsoft Exchange user's mail inbox also removes the need to switch between an incoming fax software application and an incoming electronic mail software application to read faxes or messages. As faxes are received by Microsoft Exchange and routed to the user's inbox, the centralization of information becomes a time saver for users as well as minimizes the need for an organization to train its staff on the use of a fax-only application.

The same interface is used to send and receive fax messages similar to a centralized interface for receiving electronic mail messages.

Ability to Carbon Copy Fax Recipients as Well as E-Mail Recipients

For many organizations, a big benefit of integrated faxing is the ability to distribute information to people whether they use e-mail or faxes as their standard communications system. Exchange users have the ability to select electronic mail message recipients from the messaging recipient address book, as well as the ability to select recipients that need to receive the exact same information, only via fax rather than e-mail. Exchange users can add fax recipients as TO: users or CC: users in the message transmission.

No Extra Software to Install on the Client or Manage User Names or Drivers

With Microsoft Windows NT User Manager and the Microsoft Exchange Administrator programs managing all of the functions of user administration, an organization does not need to add in more administrative training to manage a separate application program, because the administration of the integrated fax software becomes a part of the existing Microsoft Exchange messaging administration system. The integrated fax server solution to Microsoft Exchange uses the Microsoft Windows NT and Exchange administration functions, so as soon as a user is added to the NT/Exchange network, he or she can have access to network files and printers, send and receive electronic mail messages, and send and receive faxes using the same user application and interface.

Third-Party Add-ins for Exchange Faxing

Microsoft Exchange does not come with a built-in faxing solution, so any faxing function becomes a part of the add-in application. The common fax add-ins to Microsoft Exchange, like Omtools' Fax Sr., allow the user to send faxes using the Exchange client application and receive faxes in the Exchange inbox, as well as send faxes from any Windows-based application.

How to Send Faxes from Within the Exchange Client

Sending a fax using an Exchange server add-in is very similar to sending an e-mail from a Microsoft Exchange client. The integrated fax software allows users to be added to the Exchange Global Address List or the address book in the Exchange environment, as shown in Figure 16-1. Instead of having a common name for the user and an Internet electronic mail address, the fax recipient has a common name and a fax phone number to identify his or her method of information access. New users can be added to the address list and then selected as recipients of a fax, or they can have their fax number manually added to the address line of the message to be sent.

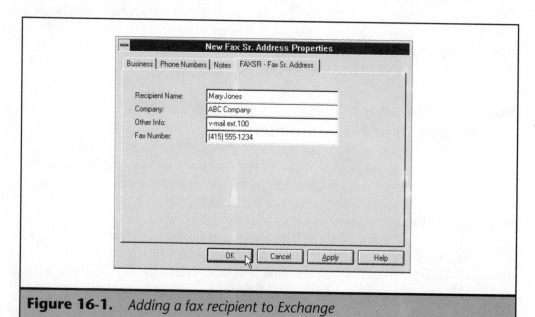

Figure 16-1.   *Adding a fax recipient to Exchange*

When a user sends a message to an e-mail recipient, he or she has the ability to select other e-mail or fax recipients. The fax client function on Microsoft Exchange supports rich text formatted messages as well as attachments. If an attachment is added to an Exchange mail message, it will be converted and faxed to the recipient.

How to Send Faxes from Any Windows-Based Application

Because the Microsoft Exchange fax solutions are part of the Windows NT networking environment, most of the third-party add-in fax solutions allow client workstations to fax from other Windows-based applications. To enable application-based faxing, typically a printer driver needs to be installed on the client workstation, similar to a printer driver used to select an HP LaserJet printer, or an Epson dot matrix printer. Once defined on the client workstation as a supported printer, the user can now print to a fax from the Windows-based application software.

When a user normally prints to a network printer, he or she would choose File | Print from the Windows application, select the printer, and select OK to print to the network printer. For network faxing, the user simply needs to select File | Print from the Windows application, select Network Fax as the printer type, and then select OK, as shown in Figure 16-2. The printer driver

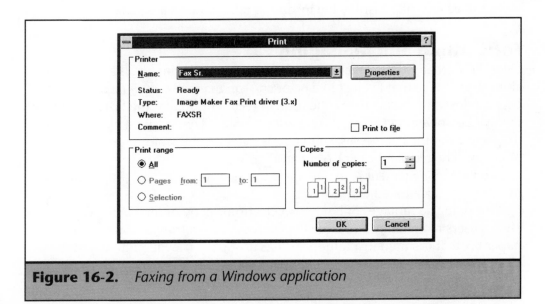

Figure 16-2. *Faxing from a Windows application*

accepts the print job, acknowledges that the job needs to be sent to a network fax server, and the message is rerouted to the Exchange fax system.

How to Receive Faxes

When an Exchange server receives a fax message, the message can be manually or automatically routed directly into the inbox of an Exchange client. Similar to a fax machine, if a fax message is received by the fax server, the message can be automatically routed to a common mailbox, such as the mailbox of a secretary or administrator. The fax cover sheet can be reviewed, and the electronic fax is then forwarded to the mailbox of the intended recipient.

For an automatic fax route to a user's inbox, the organization would need to obtain a service from its phone company that provides electronic routing of faxes. The common service is called direct inward dialing (DID), which provides each e-mail user with a personal fax number. However, all incoming faxes are channeled through only one or a few incoming phone lines. When an Exchange server with an Exchange fax software answers a call, it checks for the DID number of the incoming transmission. The phone company passes along the DID number for the recipient, which the Exchange server fax software acknowledges, maps to a user, and then automatically forwards the fax to the intended recipient. This process is depicted in Figure 16-3.

When the Exchange client receives the fax message, the message is displayed in the user's inbox just like an incoming e-mail message. The user can select the incoming message and press the ENTER key, which allows a viewer to graphically display the incoming fax on the user's screen.

Forwarding and Managing Faxes

Once the Exchange client receives and views the incoming fax, the user has the ability to manage that fax just like he or she can manage e-mail messages. The user can forward the fax to another e-mail recipient, so that the fax will appear in the inbox of another user who can view the fax. The recipient of the fax can drag and drop the fax message into a personal or public folder for future reference. The recipient can also cut and paste the fax into an external database or a contact management software application, or the user can simply choose to delete the fax altogether.

One of the advantages of having an electronic copy of the fax is that it allows users to annotate and store the fax for future retrieval. Unlike a normal paper fax that is stored in a folder and has no easy retrieval method, an electronic copy of a fax in Microsoft Exchange can have a header or annotations,

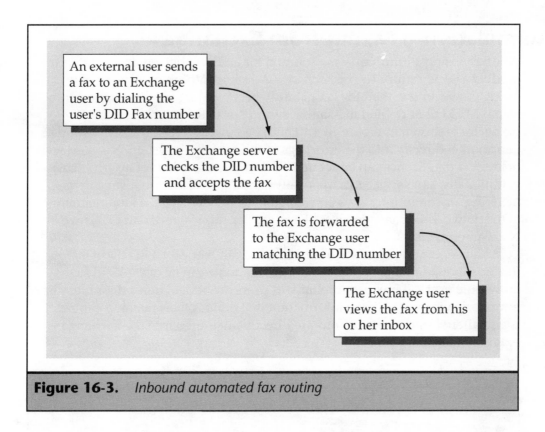

An external user sends
a fax to an Exchange
user by dialing the
user's DID Fax number

The Exchange server
checks the DID number
and accepts the fax

The fax is forwarded
to the Exchange user
matching the DID number

The Exchange user
views the fax from his
or her inbox

Figure 16-3.   *Inbound automated fax routing*

and can be saved to a public folder. At any time, the user can implement the
Microsoft Exchange Tools | Find function or a third-party search engine to
easily search for the fax and retrieve the information.

Adding Fax Messages to the Exchange Information System

Faxes in Microsoft Exchange can be dragged and dropped into folders (as part
of the folder and client management process described in Chapter 15), which
allows organizations to centrally store fax information along with electronic
mail notes, memos, and calendar appointment information into client, vendor,
employee, or other resource folders. Instead of placing some information in
folders in filing cabinets and other information in electronic messages stored
in other locations, centralizing information storage in Exchange folders greatly
improves users' ability to find the information at a later date.

Administering Faxing from Exchange

When choosing a third-party fax solution for an Exchange environment, if the product selected supports the Exchange Administrator management of the faxing environment, then the fax gateway becomes just another connector to an old MS Mail or cc:Mail messaging system, or to the Internet (a fax connector is shown in Figure 16-4). The fax connector reports all errors and information directly into the error logs of the NT Server system. Various levels of logging diagnostics can be set up to determine the extent of fax problems. Additionally, as a service to a Microsoft Exchange environment, any alerts, metering, or communications between the fax service and the administrators of the network are managed just like any other service under an Exchange or NT environment.

As a user is added to Exchange, he or she can request a DID ID so that during inbound faxing the inbound message route can be designated to the individual user's inbox. Additionally, as users are added, deleted, or their user information is modified, the information that defines their faxing components is also altered since the functions are directly integrated into the Exchange Administrator program.

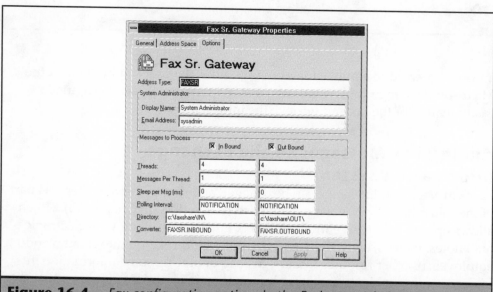

Figure 16-4. *Fax configuration options in the Exchange Administrator*

Voicemail Integration Within Exchange

A term that has been floating around the computer industry over the past few years is CTI, or Computer Telephony Integration. CTI is a process by which computer systems are integrated into telephone systems. In the past, CTI solutions were relatively limited by the restricted functionality and integration between a computer system and a phone or voicemail system. CTI used to be as simple as auto-dialing, which allowed users to have a database record on their screen with a phone number, and with the press of a button, the phone number would be dialed. However, with the integration of computer telephony into a Microsoft Exchange environment, the ability to truly merge an organization's telephony system into its computer-based system has finally become a solution that provides a variety of functional features.

What Is Voicemail Integration?

Voicemail integration into an Exchange environment occurs when an organization's voicemail becomes a part of the Microsoft Exchange messaging system. When a person normally leaves a voicemail message, that message can be retrieved and managed either with a telephone within the organization or by dialing into the company's telephone system, entering a password, and listening to the message. When a person leaves a voicemail message in an integrated voicemail/Exchange environment, the voicemail message can still be accessed and managed using any telephone (internal or external), but the message can also be managed from within the Microsoft Exchange environment.

The voice message, just like a fax message, becomes another component of the user's inbox. All of the same management features the user has to manage electronic mail messages or fax messages are also available to the user to manage voice messages.

Inbound Voice Messaging

In a voicemail-aware Exchange environment, the user's inbox accepts the voicemail message just as it would any other message object. When the user double-clicks on the message, a message playback screen appears on his or her desktop, as shown in Figure 16-5. Users then have the choice of either playing the message to their telephone handset or playing the message through a multimedia system speaker. Unlike the playback of an ordinary voicemail

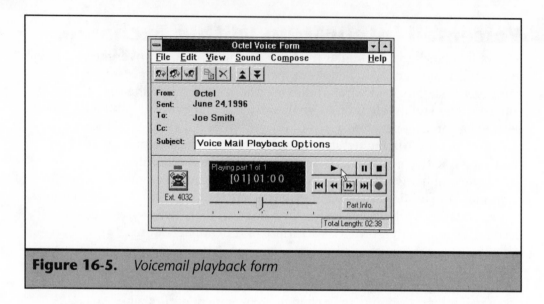

Figure 16-5. *Voicemail playback form*

message over the phone, users have much more flexibility when playing back a voicemail message using the active controls of the Exchange client playback software. Through the desktop client playback software, a user can exercise a number of controls on voicemail messages, including pausing the message, stopping the message, restarting the message, scrolling forward or backward through the message, or skipping directly to a part of the message.

Outbound Voice Messaging

An Exchange client user can leave a voicemail message for a recipient by picking up the phone handset, dialing the recipient's voicemail box number, and leaving a voice message. Because an integrated Exchange voicemail system has many of the desktop tools available to the system, an Exchange client user can leave a voicemail message for a user by launching the voicemail playback utility, selecting record, and either talking into the phone handset or into a multimedia microphone on the workstation system. The message gets recorded and the user can now send the message to the recipient just as he or she would send an electronic mail message.

Text-to-Speech

An important aspect of the Octel Unified Messaging voicemail integrated system for Exchange users is that it allows electronic mail users to send a text-based e-mail to a recipient and allows the recipient to listen to the message from any telephone. In one part of the text-to-speech function of the Unified Messaging software, users can dial into the company's voicemail system to check their messages, the voicemail attendant will notify users of how many new voicemail messages they have, how many saved voicemail messages they have, and how many new and saved electronic mail messages are in their inbox. Users can choose to listen to only voicemail messages, or can also listen to electronic mail messages in their inbox, as shown in Figure 16-6. The voice attendant reads the user the subject of the electronic mail message. The user then has the option of listening to the e-mail message synthesized by the voicemail system or can decide to skip the message and listen to the header of the next electronic message. Through text-to-speech, a user can dial into the integrated Exchange e-mail and voicemail system and collect all of his or her messages directly from within the integrated environment.

Managing Voice Messages Like Text Messages

Since voicemail messages reside in the user's inbox, the user has the ability to manage and manipulate voicemail messages just as if they were e-mail messages or fax messages. The user also has the ability to forward a voice

Figure 16-6.   *The voice attendant can read e-mail messages*

message to another user. The recipient of the voice message can listen, store, delete, or reply to the voice message. A recipient of a voicemail message can reply to the voicemail message either with a text message or with a voicemail response. Additionally, with an integrated fax solution, there's no reason why a user could not reply to a voicemail message with a fax response message. The point, however, is that there are many ways available for the organization to communicate, and also that there are many ways for the user of the system to reply or respond to information in a fully-integrated Exchange environment.

Just as users have the ability to drag and drop e-mail messages or faxes into personal or public folders and cut and paste e-mail or fax messages into databases or contact management software, they also retain this level of flexibility and information control with voicemail messages integrated into an Exchange environment. In this scenario, an organization would have a public folder for a client that has copies of e-mail messages, faxes, and voicemail messages all stored as "information" in the organization's Exchange message folder.

Integrated Virus-Checking Within Exchange

No organization groupware strategy is complete without ensuring that virus detection, protection, and eradication are formalized and implemented procedures. Never have viruses spread so quickly since the proliferation of electronic messaging, where users are sending and receiving mail messages including attachments on a frequent basis without scanning or checking the message attachment for viruses. Although the spread of most viruses is usually not done on purpose, users who neglect to check for viruses can unknowingly contract a virus on their computer system and spread it across small or even large workgroups of users as an attachment to a mail message.

To help an organization to implement a safe message access and transmission policy are the integrated virus checking systems for Microsoft Exchange. As messages are received from external or internal users, the message attachments are checked for any viruses, as shown in Figure 16-7. The more automated the process, the greater likelihood the organization will catch a virus before it spreads to other users. Two types of virus checking software are available for a Microsoft Exchange environment.

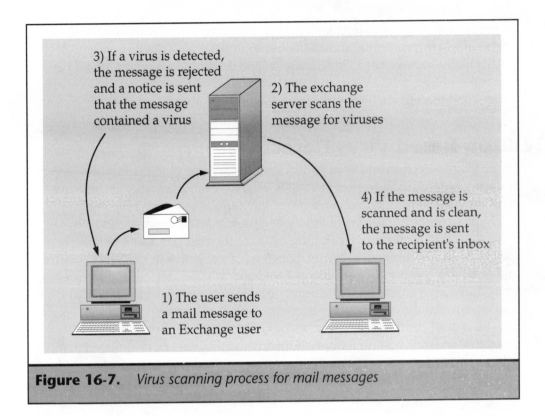

3) If a virus is detected, the message is rejected and a notice is sent that the message contained a virus

2) The exchange server scans the message for viruses

4) If the message is scanned and is clean, the message is sent to the recipient's inbox

1) The user sends a mail message to an Exchange user

Figure 16-7.   *Virus scanning process for mail messages*

Server-Based Virus Checking

The first type of virus checking software is one that is installed on the Exchange server or on a gateway server between the external environment and the internal environment. This virus detection and protection server scans all incoming and outgoing messages for viruses. When it detects a virus, the software can perform one of a number of functions. The administrator can select whether he or she wants all viruses automatically eradicated before the file is forwarded to a user, or the administrator can elect to have the file automatically rejected with a notice going back to the originator that tells that the attachment to the message he or she just sent has been rejected, and that only after the virus has been eradicated will the message reach its proper destination.

Server-based virus detection is a good, secure solution because the virus can be blocked long before it makes its way to the user's desktop. Additionally, server-based virus detection and eradication requires little if no user intervention, thus allowing the network administrator to maintain the control and management of viruses on the organization's network.

Desktop-Based Virus Detection

Other virus detection and eradication systems are installed on each desktop system. These virus detection processes provide each user with the ability to conduct virus detection and controls on the deposition of a virus, whether that might be to eradicate the virus or to leave the file untouched. Desktop-based virus detection is extremely common because the cost per user is relatively inexpensive, and for general virus detection, it's effective at detecting a virus and notifying the user of a problem. The desktop virus detection programs can be updated on a subscription basis, making it easy for an organization to implement and maintain a virus detection and eradication policy.

The crucial component to total virus control is the ability to manage programs and data scanning throughout an organization in a centralized manner, minimizing the variable that individual users provide when they attempt to conduct their own housecleaning and data management.

The Chapter in Review

- In this chapter, we've taken a look at three other add-in technologies to an Exchange environment that have become popular post-Exchange added functions. These technologies, which are faxing from within Microsoft Exchange, integrating voicemail into an Exchange environment, and the scanning of e-mail messages for viruses, can assist an organization in leveraging the full potential and capabilities of the Microsoft Exchange product.

- Faxing from a Microsoft Exchange environment is a logical progression for an organization because Microsoft Exchange provides the core infrastructure for communications. While many organizations are using Internet e-mail messaging as their standard for communications, just as many (if not more) are still using facsimiles as their primary method of communication. A user may want to send a memo to a number of users—some of the users may be able to accept the information as an e-mail message while others need to accept the information as a fax message. By making a user's task of sending or carbon-copying information to fax phone numbers just as easy as sending an e-mail, a user can expand an organization's reach of communication.

- For the administrator of an Exchange environment, there is no additional user administration necessary for the organization, because the third-party add-ins to Exchange integrate directly into the directory and information stores in Exchange. When a user is added to the Exchange environment, he or she immediately has access to faxing capabilities. All error and event logging for fax messages are managed by the same logging and message tracking process as e-mail messages.

- As the next evolution in communications extends beyond text-based messaging of e-mail messages or faxes, the integration of voicemail messaging in an Exchange environment provides the added functionality of a single location for communications. Voicemail-integrated solutions provide an organization with the ability to have voice messages received and stored in the user's Universal Inbox just as easily as the user can accept and manage text-based e-mail messages or fax memos. The integration of voice messaging enables a user to manage voice messages by simply dragging and dropping a message just as if it were a common piece of e-mail.

- Extending the capability of the Universal Inbox beyond being just a storage place for text messages, Microsoft Exchange makes it a universal depository of information where electronic messages, fax memos, voicemail messages, graphic files, word processing documents, or presentation materials can all be stored in folders. This can make the Universal Inbox the main method of data and information management for an organization.

- While an organization manipulates all of this information, the need to have a solid virus detection, protection, and management system is crucial in maintaining the integrity of the information stored in an Exchange environment. The most functional virus program in a messaging environment is one that checks for viruses both before a message is sent outside of the local messaging system, as well as before a message is received by the messaging system. These proxy-based, message-virus scans intercept a virus before it hits the desktop. This is crucial for an organization that relies on e-mails as its mode of communication.

Review Questions

Q. Why is an integrated fax solution for Exchange preferred over a standalone fax add-in solution?

A. An integrated fax solution uses the same user, security, and message management and tracking system as e-mail messages. Since users of fax and e-mail systems within an organization are typically the same, centralizing administration and management simplifies the maintainance of the communications infrastructure.

Q. How does a fax message get from a fax server to the inbox of a user?

A. An inbound fax message can be routed either manually or automatically to the inbox of a fax recipient. In a manual process, all faxes are received in and routed to a common fax message store. An administrator views the cover sheet of an incoming fax and forwards the entire fax to the intended user. The fax is received by the user in his or her inbox. Automatic fax routing can occur when an organization has direct inward dialing (DID) implemented. DID is a phone company service providing every user with a personal fax number. When the incoming fax is received by the server, the destination fax number is acknowledged and used by the server to automatically route the fax to the intended destination.

Q. How are voicemail messages treated in an integrated Exchange environment?

A. Voicemail messages are treated just like regular e-mail messages. The incoming voice message is stored in the user's inbox. The user has the ability to listen to the incoming message from any phone handset and can also manage the message from within his or her Microsoft client software. The user can reply to, forward, delete, or move the voice message just like any other message in the inbox.

Q. What is text-to-speech?

A. Text-to-speech is an add-in function to voicemail integration with Microsoft Exchange. It's the ability of a voice messaging system to convert e-mail messages into audio messages. A remote user, checking voicemail messages, can listen to just the subjects of the messages or can elect to play the entire content of all or selected mail messages.

Q. How does an integrated virus detection software within Exchange differ from a workstation-based virus detection program?

A. A workstation-based virus detection program detects the presence of a virus after one has been received and acknowledged by the workstation. In many cases, the virus has already spread. An integrated virus detection program (as in Microsoft Exchange) scans inbound and outbound mail messages before they are received by any clients. If a virus is found, the message is rejected and the sender is notified of a virus problem. Since the virus is caught before any user accesses the message, it is isolated before it can cause harm.

CHAPTER 17

Interlinking Internal and External Information with Exchange

In the past two chapters, we have explored a few of the ways that Microsoft Exchange can be leveraged to improve communications, as well as function as an organization's intranet. In this chapter, I will discuss ways to extend the functionality of Exchange to other business productivity tools that leverage Exchange's interlinking capabilities to products on the Internet, SQL database servers, project management information systems, and common desktop applications.

Exchange and the Internet

In Chapter 15 I discussed the implementation of Microsoft Exchange as an intranet solution; however, beyond its intranet uses, Microsoft Exchange has very powerful Internet capabilities as well. Exchange's Internet capabilities include selectively providing internal public folder information to Internet users as well as enabling trusted users to access their electronic mail messages over the Internet.

Because Microsoft Exchange has such robust capabilities relative to the Internet, I have dedicated an entire chapter to Microsoft's integration to the Internet. Chapter 18 covers the Internet connectivity components to Exchange.

Integration Functions of Windows-Based Applications

One function of Microsoft Exchange's interlinking capabilities begins at the desktop with the ability to link the Exchange client software to Microsoft Windows-based applications. The linking capabilities can be as simple as allowing information to be stored and retrieved from central folders in Exchange, or as complex as the direct sharing of portions of information of a database or project management GANTT chart into the Exchange environment.

Posting Documents into Exchange

As I discussed in Chapter 15, the intranet capabilities of the Microsoft Exchange environment allow an organization to use Exchange's folder and subfolder functions as a method for users to save information. Instead of saving files to the F> drive on a network server, an organization can set up a similar method to save files in a hierarchical tree, storing information directly into Microsoft Exchange, as shown in Figure 17-1.

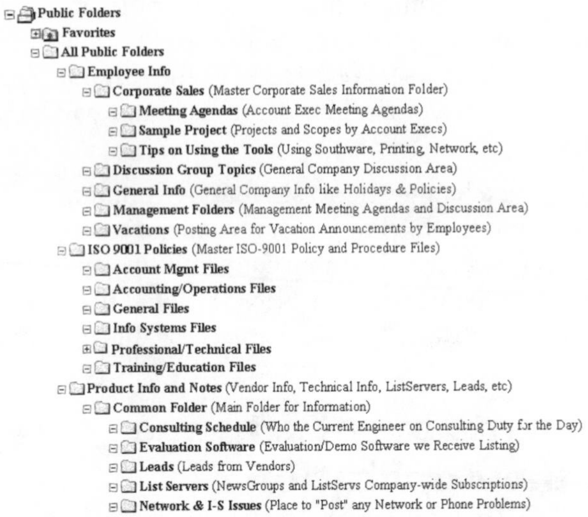

Figure 17-1. *Sample Microsoft Exchange hierarchy tree*

The advantages of storing information into a Microsoft Exchange tree instead of a network file server tree include:

- **Automatic server replication**   Because Microsoft Exchange has integrated replication capabilities of information from Exchange server to Exchange server, an organization can create an automated backup system to secure stored information across multiple servers.

- **Automated replication of information to mobile systems**   By storing template files, client data files, or other information within the Exchange directory system, organizations with remote or mobile users who need access to data files in addition to just mail messages have the ability to replicate automatically the information to the remote and mobile systems during a standard mail message upload and download.

- **Integrated access**   With mail messaging and file management in the same hierarchical platform, information can be shared across multiple applications but centrally stored and managed.

■ **Viewing** For users who need to view information, Microsoft Exchange provides viewing capabilities of text and graphics information through the use of integrated viewer applications, so that it is unnecessary for organizations to allow users full access to the original application program. Instead, viewers in Microsoft Exchange can be used for user viewing and access.

■ **Sharing** In the Exchange client/server environment, as long as the client has access to the Exchange server for the sending and receiving of electronic mail messages, the same connectivity can be used by the system to access file information. No additional file access network drivers need to be installed in order to access this information.

Sending Documents over Exchange Directly from the Application

One aspect of the functionality of the Exchange storage management system is its ability to allow mail message users to send or distribute documents in a variety of ways directly from the Microsoft Exchange application environment. A user can select the document by pressing the right mouse button, as shown here:

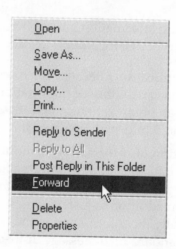

The user can elect to send the document to another message user as an attachment. A user in Exchange can also open the document and in the MAPI-aware application, select File | Send to send the open document to another messaging user.

As I discussed in Chapter 16, Exchange's ability to interlink faxing with its environment permits documents to be sent to both electronic mail users and fax recipients as an attachment. When the fax server receives the fax request with an attachment, the fax software converts the attachment and sends it as a document to a fax machine.

Maintaining the Same File Name with Different Save Dates

A feature of the file management function of posting documents into the Exchange environment is the way Microsoft Exchange stores files based on a time and date stamp-basis rather than on a file name basis. In a normal network file system, all files receive a different name as they are saved to disk, or the previous version of the file gets overwritten. As an example, a file may start off as "Company Policies" and then be saved a few weeks later as "Company Policies 2," "Company Policies 3," and so on. However, in a Microsoft Exchange environment, files are stored independently, so if a file is saved to an Exchange folder, if the file is updated and saved, the application will update the file posting in Exchange with an updated save date. The file will be displayed in the Exchange folder with the same file name but with a new date (in addition to the previously saved file with the exact same file name but a different saved date), as shown in Figure 17-2.

Integrating Exchange with Project Management

We covered the creation of GANTT charts in Chapter 10 for the project planning of a Microsoft Exchange environment, but as part of the integration capabilities of Microsoft Exchange, project plans and resource allocation can be integrated into Microsoft Exchange for scheduling, communications, and resource tracking and management.

Using Microsoft Project to Interlink Exchange Resources

Microsoft Project can be used to link schedules, tasks, resources, project communications, storage of information, and project process browsing. During a project management process, it is necessary to allocate project tasks to labor

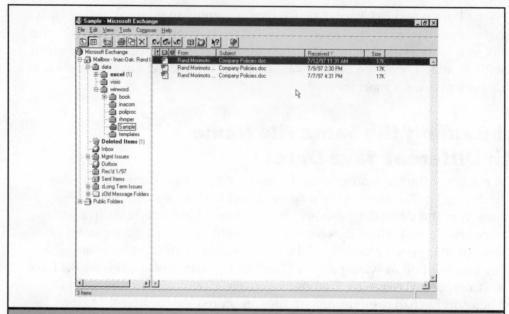

Figure 17-2. *Files saved in Exchange are automatically stamped by time and date*

resources as well as equipment resources. Normally, a project management software program requires the project manager to enter in a project step, manually enter the required resource to the resources list, and then manually send a message to the individual or post a notation for the physical resource of the allocation to this project. It would normally require a significant amount of time to enter every work order once into the project management software, and then again in the electronic messaging or scheduling software. With the integrated workgroup messaging and task management capabilities of Microsoft Project, as shown next, the amount of double entry and manual processes is decreased dramatically. As you saw in Chapter 10, project plans are crucial to an organization in developing and implementing a logical sequence of events in a project process.

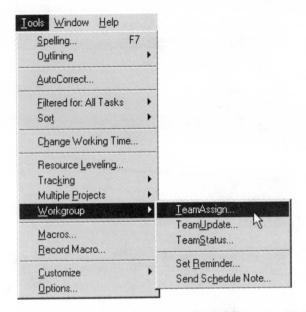

Using Microsoft Project to Assign Project Tasks

The team assign option in Microsoft Project allows a project manager to select specific tasks and assign them with the Tools | Workgroup | TeamAssign option, as shown in Figure 17-3. When this option is selected, a mail message option appears onscreen that allows the project manager to send a message to the resources notes on the task to assign the work that needs to be completed. The automated message pulls the user names from the resources section and matches the names against user names in the Microsoft Exchange Address Book. The portion of the highlighted task worksheet is added as an attachment and is prepared so that it can be sent to the resource(s) selected.

Accepting Project Assignments

The recipient of a project assignment receives a message similar to Figure 17-4 and has the option to accept or reject the project assignment, similar to a standard Microsoft Scheduler appointment invitation. The project assignment

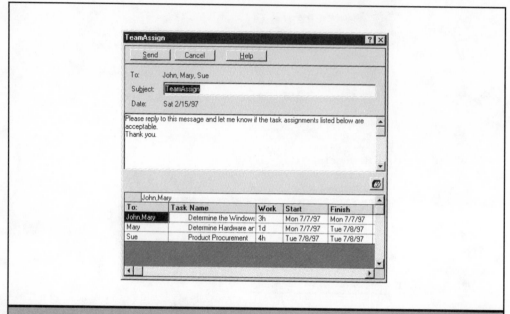

Figure 17-3. *Automatic e-mail generated by Microsoft Project to assign tasks*

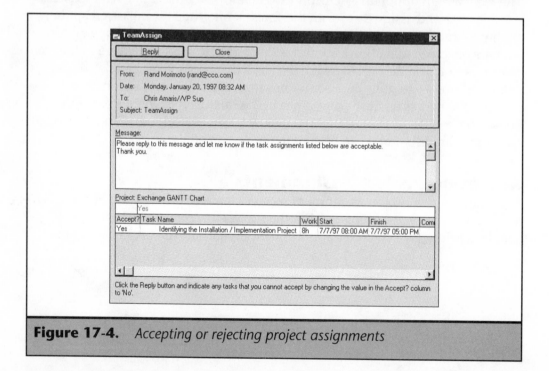

Figure 17-4. *Accepting or rejecting project assignments*

message includes each line of the project plan to which the user has been assigned as well as a Yes/No option to accept or to reject each component of the project.

When the recipient accepts the task of the workplan, a confirmation of the status is updated in the master project plan so that the project manager knows the component has been accepted, and the time, date, and assignment information is automatically updated in the recipient's Schedule file.

If the recipient denies the workplan task, the information is sent back to the project manager who would need to reassign the task to another individual.

Checking the Status of Project Components

At any time during the project, the project manager can request from the project team the status of each individual project task or set of tasks. By selecting the Tools I Workgroup I TeamStatus option in Microsoft Project, a mail message is automatically created, similar to the message shown in Figure 17-5, noting the components of the project and allowing the team member to respond on the number of completed hours on each task. The response to the status check automatically updates the project workplan, thereby providing

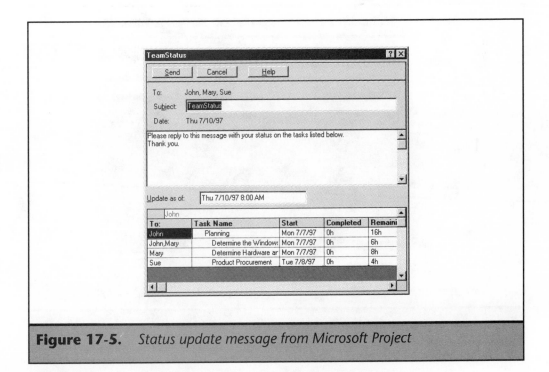

Figure 17-5. *Status update message from Microsoft Project*

rolled-up task status on the components of the project. For many organizations, a project administrator is assigned to check the status of ongoing projects and to update the status information in the GANTT chart. This is typically done through meetings or verbal requests; however, because Microsoft Exchange can be used as an electronic medium to request and respond to project workplan status, the request for information and the viewing of the requested information is both graphical and electronic to assist in automating the project process.

Sending Project Notes

Throughout a project, a project manager or project administrator may need to send notes about the project process. Rather than sending a text-based electronic message and trying to describe the desired information through the use of project notes, information can be sent graphically to a recipient from the Tools | Workgroup | Send Schedule Note option in Microsoft Project, as shown in Figure 17-6. The highlighted portions of a GANTT chart are automatically captured into a BMP graphical format, and subsequently prepared and sent to

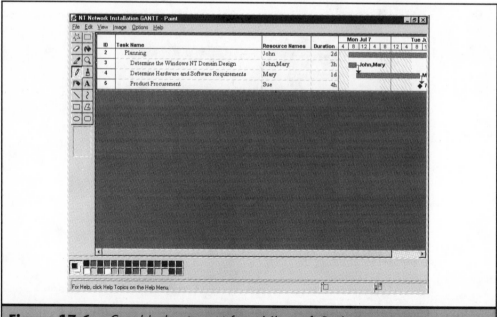

Figure 17-6. *Graphical note sent from Microsoft Project*

the recipient. The recipient can annotate the information and then reply to the originator of the information.

Project Task and Scheduling Process

The task and scheduling process between Microsoft Project and Microsoft Exchange is performed according to the following:

1. The project manager constructs the project plan with Microsoft Project, creating tasks and allocating resources and timelines to the tasks.

2. The project manager uses the workgroup task assignment feature of Microsoft Project to send e-mail messages to team members requesting that a project task or series of tasks be assigned to various team members.

3. The team members receive the tasks and review the information, and either accept or deny the task assignment. Team members select the reply option to acknowledge receipt and acceptance of the task(s).

4. The project manager receives the assigned task replies. The task information is automatically placed in the individual's task manager in Scheduler without the need to reenter it.

5. Team members then use the task manager in Scheduler to track the progress of the project tasks and note the actual number of hours they have worked on a task (or enter the percentage of the task they have completed). Tasks appear on the team members' calendars as to-do items that can be dragged and dropped to allocate time to complete the daily job responsibilities.

6. At any time, the project manager or project administrator can select the project team status option to request a status update from the team members through an automated mail message.

7. The team members receive the status update requests and can reply to the request, which will update the information from the task manager to populate the status of the project information in a response to the project manager or administrator.

8. The project manager or project administrator receives the updated status information and updates the project, so that information is automatically extracted from the project team's responses directly into the project worksheet.

Public Folders to SQL Database Information

As organizations store more and more information across various servers and electronic mediums, the ability to find, search, and manage the stored information becomes crucial. Microsoft Exchange includes a link between the Microsoft Exchange messaging environment to the Microsoft SQL client/server database system. For other client/server databases like Oracle or Sybase, links between Microsoft Exchange and those data storage management systems can be purchased as add-on applications to Exchange.

What is ODBC?

Before delving into how Microsoft Exchange folders and information can interact with a client/server database, the term *ODBC* needs to be explained. ODBC stands for Open Database Connectivity and is the common architecture used to interchange database information from clients to servers. ODBC includes the standards in which an application can log on to a database, execute SQL database access commands, acknowledge errors and error codes, and accept and translate data information. Key to ODBC is the ODBC Application Programmers Interface (ODBC API). The ODBC API provides a common database access language that enables applications to access a variety of databases such as Microsoft SQL, Oracle, Sybase, Informix, and IBM DB/2.

ODBC is comprised of four separate components:

- **Application** The application is commonly known as the front end that an individual uses to view the database. Common front-end applications include Microsoft C++, Microsoft Access, or even fields within a Microsoft Excel spreadsheet. Microsoft Exchange also acts as an application to a SQL database.

- **Driver Manager** The driver manager is the dynamic link library (DLL) that interlinks the application request and query information from the ODBC application to the driver and data source of the information.

- **Driver** The driver processes the ODBC manager requests and translates the query into the specific language set understood by the SQL database. During this translation, the information is captured and then sent to the data source.

■ **Data Source**   The data source is the database in which the information
resides. This would be the Microsoft SQL, Oracle, or other ODBC
compatible database.

An application can communicate with multiple driver managers,
which in turn draws information from multiple data sources. This can
allow information to be accessed, read, and written to multiple databases
simultaneously from the same client application, as shown in Figure 17-7.

How SQL Client/Server Databases
Link to Exchange

Microsoft Exchange provides an application interface between the Exchange
environment and Microsoft SQL. As noted earlier, other application interface
modules to other client/server databases are available from the database

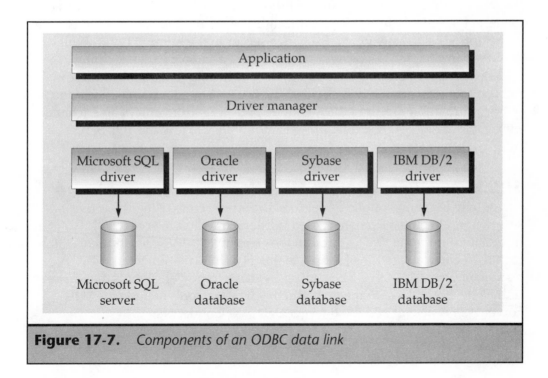

Figure 17-7.   *Components of an ODBC data link*

manufacturer for products like Oracle or Sybase. During installation, the Exchange administrator has the option to install the ODBC database link from Exchange to Microsoft SQL.

Retrieve Information from a SQL Database

A Microsoft Exchange public folder can be used to retrieve information from a SQL database. Links are created using standard SQL query calls to retrieve field-level information from a SQL database, which is then populated and can be stored in Exchange public folders. Also, through the use of any ODBC application like Microsoft Excel or Microsoft Access, users can create special front-end interface components that allow for searching and interactive dynamic queries of database information to invoke results from a data query request.

Interlinking the Web to SQL Server

As part of a completely integrated solution, content from a SQL Server can be made available to an Internet user through a series of data access options. One of the options is to activate the Exchange server to the Internet (which will be described in Chapter 18), providing Web-based access of Exchange public folders over the Internet. By activating the public folders, organizations can publish folder information over either the Internet or an intranet of selected query information captured through the application front end of an Exchange public folder request. A second option is the ability to link the SQL Server directly to the Web.

SQL Server Access from the Web

Besides the Exchange public folder to SQL Server access using the active server components of Exchange, the traditional method to access SQL information from the Web is through the creation of very sophisticated CGI (common gateway interface) scripts to link SQL information to an HTML document page. However, Microsoft provides two powerful tools that make linking the SQL Server to the Web much easier. The tools include the SQL Server Web Assistant and the Internet Database Connector.

The SQL Server Web Assistant provides a wizard that automatically generates Web pages formatted in HTML and links fields in the HTML form to actual data query results fields. The process creates a query request, format process, and data gathering function that refreshes information to the Web page at selected intervals or by manual request.

The Internet Database Connector (IDC) uses the ODBC API to send and receive information between HTML form fields and a SQL Server. The IDC provides an easy method for organizations to gain access to SQL information through a simple Web link, making data information easily accessible either to the Internet or to an intranet.

The Chapter in Review

- To round out the integration of Microsoft Exchange with other applications, this chapter explored the integration of Microsoft Exchange with Windows-based applications, SQL database servers, and with Microsoft Project for project management integration. As was covered in Chapters 15 and 16, the key to Microsoft Exchange is its ability to add functionality to an organizational process to improve the way an organization transacts business. With the ability to interconnect Microsoft Exchange into other desktop and information system environments, the true integration of Exchange as the messaging transport and conduit of an organization is tested.

- The initial interaction users have with integrating their applications with Microsoft Exchange is the ability to post messages from a Windows-based application directly into a Microsoft Exchange folder. Additionally, as an individual is using an office-based application, he or she may want to send the message to another individual in the organization. Rather than saving the file and then manually attaching the file to a mail message, Windows-based applications now have the ability for a user to initiate a File | Send option to automatically send a mail message to another user.

- A part of a unique integration function with a desktop application is the integration of Microsoft Exchange to Microsoft Project. For those who have used the Microsoft Project program, they are familiar with how Microsoft Project interacts closely with project resources. Typically the resources of a project and the scheduling of resources are disjointed processes. However, with Microsoft Exchange, the Scheduler within Exchange automatically accepts Microsoft Project workgroup functions for the assignment, configuration, and updated status of project processes.

- It is this integration between Project and Scheduler that enables an individual within an organization to communicate within and throughout a project process without having to double- or triple-enter information between the Microsoft Project GANTT chart and the Microsoft Scheduler appointment schedule.

- Finally, with the awareness that Microsoft Exchange can act as a data repository of information, data warehouses or data farms take on a whole new role in the storage, management, and maintenance of stored information. With links between Microsoft Exchange public folders and Microsoft SQL database query functions, Microsoft Exchange has the ability to accept and manage information from a client/server database.

Review Questions

Q. What is the File | Send function used for?
A. The File | Send option in Windows-based applications provides the ability for the user of the application to automatically send a document in use to another individual on the network.

Q. True or false—files stored to an Exchange folder using the same file name will automatically overwrite a previous version of the file with the same name in the folder.
A. False. Microsoft Exchange folders acknowledge file postings as individual message postings, so although a message or file may have the exact name, features, and characteristics as another message or file, if it is posted at a different time of day, the message will take on the time and date of the file every time the file is saved to the server.

Q.   Where does a user go in Microsoft Project to assign tasks?

A.   The Tools | Workgroup section of the Microsoft Project software.

Q.   What happens when a user accepts an assignment from a project manager?

A.   When a user accepts an assignment from a project manager, the response is sent back to the project manager who receives a notice of acceptance, and the accepted tasks are updated in the project as assigned to the individual.

Q.   What are the four components of ODBC?

A.   They are Application, Driver Manager, Driver, and Data Source.

CHAPTER 18

Activating Exchange, the Internet, and the World Wide Web

Lately it seems that everything in the computer industry has some tie to the Internet, whether it is the latest version of an application, a WWW address at the end of a television commercial, or a wireless Internet service provider. The latest release of the Microsoft Exchange Server software, version 5.0 contains some strategic components that make Microsoft Exchange easier to access from the Internet, and also make it easier for Exchange clients to access the Internet through Microsoft Exchange. Just about everyone has had an opportunity to surf the Internet with a Web browser to check out their favorite home page, but very few users understand much of the other Internet terminology like Active Messaging, POP3, NNTP, etc. On the other hand, there are a number of UNIX and Internet-experienced organizations that are wondering what functions the latest Microsoft Exchange Server software has and how it works in relation to those tried-and-true UNIX-based Internet messaging systems.

The intent of this chapter is to bridge the knowledge gap between users who want to know more about some of the Internet terminology components and users who want to know more about how these Internet components are integrated into Microsoft Exchange. This chapter is divided into two parts: the first part covers how users on the Internet get access to information that resides on a Microsoft Exchange Server, and the second part covers how users with the Microsoft Exchange environment can get access to information from out on the Internet. This is an approach from the outside looking in, as well as the inside looking out.

How Internet Users Can Access Information on an Exchange Server

The first section on activating Microsoft Exchange with the Internet will provide an "outside-in" approach to providing access into a Microsoft Exchange environment from the Internet. When the Internet expanded its support for virtual communications via Web browsers from anywhere the Internet connects, Microsoft's support for inbound Internet access to an Exchange environment became an important component to include in the Exchange v5.0 product. Inbound access to a Microsoft Exchange environment can be as simple as sending an e-mail message to a user on Microsoft Exchange or as complex as employees requiring full access to their e-mail inboxes as well as company folders in order to send and receive mail messages. Or, inbound communications to an Exchange environment may be an organizational strategy to provide internal and external intranet functionality by having Microsoft

Exchange public folder information available for search and reference through a standard Web browser.

Sending Electronic Mail Messages to an Exchange User

The primary reasons organizations tend to have Internet access is to facilitate Internet e-mail communications. Microsoft Exchange has always supported inbound and outbound e-mail communications with the Internet—an Internet or external user who wants to send an electronic mail message to a Microsoft Exchange user over the Internet only needs the intended recipient's Internet e-mail address. Through the implementation of the Microsoft Exchange Internet Connector (described in detail in Chapter 8), a user in the Exchange environment can easily receive electronic mail messages from Internet users.

Potential Customers Browsing Exchange Folders from the Internet

A common responsibility of most I/S organizations is the creation and maintenance of a Web server so that clients, vendors, or associates can surf the Web site to view information about the organization. Some companies set up a home page on the Internet to establish a presence and provide basic information about the organization, as shown in Figure 18-1. Some companies set up a home page as a way to advertise and market their services. Other organizations utilize the Internet as a means for commerce, whereby the organization actually sells its products and services over the Internet. In all cases, the challenge organizations face is their need to refresh the information on the Web servers frequently enough so that their products and services are appropriately and accurately advertised. In a traditional Web server environment, the information that comprises the Web server content is made up of HTML documents. Although utilities are now readily available that convert Word documents or other word processing documents to HTML, the time and effort required to manage the conversion process and upload the documents to the server can become cumbersome. Essentially, the more difficult the process is to update information, the less frequently it will be done.

Many organizations have decided to decrease the frequency of their Web server content updates. While this may be a good short-term strategy, when information is critical to an organization's success, maintaining current and accurate Web page information will always increase an organization's ability to leverage the benefits and capabilities of the technology.

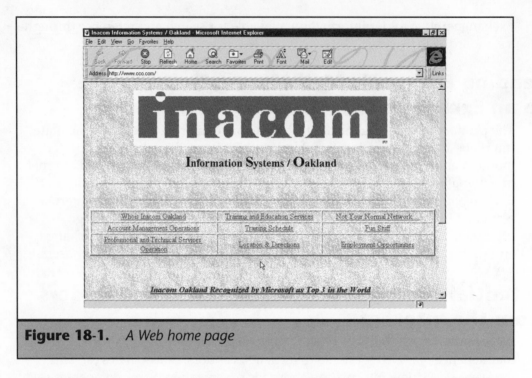

Figure 18-1.   *A Web home page*

To relieve the network administrator of the burden of frequent updates of Web server content, the new Active Platform of Microsoft Exchange v5.0 can help organizations to set up their infrastructure based on Active controls of Exchange v5.0, thus providing the Web administrator with the tools to more easily update Web server content. Instead of converting content and uploading it to a Web server, content can be dragged and dropped in its native format into a folder in Microsoft Exchange that is linked to a Web page. When a user surfs the Internet and accesses the organization's Web page, the links from that Web page to the organization's Exchange server display the stored information and will convert the information from the native Word, Excel, or other format into HTML and then will send the information to the user.

Defining the "Active" Terminology

As the Internet develops and expands at a rapid pace, keeping up-to-date on the latest terminology becomes a full-time job. Most of the press releases or product information about Microsoft Exchange Server refer to the embedded Internet controls in Exchange, with the assumption that everyone knows what the terms mean and what the benefits are to their organization. For those who haven't spent 24 hours a day keeping up-to-date, here's a quick overview of the common "Active" terms:

EXCHANGE ACTIVE SERVER COMPONENTS   Exchange Active Server Components is the name given to the entire suite of technologies that interlinks the groupware capabilities of Microsoft Exchange (electronic mail, scheduling, discussion groups, and document management) with the core capabilities of the Internet. The Internet aspect of the Exchange Active Server Components enables an organization to break the barriers of a closed proprietary corporate messaging and communications infrastructure, and to open up the resources so that its employees, clients, or strategic vendors can participate in corporate communication processes.

MICROSOFT ACTIVE PLATFORM (INCLUDING ACTIVEX)   The Exchange Active Server Components are part of the Microsoft Active Platform, which are the tools that developers use to create the links between the Internet and other environments, such as the links created between the Internet and Microsoft Exchange. The Active Platform includes technologies like ActiveX, which is a set of core technologies that provides multiplatform interoperability of functions for the ways in which information is provided by the Active Server and displayed to the user of an Active Desktop. An Active Server is a Web server that has the Active Platform Server Components installed and can take ActiveX content and send it to an Active Desktop. An Active Desktop is a user's workstation in which the browser software has been updated to accept ActiveX content and interpret the information to be displayed on the user's screen.

In comparison with the way in which an HTML document is transferred from a server to a workstation, a Web server can store an HTML document on the server, which contains all of the HTML commands including linking a document to graphic images, special background colors or textures, text font information, etc. When an HTML browser asks to view an HTML document, the server knows to send the document to the user. Once it is sent, the user's HTML browser interprets the information and displays it on the screen of the workstation. Since HTML has published specifications on type fonts, sizes, colors, and other functions, the actual fonts and color palettes do not need to be sent to the browser. This common understanding of basic features simplifies the amount of information that needs to pass from the server to the workstation about how to interpret the data it receives. The server's function of finding and sending the information for a simple HTML document is similar to the function of an Active Server, which takes ActiveX-enabled information and sends it to an Active Desktop. The information is then interpreted by the client browser using a series of published standards and functions and displays the information on the workstation screen, as shown in Figure 18-2.

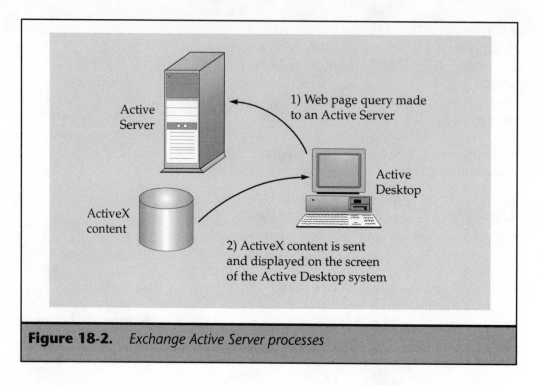

Figure 18-2. *Exchange Active Server processes*

Whereas HTML requires text to be stored in a straight ASCII text format and graphics in a GIF file format, the Active Platform allows documents and graphics to be stored in their native format. An ActiveX-enabled Web page will allow a Microsoft Word word processing document or a PowerPoint presentation to be converted "on the fly" by the Active Server and sent to the Active Desktop to be displayed on the Active Desktop screen. This process can be performed without the need for any special browser add-in or conversion tool other than an Active Desktop-aware browser like Microsoft Internet Explorer v3.0 or Netscape Navigator v3.0 or higher.

The implementation of the Active Platform allows an organization to use the ActiveX tools to create a Web page that can link files such as a PowerPoint presentation to the Web page. Both the Web page and the PowerPoint presentation (in its native format) are stored on the Active Server. When an Active Desktop accesses the Web page, the user will be able to view the PowerPoint presentation (PAGEUP/PAGEDOWN) through the slides directly from the workstation's browser software. The user needs neither a copy of PowerPoint on his or her workstation nor any special add-in viewer software.

Through the tools and functions of the Active Platform, information can be converted and transferred to a client for viewing. This ease of native information sharing between a Web server and a Web browser is true for other files, including Word documents (that can retain embedded fonts, graphics, or charts), Excel spreadsheets, or Access database information. By activating the client browser software, an organization can share information without the need to distribute applications other than the common Web browser software.

ACTIVE MESSAGING The implementation of the Active Platform in Microsoft Exchange provides an Active Desktop system user with the ability to actually log on and access his or her Microsoft Exchange mailbox through a browser over the Internet. Active Messaging includes two components, the Messaging Object Library and the HTML Rendering Object Library. The Messaging Object Library allows the client to log on to the Exchange server over the Internet, access his or her inbox and network public folders, and access the Microsoft Exchange directory, as shown in Figure 18-3. This library provides the core

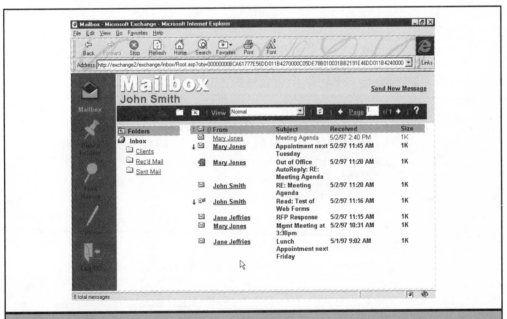

Figure 18-3. *Sample Exchange Web client over the Internet*

capabilities a user needs to send, receive, move, and delete messages as well as manipulate folders and integrated attachments. The HTML Rendering Object Library extends the rich view capabilities of Exchange to the browser client. These capabilities include manipulating message folder columns and sorting and filtering messages. In addition, users can render daily, weekly, and monthly views of their calendar information over the Internet. All of these functions are integrated into the Active Server Components with the installation of the Active Messaging Component. By integrating these functions into the Active Server, the Active Desktop client will have access to these new functions.

ACTIVE SERVER PAGES   In addition to the Active Desktop functions that provide fully-formatted server-to-client translations of Microsoft Exchange client functionality, organizations that want to stick to standard HTML client access can take advantage of the Microsoft-provided Active Server Paging capabilities of Exchange. Organizations that may have UNIX-based or terminal-based browsers optimized for HTML access may need to provide Active Messaging to these users as a requirement. Through Active Server Pages, an HTML document has embedded ActiveX script code that calls specific Active Server Components like Active Messaging Components. These components provide an HTML link to Exchange messaging using normal HTML commands and functions, enabling access by almost any HTML browser.

Microsoft Exchange v5.0 ships with an Active Server Pages application called Outlook WebView that will be covered in the next section.

Installing Active Server Components

The Active Server Components are not automatically installed along with Microsoft Exchange v5.0. To install the Active Server Components, run Microsoft Exchange SETUP.EXE on a server running Windows NT v4.0 (with Service Pack 2) and install the Internet Information Server v3.0 prior to Exchange installation. The Active Server Components can be installed on a server other than the Microsoft Exchange Server, such as a dedicated Web server or other Web application server.

To install the Active Server Components, during the Microsoft Exchange v5.0 installation, when prompted to choose a typical installation or a custom installation select the Complete/Custom Install of Exchange. There will be an option to select the Active Server Components for installation. Select the Active Server Components option and any of the component options to be

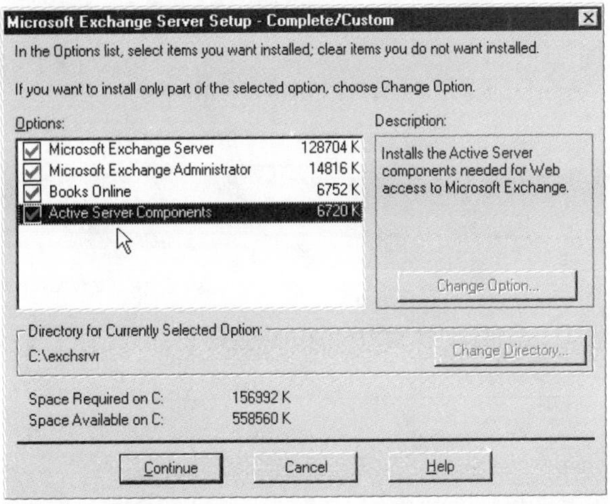

Figure 18-4. *Selecting Active Server Components to install*

installed, as shown in Figure 18-4. The Active Server Pages (*.ASP) files will subsequently be installed on the server.

To configure the Active Server Components for Exchange, from the Exchange Administrator program, select the Site | Configuration | Protocols option. The Active Server Components for Exchange are the HTTP (Web) Site Settings. By double-clicking on this option or selecting File | Properties, the options screen will become available, as shown in Figure 18-5.

- **Allowing Anonymous Access** If the organization would like to configure anonymous access to certain public folders on the network, select the Anonymous Access option on the General properties page. The administrator can also grant anonymous access to the organization's Global Address List to view user names of the organization.

- **Selecting Pubic Folders for Access** The administrator needs to select which public folders should be accessible to Internet users. By selecting the Folder Shortcuts tab and adding new shortcuts, the shortcuts added will be displayed to the anonymous users logged on to the Exchange server computer from the Internet.

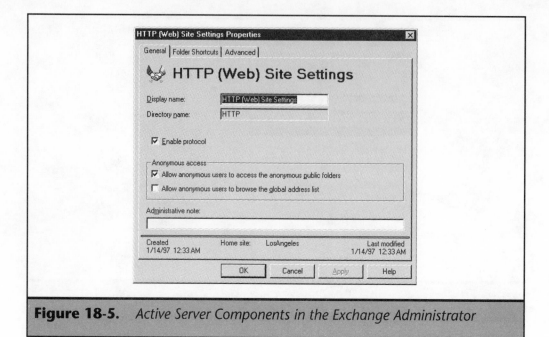

Figure 18-5. *Active Server Components in the Exchange Administrator*

■ **Limiting Address Book Views** From the Advanced tab of the HTTP (Web) Site Settings properties page, the administrator can select the extent of address book viewing on the user's desktop. If the organization is large, a limit should be placed on the address book view; otherwise, if the remote Internet user chooses to view the organization's directory, it could take a very long time for the entire directory to be displayed. By selecting the default maximum of 50 entries, the user can select and scroll through the names in smaller batches.

Employee Access to Exchange from the Internet

For an organization that wants its employees to be able to access the corporate Exchange environment over the Internet, Exchange v5.0 allows access in a few different ways. Through the implementation of Active Server Pages, an Internet-connected user would be able to access messages and public folders. Another option is to access the organization for messaging through the POP3 method.

The Web Outlook Client

The Outlook WebView is an Active Server Pages application that enables an HTML browser user to log on and securely access e-mail and public folders on the network, as well as directory information, as shown in Figure 18-6. The

Figure 18-6. *Logon screen for Web client access to Exchange*

WebView is an HTML Web page that can be put on any Active Server on the network. Using any Web browser that supports frames and Java (such as the Microsoft Internet Explorer or Netscape Navigator v2.0 or higher), users from the Internet can access this Web page which then provides logon, authentication, and mail services to the user from over the Internet.

The trusted Web Exchange client can compose messages over an HTML screen, similar to the one shown in Figure 18-7, as well as send and receive them. The Outlook WebView can also be configured to provide access to shared information folders that may have product availability reports, marketing information, technical bulletins, or other information that can be available to the organization's internal Exchange users through local public folders. In addition, the same information can be made available for external access without the necessity of storing it in multiple places.

POP3 Messaging

POP3 stands for the Internet-standard Post Office Protocol 3, which is a published set of rules for how standard messaging should be conducted in

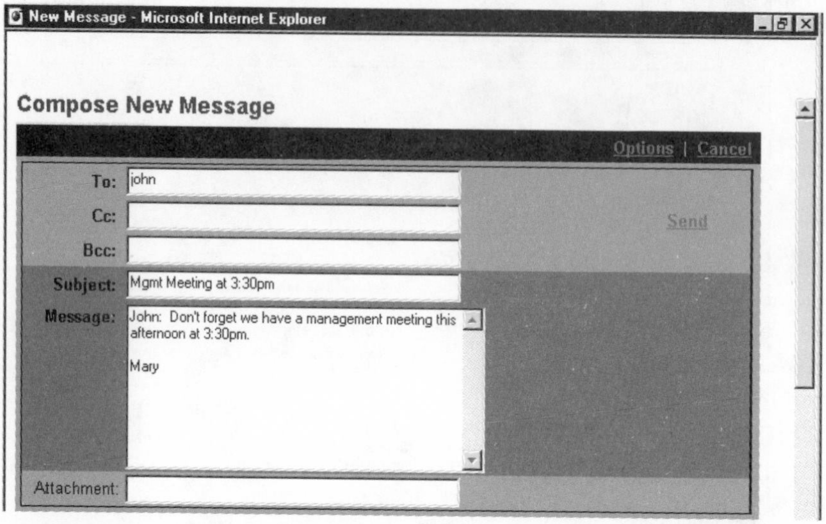

Figure 18-7. *Composing a mail message using an HTML Web client*

a UNIX environment. POP3 is to electronic messaging what TCP/IP is to transporting networking information and what SMTP is to transporting messaging information. In other words, POP3 is a common messaging server system used by many organizations in a UNIX or TCP/IP environment. It is known for ease of installation of the server services, and for the universal access by client operating systems of virtually every configuration, including all versions of UNIX, the Macintosh, DOS workstations, Windows workstations, and even dumb terminals. Common POP3 client software includes Eudora, Netscape Navigator Mail, Z-mail, and the Microsoft Internet Explorer Mail.

Prior to POP3 support in Exchange v5.0, Exchange clients had to dial into the Exchange server using a proprietary dial-up connection or set up advanced security so that a standard Exchange client could access an Exchange server over the Internet. In either case, the client still needed to access the Exchange server using the proprietary Exchange client software. However, with POP3 supported directly in Exchange v5.0, users can securely access their messages over the Internet using any POP3 client application program available. This provides users with the ability to access their mail messages at any Internet-connected workstation, whether it is at a trade show, an Internet café, or the workstation of a friend or associate.

When remote users want to access their messages from a POP3 client software, they enter the name of their Exchange server, logon name, and password. The Exchange server, with the Internet Mail Service running, authenticates the user to the server for POP3 mail services. When the POP3 client software requests messages, the request goes to the POP3 server service, which then requests that Microsoft Exchange send the client the messages from the user's inbox, as shown in Figure 18-8. Note that the POP3 client will only retrieve messages from the inbox and the user will not have access to private or public folders or to encrypted messages.

INSTALLING POP3 ON AN EXCHANGE SERVER   POP3 server support is automatically installed with the Exchange v5.0 software.

To configure the POP3 services for Exchange, from the Exchange Administrator program, select the Site | Configuration | Protocols option. By double-clicking on the POP3 (Mail) Site Defaults properties option or

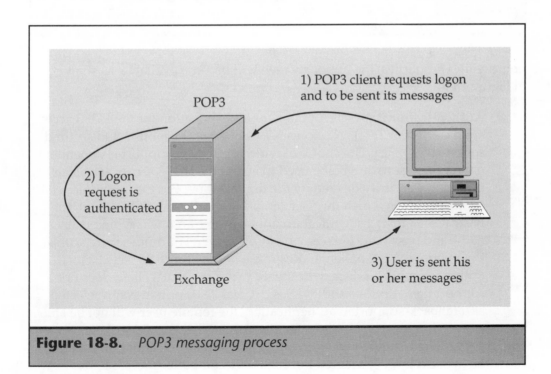

Figure 18-8. *POP3 messaging process*

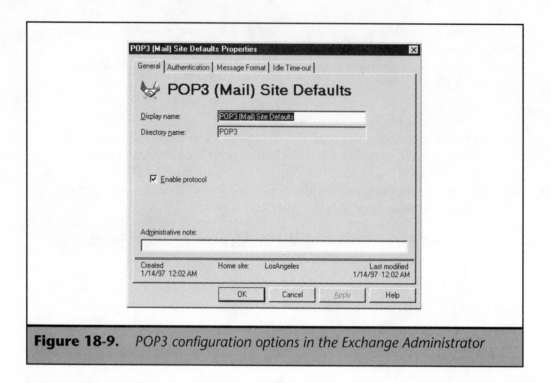

Figure 18-9. *POP3 configuration options in the Exchange Administrator*

doing a File | Properties, the options screen will become available, as shown
in Figure 18-9.

■ **Authentication Tab** The options for authentication for the POP3 access
are Basic (Clear Text), Windows NT Challenge/Response, and secured
socket layer (SSL). The choice of which options to support is dependent
on the client software being used to access the POP3 server as well as
the level of security desired by the organization. For the highest level of
compatibility in which the user can use virtually any POP3 client, the
Basic (Clear Text) authentication only requires an unencrypted user
name and password to access the POP3 server. For more secure access,
the Windows NT Challenge/Response or the Secure Sockets Layer
options should be selected. Be aware that if the POP3 client does not
support these options and the Basic (Clear Text) option is not selected
as a fallback-supported authentication, the remote user will not be able
to access the server for his or her messages. The secured socket layer
encryption is supported by many POP3 client applications and would
be the next level of secured but relatively compatible access to the
Exchange Server POP3 services. Note that the use of SSL will require

the Internet Information Server v3.0 to be installed on the Exchange server computer to provide the SSL authentication services. Lastly, the Windows NT Challenge/Response provides network security and encrypted password functions between the POP3 client and the server. This is generally not considered a universal authentication system because it requires the NT Challenge/Response support on the client; however, an organization that controls its remote workstation client software selection and for whom POP3 will be used for only trusted employee access for messaging should feel comfortable in allowing this encryption to be used for access by controlled remote users.

- **Message Format Tab** The Message Format tab on the POP3 (Mail) Site Defaults properties page allows the administrator to select the format in which messages are encoded. This would include either MIME or UUENCODE encoding plus the ability to have messages sent as regular plain text messaging or as an HTML formatted message. If the client software being used remotely is the Microsoft Internet and News software, then messages can be sent in a rich text format to allow for the viewing of fonts and other page formatting features.

- **Idle Time-out Tab** The idle time-out will disconnect a user if he or she does not respond in a predetermined time frame. Typically, 10-15 minutes is the allotted amount of time for a user to respond to the server. Remember that a user could be typing a message (which incurs no sending or receiving sequences to the server), so idle time can also occur while the user is composing a message.

ENABLING INTERNET MAIL SERVICE While POP3 is the service that allows clients to retrieve their mail messages, in order for a POP3 client to send messages, the Internet Mail Service needs to be configured and enabled. The easiest way to enable the Internet Mail Service is to run the Internet Mail Service Wizard. This wizard will step you through the configuration and installation of the service. Otherwise, you can enable the Internet Mail Service manually by selecting, from the Exchange Administrator, Site | Connections and double-clicking on the Internet Mail Service to open the service's property pages. The properties page will be displayed, as shown in Figure 18-10. Select the Routing tab, and then the Reroute incoming SMTP mail option. If this option is not selected, messages from POP3 remote clients will be received as inbound messages that will be resolved using the custom recipient's definitions and will be rejected as invalid destination addresses. However, with the Reroute incoming SMTP mail option enabled, the Internet Mail

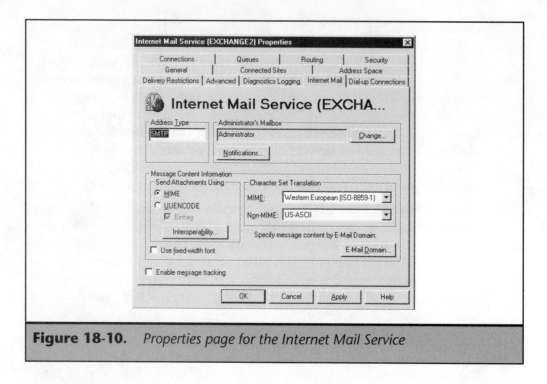

Figure 18-10. *Properties page for the Internet Mail Service*

Service will act as a smart host and reroute messages to recipients that are outside of the Microsoft Exchange organization.

ENABLING POP3 ACCESS FOR USERS To allow an Exchange client access to the network using a POP3 client from the Internet, the user's security needs to be enabled to provide the user with the POP3 services. This can be configured from the Site | Recipients options for the user, shown in Figure 18-11. By selecting the user and then selecting File | Properties, the Protocols tab provides the administrator with the option of enabling or disabling HTTP (Web) services, POP3 (Mail) services, LDAP (Directory) services, and NNTP (News) services.

LDAP

LDAP, or the lightweight directory access protocol, is another Internet protocol just like POP3, TCP/IP, and SMTP, which I have already discussed. LDAP in Exchange v5.0 allows an LDAP client to access the Exchange server's directory information, which is the list of user names, e-mail addresses, or

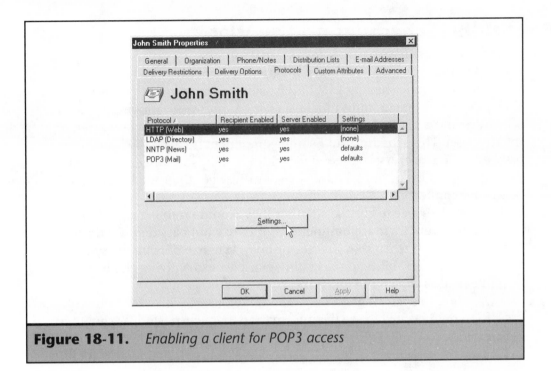

Figure 18-11. *Enabling a client for POP3 access*

even phone numbers, pager numbers, or manager name information. Although most organizations would not want all of this information available to anyone surfing the Internet, a portion of this information is useful for Internet mail users who might know the name of an individual to whom they want to send a message, but don't know that person's e-mail address. This would be similar to a "dial-by-name" directory look-up function on a voicemail system. Additionally, the use of directory information access could assist an individual who has a person's e-mail address but does not have the person's mailing address or phone number. Rather than distributing directory level information manually, much of it can be made available to an individual automatically through the use of LDAP.

A more common use of LDAP information is in the distribution of user directory information (possibly through an automated directory synchronization process) to other organizations in a directory information sharing process between organizations. In an automated process, the gateways between the two organizations would trade directory information and update user lists for both organizations.

Publishing Schedules on the Web

One last "outside-in" procedure for external information access from the Internet is an organization's ability to publish appointment schedules over the Internet. Without having to set up trusted or anonymous logons to the Exchange environment, individual users can export their appointment schedules into an HTML format that can be viewed by almost any external Internet user. This schedule publishing component is called the Microsoft Scheduler+ Internet Assistant and is included in the Exchange v5.0 client. A user can export his or her schedule by selecting File | Internet Assistant in the Scheduler application.

Users will be able to choose whether they want to publish all of the information about their appointments or if they want bars displayed across the times to represent when they are free or busy. When exporting the schedule, users also have the ability to select how many weeks of their schedule should be published, as shown in Figure 18-12.

By posting this information on a Web server, users with a Web browser and the URL would be able to see the information that was posted, as shown in Figure 18-13.

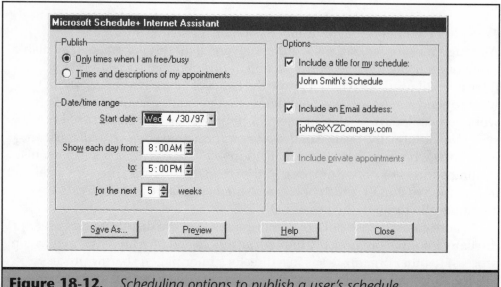

Figure 18-12. *Scheduling options to publish a user's schedule*

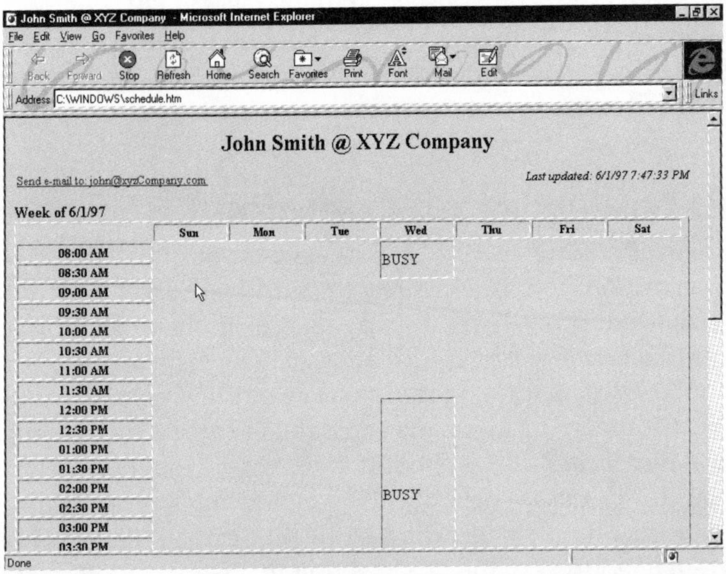

Figure 18-13. *Viewing a sample schedule on the Web*

How Users Within Microsoft Exchange Gain Access to Information on the Internet

This second section on activating Microsoft Exchange to gain access to information on the Internet is to provide an "inside-out" approach to providing access to the Internet from a Microsoft Exchange environment. This includes the ability for an Exchange client to perform a procedure as simple as sending an electronic mail message to an Internet user to one as complex as populating Exchange public folders with information as a participant in a newsgroup or as an automated information store.

Sending Electronic Mail Messages to an Internet User

A Microsoft Exchange user who wants to send an electronic mail message to an Internet user over the Internet merely needs to enter the recipient's Internet e-mail address into the To: or CC: section of the message header. Through the implementation of the Microsoft Exchange Internet Connector (described in detail in Chapter 8), a user in the Exchange environment can easily send electronic mail messages to Internet users.

Populating Folders from Common List Servers

In many organizations, the use of List Servers is a popular way for individuals to receive information from Internet resources. A List Server is an automated information distribution system set up by organizations to distribute information to subscribers. The information may be technical notes, press releases, white papers, marketing information, or other general information. List Server-distributed information is analogous to wire services, in which information is distributed and is "hot off the presses."

Individuals may elect to subscribe to a List Server. Typically, subscribing to a List Server is as simple as sending an electronic mail message to the designated e-mail address of the organization that is managing the List Server. Once he or she subscribes, the individual will receive information any time it is distributed by the List Server administrator. The List Server knows who the subscriber is by the return mail address of the user who sent the subscription request. In addition, users can unsubscribe to a List Server as easily as they subscribed to the List Server.

The problem many users encounter when they subscribe to multiple List Servers is that active List Servers can distribute tens if not dozens of List Server messages a day. This volume can greatly increase the burden of checking and sorting through mail messages to determine which messages are "real" mail messages and which messages are List Server-distributed messages. A member of many List Servers could receive dozens if not hundreds of messages a day. Rather than having many users in the organization subscribing to the same List Servers, an organization can centralize its List Server information.

Microsoft Exchange allows organizations to better configure the function of a List Server information route a few different ways. First, the organization could arrange for one user to subscribe to the List Server, set up an inbox assistant, and have messages from the List Server automatically moved to a public folder so that anyone in the organization can view and access them. The second way an organization can centralize List Server information is to set up a public folder with an Internet address and subscribe the folder to the List Server. Because Microsoft Exchange provides the ability for folders to have their own Internet address, messages sent to the designated Internet address will go directly into the folder.

Populating Folders via NNTP for USENET Newsgroups

Like all the other abbreviations in the Internet world, *NNTP*, or the network news transfer protocol, is yet another supported component in Microsoft Exchange that non-Internet experts know very little about. NNTP is the protocol by which Internet news is distributed across the Internet. On the Internet, there are thousands of newsgroups on topics ranging from French cooking to Corvette automobiles to hot air ballooning to Microsoft Exchange technical services. Over 200,000 postings to newsgroups occur each day. Users can individually log on to the Internet and read posted newsgroup messages and can also post their own comments to the newsgroup. Some newsgroups are moderated, and postings are reviewed before messages are allowed to be posted on the main newsgroup forum. Others allow users to post information directly to the newsgroup.

Microsoft Exchange provides a facility in which an Exchange server can be a local recipient of all or selected newsgroup postings so that the newsgroup information becomes folders and subfolders within the public folders section of an Exchange server. The advantages of an organization accepting and participating as a newsgroup host include the ability for Exchange users to have all of the newsgroup information sent locally to them for faster access, and the Exchange client will be able to use all of the public folder message tools available to the user, such as filtering, message grouping, and search engines. Without having to access the Internet, wait for information to display onscreen, or individually view messages, users can have the benefits of receiving newsgroup information locally that provides a more efficient access to news information.

USENET Newsgroups and Newsfeeds

USENET is the network of host computers that replicate newsgroup topics across the Internet. The hosts on USENET store newsgroup and newsfeed information. Organizations can subscribe to USENET to receive newsgroup and newsfeed information downloaded to their server(s) to improve performance for local network users' access to the information. USENET newsgroups are organized by subject. There are nearly 20,000 different global and regional newsgroups, which are broken into a hierarchy of topics. The most popular newsgroup hierarchies include:

- **alt**   alternative or controversial topics
- **comp**   computer topics
- **humanities**   humanities topics
- **misc**   miscellaneous topics that are not covered in other categories
- **news**   information about USENET
- **rec**   recreation topics such as arts, hobbies, and sports
- **sci**   science-related topics
- **soc**   social issues and topics
- **talk**   talk groups on politics, religion, or other similar discussion topics

Subscribing to Newsfeeds through Your Internet Service Provider

To establish a server link to USENET, organizations need to subscribe to USENET newsfeeds through their Internet service provider (ISP). The Internet service provider will want to know the fully-qualified domain name or IP address for the Exchange server that will be running the Internet News Service. The ISP will also want to know if you plan to use a push feed or a pull feed for inbound and outbound messages.

Newsfeeds are transferred to and from the USENET network to an Exchange server either by having a USENET host server push the information to the Exchange server or for the Exchange server to pull the information from the host server, as shown in Figure 18-14. There are pros and cons to each of the information transfer options. For large newsfeeds, a push feed is better than a pull feed since the service provider manages all of the resources necessary to determine what information needs to be pushed to the Exchange server. However, push feeds require more interaction and administration with the Internet service provider to control which newsgroup information should be configured for information distribution.

During a pull feed, the Exchange server initiates the connection with the Internet service provider and checks for new messages, which it pulls into the Exchange server. A pull feed provides the Exchange administrator with the option of choosing which information should be pulled and the management of the inbound and outbound functional control.

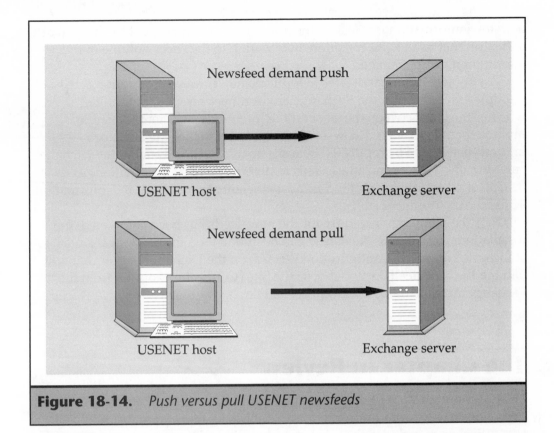

Figure 18-14.   *Push versus pull USENET newsfeeds*

Configuring the Internet News Service and Newsfeeds

To set up the Internet News Service and newsfeeds, a Newsfeed Configuration Wizard has been included with Exchange v5.0. This greatly simplifies the process by which an organization can set up newsfeed communications.

Before proceeding with the installation of the Internet News Service, additional sizing components need to be taken into consideration to ensure that the server that will become the Internet News Service server has the appropriate amount of available disk space and the performance capabilities necessary to manage the newsgroup functions. With over 200,000 messages and approximately 1.75GB of newsgroup transactions a day, both the selection of which newsgroups and the aging of messages on an Exchange server need to be reviewed before initiating full USENET newsfeeds.

As a newsfeed has the potential of transferring hundreds of megabytes of information a day, the bandwidth between the Exchange server and the Internet service provider needs to take into account how much of the total USENET newsfeeds should be transferred to the Exchange server. If all of the newsfeed information is selected, the amount of disk space and the bandwidth to the Internet need to be considered in relation to the sheer volume of the information being managed.

An organization that desires to replicate newsgroup information across multiple servers within the Exchange environment needs to determine whether the link between the site and the Internet is sufficient to handle multiple parallel USENET newsfeed updates or whether the newsfeed information should be replicated on a site-to-site basis internal to the Exchange environment. The organization needs to determine what information needs to be replicated and which method is most efficient at replicating the information across the environment.

Once the planning procedure for the newsfeeds has been completed, the installation of the NNTP Newsfeed can be initiated on the Exchange server. To launch the Newsfeed Configuration Wizard, on the Exchange server that will become the Newsfeed Server, choose the Site | Connections option from the Exchange Administrator program. Select File | New Other | NNTP Newsfeed.

The Chapter in Review

- The importance of the Internet is significant in any organization's strategy for communications both internally and externally. Microsoft Exchange includes the tools and user components necessary to provide Internet communications both from an outside-in (for external Internet users to gain access into an Exchange environment) as well as an inside-out approach (for internal Exchange users to access information from the Internet).

- The outside-in approach for communications by users out on the Internet into an Exchange environment may be as simple as sending an electronic mail message over the Internet to an Exchange user. Because Microsoft Exchange supports inbound and outbound Internet messaging, as long as the organization running Microsoft Exchange has a registered Internet domain name and has the Internet Connector and all Internet connection components set up and operational, users on the Internet can send Exchange users electronic messages.

- Remote Exchange users who need to access their mail messages also need to gain access to an Exchange environment. Microsoft Exchange includes two components to facilitate message communications over the Internet: POP3 client support and the Web Outlook client software. The POP3 client support in Exchange v5.0 allows an existing Microsoft Exchange client to access his or her inbox and messages through a standard POP3 client software such as Eudora, Netscape Internet Mail, Z-mail, etc. The other option is to support an HTML version of the Microsoft Exchange client software through the use of the Web Outlook client software. The Web Outlook client software allows a user on the Internet to log on and gain access to his or her Exchange mailbox using a standard Web browser software.

■ Microsoft Exchange clients have a number of ways that users of the Exchange environment can access the Internet with an inside-out approach. The access methods include sending mail messages to Internet users, populating public folders through the inbox assistant of a client rule, and accessing USENET newsgroups as public folders on the network.

■ Just as Microsoft Exchange users can receive mail messages from the Internet, users in an Exchange environment can also create and send mail messages to Internet recipients. With native SMTP support for Exchange, the Internet recipient's name can be entered into the To: or CC: sections of the mail message so that an Internet message can be sent to the individual.

■ Through the use of an inbox assistant rule, a user on the Exchange network can belong to a List Server group and receive mail messages on a frequent basis about updated press releases, technical bulletins, and other group list information. In addition to the redirection of a List Server group listing, a public folder can also be assigned an Internet address so that messages can be e-mailed directly to it.

■ Last, an Exchange server can participate as a USENET newsgroup server to which Exchange public folders are populated with newsgroup information. By having newsgroup information populate local Exchange folders, a large organization with numerous users participating in newsgroups will be able to provide faster access and response to the newsgroup information while minimizing the traffic necessary for each user to access the Internet to participate in newsgroups. Additionally, as an organization uses Exchange replication to replicate newsgroup information from server to server, the need for an Exchange environment to have multiple servers communicating with the Internet for newsgroup information is greatly reduced.

■ In Microsoft Exchange, Internet connectivity to improve communications from both within an Exchange environment and externally to an Exchange environment has been greatly improved because the components and tools necessary to facilitate Internet connectivity and communications have been included in the Microsoft Exchange Server software.

Review Questions

Q. What are the four client software programs that can be used to access a user's inbox for mail messages (two of which are Internet/Web-enabled)?
A. The Exchange client, the Outlook client, a POP3 client, and the Web Outlook client.

Q. What is the Active Server a component of?
A. The Active Server is a component of the Microsoft Active Platform. The Active Platform also includes the Active Desktop and Active Messaging.

Q. What "pages" are part of the Internet Information Server v3.0 that makes it a required component to run the Active Messaging portion of Microsoft Exchange v5.0?
A. The Active Server Pages are the component in IIS v3.0 that is necessary to support the Active Messaging components of Exchange v5.0, such as the Web Outlook client software.

Q. What Exchange services does the POP3 functions of the Exchange server provide?
A. The POP3 services provide remote access to a user's inbox. They do not provide access to public folders or to a user's Scheduler information.

Q. How does a user publish his or her appointment schedule?
A. From the Exchange client that comes with Exchange v5.0, the user can enter the Scheduler software and select File | Internet Assistant to export his or her appointment schedule to an HTML format.

Q. What Exchange "protocol" must be running to support the Web Outlook client?
A. The Exchange server must be configured and running the HTTP (Web) Protocol in the Site | Protocol section of the Exchange Administrator program.

Q. With LDAP, can a remote user gain access to all of an Exchange server's directory information?

A. No, the Exchange administrator has the option of selecting which components from the Exchange directory should be available to an LDAP client.

Q. What is the significance of NNTP?

A. NNTP, or the network news transfer protocol, provides the services necessary for an Exchange server to participate as a newsgroup server to accept newsfeeds from USENET Internet services.

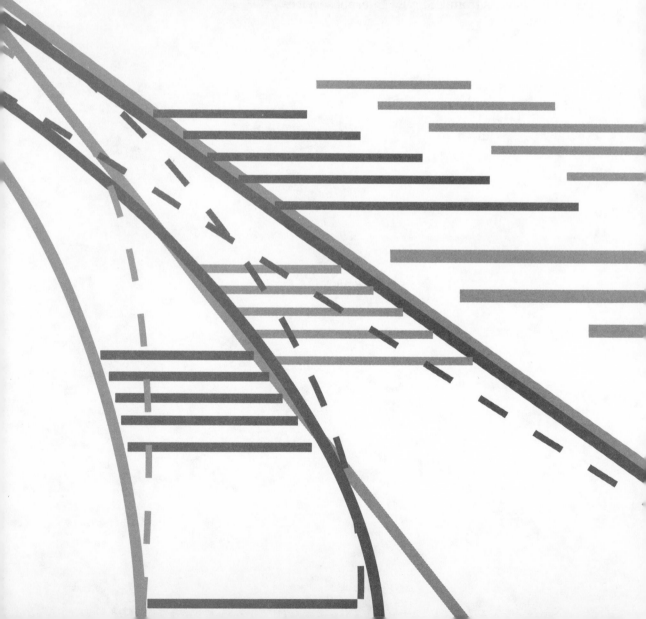

CHAPTER 19

Apple Macintosh Integration with Exchange

A s part of the universal messaging strategy for the Microsoft Exchange product, Microsoft supports the Apple Macintosh computer system. Microsoft Exchange provides support for inbound and outbound electronic mail messaging, integrated personal and group scheduling, and public folder access for the Macintosh platform, which allows organizations to conduct advanced messaging communications across multiplatform environments that may have a mixture of PC-based, UNIX or Web-based computer systems, as well as Apple Macintosh systems.

Connecting a Macintosh to a Windows NT Network

Before we can even address the client software that the Macintosh user needs to access an Exchange server, the Macintosh computer needs to be able to physically connect to the network that provides transport services between the client and the server. Because the Macintosh computer was developed separately from a UNIX or a PC-based computer system, the methods of physical networking, protocol communications, and file management are completely different between a Macintosh and an NT network. However, Microsoft Windows NT not only enables the Macintosh computer to communicate with the server, it also allows a Macintosh user to share files and printers within a Windows NT environment, so it is just a matter of configuring the operations properly to get a Macintosh to work in an NT environment.

The local area network infrastructure of an Apple Macintosh computer system evolved from AppleTalk and LocalTalk. AppleTalk is the protocol or native communication language that the Macintosh speaks in a networking environment (similar to TCP/IP or NetBEUI), and LocalTalk is the hardware platform with which the Macintosh has traditionally communicated (similar to Ethernet or Token Ring). Many people confuse these two concepts.

Apple Macintosh Networking Communication Protocols

The Apple Macintosh was designed with ease of use in mind. Back when local area networking in a UNIX or mainframe environment required IP address maps or hardware controllers plus user name lists that had to be maintained by programmers and managers, the Apple Macintosh allowed networking between other Macintosh computers as well as printers by simply plugging in the computers via a phone cable to a LocalTalk connector that came with every Macintosh computer and printer. The AppleTalk networking system required no special configuration, mapping, or software installation. The operating environment was auto-aware and dynamic, meaning that as soon as a new Macintosh computer or printer was attached to the network, the other computers and printers would immediately see the added device. When a user dropped off the network, within seconds, the device would automatically drop from the client's list of devices on the network. This new networking system greatly simplified the creation of Macintosh networks.

As Apple Macintosh computers began to be integrated into other networks, the need arose to support hardware platforms other than LocalTalk or protocols like AppleTalk. Apple began to support the Ethernet networking standard as well as the Token Ring networking standard. The two networking systems are called EtherTalk and TokenTalk because they support the AppleTalk protocol over traditional Ethernet and Token Ring physical networks.

As Apple Macintosh computers were interconnected to other network environments, the challenge became how to integrate the Apple operating system into other operating environments. Although the Macintosh network operating system was simple to set up initially, the same functions that made it simple to install and set up also made it a problem on wide area networks. The standard AppleTalk network protocol is very "chatty," meaning that there are a number of conversations that occur on the network infrastructure. Chatty Macintosh computers were blamed for excessive network traffic. As Macintosh systems were added in large numbers to wide area networks, the need to address the routing of the AppleTalk protocol and the minimization of the chatty traffic became an issue.

The original edition of the AppleTalk operating environment only supported 254 computers on a network. However, within a few years Macintosh networks grew in size, and the Macintosh began to support a new version of AppleTalk (AppleTalk-2) that supported 254 different zones of 254 different computers, or now over 64,000 Macintosh systems on a network. Each zone constitutes a separate workgroup of Macintosh computers, breaking up the communications of the Macintosh systems into smaller clusters.

With the growing popularity of TCP/IP, the Macintosh operating environment began to support MacTCP. MacTCP is a TCP/IP language that

Apple Macintosh computers can use to communicate with other TCP/IP devices such as UNIX servers or UNIX printers, or also use to surf the Internet.

Physical Connections

The physical connections of an Apple network include the support for LocalTalk, Ethernet, or Token Ring. LocalTalk is the two-wire daisychain configuration of an Apple Macintosh environment in which Macintosh computers are connected over normal telephone wiring. In this configuration, all the Apple computers and printers in a zone have the ability to communicate with each other for file and print sharing.

As the need grew to interconnect Macintosh computers with other computer systems, the need to support other hardware platforms such as Ethernet and Token Ring became important. Depending on what level of interconnectivity is desired by the organization, the Macintosh computers and the other computers in the organization can be interconnected to the same Ethernet hub or Token Ring wiring hub. While the two environments may be physically connected over Ethernet as their hardware platform, the two separate environments may not necessarily have to intercommunicate with each other. The Macintosh computers could be talking EtherTalk to each other and the UNIX systems or PC systems could be talking TCP/IP to each other on the network.

Macintosh File System

The file storage system of the Apple Macintosh system is also proprietary to the Macintosh environment. While DOS was limited to an eight-character file name, the Macintosh supported file names of up to 254 characters, including spaces and punctuation. The Macintosh file system supported the characteristics of the easy-to-use, graphical, Macintosh operating system.

Preparing the LAN for Macintosh Exchange Clients

The need to interconnect Macintosh computers to an existing Windows NT environment now requires that the hardware, the operating language, and the file system are all compatible with each other and with the Microsoft Exchange client of the Macintosh.

Macintosh Access over AppleTalk

One option for attaching Macintosh computers is to install a LocalTalk or Ethernet adapter into the NT/Exchange file server and allow the Macintosh computers to continue to talk to each other over AppleTalk, and now talk to an NT server still using a native AppleTalk infrastructure scheme, as shown in Figure 19-1. To support AppleTalk communications in a Windows NT environment, the Windows NT Services for Macintosh need to be installed on the Exchange server. The installation of the Windows NT Services for Macintosh can be found in the Start | Settings | Control Panel | Network under the Services tab. When configuring the Windows NT Services for Macintosh, the administrator would need to ensure the boot volume of the Exchange server is NTFS, a zone is created for the AppleTalk network, and the MacFile name is configured to be the same as the Microsoft Exchange Server name.

Once the Windows NT Services for Macintosh have been installed, configured, and then started, any Apple Macintosh system physically plugged into the

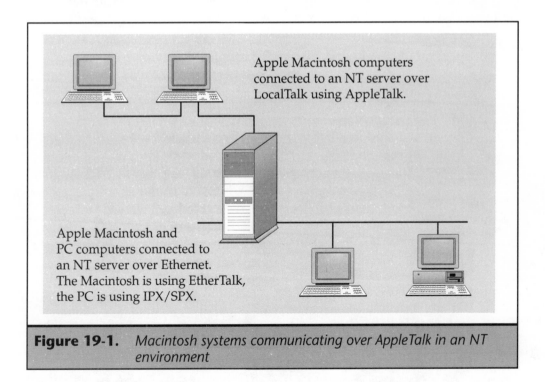

Apple Macintosh computers connected to an NT server over LocalTalk using AppleTalk.

Apple Macintosh and PC computers connected to an NT server over Ethernet. The Macintosh is using EtherTalk, the PC is using IPX/SPX.

Figure 19-1.   *Macintosh systems communicating over AppleTalk in an NT environment*

LAN connection for the server will be able to see the Exchange server as another Macintosh AppleTalk server in the Macintosh workstation's Chooser.

Macintosh Access over TCP/IP

Another option to interconnect Macintosh clients to an NT/Exchange server is through the use of a standard Ethernet connection configuration and the TCP/IP protocol, as shown in Figure 19-2. In the Macintosh environment, the TCP/IP client for the Macintosh is the MacTCP client. To support Microsoft Exchange access, the MacTCP needs to be version 2.06 or higher.

Assuming the Exchange server is configured for TCP/IP networking, once the Macintosh clients are configured with MacTCP and the Macintosh computers can ping the Exchange server, the Macintosh client is configured and ready for the installation of the Exchange client software. In a MacTCP environment, the Windows NT Services for Macintosh does not need to be installed. By standardizing on TCP/IP over Ethernet, an organization could limit the number of types of hardware routers, bridges, or hubs it needed since these can be the same hardware topology and protocol used for PC computers, UNIX workstations, mini-computers, and mainframes in the same environment.

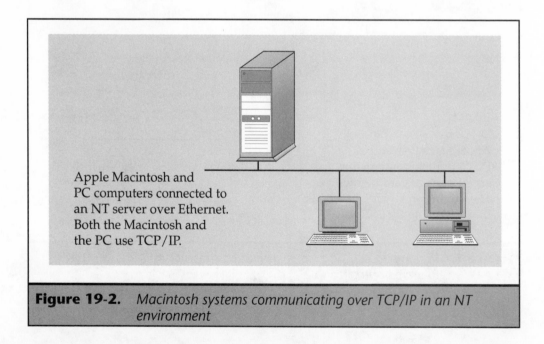

Apple Macintosh and
PC computers connected to
an NT server over Ethernet.
Both the Macintosh and
the PC use TCP/IP.

Figure 19-2.   *Macintosh systems communicating over TCP/IP in an NT environment*

The Macintosh Exchange Client

The Macintosh Exchange client supports electronic mail communications, personal and group scheduling, and public folder access in an Exchange environment. Currently, Exchange forms are not supported by the Exchange client, so the access of forms will be on a text-based information transfer rather than a full graphical user forms access.

Installing the Macintosh Exchange Client

The installation of the Macintosh client for Microsoft Exchange starts with the launch of the Microsoft Exchange Setup program on the Macintosh client CD. (Note that the Macintosh client software is installed on the same client software CD as the DOS, Windows, and Windows 95 CD versions, but when a Macintosh user accesses the same CD, the Macintosh file system displays a portion of the CD dedicated to the Macintosh client software and utilities.) After launching the setup program, the administrator will see a setup screen similar to the one pictured in Figure 19-3.

Select OK to proceed and enter in the user's name and organization for this copy of the Exchange client software installation. The installation will prompt the user to install a complete installation of the Exchange software. Select the Complete Installation option and the software will be installed on the hard drive of the Macintosh computer.

The first time the user launches the Exchange client software, he or she will be prompted through the configuration of a user profile. The user profile includes the messaging services the user has access to, including the Microsoft Exchange Server service as well as the Personal Address Book service. If the user selects the Automatically Create Profile option, he or she will be prompted through an installation wizard that will guide the user through the installation of the Exchange client software. The first screen, similar to the screen shown in Figure 19-4, allows the user to enter the name of the Exchange server and the Mailbox of the user for the workstation. The Exchange server will be the name of the MacFile name which should be the same as the name of the Microsoft Exchange Server name. The user will have the option of selecting either AppleTalk (including the Zone defined in the Windows NT Services for Macintosh) or TCP/IP. Upon completion of this first-time profile creation, the user will not be prompted through the questions again. If the user needs to change his or her profile, the Exchange Settings application can be launched, which will provide the user with the ability to delete the current configuration or to modify the current configuration as desired.

Figure 19-3. *Exchange client setup for the Macintosh*

Figure 19-4. *Exchange Setup Wizard for the Macintosh*

Electronic Mail Functionality

Once the Exchange client for the Macintosh has been installed, the Macintosh user can launch the Exchange program, which will prompt the user to enter his or her user name, domain name, and password. This is the authentication to the Exchange server, as shown in Figure 19-5. Once authenticated to the Exchange server, the user will have a standard Microsoft Exchange client screen where the user can create, reply to, reply to all, forward, or delete messages.

The Microsoft Exchange client can be broken down into three separate categories. They include the basic features of the Exchange client (including sending and receiving messages and sending attachments), message formatting features (including rich text formatting, embedding graphics into a mail message, and automatic signatures), and message management (including intelligent message rules, filtering, and folder views).

Basic Features

The most common features of all messaging programs are the ability to send, receive, reply to, forward, and print mail messages. Microsoft Exchange for the Macintosh is no exception in its inclusion of these basic features. However

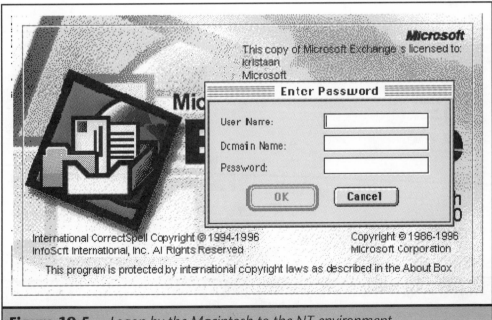

Figure 19-5. *Logon by the Macintosh to the NT environment*

basic these features appear to be, Microsoft has enhanced these features in its fully integrated groupware Exchange server environment so that it now provides a simple centralized message storage system in its Universal Inbox, better compatibility of attachments by supporting multiple file attachment formats, and easier search and reference of the creation of message recipients in the user's address book. These features are the core to workgroup communications and information management.

The Universal Inbox

The most notable function of the Microsoft Exchange client for all operating platforms is the concept of the Universal Inbox. As I discussed in Chapter 1, all information is stored on a Microsoft Exchange Server as objects, enabling the centralization of all forms of information in a single message folder. Information can consist of text messages, graphic files, word processing documents, fax documents, voicemail messages, specialized forms, and posted message information. Many organizations have replaced databases and shared subdirectories with Exchange folders. Since an Exchange folder can hold more than just text information, and the information can be searched for future reference, the Exchange folder has become the universal information depository. Figure 19-6 shows a basic Microsoft Exchange client screen.

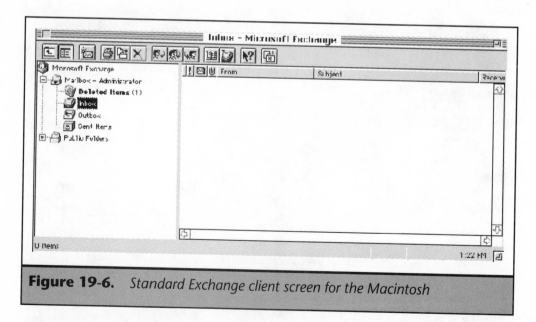

Figure 19-6. *Standard Exchange client screen for the Macintosh*

Compose, Reply, Forward, and Print Messages

These features are standard to all electronic mail packages. They are the key to creating an electronic message, responding or replying to a message, forwarding the message to another recipient, and printing the message to a printer. In the Exchange client for the Macintosh, these options are selected as button bar options.

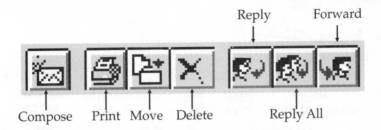

Reply   Forward

Compose   Print   Move   Delete   Reply All

- To compose a new message, click on the Compose icon on the toolbar

- To print a message, click on the Print icon on the toolbar

- To reply to a message, click on the Reply icon on the toolbar

- To reply to a message and include all carbon copy recipients, click on the Reply All icon on the toolbar

- To forward a message, click on the Forward icon on the toolbar

Attachments

The sender of a mail message in Microsoft Exchange has the ability to attach files to the message. The file(s) can be a word processing document, a spreadsheet file, a graphics image file, or any other application or data file. Files can be attached to a mail message by selecting Insert from the Exchange client software. Note that unlike a PC Windows Exchange client in which the user can drag and drop files from the Windows File Manager software into an Exchange client message or folder, the Macintosh version of the Exchange client does not support object linking and embedding (OLE) in this manner. Files in a Macintosh client need to be inserted as attachments, not dragged and dropped. However, files and messages "within" the Macintosh Exchange client can be dragged and dropped between Exchange folders internal to the Exchange directory.

Global and Personal Address Books

In an Exchange environment, there is a Global Address Book that contains the addresses of all of the e-mail recipients in the organization, and individual users also have their own Personal Address Book in which they can add addresses to their personal address list. Addresses are created by selecting the type of address (Internet, X.400, fax, MS Mail, etc.) and entering information into the fields needed for the address.

cc:s and bcc:s

Carbon copies (cc:) and blind carbon copies (bcc:) are both ways for a user to send a copy of a message to someone other than the actual intended recipient. The message may be sent to invoke a response or it may just be for the recipient's reference. If the recipient resides in the sender's address book, the name can be pulled from the address book or the e-mail address can be manually added at the time the message is sent by typing the user's electronic mail address.

Message Formatting

As electronic mail messaging has evolved, users have become more sensitive to how their mail message looks, so the need to improve the way messages are created and formatted became an important focus of the Microsoft Exchange client software. Since rich text formatting has been a standard function of the Macintosh operating system environment from the beginning, these features of the Exchange client were simply integrated into the standard message formatting features of the Macintosh version of the Exchange client software.

Message Management

Now that the electronic mail user can create sophisticated mail messages with embedded graphics, colors, variable fonts, and attachments as well as receive sophisticated mail messages, the user's ability to manage all of these messages has become very important. The Exchange client software contains message management features that help users sort their messages, view messages by user definable groupings, or automatically respond to or act on messages based on their characteristics. These features help the users of Microsoft Exchange client for the Macintosh find and categorize their messaging information, which are a few of the basics of workgroup and groupware information management.

Out of Office Assistant

The Out of Office Assistant is a server-based rule supported by the Exchange client that allows recipients to respond automatically to messages if a particular event occurs. The event may include a vacation (in which case the recipient would want to notify the sender of an e-mail that he or she will be gone until a specific date). There are a variety of options and triggers for the out-of-office response.

When a message is sent to a person with an out-of-office rule set for his or her system, the sender of the message will receive the notice created by the recipient of the message. These rules in Microsoft Exchange are server-based, so they are active even if the creator of the rule is not logged into the system. The Exchange server manages these rules and applies them when the conditions of the rule are triggered. Additionally, Microsoft Exchange rules are intelligent, so when a sender receives a copy of a notification that the recipient is out of the office for a period of time, any subsequent messages to that recipient will not invoke additional out-of-office notices. The sender will only receive one out-of-office notice from that recipient, minimizing the number of spurious message responses replicated over and over.

Inbox Assistant

The inbox assistant enables a series of triggers to invoke a specific result. The trigger may include moving all electronic messages received from a specific sender into a specific user folder. An inbox assistant trigger may also involve invoking a pager to notify the recipient of an inbound urgent electronic message, or the trigger may cause a message to be prioritized when read. The inbox assistant functions whether users have their workstations turned on or not, since it is also a server-based rule.

Client-Based Filtering

Users have the ability to select which electronic mail messages they would like to filter (to see or to not see) within a folder. Users have the option of selecting from a series of filtration options, such as by the sender's name or by the recipient's name. Users can select filtration by the size of the file or by a date range of the receipt of the message. This option is frequently used by individuals who receive dozens of mail messages and only want to see the messages from a particular sender, or only see messages related to a particular subject topic, or only messages received during a one-week period. Filters can be invoked on any folder in Microsoft Exchange.

Scheduling Using the Macintosh Exchange Client

Scheduling with the Exchange client is a new function that has been added to Exchange v5.0. The Scheduler component of Microsoft Exchange for the Macintosh allows a user to enter and keep track of personal appointments, such as meeting dates, scheduled reminders, vacations, and holidays. Since users are integrated into the Microsoft Exchange Server enterprise-wide environment, they have the ability to make their personal schedules available to view by others in Microsoft Exchange, which forms the first workgroup-enabled process. The Exchange Scheduler facilitates this process by providing a number of calendar features and capabilities.

Personal Appointment Scheduling

Microsoft Exchange users can easily create and maintain a personal appointment calendar or schedule. Users have the option of entering one-time appointments or events or recurring events (such as weekly Friday meetings, or a first-Tuesday-of-the-month conference call). The procedure for inserting appointments is the same whether it is a single or recurring event. To add an appointment:

1. Insert an appointment from the Scheduler client software.

2. Enter the date, time, and description of the appointment.

3. If the appointment is recurring, select the Make Recurring option and enter the characteristics of the recurring appointment.

The main appointment screen has a few options to choose from. By selecting the Set Reminder For option, users will be notified on their desktop screens of an upcoming appointment. If the user selects the Private option, the appointment will be marked as private and the appointment description will become unavailable to other workgroup members. This function allows users to enter private notations or appointments without worrying that the entire organization will know about personal events entered into their calendars.

Setting Privileges for Appointment Calendar Access by Others

Once users enter their personal appointments into their personal calendars, they can make their calendars available to be viewed by others within the organization. By default, an individual's calendar is inaccessible to anyone in the Microsoft Exchange organization. In order to grant other users access to their calendars, they must configure the access permission. The available permissions are as follows:

- **None** No access to the user's calendar
- **Read** Ability to read appointments (non-private appointments only)
- **Create** Ability to read non-private appointments and create appointments for the user
- **Modify** Ability to read non-private appointments, create appointments, and modify existing appointments in a user's calendar
- **Delegate** Ability to read non-private appointments, create and modify existing appointments, and to invite others to appointments on behalf of the user
- **Owner** Full rights to read, create, modify, and invite users to appointments
- **Delegate Owner** Full rights to a delegated user(s) to read, create, modify, and invite people to appointments on behalf of the user

To allocate these rights to others, users would need to determine which privileges they wish to give to others in the workgroup, and then set those privileges in their schedule. To do so:

1. Set the access permissions of the Scheduler program.
2. Add and select the individual(s) or group(s) to be defined for special privileges.
3. Select the user role of none, read, create, modify, delegate, owner, or delegate owner.

Once the privileges are assigned for an individual's calendar, other users with access privileges will be able to read, create, or modify appointments according to the access permission designation.

Group Scheduling

Regardless of whether a user has been given the right to read, create, or modify appointments, all users have the ability to invite others to appointments. The Scheduler software does not automatically book an individual to an appointment unless that individual has the right to create appointments for the attendees; however, the attendees will, at minimum, receive an invitation to an appointment that they can either accept or deny.

To invite others to an appointment, the user would follow the procedure for creating a personal appointment, and enter in the time, date, and description of the appointment. In order to invite others to the appointment, the user would now select the Attendees tab and invite others to the appointment. The user can select required attendees as well as optional attendees. The designation of required and optional attendee is not enforced by Microsoft Exchange, but it does allow the invitee to know how urgently his or her presence is requested at the meeting.

Another way to invite a group of users to attend an appointment is to use the Planner option in the Scheduler software. By showing both the available and busy schedules of potential invitees in a graphical format, the Planner option can help determine an appointment time that won't conflict with anyone's prior engagements. You can use the Planner option when you create an appointment: before entering the time and date, select the Planner tab on the appointment option screen. Click on the Invite button and select the desired attendee(s) to the appointment. All attendees' available and busy schedules are shown onscreen. The user can now select an open appointment time for all attendees.

Once a Planner-defined appointment is selected and the user selects OK, an e-mail message is created that invites all attendees to the appointment. When the user selects the Send button, the invitations are distributed.

Resource Scheduling

In addition to scheduling appointments for individuals and groups of individuals, Microsoft Exchange also supports the scheduling of resources that may be necessary for the appointment (such as a conference room), or for an individual user (such as use of a company vehicle). Resources are created by the Microsoft Exchange administrator just like an electronic mail/schedule individual is created. The difference between a resource and a user is that a resource does not have an e-mail message box in which to receive invitations to appointments. The resource has a schedule that is viewable by users of the workgroup who have been granted permission to schedule the resource (read, create, or modify the resource availability).

When users are booking an appointment using the appointment option from the Scheduler program, they would select the resource exactly as they would select other attendees to the appointment: directly from the organization's Global Address List.

Using Public Folders

The public folders and folder replication of Microsoft Exchange comprise the heart of its group communications infrastructure. The public folders in Microsoft Exchange are storage folders available to a defined group of Microsoft Exchange users. Users can drag and drop e-mail messages, word processing documents, and graphic files into public folders designed for a number of users just as they can drag and drop similar files to universal private folders (as described in Chapter 2).

Creating Public Folders and Public Folder Security

A public folder is created by the Microsoft Exchange administrator or by any user who has been given the right to create public folders for the organization. The security and access to these folders are also created by the Microsoft Exchange administrator or by the original creator of the folder.

Managing Information Within a Public Folder

As long as a user has privileges to the public folder, he or she can drag and drop information into the folder such as e-mail messages, documents, and graphic files. A core functionality of public folders is their ability to share information across a workgroup of users. This may include a folder full of common document templates used by the organization, a clustering of company policies and procedures, or a consolidation of e-mail message information like a common newsgroup store. Files can be inserted and placed into an Exchange public folder by a Macintosh client. To insert a Macintosh file, the Macintosh user simply needs to view the Macintosh file folder onscreen, as shown in Figure 19-7, select a file, and then insert the file into the Exchange environment.

Because the information in any folder in Microsoft Exchange can consist of a variety of types of information shared by a defined group of users, the possibilities of this capability are extensive, and they are key to the intranet and workgroup communications that have been highlighted throughout this book.

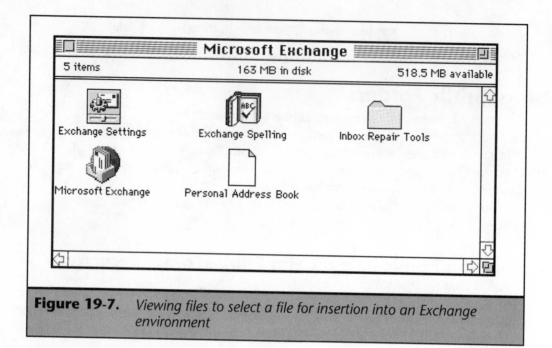

Figure 19-7. *Viewing files to select a file for insertion into an Exchange environment*

Interoperability Within a PC Environment

The interoperability of the Macintosh with other operating systems like DOS, Windows, Windows 95, Windows NT, or UNIX is made simple in a Microsoft Exchange environment. Because Microsoft Exchange is an object-based client/server messaging and storage system, there is no underlying file system standard used when messages or attachments are shared between computers of different operating systems.

Exchanging Files

In order for a Macintosh computer to share a file with a PC computer, the file needs to be attached to a mail message and then sent to the PC computer, or vice-versa. The file should be in a document format that can be read by the other system's application program, for example, an Excel v5.0 spreadsheet file on the Macintosh can be read by an Excel 97 in a Windows 95 environment without a problem. Even if the file format is not completely compatible, through Exchange views, files can be viewed through the Exchange client.

The Chapter in Review

- In any enterprise messaging system, the need to include Apple Macintosh support is crucial, but there are usually challenges when integrating Macintosh systems into other LAN or WAN environments generally because of hardware connection and network communication protocol differences of the Macintosh computer. With Microsoft Exchange, however, which runs under a Windows NT environment, the issue of support for Macintosh computers is greatly simplified. This is primarily due to the fact that Microsoft Exchange is a client/server environment that supports a number of different communication protocols.

- The key to connecting Macintosh computers to an NT or an Exchange environment is the ability to physically connect the computers together. Through the use of standard Ethernet or Token Ring hardware connections, a Macintosh computer can be easily added to a Windows NT networking environment. Once physically connected, the next step is to ensure that protocol communications between the Macintosh computers and the Exchange server are compatible. The Macintosh computers can communicate to the NT environment either through the AppleTalk protocol or through another protocol like TCP/IP. If the Macintosh systems communicate through AppleTalk, the NT environment needs to run the Windows NT Services for the Macintosh. If the Macintosh systems communicate through TCP/IP, the Macintosh systems need to run a protocol like MacTCP to communicate with the Exchange server.

- Once connected, the Macintosh system can load the Microsoft Exchange client for the Macintosh, which then communicates with the Exchange server as a client/server system. The Exchange client software for the Macintosh supports the sending and receiving of mail messages, personal and group appointment scheduling, the sending and receiving of attachments, inbox and out-of-office rules, rich text formatting, and dozens of other messaging and groupware capabilities.

- The Macintosh computer can also share public folders with other computers in the Exchange environment, thus participating in file and message sharing groupware capabilities with Exchange. Since the

Microsoft Exchange environment considers messages and files as objects, any information stored in public folders in Microsoft Exchange can be opened, viewed, or edited by any client platform system as long as the client has native access to the files. Thus if a Macintosh user saved a file using Microsoft Word for the Macintosh into a public folder, that file can be opened by a Microsoft Word for Windows user, edited, and resaved to the folder. There is no need to set up compatible file transfer protocols, high-capacity file storage systems, or other processes to share information throughout a diverse client workgroup.

- Microsoft Exchange's strength in an enterprise messaging system is its ability to support a variety of different client operating systems and the subsequent ability of the various clients to access common information and participate as a truly diverse workgroup environment.

Review Questions

Q. What protocols can a Macintosh use to access an Exchange server?
A. The Macintosh can access the Exchange server through any standard protocol supported by Exchange, including TCP/IP, AppleTalk, IPX/SPX, and NetBEUI.

Q. Where is the Macintosh client software located for installation?
A. The Macintosh client software resides on the same Exchange client CD-ROM as Exchange.

Q. Does the Macintosh client support rich text formatting documents?
A. Yes, the Macintosh client supports virtually all of the formatting and message management capabilities of the other Exchange client software, including rich text formatting.

Q. How does a Macintosh user share word processing documents through Exchange with a non-Macintosh user?
A. Since Microsoft Exchange supports the saving of information as universal objects on the Exchange server, any client with access to the Exchange server can retrieve files and view them as long as the individual has the appropriate security privileges and software to open and view the common shared file.

Q. In which version of Microsoft Exchange did personal and group scheduling for Macintosh users begin to be supported?

A. Personal and group scheduling began support for Exchange in version 5.0. In Exchange v5.0, Macintosh users can open, view, and schedule appointments for other Exchange users on the network as long as they have access security privileges.

CHAPTER 20

Remote Access, Telecommuting, and Mobile Computing with Exchange

O ne of the biggest challenges organizations face is their need to provide data access to employees, clients, and strategic vendors from anywhere individual users reside or work. In the early days of the computer industry, the computer equipment that was used to access company records and data information fit in the size of a room, so the ability of users to travel with or access the information was limited. Furthermore, information was typically stored in paper format (in filing cabinets), so users by default had limited availability to that information. Today, portable laptop computers have the capabilities of huge desktop systems, and users demand access to information any time from any place. Clearly, users' need to travel with or access vital company information remotely has become a growing organizational need.

The Demand to Access Information Remotely

Data demands continue to increase as organizations increasingly use electronic methods as one of their primary modes of communication. As I have described throughout this book, the means to communicate as an electronic workgroup, the ability to route documents or schedule projects, and the capability to share in discussion groups have made the electronic medium of communications a significant component in an organization's communications requirement.

Individuals typically fall into one of three categories in need of information access. One type of individual includes the telecommuter, who works from home on a permanent or temporary basis as his or her remote site for doing business. A second type is the individual who works in a remote office and who needs full-time access to information during business hours at another location, which functions as the primary site for data access. The third type is a person who travels frequently and may be in a hotel, airport, or client site and needs access to information stored on servers back at the office.

Telecommuting

In the past few years, telecommuting has become a very popular way for organizations to provide offsite offices for their employees. Telecommuting allows employees to work from home or from a local office to do business instead of traveling to the main corporate office. It also minimizes the need for the individual to drive to work every day and it can also allow employees to work flexible hours and limit their travel to the office at times that are not traditional commute hours.

Although telecommuting is a great way for individuals to spend less time in a car and more time getting work completed, the challenge is to provide employees with the tools and resources at home as they would normally have at the office. For some organizations it may be as simple as providing the user with a telephone and a phone directory of clients. However, for some organizations, it may require access to a mainframe computer system, a local area networking system, e-mail messages, electronic schedules, or other data information systems.

The telecommuter may occasionally work in the main corporate office and will need to have access to the same information at the office as he or she does from home. For example, this may be a telecommuter who works from home from 8 A.M. until 10A.M., travels to the office after the traffic has died down, and works in the office until the early afternoon, when he or she goes home and telecommutes for the rest of the afternoon. This process now requires that an organization provides full-time capabilities to this individual in multiple locations.

Remote Site Access

The second type of remote access user permanently works at a remote site office. This may be a satellite office of the main company where the employee or employees work in an office that may be too small to warrant a full network file server and wide area connection configuration; however, the user needs may be as sophisticated as those of the users who reside in the main business office. These remote site users need access to electronic mail messages, office memos, database information, document routes, appointment schedules, and client information.

Because the individuals reside in a static office, the options for remote access can be a relatively long-term investment; thus higher performance capabilities can be considered since the user or users are situated in a single location.

Business Traveling

The third type of remote access user is a business traveler who may work in the office on a regular basis but travels and needs access to information from hotels, airports, client sites, or even unplugged and standalone on an airplane.

The challenge of information access for this type of employee is the need to have access from phone equipment of varying quality and performance speeds as well as the ability to store and forward information offline, because the employee may need to store information on the laptop hard drive while he or she is disconnected from the main office.

A business traveler's needs combine full-time office access to full-time remote slow speed access from any hotel room or airport, to offline access while disconnected from the main network.

Types of Remote Communication Solutions

Just as there are different types of individual access needs to a network of information, there are different methods of accessing the information from remote locations. The three common methods of information access include remote node, remote control, and store and forward. Unfortunately, the three needs for information access and the three methods of information access do not correspond one-to-one, so there is a need to evaluate the benefits and the limitations of each method of information access to determine which method or methods of communication are appropriate for the individual.

Remote Node

Remote node, as shown in Figure 20-1, is a method in which a remote user becomes a node on the network. The remote user's connection and access is exactly like the connection and access of a user who actually resides on the main system network. The user can log on to the network and access data files using drive letters common to the organization's local area network user connection.

The characteristics of a remote node configuration include:

- Users have programs on their remote system
- Data can reside on the network or on the user's remote system
- Users dial in remotely to the network to access information they need to transfer down to their remote system or back to the network
- Users disconnect when session is completed

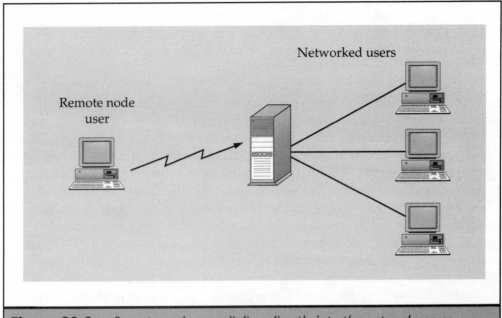

Figure 20-1.   *Remote node user dialing directly into the network server*

One of the advantages of a remote node system is that the user has offline use of his or her application because the program resides on the user's local hard drive. Additionally, the normal network "drive letters" remain the same since the user is a node on the network. Lastly, the data can remain on the centralized network system since the user can open or save information to the file server just as if he or she were a user on the network itself.

A disadvantage of a remote node system is that access performance is slow and the programs the user accesses are distributed across all remote users' workstations. Because the remote user is typically accessing the system over a dial-up type connection, the data access is rated in Kbps such as 14,400Kbps or 28,800Kbps whereas a normal network-attached workstation communicates in Mbps. A typical Ethernet network communicates on average at 3Mbps, or almost 100-200 times faster than the normal telephone modem. If it normally takes one second to retrieve a file, it could easily take up to a minute for the remote user to retrieve that same file. Even with some of the newer ISDN-type phone systems that are digital phone access systems, the maximum speed is still 128Kbps or 20-30 times slower than being on a local network. This access speed needs to be taken into account for applications that typically take 10-20 seconds to search and find information on a network, which for the remote user can translate to minutes if not hours to invoke a single response from a database or other access information method.

Because a software program normally takes 15-20 seconds to load on a network, storing the application program on the user's local hard drive becomes a necessity, or the remote user could be faced with a 20-minute wait to load the main screen for Microsoft Word if the program were launched over the dial-up phone connection. Many organizations have difficulty managing remote copies of software because users who have software installed on their remote node system need to have a way to refresh the application program when the organization updates the software used at the main office. Although an organization may be able to add users one at a time over an extended period of time for remote access, if the same organization upgrades the main database or a messaging program or word processing program at the main office, upgrading or updating remote users may need to occur simultaneously.

Remote node is a good method to use when the information being accessed is clearly identified and small enough in content that the speed of the application accessing the information can complete the transaction in a reasonable amount of time. This method is typically used by individuals wishing to access a word processing file or spreadsheet document by downloading the file to their remote system, working offline, and then uploading the information back to the main network. A remote node system is also a way for true client/server applications to send and receive information, since the online access is the only interaction between the client and the server and the bulk of the processing occurs either locally at the client or remotely at the server.

Remote Control

Remote control is a method in which a remote user sends and receives only screen and keyboard images between the remote system and the main office. It is called remote control because usually a user is taking control of a remote system to gain access to information, as shown in Figure 20-2. Since only the keyboard and screen images are passed over the data line, a slow communication phone line is typically adequate to send and receive screen and keyboard images. The actual processing performance is managed by the system at the main office from which the remote user is taking control.

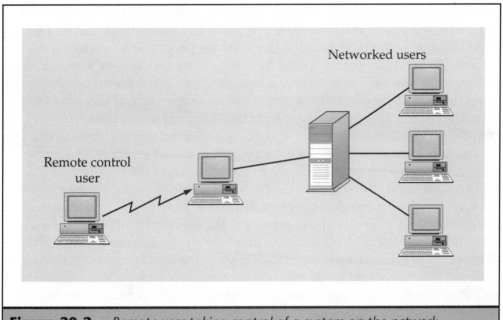

Figure 20-2. *Remote user taking control of a system on the network*

The characteristics of a remote control configuration include:

- Remote user runs a remote access application program on his or her remote system

- There is a computer sitting at the main office that waits for remote users to dial in using a remote access program that will allow them to take control of the system

- Only keyboard and screen images transfer between the office and the remote user, which allows performance to be relatively fast

An advantage of a remote control system is that there is fast access to applications since only the keyboard and screen images pass over the modem/phone line, no applications reside on the remote laptop or computer systems, and the administration and upgrading of applications is easier because the information is centralized at the main office. The remote system is only running a remote access program, so application support for the remote user is limited only to the remote access program itself. If the user has problems with the word processing software he or she is accessing, or if his or her mainframe access does not work, the network administrator can fix the system that is located at the main office since the programs and actual access process reside on the system at the office, not on the remote user's system. Additionally, when the organization needs to upgrade software, because the computer with the application program resides in the office of the organization, the upgrading process can be completed at any time. The next time the remote user accesses the system, he or she will see the new version of the software onscreen. The administrator does not need to worry about how to upgrade the software residing on the remote systems of the remote users.

The disadvantage of a remote control session is that the user must be connected to the remote control server in order to have access to information. Since the remote control user does not have the main application programs on his or her local hard drive, the minute the remote user disconnects from the network, he or she no longer has a local copy of the word processing software, database software, or other information that was accessed.

For many organizations, a remote control system is a desirable method that limits which information is distributed to locations in which the administrator has neither access nor control. For other organizations, a hybrid of a remote control and a remote node system is implemented so that users have access to some information over remote control (such as to accounting information, or to a main customer database), but other information is accessed on a remote node basis (like word processing information, subsets of the main database, or personal data information). More information about options and solutions will be given later in this chapter.

Store and Forward with Data Synchronization

A store and forward method of communications is one in which a remote user works offline on his or her local system, composes or edits information, and then connects to the network to send and receive information he or she has been working on and storing. This method of communication is very common to electronic mail systems, in which remote users can write electronic mail messages and "send" the messages offline (which does nothing more than collects the messages and queues them up for future delivery). Then, when the user connects to the network the messages that were queued up are sent, and any messages waiting for the remote user are delivered. Some of the more sophisticated messaging systems like Microsoft Exchange can actually synchronize the information between the remote system and the network system. Most electronic mail programs send and receive information as a store and forward process; however, if a user deletes a message remotely, moves the message to a different file folder, or edits a message, the program will not update the information on both sides of the link. Thus, any changes to messages or folders are not translated to the same changes made at the main office. Microsoft Exchange, however, has full synchronization of local and remote folders and messages. When a Microsoft Exchange user deletes a message remotely, the message is deleted on the network. When a Microsoft Exchange user moves a message to a separate folder, the message is moved both locally and remotely. When the Exchange user goes to the office and runs Microsoft Exchange, the user sees everything on the local network exactly as the user moved, modified, or changed information on the remote system.

The characteristics of a store and forward configuration include:

- User has a store and forward application on his or her remote system
- User writes messages, makes changes to information, and logs on to the network, and any changes are updated on the main network system
- User disconnects when he or she has completed the store and forward session

The advantages of a store and forward system include the user's ability to work offline and that any work conducted offline is updated to both the local and the remote copies of the software. For individuals who travel and may be on an airplane or in a location that does not provide easy access to online information, a store and forward system can allow them to work offline. Later, when the user is near a telephone or can connect to the network, the information is updated on both sides of the link.

Accessing Microsoft Exchange Remotely

For a remote user on Microsoft Exchange, the access solutions take on a variety of combinations of the remote node, remote control, and store and forward functions to meet the needs of the telecommuter, the remote site office user, or the traveling businessperson. As noted previously, the access process of the Exchange user may include more than one access method because the user may access some information in one method and other information in another.

Dial In to RAS for Exchange Access

Microsoft Windows NT provides a remote access system called Remote Access Server, or *RAS*. RAS is a remote node system in which a user dials into an NT server configured with RAS and becomes a node on the network. RAS supports standard modem speeds (9,600bps, 14.4Kbps, 28.8Kbps, 33.6Kbps, etc.), ISDN dial-up speeds (56Kbps, 112Kbps), or even RAS over an Internet connection.

The components of a RAS connection include the RAS server, the RAS client, and the communication link between the server and the client.

RAS Server

As previously mentioned, Windows NT comes with the RAS server software as part of the core Microsoft Windows NT Server program. A RAS server is nothing more than a PC computer running Windows NT Server software, and the RAS component of the Windows NT Server software, with telephone modems attached for remote users to dial into the RAS server. Because a RAS server is nothing more than a modem gateway (which is a relatively slow-speed means of communications), the processing performance of the server can be that of an 80486 or lower-end Pentium system. The critical components in a RAS server, besides having a dependable system as the server to minimize hardware failures, are the modems and the connections the modems have to the RAS server. A RAS server can use internal modems to the computer system; however, most systems are limited by the number of add-in expansion slots available or the number COM port settings that the internal modems provide. Usually a RAS server is limited to two internal modems. Most computer systems have two external serial ports where external modems can be attached, and generally a computer system can have two internal modems, or two external modems, or one of each, but not four total modems. In order to get beyond this limit of two modems to a system, an organization can purchase a multiport serial board. The most common multiport serial boards are made by Digi International. The boards come in 2-port, 4-port, 8-port, 16-port, or 32-port sizes with the option of adding multiple boards to a single server. Using external modems and a multiport serial board, an organization can have a number of modems connected to a single system for RAS access.

The speed of the modems will determine the upper limit of the performance access speed by which users can dial in and gain access to the network. Obviously, a 33.6KB modem will be significantly faster than a 14.4KB modem, and since modems are downward-speed compatible (where a 33.6KB modem can support a remote user dialing in with a 14.4KB modem or a 28.8KB modem), having the fastest modem on the server provides the widest range of dial-up flexibility.

One of the serial port options for a system is the speed of the serial port itself. Not all serial ports are the same. Some older serial ports with 8250 or 16450 serial chips only support 9,600bps or 19.2Kbps speeds reliably. To support higher speeds, a serial chip should have a 16550 UART that can support speeds of up to 128Kbps. This is important since a 33.6Kbps modem plugged into a port that only supports up to 19.2Kbps will either not work or will tend to have frequent line drops on connections. Additionally, a smart versus a dumb multiport serial board makes a big difference as well. Some low-cost multiport serial boards are nothing more than multiple serial ports on a single adapter card. When the card is communicating with four simultaneous sessions at speeds up to 33.6Kbps, some cards cannot support that much communication traffic and errors occur. Smart multiport serial adapters have processors built into the serial card to manage multiple simultaneous communication links on a single card. It is important to confirm the maximum speed at which a serial port can handle RAS communication links and also whether the adapter has a processor on it to manage multiple simultaneous RAS communication links.

A RAS server, however, does not necessarily need to be a Windows NT server. There are a number of companies that make standalone remote node dial-up devices that can provide a dial-up RAS connection to a network. The company that people hear of most often is called Shiva, the makers of the LanRover product. Most network wiring hub manufacturers have also started to sell remote access standalone boxes, including Cisco, 3Com, and Bay Networks.

The standalone boxes typically have options about the number of ports or modems the box comes with, the speed of the modems, and the expandability of the box. Most modem servers have the option of 4, 8, 12, or 16 modems or ports per box. Choosing whether you want to have the modems included in the box or selecting one that has only ports where you connect your own external modems differentiates many of the options available. For many, the decision to buy a box with modems included means the elimination of compatibility or integration problems between a box and external third-party modems. For others, the decision to buy the box with only serial ports allows an individual to purchase the type of modems desired, whether they are 28.8KB modems, 33.6KB modems, ISDN modems, or a combination of modems.

RAS Client

The client support for RAS includes Windows v3.1, Windows for Workgroups, Windows 95, Windows NT, and Macintosh. As an RAS client, the remote user has a computer system, RAS client software, and a dial-in modem to the RAS server. The RAS client establishes a connection to the network by dialing into the RAS server and entering a logon name and password. The configuration of the RAS client can be a connection as an IPX, NetBEUI, and/or TCP/IP client. A TCP/IP client can participate as a remote DHCP client, similar to a DHCP LAN-based client described in Chapter 6.

Communications Link between the RAS Server and the RAS Client

The communications link between the RAS client and the RAS server can be anything from a dial-up asynchronous modem (14.4KB 28.8KB, 33.6KB, etc.), an ISDN modem, or a RAS client over the Internet. A standard dial-up or ISDN connection requires only a compatible modem on each end of the connection: one to dial, and one to receive the communication. A RAS connection can also take place over the Internet, in which case a remote client actually connects to the Internet, and using Point-to-Point Tunneling Protocol (PPTP) the RAS client can establish a secured connection to an RAS server over the Internet. PPTP is a method to route Point-to-Point Protocol (PPP) packets over a TCP/IP network by encapsulating the PPP, TCP/IP, IPX, or NetBEUI packet.

Configuring the Remote Exchange User

The configuration of the remote Exchange user requires the configuration of the RAS server, the RAS client, and the remote Exchange client software.

CONFIGURING THE RAS SERVER   For the installation of RAS on a Windows NT Server, the Remote Access Server software is installed through the Control Panel. By selecting Start | Settings | Control Panel | Network and then the Services option, Add Services and the Remote Access Server, the RAS services will be installed. After the software has been installed, the administrator needs to configure the Remote Access Server by selecting the modem type and the communication port to be used, as shown here:

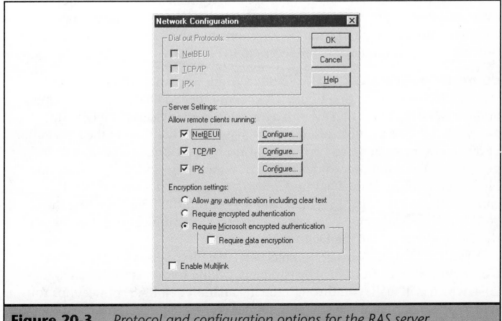

Of the configuration options, the main options that need to be selected are in the network configuration section of the RAS configuration utility. The options, as shown in Figure 20-3, include selecting the protocols that should be supported remotely (such as NetBEUI, TCP/IP, and IPX), the type of security

Figure 20-3.   *Protocol and configuration options for the RAS server*

encryption desired, and whether the connection will be a multilink connection (meaning that a number of modem connections will be running between the RAS client and the RAS server to aggregate multiple connections for faster performance). For each of the protocols that should be supported, the allocation of remote addresses, like IP addresses or IPX addresses, can either be defined by the administrator in this portion of the RAS configuration software for allocation to the remote users, or the remote client can request a predetermined address prior to his or her connection to the RAS server. The strategy for address assignment varies, but for organizations with a large number of remote users who may only be online for a short period of time and then disconnect, the ability to have the RAS server or DHCP dynamically assign addresses provides better flexibility in administering remote user addresses on a connection basis rather than on a per-user basis.

If a number of modem lines for the RAS server are similarly configured and are allocated for the RAS connection by remote users, the modem lines can be configured in a hunt group by the phone company. A hunt group allows the organization to have one primary RAS dial-up phone number that it can provide to the remote users. When the primary line is busy, it rolls over to the next phone line in the hunt group. If that line is busy it continues to roll over until it finds an available phone line. This service from the phone company can minimize the number of phone numbers that need to be provided to the remote users for access to the system.

CONFIGURING THE RAS CLIENT   Under Windows 95 and Windows NT Workstation the installation of the RAS client is called Dial-up Networking and is part of the operating system. However, in many cases the Dial-up Networking option is not automatically installed at the time of the installation of the operating system. To verify if Dial-up Networking has been installed, go into the My Computer folder on the desktop; there should be a Dial-up Networking folder. If the Dial-up Networking option does not exist, it can be installed by going into Start | Settings | Control Panel, selecting the Add/Remove Programs, Windows Setup tab, Communications, Details, and then selecting to install the Dial-up Networking.

Once the Dial-up Networking has been installed, select the Make New Connection Wizard from the Dial-up Networking folder as shown in Figure 20-4, which will walk you through the installation of a RAS connection. You will have the option of selecting the modem type in your remote computer, the communication port, and the phone number of one of the modems in your RAS server. Once the basic configuration has been set, the next set of options are configured by selecting File | Properties in order to select the protocols and

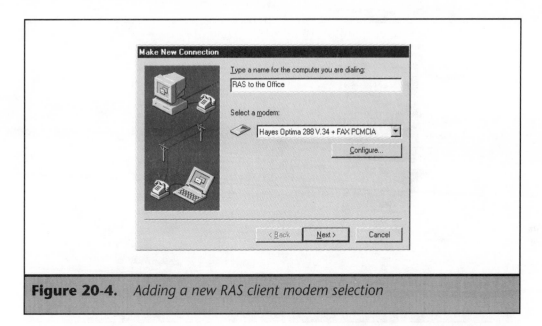

Figure 20-4.   *Adding a new RAS client modem selection*

encryption type to be used. The protocol and encryption type settings should match the configuration of the RAS server.

Once the RAS client is configured, the remote user can double-click the Remote Access icon to dial out to the RAS server.

CONFIGURING THE EXCHANGE CLIENT SOFTWARE   To configure the Microsoft Exchange client software for remote synchronization of the user's mailbox, during the installation of the Microsoft Exchange client software, the user will be asked whether the profile will be used for remote access, as shown in Figure 20-5. Select "yes" for this option and then the user will be prompted for the location in which to store his or her offline store (or OST file). The offline store is a file that holds a remote copy of the user's folders and mail messages. This file can potentially grow to tens of megabytes in size based on the number of messages the user replicates to his or her local system. The first time the remote user launches Exchange, the user needs to synchronize the mailbox by selecting Tools I Synchronize. This will initialize the user's OST file for the first time so that future remote access updates can be completed.

Using Store and Forward with Synchronization for Exchange

When a Microsoft Exchange client establishes a connection to a RAS server, the client has the ability to synchronize his or her mailbox and schedule.

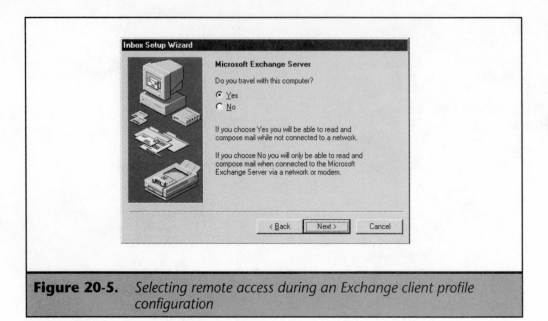

Figure 20-5. *Selecting remote access during an Exchange client profile configuration*

Just as in the store and forward process described earlier in this chapter, the remote user has the ability to write electronic mail messages or perform mailbox and message maintenance offline on his or her remote system. When the remote user establishes a RAS connection to the network, the user can select Tools | Synchronize | All Folders, as shown here:

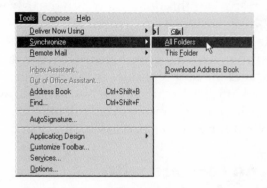

This function will send any messages queued up in the user's Outbox, and update all of the user's offline storage folders. To synchronize the user's schedule, the user can enter the Scheduler client and select Tools | Options and the Synchronize tab, and then select "synchronize now."

Remote Control for Exchange Access

The second way for an Exchange user to gain access to his or her mailbox is through a remote control process. As described earlier in this chapter, a remote control process for remote access provides the user with the ability to take control of another system with keyboard and screen images passing over the remote connection. In many cases, a remote control process may be preferable to a remote node or a store and forward messaging process. This may be a situation where the remote user needs to participate as a member of an online discussion group, in a secured document routing process, or other messaging or communication process that typically requires the user to be on the network to communicate. With a remote control session, the organization has the option of setting up a one-to-one connection or a many-to-one connection for remote access, as shown in Figure 20-6.

One-to-One Remote Control

A one-to-one remote control session is one in which a remote user dials in and accesses a computer attached to the network and takes control of the system. A common application that supports one-to-one remote control is a product like pcAnywhere. The pcAnywhere host component of the program installs on a computer on the network, which can be configured with the Microsoft Exchange client software. When a pcAnywhere remote client dials into the host computer and enters a logon and password to the computer, the remote user has access to any of the applications available on that system just as if he or she was sitting at the keyboard console of the host computer. The user can access Microsoft Exchange, send messages, read messages, and participate in discussion groups.

Many-to-One Remote Control

An organization with a number of users requiring remote access would find it very costly and time-consuming to have a one-to-one connection for each remote dial-up user, so in these cases a many-to-one approach tends to be more functional. In a many-to-one approach, a single system is set up and multiple users can dial into the system and conduct independent remote

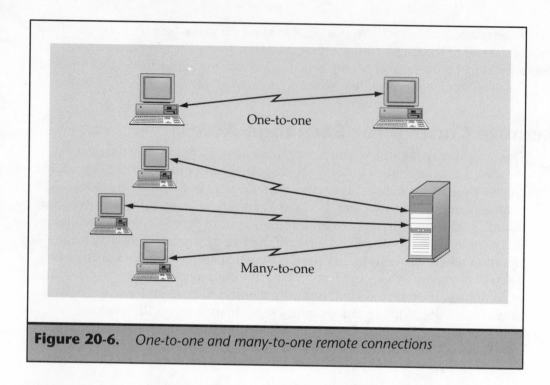

One-to-one

Many-to-one

Figure 20-6. *One-to-one and many-to-one remote connections*

control sessions. A product that provides this type of functionality is Citrix WinFrame, as shown in Figure 20-7. The Citrix WinFrame program is a Windows NT application server software program that enables multiple users to carry on independent Windows sessions while sharing the same host system and application software programs.

Similar to a RAS server, the Citrix WinFrame server has the WinFrame software installed on a system with modems attached. In the case of the WinFrame server, however, the performance of the system will dictate the speed of each remote user's session speed because multiple users will be accessing the system simultaneously. If the host system is a 133MHz Pentium computer with one user connected, the remote user will get 133MHz speed. If two users are connected simultaneously, each user will receive approximately 67MHz speed. Four users will receive the equivalent of a 66MHz 80486 computer. Because Windows NT supports multiple processors, a remote control server can support 30-40 simultaneous connections with relatively high performance for each session.

Figure 20-7. *Citrix WinFrame logon screen*

Maximizing Groupware Capabilities While Minimizing Administration

Many organizations are viewing remote control as a potential long-term solution for the problem of remote users. While there is a need for users to have offline access to information or local storage of applications and data, the growing need for an organization to manage the vast distribution of information on mobile or remote systems makes the process more and more difficult to manage and maintain. Although a remote control system requires the user to be online during the access link and limits the user's freedom to access information offline, the cost and function to administer and manage a distributed remote or mobile infrastructure can become prohibitive for many organizations.

PROVIDING REMOTE CONTROL ACCESS TO THE LAN   By providing remote control access to a network, an organization can provide electronic mail messaging, scheduling, document routing, faxing, and voicemail integration to remote users just as if he or she was a local user on the network. If the workstation functionality works for a local network-attached user, the same functionality will work for a remote control user on the network.

ADMINISTERING REMOTE CONTROL USERS   Since all files and applications remain on the network during a remote control session, the distribution of company information is limited to the local environment. This minimizes the need to support the operation of software on remote systems as well as the threat of unauthorized distribution of company information, as data is contained within the local operating environment.

PROVIDING REMOTE CONTROL OVER THE INTERNET   One additional option for a remote control solution is the ability to gain access to company resources in a remote control process over the Internet. Through the use of Citrix WinFrame over the Internet, an organization can allow a remote control client to access information using secured access controls. Essentially, through the use of WinFrame over the Internet, an organization can provide remote access with all forms, discussion group management, and document routing management capabilities available to the client.

Access Exchange through the Internet

The third way available for Exchange clients to access their messages is over the Internet. As we explored in Chapter 18, there are a few options available in Exchange v5.0 that provide Internet access, such as POP3 client access or the use of the Web Outlook client from a Web browser package. Additionally, I addressed earlier in this chapter the use of RAS over the Internet with PPTP. And lastly, in the preceding section, we explored the option of using Citrix WinFrame for remote control access over the Internet. The benefits of the Internet for remote access communications are growing as the cost to connect to the Internet decreases and the functionality of Internet-enabled applications increases dramatically.

The Chapter in Review

- As more and more information is commonly stored on network file servers and the demand for users to share information grows, the need to gain access to information from anywhere becomes a priority. There are a variety of demands users have when accessing information remotely: they need access to information when they are at home, in a hotel room, at a client's office, or at another company office.

- The ways in which users access information remotely varies depending on the type of information users need to access and the frequency of their access. For users who are telecommuting and who need flexible hour access to information, the remote access infrastructure needs to be able to support a user who requires full-time information access for short periods of time during the day. Telecommuters may also need access to the same information when they are in the office as they do when they are at a remote site. This requires an organization to provide nearly full-time access in at least two locations for these individuals. A common type of access for telecommuters is the remote control method of communications. A remote control provides users with the ability to gain access to almost all applications they would normally have at the office, as the remote users are doing nothing more than taking control of a computer (or a session on a remote control server) to pass screen and keyboard images between the host and the client user. This allows the organization to provide full access to all of the applications that users require without having to load users' remote computers with the programs and software for this access. When the organization decides to upgrade software, it only needs to update the software on the local host system or server, and does not need to figure out how to get new updated programs on all of the hard drives of remote computers.

- Users who are traveling have very different needs than telecommuters. Travelers need access to information while they are disconnected from the network while on an airplane or in an airport as well as access over virtually any dial-up connection found in a hotel. Basically, these disconnected users need access to programs and information while they are offline. This means that the programs they need, such as the e-mail program, word processing program, or other commonly used applications must be loaded onto their laptop hard drives. When users are working offline, they can easily gain access to the programs and do their work. When they connect to the network either over a dial-up phone line or by docking into the company's network, they can update their information with the network.

- The updating process can be simplified by synchronization. Normally, a remote node user who was described in the previous paragraph needs to identify which files the user was working on and manually copy the files up to the server, or copy files from the server to the user's remote workstation. Through the user of automated synchronization, any files saved or updated on the remote computer can be automatically updated to the server, or any files modified on the server can be automatically updated on the user's remote workstation. Through this process, a user can maintain automatic synchronization of information, which is the way Microsoft Exchange supports the replication and the synchronization of information between an Exchange server and an Exchange client. As a user updates or modifies mail messages, he or she can be automatically updated with the server, and vice-versa.

■ The components needed to allow remote Exchange users to access their mail messages and synchronize their mailboxes are available through the Remote Access Server (RAS) that comes with Microsoft Windows NT. RAS can be run on a Windows NT server or it can run on a dedicated standalone remote access server box (like a Shiva LanRover box). Network security and access privileges are set up to limit the remote user's access to network resources. The remote Exchange client has the client component for RAS (called Dial-up Networking for Windows 95 and Windows NT Workstation users) that provides dial-up access to the RAS server. Once connected over RAS, the remote workstation user can synchronize his or her mailbox and messages with the Exchange server.

■ Remote access to a network is not simply a process that involves allowing any user access to a network. Strategies need to be created to provide the right type of remote services for users so that they can gain access to the information they require as efficiently and as effectively as possible. However, the administrator of the network also needs to take into consideration the effect remote access places on the administration of the remote user and the remote user's services. This includes the ability of the administrator to update application software and create remote user functions that provide a long-term strategy for the entire organization to maintain an effective way to network resources remotely.

Review Questions

Q. Why has remote access become so important for organizations?

A. Because more and more information is being stored electronically, and without having access to the network remotely, mobile or remote users lose their primary method of communications and information access to the organization.

Q. What are the three most common reasons users need remote access to information?

A. Users access information as telecommuters, as remote site users, or as traveling remote users.

Q. What are the three methods for remote access?

A. Remote node, remote control, and store and forward with synchronization.

Q. What does a user need to have remote access using RAS?

A. RAS communications require a RAS server, an RAS client, and a form of communications between the two such as a dial-up phone line, digital ISDN dial-up line, or an Internet connection.

Q. What is PPTP?

A. PPTP is the Point-to-Point Tunneling Protocol that allows secured RAS access over the Internet between a client and a server.

Q. How does remote control provide easier administration for the administrator of an organization?

A. The software for a remote control system resides on a local host system of the organization, not on the hard drive of the remote computer itself. This allows the administrator to conduct upgrades, updates, and perform maintenance and diagnostics on the local host system without having to gain access to each remote system any time an update needs to be conducted. Furthermore, there is less of a chance for a user to damage information stored in a remote control configuration since the user does not actually have the application programs loaded on his or her remote system.

Q. Why is a remote node system a good solution for electronic mail users?

A. A remote node system enables the user to have the electronic mail program reside on his or her local system, thus allowing the user to create mail messages offline, queue up messages, and then connect and synchronize the messages when he or she has the opportunity to connect to the organization's network. Users do not need to be connected throughout the procedure in order to gain access to their mail messages.

Q. Which solution is better for an organization, a remote node or a remote control system?

A. Most organizations have a need for both a remote node and a remote control system. Many users' needs may include both a remote node and remote control access process, as well. The remote control is best suited for users to access any and all applications without the need for the organization to provide its remote users with software to install and support on their remote systems, and the remote node system provides users with offline access to electronic messages or word processing work while they are disconnected from the network.

PART FIVE

Appendixes

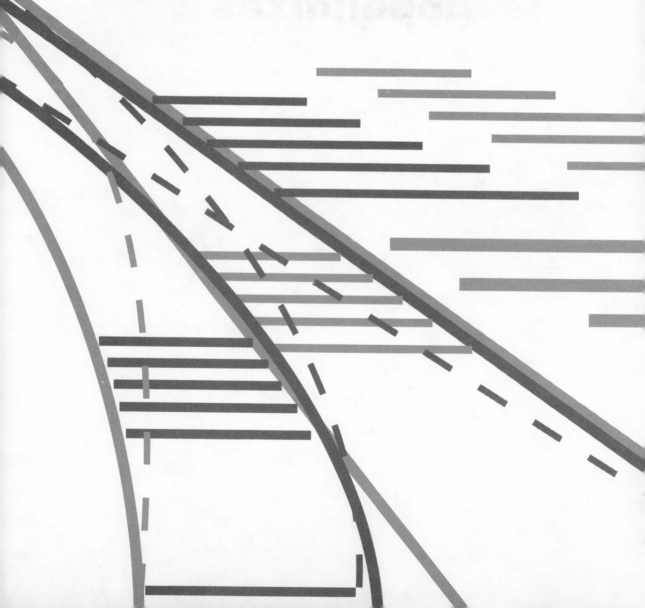

APPENDIX A

Glossary of Terms

Access Control List (Chapter 6)

The Access Control List, or ACL ("ah-kul") is a Microsoft list which controls access to resources. It is the security system that the administrator of the network uses to enable or disable user access to the resources of the network.

Access Rights List (Chapter 6)

The Access Control List in a Banyan Vines environment is called the Access Rights List (ARL). The ARL provides user and resource administration security access and designates what files, directories, and resources a user should access.

ACL (Chapter 6)

See Access Control List.

Active Desktop (Chapter 18)

Active Desktop is an initiative by Microsoft to provide Web-aware applications to every desktop system. As seen in many of the Office 97 applications including the Outlook 97 client, a user's workstation can have browser software that has been updated to support ActiveX content and interpret the information to be displayed on the user's screen.

Active Messaging (Chapter 18)

Active Messaging includes two components, the Messaging Object Library and the HTML Rendering Object Library. The Messaging Object Library provides the client with the ability to log on to the Exchange Server over the Internet, access his or her inbox and network public folders, and access the Microsoft Exchange directory. This library provides the core capabilities to allow a user to send, receive, move, and delete messages as well as manipulate folders and integrated attachments. The HTML Rendering Object Library extends the rich view capabilities of Exchange to the browser client. This includes manipulating message folder columns, and sorting and filtering messages. Users have the ability of rendering daily, weekly, and monthly views of their calendar information over the Internet.

Active Platform (Chapter 18)

The Microsoft Active Platform is a set of tools that developers use to create the links between the Internet and other environments like Microsoft Exchange. The Active Platform includes technologies like ActiveX.

Active Server Components (Chapter 18)

The Exchange Active Server Components is the name given to the entire suite of technologies that interlinks the groupware capabilities of Microsoft Exchange (electronic mail, scheduling, discussion groups, and document management) with the core capabilities of the Internet. The Internet aspect of the Exchange Active Server Components provides the ability for an organization to break the barriers of a closed proprietary corporate messaging and communications infrastructure, and to open up the resources so its employees, clients, or strategic vendors can participate in corporate communication processes.

Active Server Pages (Chapter 18)

Active Server Pages is a technology integrated into the Microsoft Internet Information Server that provides the services necessary to activate Active Server functions within Microsoft Exchange. The Active Server functions in Microsoft Exchange include providing a Web-based client, like the Web Outlook Client, that provides Internet access to any user with a Web browser client software where the DOS, Windows, or Macintosh version of the software is not compatible.

ActiveX (Chapter 18)

ActiveX is a set of core technologies that provides multiplatform interoperability of functions of how information is provided by the Active Server and displayed to the user of an Active Desktop.

All-in-One Mail (Chapter 9)

All-in-One Mail is a groupware messaging system provided in a DEC minicomputer environment. The product is now known as TeamLinks. Users of the messaging system in a DEC environment can connect to a Microsoft Exchange environment through the implementation of an X.400 connector for message interchange.

Alpha Processor (Chapter 7)

The Alpha processor is a RISC-based processor in higher-end Digital servers that provides processing capabilities 20-30 percent faster than comparable Intel-based processors. Digital has two processor generations available, the 21064 and the 21164, with speeds ranging from 200 megahertz to 350 megahertz.

AppleTalk (Chapter 19)

AppleTalk is the standard protocol used by Apple Macintosh computers in a local area networking environment. AppleTalk is synonymous to TCP/IP as a protocol. Microsoft Windows NT provides support for AppleTalk through the implementation of the Microsoft Windows NT Services for the Macintosh that is included with Windows NT.

ARL (Chapter 6)

See Access Rights List.

Asynchronous Modem (Chapter 9)

An asynchronous modem is a standard dial-up modem. Today, the standard speeds for modems are 14.4 kilobit, 28.8 kilobit, or 33.6 kilobit. Modems send data over phone lines, converting it from digital to analog and back again.

ATEC (Chapter 10)

See Authorized Technical Education Center.

Attachment (Chapter 2)

An attachment is a file added to an electronic mail message sent along with the message. Rather than sending just a text message, an electronic mail user can attach a word processing document, graphic file, sound file, or other information along with the mail message. The receiver of the message and attachment can launch a program to access the attached file.

Authorized Technical Education Center (Chapter 10)

An Authorized Technical Education Center, or better known as an ATEC ("ay-tek"), is a training center that offers Microsoft training classes ranging from desktop applications, like Microsoft Windows 95 or Microsoft Word, as well as server-based applications such as Microsoft Exchange administration, Microsoft Windows NT networking, and the like. An ATEC employs instructors that have received extensive training and have passed certification courses to demonstrate competency in providing training in the course curriculum.

Backbone (Chapter 4)

In a local area or a wide area network, a backbone is the trunk or cluster where the file servers, gateways, and host systems in the organization are connected to provide the infrastructure of the data communication and information system for the organization. The backbone receives it name from the cable trunk line where all of the major devices on the network are connected.

Backup Domain Controller (Chapter 4)

A backup domain controller, or commonly called the BDC, is a component of the Windows NT user and resource security system that maintains a copy of the domain security from the primary domain controller. The BDC provides distributed logon access authentication to users on the network as well as a fault tolerant replica of the network security information in the event of a primary domain controller failure.

Banyan Systems (Chapter 6)

Banyan Systems is a Massachusetts-based company whose network operating system, Banyan Vines, is widely respected for its sophisticated directory services called StreetTalk that can support wide area networks in the tens and hundreds of thousands of users.

Baseline (Chapter 10)

The baseline on a project plan is the amount of time or money required in each phase. The baseline can then be compared with actual project costs and installation dates to see how closely the implementation is following the work plan.

bcc: (Chapter 2)

See Blind Carbon Copy.

Bindery (Chapter 6)

Under Novell NetWare v3.x, the user name and security information are stored in what Novell calls a Bindery. The Bindery is a database of user names, passwords, and security rights that a user is assigned for access to file servers. It also includes a database of security access by users for specific files on file servers throughout the network.

Blind Carbon Copy (Chapter 2)

When a user sends a copy of a mail message to an individual and wants to send a copy to another user without the original recipient knowing, the second recipient receives what is known as a blind carbon copy. It is indicated in the address header by bcc:.

Broadcast Storm (Chapter 8)

There are a number of different uses of this term; however, in the context of this chapter, a broadcast storm refers to the mass distribution of mail messages to hundreds if not thousands of electronic mail users. A messaging broadcast storm may be generated on purpose during the mass distribution of an electronic message to a number of recipients, or it could be an accidental reply to all recipients of a message distribution list.

Business Process Re-Engineering (Chapter 5)

Business process re-engineering (BPR) has become a popular process in the information technology industry as organizations find that they need to change the way they do business to either maintain their competitiveness or to surpass their competition.

CAPTURE (Chapter 6)

In a Novell network, the CAPTURE command allows a user to redirect printing to a network printer (for example, CAPTURE /Q=LASERPTR). Compatibility from a Windows client to access Novell resources emulates the CAPTURE command so that the clients on an NT network can access printers on a NetWare network.

Carbon Copy (Chapter 2)

Just as in a common letter where a copy of the message is sent to one or more recipients other than the main addresee, in the computer electronic messaging

business, a carbon copy is a copy (cc:) of a message to another individual or group of individuals. Typically, the recipient of a message is requested to respond to the message, whereas carbon copy recipients are not required to respond to
the message.

CAST (Chapter 12)

CAST is a security system that uses 40- and 128-bit encryption algorithms to encode electronic messages as they transfer from user to user of the messaging environment. CAST was created by Carlisle Adams and Stafford Tavares, thus the achronym. Microsoft Exchange supports both CAST and DES encryption standards.

cc: (Chapter 2)

See Carbon Copy.

cc:Mail (Chapter 8)

cc:Mail is a direct competitor of the Microsoft Mail file-based electronic messaging system, and is sold and distributed by IBM/Lotus Software, formerly Lotus Software. Because of cc:Mail's popularity, Microsoft Exchange provides a series of tools for users of cc:Mail to integrate or migrate their existing messaging system to Microsoft Exchange.

CGI (Chapter 17)

See Common Gateway Interface.

Clustering (Chapter 13)

When an organization needs uninterrupted networking operations or more processing power than a single network file server can provide, it can implement a cluster of servers. Clustered servers share a common hard drive subsystem, so that if one server fails, the other server continues to be operational. The failed system can be repaired and reconnected to the environment while maintaining a continued operation of the networking operation. In the next generation of server clustering (due out mid to late 1997), the clustered server pair will also provide combined server processing performance in addition to just server failure prevention.

CPU (Chapter 7)

Central Processing Unit. This is the primary computer chip that processes the data. For example, it might be an Intel Pentium or a Digital Alpha processor chip.

Collabra Share (Chapter 9)

Owned by Netscape Communications, Collabra Share provides groupware intranet capabilities to the Netscape family of products. Collabra Share is known for its ability to provide an organization with file or document sharing, discussion group communication management, and shared resource management.

Common Gateway Interface (Chapter 17)

The common gateway interface, or commonly known as CGI, is the scripting language used to link an Internet home page with other Internet functions to process a series of tasks. A CGI script may take data typed into a form and send that information into a SQL database. A CGI script could be used to launch an application.

Computer Telephony Integration (Chapter 16)

Computer Telephony Integration, or CTI, is the interconnection between an organization's computer network and its phone system. It could be as simple as connecting the phone system so that it dials the phone number selected by the user from a database. With Microsoft Exchange, CTI includes the ability to integrate an organization's voicemail system into Microsoft Exchange so that the users of the voicemail system can retrieve, forward, or send voicemail messages directly from the Microsoft Exchange client software.

Concatenating Names (Chapter 12)

Concatenating means to link structures together. Concatenating names means to take two or more names and create one out of them. Microsoft Exchange will concatenate a common name and surname to create a user's e-mail name. For example, Jill Smith might become jsmith in an e-mail system where the first letter of the individual's name is concatenated with the individual's last name.

Connectors (Chapter 8)

A term used within Microsoft Exchange to describe a gateway that is tightly integrated into the core Microsoft Exchange communication system. Connectors tend to support a broader range of message and communications links that include e-mail and schedule interchange, and user list name directory synchronization. The connector resides within the Exchange services for better services management.

Cryptography (Chapter 12)

Cryptography in Microsoft Exchange is used to encrypt messages and information within the Exchange environment to secure communications between users or between Exchange servers. Microsoft Exchange supports both the DES and the CAST encryption standards.

CTI (Chapter 16)

See Computer Telephony Integration.

Data Encryption Standard Security Algorithm (Chapter 12)

The Data Encryption Standard security algorithm, or DES, is a 64-bit/56-bit encryption standard used in Microsoft Exchange to secure communication between users. The encryption process requires a Key Management Server on the Exchange network to encode and decode messages within an Exchange environment.

Dedicated Server (Chapter 4)

A dedicated server is a computer system that operates as a file server within the organization. Microsoft Windows NT Server is primarily a dedicated server environment; however, some smaller organizations may choose that a user have the organization's file server as his or her workstation. This would make the file server a nondedicated server.

Demand-Push/Demand-Pull (Chapter 5)

In an electronic messaging environment, e-mails are said to be pushed to users (demand-push) because the sender of the message creates the messages, selects the recipients from a user list, and sends the information. In a groupware or intranet environment, information is said to be pulled by the users (demand-pull) as they search for the information they require and pull the information into their desktop to be viewed when they need it.

DES (Chapter 12)
See Data Encryption Standard Security Algorithm.

DID (Chapter 16)
See Direct Inward Dialing.

Digital Encryption (Chapter 2)
Digital encryption is when message files are encoded by a sender before being sent to a message recipient. When the recipient receives the message, he or she needs to enter an encryption code to unencode the message. Microsoft Exchange supports both DES and CAST encryption standards.

Digital Signatures (Chapter 2)
Microsoft Exchange provides an authentication process known as digital signatures to authenticate the sender of a message. During the authentication process, the sender must enter a password to confirm that he or she is the originator of the message and the actual individual who owns the mailbox for the user. The recipient can validate the information by checking for the encoding, or digital signature, of the message.

Direct Inward Dialing (Chapter 16)
Also commonly called DID ("dee-eye-dee"), DID is a service provided by the phone company that allows an organization to provide unique fax numbers for each of the individuals within its group to all be directed to a single phone line (or a series of designated incoming phone lines). When a network faxing software system is integrated into the system, the fax software listens to the incoming fax call and, from the DID call sequence, can determine the individual recipient of the fax. This allows the fax software to route the message directly to the intended recipient.

Directory Service Manager for NetWare (Chapter 6)

The Directory Service Manager for NetWare, or DSNM, is an add-on to Microsoft Windows NT that synchronizes a Novell NetWare user list into a Microsoft Windows NT user list for the purpose of maintaining an automated link between the two environments. When an organization uses the DSNM and changes information about a user in the Novell network administration software, the user information is automatically updated in the Windows NT administration software.

Directory Store (Chapter 1)

The directory store in Microsoft Exchange keeps track of the users on the Exchange server, monitors the security rights of the users in regard to their access to information in public folders or individual messages, and maintains all of the address information for internal and external users on the network. The directory store is queried any time there is a transaction on the Exchange server to verify whether a user, resource, or folder store resides on the current server or another server in which the Exchange server has information.

Directory Synchronization (Chapter 9)

The process in which the user names from one post office system are updated with those of another post office system, thus maintaining a current list of users in the organization's address book.

Directory Synchronization Server and Requester (Chapter 9)

In a Microsoft Mail system, the process to synchronize the user directory between multiple post offices is called DirSync. The DirSync Requester Server post office sends its post office address to the DirSync Server. The DirSync Server compiles all the addresses it receives from all DirSync Requester Servers. From that compilation it creates a global address list (GAL) for the organization, which is then sent to all requester post offices. When the requester receives the GAL, it updates its list of users in the organization with the new information it has received.

Disk Fault Tolerance (Chapter 7)

In a process to minimize system failures, high availability file servers have a system called disk fault tolerance that maintains a duplication process of hard disk information. Information can be mirrored or duplexed, meaning that there is a second hard drive to which information is written simultaneously, thus providing two hard drives with the exact information as a security measure in the event of a hard drive failure. Newer disk fault tolerance processes like RAID provide similar redundancy but for larger disk subsystems.

.DLL File (Chapter 7)

A dynamic link library file, or .DLL file, is an application program used in a Microsoft Windows environment that provides a function to the operation of a Windows session. A .DLL file may be invoked to sort names in a list, or process information before being printed, or invoke a process to quickly search and retrieve information from a database. In an old DOS environment, these add-in programs were called memory resident or TSR (terminate and stay resident) programs that invoked a process when requested; however, in a Windows environment, since memory is not limited to just 640KB, a program file can be invoked in the memory space without the interaction of the system user.

Domain Controllers (Chapter 10)

A domain controller is specific to an NT network. It is the server (either a primary domain controller or a backup domain controller) that authenticates logons, and maintains the master database and network security.

Domain Name System—DNS (Chapter 6)

The DNS is an Internet process for translating server names into IP addresses. Since names are easier to remember than a string of four numbers separated by periods (like 204.31.169.77), the DNS makes it easier to successfully search for an Internet resource like http://www.inaoak.com.

Downstream Post Office (Chapter 9)

A downstream post office manages gateway functions that reside on a different post office. It is used to consolidate server processes into a primary system with secondary systems just forwarding messages to the primary post office for processing. Many organizations use the downstream post office process when they have multiple mail post offices; however, they only have one connection to the Internet. All of the subordinate post offices send their messages upstream to a primary post office for outbound Internet messages, and incoming Internet messages get forwarded from the primary post office to the downstream post office of the recipient.

Dynamic Host Configuration Protocol— DHCP (Chapter 6)

DHCP stands for Dynamic Host Configuration Protocol. It is a protocol that assigns IP addresses dynamically so that an organization does not need to statically assign IP addresses to each user.

Electronic Forms Designer (Chapter 15)

The Electronic Forms Designer software in Microsoft Exchange enables users to create forms with questions and fill-in fields that provide a structure to messages sent within the organization. The Electronic Forms Designer software is included free with Microsoft Exchange and comes as a 16-bit version that is compatible with all Microsoft Exchange clients, or a 32-bit version that works with all Microsoft Outlook clients.

Electronic Messaging or Electronic Mail— E-mail (Chapter 1)

E-mail is the common term for electronic messaging. Electronic mail applications manage the receipt and distribution of mail messages both within the organization and between the organization and outside networks. E-mail generally refers to text messages sent electronically over computer systems from one computer user to another. The users can be within an organization, in another country, or at any point in between. E-mail messages may contain file attachments created in a multitude of applications such as charts, graphs, and images.

E-mail (Chapter 1)

See Electronic messaging.

Ethernet (Chapter 7)

Ethernet is a common physical network communication system for local area networks. There are two common types of Ethernet cabling available. One is called 10BaseT ("ten-base-tee") and the other is called Coax. Most organizations install twisted-pair phone type cabling for network connections, thus 10BaseT is the popular standard for Ethernet cabling. In addition to cabling, in an Ethernet environment an organization needs to have a network adapter, as well as an Ethernet hub, in each workstation or file server. The Ethernet hub is the central connection where all Ethernet cables connect to form a star cabling scheme.

EtherTalk (Chapter 19)

EtherTalk is the protocol used by Macintosh computers that is an encapsulation of the native AppleTalk protocol within an Ethernet communications stream. EtherTalk allows a Macintosh to share computer, file, and printer resources with other Macintosh computers over the Ethernet hardware standard. Microsoft Windows NT supports EtherTalk communications through the use of the Windows NT Service for the Macintosh add-in that comes free with Microsoft Windows NT.

Eudora (Chapter 18)

Qualcomm's Eudora is an SMTP/POP3 mail client available for Macintosh, UNIX, and Windows clients, and is commonly referred to (along with Z-Mail) as the standard POP3 messaging client available.

Event Viewer (Chapter 13)

The Event Viewer is the logging software that tracks system, application, and security errors in a Windows NT environment. For Windows NT, the Event Viewer logs when the server is activated, any hardware errors such as fatal disk failures or controller adapter failures, and tracks security violations of intruders or invalid user logon attempts to the network. Since Microsoft Exchange integrates directly into Microsoft Windows NT, the Event Viewer is used to track the routing of electronic mail messages, security errors of electronic mail users, or notification of add-ins to Exchange on the processing of message information.

Firewall (Chapter 4)

A firewall is a hardware device or software program that limits the access of information from external users. A firewall is set up to block specific information, such as unauthorized query requests into an organization, from passing through its structure. A firewall is the first defense an organization has to prevent hackers from damaging an organization's information.

FPNW (Chapter 6)

FPNW is defined as File and Print Services for Netware. This is an optional Windows NT add-in that allows an NT server to look like a Novell NetWare server to NetWare clients.

Fully Trusted Domain Model (Chapter 4)

In a fully trusted domain model, two or more domains are independently administered, but fully trust each other for the access of domain resources. A trust between domains allows users from one domain to gain access to resources in another domain based on administrator-defined parameters. A fully trusted domain is commonly used by organizations administered in regions or divisions. Because each domain is independently administered, the administrators for each domain have full control to add, delete, and modify users within their domains. Each domain has one primary domain controller and can have multiple backup domain controllers, file servers, and domain resources.

GANTT Chart (Chapter 10)

A GANTT chart is a tool used by project managers that summarizes a project based on the sequence of events. It helps project managers track information, through text and graphs, about the individual tasks that comprise the project plan. GANTT charts are created electronically by using a project management application such a Microsoft Project.

Gateway (Chapter 9)

A gateway is a stand-alone PC that looks in the e-mail server for messages that are being directed for transmissions to another network within the organization, or to a mail system outside the organization, such as the Internet.

Gigabyte (Chapter 7)

In mathematical terms, a gigabyte is 1,000,000,000 bytes; however, in relative computer terms, hard disk drives are measured in gigabytes of disk space. A typical network file server may have 4 gigabytes or 8 gigabytes of disk storage, and most personal computers are now coming with one or two gigabytes of hard drive storage. With the average five-page word processing document taking up 50,000 bytes (or 50 kilobytes of disk space), the average home computer system can store 20,000 word processing documents.

Groupware (Chapter 1)

Groupware is a term for LAN-based software that typically includes e-mail, scheduling, and discussion threads. Discussion threads are "conversations" that take place electronically. One person writes a message to the team and the entire team reads it. If someone responds, all other team members can see the response. It allows for a discussion to take place without having users in the same place and without users communicating at the same time.

Groupware is often used throughout an organization to support virtual workgroups. Virtual workgroups are a team of staff that is tasked to complete a project. But instead of requiring face-to-face meetings, this software allows for computer documents to be shared by other team members in order to further complete their task, as with discussion threads. Groupware is said to allow projects to be completed faster and with less effort than in the past.

GroupWise (Chapter 8)

GroupWise is the Novell Inc. groupware application that is a direct competitor of the Microsoft Exchange messaging environment. GroupWise includes electronic mail, personal and group scheduling, personal address book, discussion groups, task management, and document management. Microsoft Exchange provides a migration tool to assist organizations in converting their user names and mailboxes from Novell GroupWise to Microsoft Exchange.

Hierarchy (Chapter 4)

The reference to a hierarchy in Microsoft Exchange is in the folder structure an organization uses to store public and private messages. Similar to sub-directories in an MS-DOS environment, folders within Microsoft Exchange take on the hierarchy of a branch, trunk, and root file system.

Hot Spare Server (Chapter 13)

In an environment where server downtime is unacceptable, an organization may implement a backup procedure that involves the use of a hot spare server. The hot spare server will be a fully configured file server with similar hard disk storage space and system processor capabilities. In the event of a primary system failure, the hot spare server will replace the failed system, potentially by having faulty components in the primary server replaced by components from the hot spare server to minimize system downtime.

HTML (Chapter 15)
See Hypertext Markup Language.

Hypertext Markup Language (Chapter 15)
The Hypertext Markup Language, or HTML, is the standard document language used in the creation and implementation of Internet home pages. Because HTML is a published standard, anyone who creates content on a Web page creates the information in the standard HTML document creation language. When a user browses the Web page from the Internet, the individual's browser, regardless if it is a Windows, Windows 95, Macintosh, or UNIX browser, displays the contents of the Web page on the individual's screen. It is this commonality that makes using the Internet independent of the operating environment.

IBM Profs (Chapter 1)
IBM Profs is the electronic mail system used on IBM mainframe computers. Millions of users use IBM Profs on a daily basis as they use their connection to the mainframe for normal information access. Microsoft views both the industry trend toward downsizing and the migration to desktop personal computers from centralized mainframe systems as an opportunity to convert the millions of Profs users into Microsoft Exchange users.

IDC (Chapter 17)
See Internet Database Connector.

Information Store (Chapter 1)
The information store in Microsoft Exchange includes the private information store that contains information about the users' mailboxes, and the public information store that contains information about the public folders. The information store is similar to the table of contents of a book, and has a list of all mail messages in each user's inbox and personal folders that point to messages residing in the message database. The message database is separate from the information store and is the depository for all messages on the Microsoft Exchange Server. When a message is created, deleted, or modified, the information store maintains a log of the transaction and updates or modifies its link to the message database and the data in the message database.

Integrate (Chapter 6)

In the computer industry, the word integrate refers to the ability of an organization to interconnect various types of components, from desktop/user applications to desktop and network computer equipment. Integrate also refers to the ability to configure electronic messaging and communication systems, as well as to configure a complete computer technology information solution.

Internet (Chapter 1)

Also known as the information superhighway, the Internet is the world's largest computer network. It consists of thousands of smaller networks in many different countries all interconnected to each other. Originally, it was intended for government and academic use, and there was intentionally no central hub or computer system to manage it, with the theory that it may need to serve as a communications tool in the event of a war. Recently, commercial businesses have been allowed to participate, which has yielded unprecedented growth.

Online services such as the Microsoft Network and America Online have allowed any computer user to have access to Internet e-mail. With the Internet, e-mail can be exchanged between people around the world at a very reasonable cost. Another reason for the growth has been the development of Web browsers such as Internet Explorer and Netscape Navigator. This provides the ability for anybody to publish an unlimited amount of information at a very reasonable cost. The browsers allow end users to look up information, similar to how people might do research at library on a topic of interest to them.

Internet Database Connector (Chapter 17)

The Internet Database Connector provides an easy method for an organization to gain access to SQL information through a simple Web link, making data information accessible either to the Internet or to an intranet.

Internet Mail Service (Chapter 18)

The Internet mail service is the function in Microsoft Exchange that authenticates a remote trusted Internet mail user to the Exchange server for POP3 mail services. When the POP3 client software requests messages, the request goes to the POP3 server service which then requests Microsoft

Exchange to send the client the messages from the user's Inbox. All of these functions are managed by the Internet mail service.

Internet Service Provider (Chapter 18)

An Internet service provider is a company that provides organizations with a connection between the organization's local area network and the Internet. These providers can be seen as the on-ramp to the information superhighway. Some of the commonly-known personal Internet service providers include companies like America Online or the Microsoft Network (MSN). Commercial providers that connect businesses to the Internet include organizations like PSInet, Netcom, or UUnet.

Intranet (Chapter 1)

An intranet is an internal groupware system that allows users to share internal company information such as policies, procedures, or discussion group information.

IP Address (Chapter 6)

The Internet Protocol (IP) address is a unique station identification for a computer on a TCP/IP network. An organization must get a series of IP addresses by registering with the InterNIC. Every organization must have a unique IP address for messages to successfully be sent on the Internet (just as every business must have a unique address for US mail to reach it).

IPX/SPX (Chapter 4)

Novell developed and standardized IPX/SPX as their communications protocol. For Windows NT to be compatible with Novell networks, Microsoft had to speak the same protocol (IPX/SPX) language as Novell, so the NWLink protocol set allows a Windows NT server to speak the basic core language of the two environments.

ISDN (Chapter 20)

Integrated Services Digital Network, ISDN, is a digital dial-up phone service that takes the normal telephone line maximum thruput of 33.6 kilobit per second and boosts the capability to 128 kilobit per second. Because ISDN is digital, it provides higher thruput of communications. Additionally, because ISDN is a dial-up service, the initiator of an ISDN call can dial any ISDN recipient. Unlike digital lease lines that are fixed from point to point, ISDN provides a selection of destination locations. In many parts of the country, ISDN phone line services cost the same as regular phone calls, so organizations are installing ISDN to get faster thruput for approximately the same cost per minute.

ISP (Chapter 18)
See Internet Service Provider.

Key Management Server—KM Server (Chapter 12)
The Key Management function manages the allocation and authentication of the digital signatures and digital encryption on the network.

Large Internet Packet—LIP (Chapter 6)
In NetWare 4.*x*, LIP allows for the size of internet packets to be larger than the former maximum size if the router can support it. The previous maximum packet size was 576 bytes; however, some networks, such as Ethernet and Token Ring, can support larger packets. LIP allows the workstation to determine the largest packet size that its network can support and send packets up to that size.

LDAP (Chapter 18)
See Lightweight Directory Access Protocol.

Least Cost Routing (Chapter 16)
In telephone systems as well as wide area network communications, the ability to route information across the backbone of a network has a lower cost than dialing long distance. Least cost routing takes advantage of established network infrastructures to minimize the cost of the call. For example, if an organization has an office in San Francisco and an office in New York City with a wide area lease line between the locations, and a user in San Francisco needs to send a fax to a user in Boston, rather than having the San Francisco fax server send the fax long distance from San Francisco to Boston, a least cost route function in the fax system will allow the fax to be transported from San Francisco to New York over the company's lease line, and then it'll be faxed from the New York office to the Boston office.

Licensing (Chapter 7)

Software licensing is a necessary requirement for all organizations for evaluating their usage and for complying with the legal requirements of the software. Microsoft Exchange comes as a server as well as a client component, called client access licenses (CALs). An organization needs to purchase the appropriate number of software licenses for the users in the organization using the Microsoft Exchange product.

Lightweight Directory Access Protocol (Chapter 18)

LDAP is another Internet protocol just as POP3, TCP/IP, and SMTP have been defined so far. LDAP in Exchange v5.0 provides the ability of an LDAP client to access the Microsoft Exchange Server's directory information. The directory information on an Exchange server is the list of user names, e-mail addresses, or even phone numbers, pager numbers, or manager name information. While most organizations would not want all of this information available to just anyone surfing the Internet, a portion of this information is useful for Internet mail users who know the name of an individual they want to send the message to, but who do not need to know the person's e-mail address. This would be similar to a "dial-by-name" directory look-up function on a voicemail system. Additionally, the use of directory information access could assist an individual who has a person's e-mail address but not the person's mailing address or phone number. Rather than having to distribute directory level information manually, much of this information can be made available to an individual automatically through the use of LDAP.

Linked Processes in a Project (Chapter 10)

Some processes are sequential and can only be started once a specific event has taken place. In other words, the delay of a preceding event can affect whether the next sequential task can be completed. For example, the configuration of a server cannot be completed until the equipment arrives. Similarly, the equipment cannot arrive until a purchase order is placed, and, the equipment cannot be ordered unless its configuration is determined. Each of these tasks is linked, and a delay or change in any of them will affect the initiation of the final task. As an example, the configuration of the server cannot be started without the receipt of the equipment. Thus, the required task must be completed, or the preceding task is said to be "linked" to the current task. The project management software has the ability to link tasks in this way so that a delay or change in preceding tasks can be made, and the subsequent effect upon the balance of the project can be visually displayed for analysis.

Link Monitor (Chapter 13)

The link monitor in Exchange can be configured to check for problems with the transportation of message or network connections with other servers or other messaging systems (internal and external) to ensure that valid communication links are active. Link monitors are configured in the Exchange Administrator program and can perform *pings* to other messaging systems or servers with the anticipation of a response. If a threshold is reached without a response, the remote device can be declared offline. When this occurs, an alert can be generated in the form of an electronic message sent to a designated individual or group of individuals on the network, or the alert can be logged on a server in the network domain. In either case, the alerts may be linked to an external pager system to inform the administrator of a system failure or potential problem.

List Server (Chapter 18)

A List Server is an automated information distribution system set up by organizations to distribute information to subscribers. The information may be technical notes, press releases, write papers, marketing information, or other general information. List Server-distributed information is analogous to wire services where information is distributed and is "hot off the presses." Individuals may elect to subscribe to a List Server. Typically subscribing to a List Server is as simple as sending an e-mail message to a designated e-mail address for the organization that is managing the List Server. Once subscribed, the individual will be sent information any time information is distributed. The List Server knows who the subscriber is by the return mail address of the user who sent the subscription request. A user can unsubscribe from a List Server just as easily as he or she subscribed to it.

LOADSIM (Chapter 7)

To assist organizations in determining whether they have properly sized the Microsoft Exchange file server for their environment, Microsoft includes a load simulation utility, loadsim.exe, with Microsoft Exchange. The LOADSIM program will simulate all messaging and groupware functions including sending, receiving, replying to, saving, deleting, and forwarding e-mails; user interaction with public folders; personal and group appointment scheduling; and electronic form access and use.

Local Area Network—LAN (Chapter 1)

A LAN ("lahn") is a data communications network that covers a relatively small area, for example, within a building or a campus. At a minimum, it is made up of a communications link, a server, a workstation, and a network operating system. LANs allow any user with physical and security access to use shared network resources such as file servers, applications, printers, and electronic mail systems.

LocalTalk (Chapter 19)

LocalTalk is the original form of networking hardware that Apple Macintosh computers used to communicate with each other. Synonymous with Ethernet or Token Ring, AppleTalk requires an adapter in each computer system and a cable connecting the systems together. LocalTalk was designed to support the interconnection of Macintosh computers through regular silver satin phone cable, thus making the cost of networking Macintosh computers affordable. Most organizations have replaced their LocalTalk connections with EtherTalk to improve the performance by approximately 10-15 times.

Login/Logon (Chapter 4)

The logon process (also sometimes called the login, log-in, or log-on process) is used by individuals to gain access to a computer system or file server to authenticate their security access to the system. A logon requires a user name and a password that matches the security system of the network.

Lotus Notes (Chapter 8)

Lotus Notes is the groupware application by IBM/Lotus Software. Lotus Notes includes electronic messaging, group discussions, a database and data development language, and document routing capabilities. Lotus Notes latest release, Lotus Domino, includes the ability to link Lotus Notes information to the Internet. For organizations that have both Lotus Notes and Microsoft Exchange, there are companies that make gateways between the two for the sharing of messages and information, and migration tools exist to convert from Lotus Notes to Microsoft Exchange.

MacTCP (Chapter 19)

MacTCP is the TCP/IP language supported by Apple Macintosh computers. Normally a Macintosh communicates over the AppleTalk language; however, because of limitations of the AppleTalk protocol, many organizations switch to Ethernet for their hardware and use MacTCP as their communications protocol. MacTCP allows a Macintosh computer to communicate with an Exchange server over TCP/IP.

Maildata (Chapter 9)

The maildata is where messages and attachments on a Microsoft Mail network are stored.

Mail Message File—MMF (Chapter 9)

The Mail Message File (MMF) is where Windows clients access messages and attachments on the MS Mail on the server.

Mainframe (Chapter 1)

Before PCs and LANs were invented, mainframes were commonly used by organizations to process data. Mainframes systems are transaction oriented; that is, a user interacts with an application that stores its information on the mainframe system throughout the transaction process.

Mapping (Chapter 6)

To access files on a Novell network, NetWare individuals use the map command to specify a drive letter to a Novell drive share (ex MAP F:=MYSERVER\DISKC:). The Windows NT client software needs to be able to emulate the Novell map command so that it can be compatible with file access to a Novell NetWare network.

MCI Mail (Chapter 1)

MCI Mail was one of the first public messaging systems that allowed organizations to send and receive e-mail messages across geographically dispersed locations. Users of MCI Mail were able to dial in to the MCI Mail system and create, read, and delete mail messages. With network-based messaging systems like Microsoft Exchange, organizations can send and receive mail messages with other MCI Mail users through gateways between Microsoft Exchange and MCI. Many organizations find that the security of a message sent over MCI to be higher than that of one sent over the general Internet since MCI Mail is a private messaging network.

Message Transfer Agent—MTA (Chapter 9)

The message transfer agent is the component that routes a message between other Exchange servers or to other agents that may manage routing of messages to the Internet, to a fax modem, or to other external services. The message transfer agent handles all message routing internal and external to the Exchange server. If an organization has more than one MS Mail post office, it probably has an external gateway to route messages from one post office to another. This external gateway is also known as a message transfer agent (MTA.).

Microsoft—MS (Chapter 9)

Microsoft is the manufacturer of DOS, Windows, Windows NT, Exchange, and many other software applications and products.

Microsoft Certified Professional (Chapter 10)

A Microsoft Certified Professional is a specialist who passes a core Microsoft Windows NT certification test as well as a specialization exam. In the case of a Microsoft Exchange certification, an individual would take the Windows NT Enterprise Networking exam as well as the Microsoft Exchange Server exam. The content knowledge required to pass these exams is taught in the ATEC training courses on the products and technologies.

Microsoft Certified Solution Developer—MCSD (Chapter 10)

A Microsoft Certified Solution Developer is required to pass a series of exams including core Microsoft Windows NT certification tests, plus have a focus on application development tools such as C++ or Visual Basic. The certification is mainly for developers, whose expertise will be in the creation of application-based solutions.

Microsoft Certified System Engineer (Chapter 10)

A Microsoft Certified System Engineer is required to pass a series of exams including core Microsoft Windows NT certification tests as well as a number of electives. The certification is more comprehensive across a handful of specializations, demonstrating the individual's technical expertise in a variety of fields and practices.

Microsoft Consulting Services—MCS (Chapter 10)

Microsoft Consulting Services (MCS), a division of Microsoft, works with large organizations or with organizations that have very unique or extremely strategic Microsoft integration implementation needs. MCS works on a consultative arrangement with clients in conjunction with specialized Microsoft Solution Providers to assist clients with their Microsoft Exchange plans or implementation needs.

Microsoft Mail for AppleTalk Networks (Chapter 8)

Microsoft Mail for AppleTalk Networks was Microsoft's e-mail system for Macintosh computers. Purchased in 1995 by Quarterdeck, Microsoft Mail for AppleTalk Networks has become Quarterdeck's Mail for Macs. The Microsoft Mail for AppleTalk Networks provides e-mail services for organizations that have predominately Apple Macintosh computers. Microsoft provides migration tools and a gateway between the Microsoft Mail for AppleTalk to Microsoft Exchange.

Microsoft Mail for PC Networks (Chapter 8)

The Microsoft Mail for PC Networks, better known as Microsoft Mail, or MS-Mail, was the e-mail messaging standard from Microsoft prior to Microsoft Exchange. Microsoft Mail provides a reliable e-mail system for LANs and WANs as well as the optional interconnectivity to the Internet, MCI Mail, or message faxing.

Microsoft Solution Providers—MSP (Chapter 10)

Microsoft has a number of independent organizations around the globe called Microsoft Solution Providers that specialize in working with Microsoft products and technologies. Each Microsoft Solution Provider has specialties that range from design planning, installation, training, application development, or support services on a variety of Microsoft products. These range from desktop application products like Windows 95 or Office 97 to the Microsoft BackOffice products like Microsoft Exchange, System Management Server, and SQL Server, and even to organizations specializing in application tools such as C++, ActiveX, or Microsoft Access.

Microsoft Solution Provider Member (Chapter 10)

Microsoft has two levels of solution providers. The first level is referred to as Microsoft Solution Provider Members. There are over 11,000 Solution Provider Members worldwide who specialize in Microsoft products and technologies.

Microsoft Solution Provider Partner (Chapter 10)

A partner-level solution provider is in the top ten percent of solution providers who have committed to a higher level of technical certification and additional training on Microsoft products. Solution Provider Partners receive priority technical assistance from Microsoft as well as additional training and resource allocation. If they are experienced in a product line or technology, Microsoft Solution Provider Partners can be among the best resources available on Microsoft technologies.

Migration (Chapter 6)

When an organization decides to convert from one system to another, the process is called migration. A migration process may involve a conversion from Novell NetWare to Microsoft Windows NT, or a conversion from Microsoft Mail to Microsoft Exchange.

Migration Tool for NetWare (Chapter 6)

The Migration Tool for NetWare (nwconv.exe), converts Novell network security information such as a user's login name, file access, and group information to Microsoft Windows NT equivalent items. The Migration Tool for NetWare is used by an organization that wants to populate an NT server with the login names and basic security information of a previous NetWare network, or by an organization that has a longer-term strategy involving a co-existence of NetWare and NT, synchronized by Directory Services Manager for NetWare on an ongoing basis.

MIME (Chapter 8)

See Multipurpose Internet Mail Extension.

Mini-computer (Chapter 1)

Mini-computers were designed to provide similar services as a mainframe computer, but for a smaller workgroup of users or to manage a specialized process or service. Some of the major mini-computer systems include the IBM AS/400 or the DEC Vax.

MMF (Chapter 1)

See Mail Message File.

Modem (Chapter 20)

Technically, a modem is a device that *mo*dulates and *dem*odulates information from a digitally-based computer communications system to an analog communications system so that it can be transported over analog telephone lines. Modems are the primary method for mobile and remote computing because of the availability of phone lines everywhere that can be used to transmit and receive information. Typical modem speeds are 14.4, 28.8, or 33.6 kilobits per second.

MTA (Chapter 1)

See Message Transfer Agent.

Multiple Master Domain Model (Chapter 4)

The multiple master domain model consists of two or more single master domains that have centralized user security management in each of the single master domains. Every user is created and maintained in one of these first-tier master domains. The second tier consists of resource domains that manage file servers, printers, and other domain resources. In this model, the first-tier master domains are connected to every other master domain in a two-way trust relationship. The second-tier resource domains trust the first-tier master domains and can trust other resource domains, but the first-tier master domains do not trust the second-tier resource domains.

Multipurpose Internet Mail Extension (Chapter 1)

The multipurpose Internet mail extension (MIME) under RFC 1521 defined how actual message body parts and their contents should be managed in a message transfer. MIME allows different kinds of data to be sent as different body parts; thus text, word processing document attachments, audio files, and graphical images are independently tagged, separated, converted, sent, and reassembled.

NCP (Chapter 6)

NCP refers to Netware Core Protocol. It is an application layer protocol and is Novell NetWare's internal language for communications between servers and workstations. It provides a means of requesting file and print services, accessing NDS and the bindery.

NetBIOS (Chapter 6)

NetBIOS stands for Network Basic Input/Output System. It provides a method of communication between an application and the network. The NetBIOS name is the name a user calls the workstation the first time it is configured. For example, it could be JanetsPC or JimsWS.

NetBEUI (Chapter 4)

Pronounced "net-boo-eee", NetBEUI is the default communications protocol used by Microsoft Windows NT to communicate from system to system within the network. Microsoft Exchange can communicate with each other or with Exchange clients over NetBEUI. NetBEUI is more efficient than other mediums because the query and request are handled at the core server-to-server level of communications. In a small network or in a relatively closed single site/single domain environment, NetBEUI is more efficient than something like TCP/IP for the server-to-server or client-to-server communications, and can provide the fastest Exchange communications performance of any of the various options.

NetWare Directory Services—NDS (Chapter 6)

In a Novell NetWare v4.x network, the NetWare Directory Service (NDS) maintains a list of all network resources including users, printers, file servers, file access, file security, and resource management on the network. The NDS is the core to the security and resource management system in a NetWare environment.

Network Adapter (Chapter 7)

The network adapter is the physical device that connects a user's workstation to a file server for information sharing.

Network File System—NFS (Chapter 6)

NFS was developed to provide file sharing between UNIX-based systems. In an environment, there is an NFS server and an NFS client. The NFS client is said to "mount" an NFS server to gain access to the files on the server system. In an NT environment, through third-party utilities, an NT server can emulate an NFS server and allow UNIX workstations to mount an NT server for file sharing.

Network News Transfer Protocol (Chapter 18)

NNTP is the protocol in which Internet news is distributed across the Internet. On the Internet, there are thousands of newsgroups that people participate in on topics ranging from French cooking to Corvette automobiles to Hot Air Ballooning to Microsoft Exchange technical services. Over 200,000 postings to newsgroups occur each day. Users can individually log on to the Internet and read posted newsgroup messages or the user can post their own comments to the newsgroup. Some newsgroups are moderated where postings need to be reviewed before they are posted on the main newsgroup forum. Others just allow users to post information directly to the newsgroup.

Newsfeed (Chapter 18)

Newsfeeds are information streams on categorized topics that are distributed to users or organizations that want information about a particular topic or category. With a pull feed, the Exchange server initiates the connection with the Internet service provider and checks for new messages and pulls messages into the Exchange server. A pull feed provides the Exchange administrator the option of what information is desired to be pulled and the management of the inbound and outbound functional control.

NFS Host (Chapter 6)

An NFS host server is one that publishes the contents or a portion of the content of the server disk storage information for access by other users on the network.

NFS Mounting (Chapter 6)

A system that has NFS mounting capabilities can mount an NFS host server's shared disk space.

NNTP (Chapter 18)

See Network News Transfer Protocol.

Nwadmin Utility (Chapter 6)

This is the utility in a Novell NetWare v4.x environment that is used to manage the Novell Directory Services. The nwadmin utility is used to add, modify, and delete users in a NetWare v4.x environment, and it allows the network administrator to specify which files the user should have access to and the level of privileges to the files (read, write, create, modify, or delete).

NWLink (Chapter 6)

NWLink is a network protocol that supports NT/NetWare communications. This allows for the two network operating systems to communicate successfully.

Object Linking and Embedding (Chapter 2)

The Microsoft Exchange client supports object linking and the embedding of information directly into the body of the e-mail message. Rather than attaching the entire contents of a file to a document, Exchange allows for the ability to insert a link to a document that points to a common storage location without sending the entire document. This significantly minimizes the amount of messaging traffic on the network, the storage space that multiple copies of the same file create, and the number of multiple versions of a file that would exist on the network. Object embedding allows a selected portion of a document to be visually stored in an Exchange message. This portion of the embedded document can be double-clicked to open the full document for editing, viewing, or printing.

ODBC (Chapter 17)

ODBC stands for Open Database Connectivity and is the common architecture used to interchange database information from clients to servers. ODBC includes the standards in which an application can log on to a database, execute SQL database access commands, acknowledge errors and error codes, and accept and translate data information. Core to ODBC is the ODBC Application Programmers Interface (ODBC API). The ODBC API provides a common database access language that enables applications to access a variety of databases such as Microsoft SQL, Oracle, Sybase, Informix, or IBM DB/2.

ODI Client (Chapter 6)

Technically, ODI (pronounced "oh-dee-eye") stands for open datalink interface. It is the common name for the client driver or client access software to gain access to a Novell network file server. When a workstation loads the ODI client software, they are loading the protocol drivers and LAN connectivity drivers to provide the communications with Novell networks. Microsoft Windows NT has an add-in called File and Print Services for NetWare that allows a Novell ODI client to access a Windows NT file server by making the Windows NT server look like a Novell file server. This can minimize the need of an organization to convert workstations' client access software during an initial migration to NT.

OLE (Chapter 1)

See Object Linking and Embedding.

Online Standby Server (Chapter 13)

An online standby server is a system that operates in tandem with the primary server of the network which typically saves information simultaneously to the standby server. In the event of a primary server failure, with a few minor changes to the standby server configuration, the standby server can be brought online within 30-60 minutes as the new primary server, and with no loss in stored information.

Organization (Chapter 4)

The topmost component in the Microsoft Exchange hierarchy is the Microsoft Exchange organization name. The organization name is typically some level or

representation of the company name (like XYZCorp). The organization is the
largest grouping for an Exchange enterprise. When selecting the name of the
organization, it is critical to select a distinctive name that won't create a
compatibility problem with external mail systems or even versions of the
Microsoft Exchange client software. Once selected, the organization name
cannot be changed without completely reinstalling the entire Microsoft
Exchange Server software. However, the organization name has no
direct bearing on the organization's Internet domain name (like
@xyzcorp.com) because the Internet domain name for the organization
can be defined separately.

Outlook Client (Chapter 2, 3)

There are two client programs available for Exchange, the Exchange client and
the Outlook client. The Outlook client is a completely Win32 version of the
client software that runs on Windows 95 and Windows NT Workstation.

Outlook Web View (Chapter 18)

The Outlook Web View is an Active Server Pages application that enables
HTML browser users to log on and securely access their e-mail and public
folders on the network, as well as directory information. The Web View is an
HTML Web page that can be put on any Active Server on the network. Using
any Web browser that supports frames and Java (such as the Microsoft Internet
Explorer or Netscape Navigator v2.0 or higher), users from the Internet can
access this Web page which then provides logon, authentication, and mail
services to users from over the Internet. The trusted Web Exchange client can
compose messages over an HTML screen to send and receive messages. The
Outlook Web View can also be configured to provide access to shared
information folders that may have product availability reports, marketing
information, technical bulletins, or other information that can be available to
the organizations internal Exchange users through local public folders, or the
same information can be available to external access without having the need
to store information in multiple places.

Pagefile (Chapter 7)

A pagefile, also known as virtual memory, is the space reserved on a hard
drive for use whenever the system runs out of RAM. For example, if a user has

16MB of memory, has loaded six applications, and tries to launch a seventh application without sufficient memory, the system will use the pagefile to swap some of the other applications out of memory into this virtual disk file, thus opening up the RAM for the current application to load. When the user toggles to the application that happens to have been stored in memory, other components of applications are temporarily swapped into memory.

Parallel Processes in a Project (Chapter 10)

Some processes within a project can be completed concurrently without placing overwhelming demands on project resources. Parallel processes may occur when work is being completed in multiple locations or workgroups simultaneously. An example would be work being completed in multiple cities at the same time, and the two processes can take place in parallel, which results in an overlap of installation dates for these tasks. If use of the resources needed to complete the work does not overlap, completing tasks simultaneously can minimize the time necessary to finish the task, phase, or project.

PathWorks (Chapter 6)

PathWorks is network operating system used in DEC networking that is synonymous with Microsoft Windows NT Server, Novell NetWare, or Banyan Vines. Microsoft Exchange integrates into a PathWorks environment providing electronic messaging and groupware services to an infrastructure based on the DEC PathWorks operating system.

Pentium Processor (Chapter 7)

The Pentium processor is the 32-bit processor by Intel Corporation that is the most common desktop processor used in file server and workstations today. The Pentium processor is supported as a single processor or as a multi-processor version for Windows NT providing an organization the ability to scale its performance demands based on the speed and number of processors in its workstation or server.

PerfMon (Chapter 13)

See Performance Monitor Utility.

Performance Monitor Utility (Chapter 13)

The Microsoft Performance Monitor utility (also commonly called PerfMon) provides the Microsoft Exchange administrator with a tool to monitor dozens of statistics and operations on the network. PerfMon tracking options typically fall into three categories that include percentages, high counts, and events per time.

Personal Address Book—PAB (Chapter 9)

This is where Exchange stores a user's Personal Address Book, which consists of e-mail addresses that the user has saved for future reference but has not published for use by other users.

Personal Computer—PC (Chapter 1)

A personal computer is a computer system that provides independent processing and storage capabilities for users to run personal applications like word processing, graphics, or electronic messaging.

Ping (Chapter 6)

To verify if a TCP/IP Internet address is valid, a user can initiate the ping command that verifies if the destination address is available. If it is available, the response will be the number of milliseconds it took to get the ping to and from the destination. Ping is commonly used to confirm connectivity between IP locations.

Point-to-Point Protocol (Chapter 2)

The point-to-point protocol, also known as PPP, is a common remote communications process used to establish connections between a remote user and a networking environment. The Microsoft Remote Access Server (RAS) provides PPP support for remote clients to log on and access a Microsoft Windows NT environment.

Point-to-Point Tunneling Protocol (Chapter 20)

The point-to-point tunneling protocol, or PPTP, provides a remote user with a secure remote access connection over the Internet. PPTP is a method to route point-to-point protocol (PPP) packets over a TCP/IP network by encapsulating the PPP packet, or the TCP/P, IPX, or NetBEUI packet.

POP3 (Chapter 7)
See Post Office Protocol.

Post Office (Chapter 9)
A post office is where e-mail messages are stored on a network for distribution to the proper recipient.

Post Office Protocol (Chapter 18)
POP3 stands for the Internet-standard Post Office Protocol 3 that is a published set of rules for how standard messaging is conducted in a UNIX environment. POP3 is to electronic messaging as TCP/IP is to the rules for transporting networking information, and as SMTP is to the rules for transporting messaging information. POP3 is a common messaging server system used by many organizations in a UNIX or TCP/IP environment. It is known for its ease of installation of the server services, and for the universal access by client operating systems of virtually every configuration including all versions of UNIX, the Macintosh, DOS workstations, Windows workstations, or even dumb terminals. Common POP3 client software include Eudora, Netscape Navigator Mail, Z-mail, or the Microsoft Internet Explorer Mail. When remote users want to access their messages from a POP3 client software, they enter the name of their Exchange server, LOGON names, and passwords. The Exchange server, with the Internet Mail Service running, authenticates users to the server for POP3 mail services. When the POP3 client software requests messages, the request goes to the POP3 server service which then requests Microsoft Exchange to send the client the messages from the user's Inbox. Note that the POP3 client will only retrieve messages from the Inbox and the user will not have access to private or public folders or to encrypted messages.

Posting Information (Chapter 5)
Normally, when a user wants to save information from an application program, he or she would use the save command to store the information in a directory or a subdirectory on a network. Using Microsoft Exchange, the same user can post information to a Microsoft Exchange folder instead of saving the information to a file server or workstation hard drive.

PPP (Chapter 2)

See Point-to-Point Protocol.

PPTP (Chapter 20)

See Point-to-Point Tunneling Protocol.

Primary Domain Controller (Chapter 4)

A primary domain controller, or commonly called the PDC, is a component of the Windows NT user and resource security system that maintains the master copy of the domain security information. The primary domain controller provides distributed logon access authentication to users on the network and is supported by backup domain controllers to replicate the network security information in the event of a primary domain controller failure.

Project Plan (Chapter 10)

A project plan is the process by which an organization intends to implement a project or solution. Some components of the project plan include scope of work, work plan, phases, tasks, resources, milestones, parallel and linked processes, major phases of the project, major components of each phase, detailed components of each phase, and project milestones.

Protocol (Chapter 6)

A protocol defines how data will be communicated between two or more systems. The purpose of defining a protocol is to allow the systems to know when all of the data transmitted was not received. As with human languages, protocols establish rules that allow each side to communicate effectively.

Profs (Chapter 8)

See IBM Profs.

Prototyping Phase (Chapter 10)

After an organization completes the planning portion of a project, the next step is the prototyping phase, which validates the design plan to ensure that the solution can be completed as expected. The prototyping phase would include setting up a test server and workstations to confirm the successful communications between the client and the server, to confirm user expectations of the system functionality, and to validate the time necessary to complete the installation process.

RAID-1 Disk Mirroring (Chapter 7)

In a RAID-1 implementation, hard drives in the system are duplicated and information is written to both sets of hard disks simultaneously. In the event that one hard drive or hard drive set fails, the other drive or drive set continues to operate. Disk storage purchase requirements should double the amount of available disk space desired. Thus, if an organization requires 4GB of disk space and would normally purchase one 4GB hard drive, it would purchase two 4GB hard drives and mirror the drives to create a replication of information stored.

RAID-2 Disk Mirroring (Chapter 7)

In a RAID-2 implementation, both the hard drives and the hard drive controllers are duplicated in a system. The same double disk purchase requirements apply as in the disk redundancy above; however, the organization would also purchase a redundant hard drive controller for the system. In the event of a failure of either one of the hard drives or hard drive sets or the hard drive controller, the redundant set would continue system operation without interruption or loss of information.

RAID-5 Disk Mirroring (Chapter 7)

In a RAID-5 implementation, an organization would require a file server and hard drive controller that supports RAID-5 disk redundancy. A RAID-5 disk redundancy system requires at least three hard drives. In an N+1 model, the equivalent of one drive in the RAID-5 configuration retains a mathematical representation of the fault tolerance parity information. This fault tolerant component is distributed across all of the hard drives in the RAID-5 drive set. In the event that any one of the drives in the set fails, the RAID-5 environment continues to run without interruption or data loss. A RAID-5 configuration is more economical than a disk mirror or duplexing system that requires an exact one-to-one relationship between drives. If the subsystem involves three 4GB drives for 12GB of usable disk space, a RAID-5 configuration would require just one extra 4GB drive to make up the RAID-5 N+1 configuration. However, in a mirror or duplexing scenario, the three 4GB drives would need to be matched with three additional 4GB drives to provide the one-to-one relationship of the mirrored or duplexed configuration.

RAID-6 Disk Mirroring (Chapter 7)

A RAID-6 configuration is similar to a RAID-5 configuration in which there is an N+1 relationship of drives (one extra drive for a series of data drives). However, RAID-6 includes one additional drive, which is an online spare in the environment. In the event that one drive in a RAID-5 subsystem fails, the system continues to operate, but if a second drive fails, all data will be lost and recovery would need to be performed from the last tape backup. With an online spare drive, when the first drive in the subsystem fails, the extra online spare drive will automatically substitute for the failed drive and begin recovery of the RAID-5 configuration. Once recovered to a RAID-5 configuration, an additional drive can fail and the system will still be operational, thus allowing for the potential of an additional failure. In effect, a RAID-6 configuration can have two drives in the drive set fail before the environment is in a fault situation in which data can be lost.

RAM (Chapter 7)

In a Windows NT environment, server RAM (pronounced "rahm"), or random access memory, plays as important a role as processor speed in determining the capabilities of the server-to-manage network resources. The more memory in a Windows NT Server, the more caching on the server disk storage is available, which in turn improves the performance of the network file server. In a network environment in which there are hundreds of users accessing the same file server, if the server has more memory in the system, it can potentially service disk read and write requests from RAM rather than having to constantly access the hard disks in the server. Because memory is rated in nanoseconds and hard drives are rated in milliseconds, the difference in access performance is significantly improved for the cached information access.

RAS (Chapter 20)

See Remote Access Server.

Remote Access Server (Chapter 20)

Windows NT comes with the Remote Access Server software, or RAS (pronounced "rahz"). A RAS server is nothing more than a PC running Windows NT Server software (the RAS component of the Windows NT Server software), and has telephone modems attached for remote users to dial into the RAS server. Remote users within a Microsoft Exchange environment use RAS to access the Exchange system to send and receive mail messages.

Remote Control (Chapter 20)

Remote control is a method by which a remote user sends and receives only screen and keyboard images between the remote system and the main office. It is called remote control because usually a user is taking control of a remote system to gain access to information. Because only the keyboard and screen images are passed over the data line, a slow communication phone line is typically adequate in sending and receiving screen and keyboard images. The actual processing performance is managed by the main office system of which the remote user is taking control. The characteristics of a remote control configuration include the remote user running a remote access application program on his or her remote system, a computer sitting at the main office waiting for someone to dial in using a remote access program to allow the user to take control of the system, and only keyboard and screen images transferring between the office and the remote user (thus performance is relatively fast).

Remote Node (Chapter 20)

Remote node is a method by which a remote user becomes a node on the network. His or her connection and access is exactly like the connection and access of a user that actually resides on the main system network. The user can log on to the network and access data files using drive letters common to the organization's local area network user connection. The characteristics of a remote node configuration is one where a user has programs on a remote system, where data can reside on the network or on the user's remote system, where the user dials in from a remote to the network to access information needed to transfer down to the remote system or back to the network, and where the user disconnects when the session is completed. The advantage of a remote node system is that the user has offline use of an application because the program resides on the individual's local hard drive. Additionally, the normal network "drive letters" remain the same because the user is a node on the network. Finally, the data can remain on the centralized network system because the user can open or save information to the file server just as if he or she were a user on the network itself.

Remote User (Chapter 9)

A remote e-mail user is one who is not attached to the network via a network adapter. In order to send and receive messages, the user must dial in to the network via phone lines.

Replication (Chapter 4)

Part of Microsoft Exchange's enterprise view of messaging and communications is the ability to replicate information from server to server. The replication of information may be for the purpose of providing the information across a wide area link so that the users on the other side do not have to go across a slow data communication link to access information. The replication of information may also be a form of information load balancing, in which high-demand information is replicated to multiple servers within a site, so that users can access the same information from different servers without the degradation caused by too many users accessing the same common information resource depository. Last, replication could be a component of a data information fault tolerance system in which high-profile information may be required to be distributed to another location within the same site (or to a different site), so that the information can be made available even in the event of a primary Exchange server failure.

Resources

Resources are components of a project plan that can be anything needed for a project, such as people, equipment, time, or money. A project's resources are typically allocated at its start, and the success of the project is often dependent upon whether the resources are used as efficiently as possible without last-minute, unplanned demands for additional resources. Some resources are scarce, such as a high-level engineer's consultation time, which needs to be managed carefully so that the utilization of the resource can be maximized.

Resource Domain (Chapter 4)

A resource domain is a component of the domain security model in Microsoft Windows NT. This domain would commonly retain resources such as printers, file servers, or communications gateways. Security access is provided to users of the user domain to all or part of the resources residing in the resource domain.

Rich Text Format—RTF (Chapter 9)

Rich text format is when text-based information, such as boldface, underlining, column setup, large fonts, small fonts, varying font typestyles, or different colors, is enhanced. The ability for an application to exchange information in a rich text format allows an organization to interchange information in the same look and style as the document was sent. Microsoft Exchange supports full rich text formatting capabilities.

RISC Processor (Chapter 7)

RISC stands for reduced instruction set chip and is a type of processor chip that can run faster than non-RISC processors. The Digital Alpha chips, as well as the Pentium Pro processor chips, are RISC-based systems that provide organizations with the scalability to support more users or to process information faster on a Microsoft Exchange server.

Scalability (Chapter 7)

This is the ability to purchase and/or use one system today and have the ability to use a more powerful system as the demands of the organization increase.

SchDist (Chapter 8)

The utility in Microsoft Mail that provides the free and busy time schedule distribution for users' personal schedules across multiple post offices.

Scope of Work (Chapter 10)

The scope of work of a project is a compilation of its goals, expectations, available resources, required resources, expected effort for completion, and available budget that is written down, specifically outlining what the project is expected to entail. In many cases, the scope of work consists mainly of the originator's brainstormed ideas in outline form. Essentially, it delineates the conceptual view of the project and provides as much information about the project as possible.

Search Engine (Chapter 15)

A search engine is an add-in to Microsoft Exchange that provides a user with the ability to look-up information stored on an Exchange server. The information may be e-mail messages or a series of word processing documents. The search engine will quickly search and find the information and provide the user with a list of potential matches.

Security Account Managers—SAMs (Chapter 4)

The security account manager stores the security information in a Microsoft Windows NT domain environment. It maintains a list of the users, and their passwords and access rights to information and resources within the domain.

Server Clustering (Chapter 7)

Multiple servers providing resource distribution in excess of the capability of a single server in the environment make up server clustering. During a server clustering process, the demands of the workgroup are distributed simultaneously across multiple servers within the organization. The cluster can access and manage resources within the organization at performance levels higher than ever achieved on a single server environment.

Server Monitor (Chapter 13)

The server monitor checks for the existence of other Exchange servers in the organization. It may be used to confirm that a server designated as a public information store for the environment is still operational. While the public information store server provides public information storage capabilities to the organization, it does not have general electronic messaging capabilities that can be traced in something like the link monitor.

SETDRIVE (Chapter 6)

Banyan Vines users access network resources such as disk shares through the use of the SETDRIVE commands. Similar to a Windows NT network NET USE command to access file shares, the SETDRIVE utility is used as a counterpart in a Banyan Vines environment.

SETPRINT (Chapter 6)

Banyan Vines users access network resources such as printers through the use of the SETPRINT command. Similar to a Windows NT network NET USE command to access printers, the SETPRINT utility is used as a counterpart in a Banyan Vines environment.

Simple Message Transfer Protocol (Chapter 1)

Simple Message Transfer Protocol (SMTP) is defined in RFC 821 according to how an Internet mail message is transferred. The Internet Connector for Microsoft Exchange utilizes RFC 821 as messages are passed between the Exchange server and another mail message server. Exchange also supports RFC 822, which defines the message content including formatting, headers, and text. When a message includes a nontext attachment, the information must be converted to a 7-bit ASCII standard before it can be transported over SMTP. The most common way of handling this nontext information is by encoding and decoding the information (UUENCODE/UUDECODE).

Single Domain Model (Chapter 4)

The simplest of all of the domain models is the single domain model. As the name suggests, there is only one domain in this configuration. All users, file servers, printers, and domain resources belong to the single domain. When users log in to the domain, their access rights are centrally managed and administered. Their privileges to resources in the domain (such as printers or file directory shares) are also centrally administered and allocated. This domain will have only one primary domain controller, but it can have multiple backup domain controllers, file servers, printers, and other resources. Adding a user to the domain gives that user rights to all resources in the domain as long as the user has been granted the central rights to access the resources.

Single Master Domain Model (Chapter 4)

The single master domain model has two or more separate domains that are all centrally administered for users but that have distributed administration for file servers and domain resources. The single master domain has one domain that maintains all user names and user security for the entire domain. The centralized administration of the users allows an organization to maintain a single security system. Resources have distributed administration so file servers, printers, and domain resources can be administered by local administrators within the organization. When users log in to the domain, they are authenticated by the centralized user domain and are then given access to the file servers, printers, and other domain resources within their local domain. The single master domain allows resources to be grouped and managed locally.

Site (Chapter 4)

The site name in the Microsoft Exchange hierarchy is typically some level or representation of a geographic designation for the company, like a region (Western, Northeast, Europe), a city (San Francisco, London, Tokyo), or a building (Bldg. 1A, 5-East), or by a function or department name (like Marketing or Finance). Similar to selecting the name of the organization, choosing a distinctive name for the site, without creating a problem of compatibility with external mail systems or even versions of the Microsoft Exchange client software, is critical. Once selected, the site name cannot be changed without completely reinstalling the entire Microsoft Exchange software. Like the organization name, the site name has no direct bearing on the organization's Internet domain name (for example, @xyzcorp.com), as the Internet domain name for the organization can be defined separately.

Site Connector (Chapter 4)

The Site Connector for site-to-site communications is the preferred method to interconnect multiple sites as long as the link is a permanent connection of a relatively high bandwidth medium. The Site Connector uses RPC to connect the two sites together and to exchange information. RPC does not require any transport protocols to be set up or configured. All messages go directly from one server to the other without being translated into X.400 or SMTP, or any other format.

Sizing a Server (Chapter 7)

Sizing a server is an expression used when determining the number of file servers needed and the appropriate processor performance required to manage the demands of the environment. That includes determining the amount of disk space required, the processor speed required, the amount of memory required, and the operating system to be used.

SMTP (Chapter 1)

See Simple Message Transfer Protocol.

Stand-Alone Computer (Chapter 9)

A stand-alone computer is one that is not attached to the network or other networked environment. Stand-alone computers usually have a network adapter installed and connected through cabling to a wiring hub to allow the computer to participate as part of a network.

Store and Forward Messaging (Chapter 20)

A store and forward method of communications is one where a remote user works offline on a local system, composes information or edits information, then connects to the network to send and receive information he or she has been working on and storing. This method of communication is very common to e-mail systems where a remote user can write electronic mail messages and "send" the messages offline (which does nothing more than to collect the messages and queue them up for future sending). Then, when the user connects to the network, the messages that were queued up are sent, and any messages waiting for the remote user are received by the user.

Store and Forward Messaging with Synchronization (Chapter 20)

Some of the more sophisticated messaging systems like Microsoft Exchange provide a store and forward messaging process but also include the synchronization of the information between the remote and the network systems. Most e-mail programs send and receive information as their store and forward process; however, if a user deletes a message remotely, moves the message to a different file folder, or edits a message, the program will not update the information on both sides of the link. Thus, any changes to messages or folders are not translated to the same changes made at the main office. Microsoft Exchange, however, has full synchronization of local and remote folders and messages. When a Microsoft Exchange user deletes a message remotely, the message is deleted on the network. When a Microsoft Exchange user moves a message to a separate folder, the message is moved both locally and remotely. When the Exchange user goes to the office and runs Microsoft Exchange, the user sees everything on the local network exactly as if the user moved, modified, or changed information on the remote system.

StreetTalk (Chapter 6)

Banyan's design of directory services is called StreetTalk. Where many directory services models are limited to networks of less than 256, 2500, 10,000, or 20,000 users, Banyan Vines, utilizing the StreetTalk directory services, commonly manages wide area networks with 20,000, 50,000, 100,000, or more users. StreetTalk uses an Organization, Group, and User structure for the naming of users on the network.

Swapfile (Chapter 7)

A swapfile, or pagefile, is used in the event that the server runs out of memory and needs to use virtual disk storage to manage server operations.

Synchronization (Chapter 6)

This term is used in a variety of settings. Basically, it refers to the ability to replicate and maintain common information in two or more locations. A remote user may synchronize his or her laptop data to a server. A network may synchronize its user names with the names of another network, or an e-mail system may synchronize its user list with the user list of another mail system.

Syscon (Chapter 6)

The utility used to manage the Bindery is SYSCON.EXE. The Syscon utility is used to add, modify, and delete users in a NetWare v3.*x* environment. This utility also allows the network administrator to specify which files the user should have access to and the level of privileges to the files (read, write, create, modify, or delete).

System Attendant (Chapter 1)

The system attendant is the management component that directs messages through the information store, the directory store, and the messaging transfer agent, and rebuilds the routing tables as information is changed in the directory store. The system attendant also manages the server and link monitors that track message logging.

Tasks (Chapter 10)

Tasks are the steps of a project that need to be completed. There are typically two levels of tasks that can be identified. Some tasks are major components of a phase of a project, and some are minor details within a phase of a project. Major tasks are categories that typically have a number of detailed steps that are associated with the specific task.

T1 Lease Line (Chapter 4)

A T1 lease line communicates at the speed of 1.54 megabits per second. T1 communication lines are common links between multiple locations in a wide area network configuration. T1 connections provide approximately one-half the speed of a normal network connection, unlike a telephone dial-up connection that is $1/100^{th}$ the speed of a normal network connection. T1 lines, however, are very expensive for wide area networks that span multiple states or countries, which can be cost prohibitive. An organization needs to evaluate its need for communication speed and the cost of the link.

TCP/IP (Chapter 6)

This stands for Transmission Control Protocol/Internet Protocol. TCP/IP is the protocol standard of the Internet and is now supported by most other network operating systems. TCP/IP allows for dissimilar networks to communicate with each other. The TCP part provides the transport control; the IP part provides the routing mechanism or the address where the message should be sent.

Telecommuting (Chapter 20)

Telecommuting is when an individual works from home or from a local office to do business instead of driving into the main corporate office. Telecommuting minimizes the need for the individual to drive to work every day, or it can provide the individual with flexible hours to limit travel to the office at times that are not traditional commute hours.

Token Ring (Chapter 7)

Token Ring is a type of physical interconnection standard for computers and printers in local area networks. All network systems in a ring are centrally connected. Token Ring stipulates that all systems get a chance to hold the token. The system holding the token is the only system that gets to speak on the network for the duration that it holds the token. There are many different kind of cabling systems that can support token ring. The theoretical maximum speed of token ring ranges from 4Mbps to 16Mbps (megabits per second).

TokenTalk (Chapter 19)

TokenTalk is the protocol used by Apple Macintosh computers communicating over Token Ring. It is the variation of AppleTalk for Token Ring.

Transaction Rollback (Chapter 1)

Microsoft Exchange provides a function, called transaction rollback, that ensures that when information is written to a Microsoft Exchange database, the information is written in its entirety; otherwise, the entire portion is rolled back to prevent database corruption.

Virtual Memory (Chapter 7)

See Pagefile.

Visio (Chapter 1)

Visio is a common graphical development tool made by Visio Corporation and is used by many companies to develop network diagrams, flow charts, or organization charts. Visio comes with templates for diagramming a variety of different types of graphical charts.

Universal Inbox (Chapter 2)

The concept of the universal inbox is the key to Microsoft Exchange's popularity as a solution for the intranet. The user's mailbox in Microsoft Exchange can accept e-mail messages, fax messages, word processing documents, voicemail messages, graphics files, or schedule requests to be stored in the mailbox. With this flexibility of information storage, an organization can use folders and mailboxes as a depository for any type of corporate information.

UNIX (Chapter 6)

UNIX is a network operating system that provides the interconnection between computers, terminals, and printers. UNIX is a competing network operating system with Windows NT and there is frequently a need to interconnect UNIX systems with LAN- or WAN-based PC systems.

URL (Chapter 2)

A URL, or Uniform Resource Locator, is an Internet term used to describe the Web address of a home page or Web page. This may be something like http://www.microsoft.com, which is the Microsoft Exchange Web page.

USENET (Chapter 18)

USENET is the network of Internet host computers that replicate newgroup topics across the Internet. The hosts on USENET store newsgroup and newsfeed information. Organizations can subscribe to USENET to have newgroup and newsfeed information downloaded to their server(s) to improve performance for local network users' access to the information. USENET newsgroups, numbering nearly 20,000 globally, are organized by subject, and are broken into a hierarchy of topics. The most popular newsgroup hierarchies include alt (alternative or controversial topics), comp (computer topics), humanities (humanities topics), misc (miscellaneous topics that are not covered in other categories), news (information about USENET), rec (recreation topics such as arts, hobbies, sports, etc.), sci (science related topics), soc (social issues and topics), and talk (talk groups on politics, religion, or other similar discussion topics).

UUENCODE (Chapter 8)

UUENCODE is a process of converting a binary file (like a word processing document, spreadsheet file, or graphic file) into a 7-bit ASCII file that can be transmitted over the Internet. Since the Internet supports only ASCII file transfers, the conversion process to go from binary to ASCII is called UUENCODE, and the term to reconvert the file from ASCII to binary is called UUDECODE. Microsoft Exchange will automatically UUENCODE attachments before sending them to the Internet, and it will automatically UUDECODE attachments after receiving them. Some older gateway products require that UUENCODING and UUDECODING to be perfomed manually.

Vines Operating System (Chapter 6)

The network operating system of the Banyan Systems Corporation is the Banyan Vines Operating System. Banyan Vines has been known for years for its directory services and scalability for managing very large networks. Microsoft Exchange supports electronic messaging over Microsoft Exchange in a Banyan Vines environment, and there are tools that assist an organization to migrate from Banyan Vines to Windows NT.

WarpServer (Chapter 6)

WarpServer is the IBM Software network operating system. Microsoft Exchange supports electronic messaging over Microsoft Exchange in an IBM

WarpServer environment, and there are tools that assist in the integration of IBM WarpServer into a Microsoft Windows NT environment.

Windows for Workgroups—WFW (Chapter 9)
A version of MS Windows that allows for peer-to-peer networking.

WINMSD (Chapter 14)
WINMSD is the Microsoft Windows NT version of the Microsoft Systems Diagnostics utility. The WINMSD can be run from any Windows NT desktop and will provide the user or network administrator with the ability to determine the amount of memory, disk storage capacity, versions of DLL drivers being used, processor speed, and other hardware and software characteristics of the system.

WINS (Chapter 6)
Windows Internet Naming Service is Microsoft software that helps users find computers on their Internet network or on the Internet. The WINS server runs under NT and is a database of user names and their IP addresses.

Wizard (Chapter 9)
A series of computer screens that assist users in completing a task. Many functions in Microsoft now have wizards that are provided to make the installation or operation of that function in Exchange easier.

WordMail (Chapter 2)
Within the Microsoft Exchange or Outlook 97 client, users have the ability of selecting WordMail as their basic message creation tool. Rather than using the standard Exchange or Outlook message form, using Microsoft Word allows the e-mail user to take advantage of Word functions such as macros, templates, find tools, tables, or Word art. A user has the ability of selecting to use the standard mail form to send and receive messages, or of using Word as the message editor.

Workflow (Chapter 10)
An organization processes work by following a series of steps until the task is completed. This path is called workflow.

Workplan (Chapter 10)

The workplan of a project takes the scope of work and forms the guideline to which the GANTT chart is developed. The GANTT chart is the sequential text and graphical representation of the project process or of the project's entire workplan. The workplan identifies the requirements of the project and the resources that will be necessary to complete it.

X.400 (Chapter 1)

X.400 is a widely recognized and accepted set of standards for electronic messaging and communications. Microsoft Exchange has built-in support for X.400 and is U.S. GOSIP-certified for both the 1988 and the 1984 standards. Microsoft Exchange's support for X.400 means that information from Microsoft Exchange can communicate better with other messaging systems because of standard industry transports such as X.25, TCP/IP, and TP4. Also, the parts of an Exchange message (from the textual body part through attachments) are of standard definitions. Last, the addressing of the sender and recipient use X.400 naming schemes such as Country Code, ADMD, PRMD, Organization Name, and Common User Name.

Z-mail (Chapter 18)

Z-mail is a cross-platform e-mail program by NetManage Inc., that enables an SMTP or POP3 mail client to work in over a dozen versions of UNIX, in the Windows environment, or on a Macintosh computer. Z-mail and Eudora are commonly referred to as the standards in POP3 or SMTP e-mail clients.

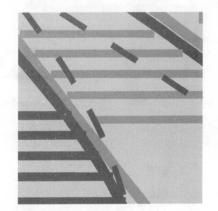

APPENDIX B

What's New in Exchange v5.0

T his book was written with Microsoft Exchange v5.0 in mind, so from Chapter 1 through Chapter 20, I have integrated Microsoft Exchange v5.0 components throughout its content. For those who have Exchange v4.0 or who have evaluated Exchange v4.0 and want to know what is in Exchange v5.0, the following is a summary of v5.0's new features, along with a cross reference to the corresponding chapter where each feature can be found.

New Internet Components

The following are new components in Exchange that enhance Microsoft Exchange's Internet capabilities (from Chapter 18):

- **Active Server Components** The Active Server Components in Exchange v5.0 provide Active Messaging that allows message access to an Exchange server from the Internet.

- **HTML Support** Information in Exchange public folders can be viewed using a native HTML browser.

- **POP3 Protocol Support** Mail messages for Exchange clients can be accessed using a standard POP3 client. This eliminates the need for using the Exchange client remotely.

- **NNTP Protocol Support** The network news transfer protocol (NNTP) provides inbound and outbound newsfeeds from USENET newsgroups into an Exchange server.

- **LDAP Protocol Support** The lightweight directory access protocol provides directory information to LDAP clients.

- **SSL Protocol Support** The secured socket layer security provides encrypted communications that are integrated as an option for POP3 mail message security.

- **Internet Mail Service Wizard** To automate the installation of Internet mail services on an Exchange server, the Internet Mail Service Wizard installs the services that facilitate the sending and receiving of SMTP mail messages.

- **Newsfeed Configuration Wizard** To simplify the installation of the USENET newsgroup communications, the Newsfeed Configuration Wizard automates the installation process.

New Migration Components

The following are new migration components intended to provide easier migrations from other messaging environments (from Chapter 9):

- **Novell GroupWise Migration Wizard** This wizard automates the migration from Novell's GroupWise software into a Microsoft Exchange environment. In Chapter 9, I describe the general support of Microsoft Exchange for the source extractor and migration wizards for this and other referenced migration.

- **Netscape Collabra Migration Tools** To easily migrate from a Netscape Collabra Share environment to Microsoft Exchange, the Netscape Collabra Migration tools simplify the process.

- **UNIX Mail Migration Tools** The UNIX mail migration tools simplify the migration to Microsoft Exchange from UNIX sendmail systems.

New Connector/Gateway Components

The following is an enhancement to provide better support for inbound and outbound messaging with an existing messaging environment:

- **Lotus cc:Mail Connector (Chapter 9)** The Lotus cc:Mail Connector provides an inbound and outbound messaging gateway between Microsoft Exchange and existing cc:Mail environments. The cc:Mail Connector also provides directory synchronization between Exchange and cc:Mail environments.

New Server Components

The following are additions to the Exchange Server software to provide enhanced administration or functions in Exchange v5.0:

- **Address Book Views (Chapter 2)** The administrator can select user names from the global address list to distribute names in separate address book views.

■ **Attribute Filtering for Intersite Replication (Chapter 3)**
Administrators can now choose which directory attributes or properties
are replicated to other Exchange sites. By minimizing the replication of
ancillary information, the time to synchronize the global directory and
the size of the directory database are decreased.

New Client Components

The following are new editions in Exchange v5.0 that provide enhanced
functionality for Exchange client users:

■ **Apple Macintosh Client for Schedule+ (Chapter 19)**   The Apple
Macintosh client shipped with Exchange v4.0, but in Exchange v5.0, the
Schedule+ component was added to provide Macintosh users the
ability to participate in company-wide personal and group scheduling.

■ **Message Screening (Chapter 15)**   Messages can be manually screened
before the message is automatically put into a Public folder.

■ **Adding Subfolders to Favorites Folders (Chapter 15)**   Subfolders can
now be linked under the Favorites folder allowing for easier view of
information from the favorites list.

■ **Hiding Selected Public Folders (Chapter 15)**   Public folders can be
selected to be hidden from specific users on the network.

■ **Exchanging Security Keys between Organizations (Chapter 12)**
Security keys can be exchanged between users of separate
organizations, thus extending the capability of digital encryption and
digital signatures beyond a local server site.

■ **Publishing Schedules on the Internet (Chapter 18)**   Schedules for
users can be exported into an HTML format that can be accessed over
the Internet from regular Web browsers.

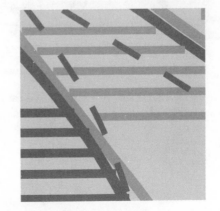

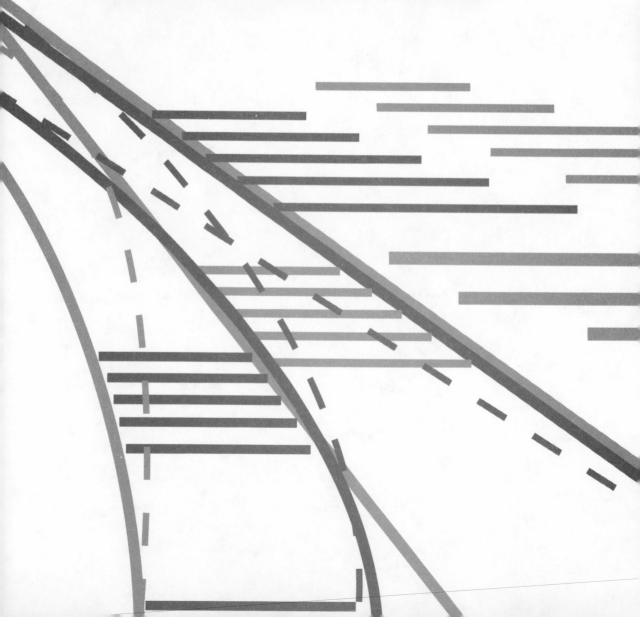

APPENDIX C

Upgrading from Exchange v4.0 to v5.0

Exchange v5.0 Requirements

Exchange v5.0 has the same hardware and compatibility requirements as Exchange v4.0. The only major change is that you need to run Exchange v5.0 on a current version of the Microsoft Windows NT software. The supported versions are:

■ Windows NT v3.51 with Service Pack 5

■ Windows NT v4.0 with Service Pack 1

If you plan to install the Active Server Components (described in Chapter 18) for Internet functions with an Exchange Server, the Active Server Components require:

■ Windows NT v4.0 with Service Pack 2

Service Pack Upgrade Notation

Any time a service pack is installed on a server within a domain, the primary domain controller (PDC) must also be updated to the same version or higher of the service pack. When a server or a backup domain controller communicates with the primary domain controller, there are specific updates to domain management services that are installed and that need to remain consistent on the primary domain controller to prevent problems from occurring.

Upgrading to Exchange v5.0

The upgrade from Microsoft Exchange v4.0 to Exchange v5.0 should be conducted only after completing an entire backup of the Exchange v4.0 Server including programs, logs, and the information and directory store (see the Windows NT and the Microsoft Exchange manuals on Exchange Server backup and restoral). Begin by following these steps:

1. Make sure there is at least 40MB of available disk space on the hard drive of the Exchange Server.

2. Make sure the version of Windows NT is one that is supported as noted earlier in this appendix.

3. Insert the Exchange v5.0 CD into the CD-ROM drive of the server and run SETUP from the \SETUP\{*platform*} directory.

Installing an Exchange v4.0 Server into an Exchange v5.0 Site

When an Exchange v5.0 server is installed into or upgraded in an Exchange v4.0 site, the directory schema, different in the two versions, is automatically updated for the site to an Exchange v5.0 configuration. If a new Exchange v4.0 server is added to an Exchange v5.0 site or to a site where the schema has been automatically updated to v5.0 after a v5.0 server was installed in the site, the following procedure needs to be conducted:

1. Copy the contents of the Exchange v4.0 platform files (and subdirectories) (\SETUP\{*platform*} to a subdirectory on the server hard drive (ex: \EXCHCODE)).

2. Copy the contents from the \SUPPORT\EXCH40\{*platform*} of the Exchange v5.0 CD to the same subdirectory on the server hard drive—this will overwrite some of the Exchange v4.0 files.

3. Run the SETUP program of the updated Exchange v4.0 code software from the hard drive of the server to add this new v4.0 server into the v5.0 site.

Upgrading the Key Management Server to Exchange v5.0

The Key Management Server in Exchange v5.0 is also an updated version of the software. To upgrade the Key Management Server from v4.0 to v5.0:

1. Run the SETUP program of the Key Management Server software on the Exchange v5.0 CD (in the \EXCHKM directory).

2. When prompted to replace an existing version of the software, select OK.

3. Choose "Typical Installation" to install the software.

 NOTE: *As with any upgrade or update, make sure to make a complete backup of the data and security information before proceeding. The upgrade will maintain the security key through the upgrade; however, the KM Server security information should be backed up prior to the upgrade process.*

APPENDIX **D**

Internationalization of Microsoft Exchange

As an enterprise-level messaging, intranet, and communication infrastructure application, the Microsoft Exchange product must have the ability of being a globally supported product. This involves multilanguage support, considerations for variable wide area network link connections (communications speed and quality), and sensitivity to United States, French, and other global security and data encryption laws and policies.

When designing and deploying Microsoft Exchange in an international environment, the following components need to be taken into consideration:

- **Multilanguage Support (Chapter 1)**   Starting with Microsoft Exchange v4.0 Service Pack 2, code pages for the interchange of messaging information between all of the versions of the Microsoft Exchange product were included and can be installed on each Exchange server. The code pages allow the Exchange Server software to support the acceptance of extended character sets and foreign character set conversions between the versions of the Microsoft Exchange Server software. While this does not translate text from German to English or Japanese to Swedish, it does provide the ability of the versions of Microsoft Exchange to accept messages created in a foreign language. For international companies that have translators or translation software programs, the inbound messages in Exchange are in a format that can be translated instead of either rejected or displayed with indecipherable text.

- **Variable Communication Line Speed Support (Chapter 4)**   The phone companies have different phone line standards as well as standard communication speeds. For example, in Europe, the phone modulation standard is CCITT, whereas in the United States, it is the Bell standard. This difference means that a dial-up modem that works in the United States may not work in Europe unless the modem supports both the Bell and the CCITT standards. Most modems today support these options; however, many older modems or specialty modems do not support the varying standards. Additionally, in the United States, long distance digital circuits are rated in 56-kilobit increments although the full digital circuit should be rated in 64-kilobit increments. This is because the 8-kilobit variance used by the American phone companies has traditionally been for framing, sequencing, and diagnostics. Most other countries provide the full 64-kilobit digital circuit as their standard increment for digital communications. Many of the local line phone companies in the United States, sometimes called the "baby-Bells" (like Pacific Bell), are starting to provide the full 64-kilobit line services as their standard digital line increment. When connecting lines between countries or even between long distance phone services within the United States, the equipment and line speeds of the locations need to be taken into account. Obviously, the lowest common denominator (usually 56-kilobit speeds) needs to be selected between locations if that is the fastest speed being transmitted from one of the two sites in a point-to-point connection.

■ **Wide Area Network Quality and Reliability (Chapter 5)**   When designing line speed connections in a wide area network environment, the quality and the reliability of phone lines between locations need to be addressed. While a site may require a high-speed phone line connection because of the demands of the workgroup or workflow requirements, the availability of reliable high-speed circuits may not exist or may be prohibitively costly for the site. When designing the wide area links, not only should the demands of the organization's workgroup be taken into account, but also the availability of communication services.

■ **United States Security Encryption Export Laws (Chapter 12)**
The United States prohibits the export of any software that includes high-level encryption, thus the international versions of Microsoft Exchange support only up to 40-bit encryption. For organizations installing Microsoft Exchange with encryption internal to the United States, levels can be set to 64 bit or 128 bit. If the organization plans to encrypt and send information internationally, it should be kept in mind that the version of the Key Management Server and encryption level should be set for 40 bit. Although an organization can unencrypt messages as it converts from a 64- or a 128-bit standard to a 40-bit standard, taking international communications into account *before* encryption processes are implemented will eliminate the effort needed to convert messages and server software versions. Additionally, whenever updates or upgrades are conducted between versions of Exchange software in an environment that utilizes encryption, the administrator of the Exchange environment *must* verify that the organization is upgrading to a version of the Exchange software that is of the same level of security encryption as the current version of the software installed. If an organization is running the 64-bit United States version of Exchange and does a service pack upgrade or version upgrade that has a 40-bit version of Exchange, *all* messages that were encrypted prior to the upgrade will not be able to be recovered. The

organization must do a service pack or version upgrade to the exact level of encryption as it had prior to the upgrade.

- **French Security Encryption Usage Laws (Chapter 12)**   The French government forbids the use of encryption codes in any forms of nongovernment communications; therefore, the Microsoft Exchange software in the French language does not come with the Key Management Server software, and all options for encryption and digital signatures have been eliminated from the client components of the software. When an Exchange user communicates with an Exchange user in France, the option to encrypt or encode information is not allowed in the Exchange software.

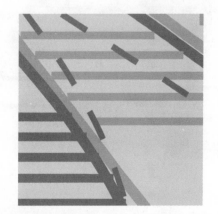

APPENDIX E

Third-Party Applications Available

The following are companies mentioned in this book that provide add-in products or services for the Microsoft Exchange Server product:

Desktop Applications

Microsoft Corporation
1 Microsoft Way
Redmond, WA 98052
Desktop: (800) 936-4100
Business Solutions: (800) 936-4400
http://www.microsoft.com

> **Products**:
> Microsoft Windows 95
> Microsoft Project
> Microsoft Office 97

Qualcomm Inc.
6455 Lusk Blvd.
San Diego, CA 92121
(800) 544-4977
(619) 587-1121
http://www.qualcomm.com

> **Product**:
> Eudora Pro Mail

NetManage, Inc.
10725 N DeAnza Blvd.
Cupertino, CA 95014
(408) 973-7171
http://www.netmanage.com

> **Product**:
> Z-Mail

Visio Corporation
520 Pike Street Ste. 1800
Seattle, WA 98101
(206) 521-4000
fax: (206) 521-4501
http://www.visio.com

   Product:
   Visio Diagramming Software

Document Routing

KeyFile Corporation
22 Cotton Rd.
Nashua, NH 03063
(800) 453-9345
(603) 883-3800
fax: (603) 889-9259
http://www.keyfile.com

   Product:
   KeyFlow for Exchange

Faxing

Omtool
8 Industrial Way
Salem, NH 03079
(800) 886-7845
(603) 898-8900
fax: (603) 890-6756
http://www.omtool.com

   Product:
   Fax Sr.

Mail Gateways

Attachmate
3617 131st Ave. Southeast
Bellevue, WA 98006
(800) 426-6283
http://www.attachmate.com

Product:
Attachmate Mail Gateway

Remote Access

Citrix Systems Inc.
6400 NW 6th Way
Ft.Lauderdale, FL 33309
(800) 437-7503
(954) 267-3000
http://www.citrix.com

Product:
Citrix WinFrame

Search Engines

Fulcrum Software
785 Carling Avenue, 9th Floor
Ottawa, Ontario K1S 5H4 Canada
(613) 238-1761
fax: (613) 238-7695
http://www.fulcrum.com

Product:
Fulcrum Find!

Voicemail Integration

Octel Communications
1001 Murphy Ranch Road
Milpitas, CA 95035
(408) 321-2000
http://www.octel.com

Product:
Unified Messaging

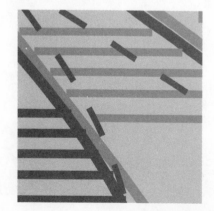

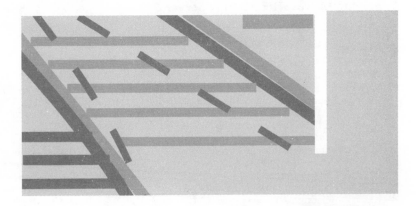

Index

E

T

X